OXFORD MEDIEVAL TEXTS

General Editors

D. E. GREENWAY   B. F. HARVEY

M. LAPIDGE

WULFSTAN OF WINCHESTER

The Life of St Æthelwold

WULFSTAN OF WINCHESTER

The Life of St Æthelwold

EDITED BY

MICHAEL LAPIDGE

AND

MICHAEL WINTERBOTTOM

CLARENDON PRESS · OXFORD

This book has been printed digitally and produced in a standard specification in order to ensure its continuing availability

OXFORD
UNIVERSITY PRESS

Great Clarendon Street, Oxford OX2 6DP

Oxford University Press is a department of the University of Oxford.
It furthers the University's objective of excellence in research, scholarship,
and education by publishing world-wide in

Oxford New York

Auckland Bangkok Buenos Aires Cape Town Chennai
Dar es Salaam Delhi Hong Kong Istanbul Karachi Kolkata
Kuala Lumpur Madrid Melbourne Mexico City Mumbai Nairobi
São Paulo Shanghai Taipei Tokyo Toronto

Oxford is a registered trade mark of Oxford University Press
in the UK and in certain other countries

Published in the United States
by Oxford University Press Inc., New York

Reprinted 2004

ISBN 978-0-19-822266-8

PREFACE

The present book, which presents the first critical edition of Wulfstan of Winchester's *Vita S. Æthelwoldi*, was conceived jointly some ten years ago and planned as a work of collaboration. In the event, MW has been primarily responsible for the Latin text and translation, ML for the Introduction, Notes to the Text, and Appendices; but we have overseen each other's work at every stage and derived the kind of enjoyment and enlightenment which collaboration between scholars in different fields can often bring.

It is a pleasure, and also a necessity, to record our gratitude to those who have helped us in various ways. MW's wife Nicolette attended to the style of the English translation. ML drew continually on the learning of David Dumville and Simon Keynes, not only in specific matters concerning Anglo-Saxon manuscripts and history, but also more generally in countless aspects of Anglo-Saxon studies. Their generous assistance is reflected in some way on nearly every page of the book. Several other colleagues supplied ML with precise information on individual liturgical points: David Chadd, Alicia Corrêa, Robert Deshman, Helmut Gneuss, and Peter Jackson. Pauline Thompson kindly made available a typescript of her edition of Gregory of Ely's poem on St Æthelthryth before its publication, as did Ardis Butterfield her unpublished dissertation on the Middle English 'Life of Adelwolde'. Jill Mann helped to eliminate many errors from the edition of the 'Life of Adelwolde' printed as Appendix C. And in the final stages of preparation Leofranc Holford-Strevens saved us from countless errors and enriched the text in many ways. To all of these we express our thanks.

M.L.
M.W.

September 1989

CONTENTS

ABBREVIATIONS

AB	*Analecta Bollandiana.*
AH	*Analecta Hymnica Medii Aevi*, ed. G. M. Dreves and C. Blume, 55 vols. (Leipzig, 1886–1922).
ASC	The Anglo-Saxon Chronicle (see also Bately, *MS A* and Plummer, *Two Chronicles*).
ASE	*Anglo-Saxon England.*
Bately, *MS A*	*The Anglo-Saxon Chronicle, A Collaborative Edition*, iii: *MS A*, ed. J. Bately (Cambridge, 1986).
BCS	W. de G. Birch, *Cartularium Saxonicum*, 3 vols. (London, 1885–93) with index (1899).
Bede, *HE*	*Bede's Ecclesiastical History of the English People*, ed. B. Colgrave and R. A. B. Mynors (OMT 1969).
BHL	[Bollandists], *Bibliotheca Hagiographica Latina*, 2 vols. (Brussels, 1899–1901), with suppl. by H. Fros (1986).
Bibl. mun.	Bibliothèque municipale.
Bishop Æthelwold	*Bishop Æthelwold: His Career and Influence*, ed. B. Yorke (Woodbridge, 1988).
BL	British Library.
BN	Bibliothèque Nationale (Paris).
Burton	*Charters of Burton Abbey*, ed. P. H. Sawyer, Anglo-Saxon Charters, ii (London, 1979).
CCM	*Corpus Consuetudinum Monasticarum* (Siegburg).
CCSL	*Corpus Christianorum, Series Latina* (Turnhout).
Chron. Abingdon	*Chronicon Monasterii de Abingdon*, ed. J. Stevenson, 2 vols., RS (1858).
CLitLA	K. Gamber, *Codices Liturgici Latini Antiquiores* (2nd edn., Fribourg, 1968).
Councils & Synods	*Councils & Synods with other Documents relating to the English Church*, ed. D. Whitelock, M. Brett, and C. N. L. Brooke, 2 vols. (Oxford, 1981).
CPB	*Corpus Pontificalium Benedictionum*, ed. E. Moeller, 4 vols., *CCSL* clxii, clxiiA–C (1971–9).
CSEL	*Corpus Scriptorum Ecclesiasticorum Latinorum* (Vienna).
DACL	*Dictionnaire d'archéologie chrétienne et de liturgie*,

	ed. F. Cabrol and H. Leclercq, 15 vols. in 30 (Paris, 1907–53).
DHGE	*Dictionnaire d'histoire et de géographie ecclésiastiques*, ed. A. Baudrillart *et al.* (Paris, 1912–).
DTC	*Dictionnaire de théologie catholique*, ed. A. Vacant, E. Mangenot, and E. Amann, 15 vols. (Paris, 1903–50).
EETS	Early English Text Society (London).
os	Original Series.
ss	Supplementary Series.
EHD	*English Historical Documents I:* c.*500–1042*, ed. D. Whitelock (2nd edn., London, 1979).
EHR	*English Historical Review*.
Gelling, *ECTV*	M. Gelling, *The Early Charters of the Thames Valley* (Leicester, 1979).
Gerchow, *Gedenküberlieferung*	J. Gerchow, *Die Gedenküberlieferung der Angelsachsen* (Berlin–New York, 1988).
Gneuss, *Hymnar*	H. Gneuss, *Hymnar und Hymnen im englischen Mittelalter* (Tübingen, 1968).
Gneuss, 'Liturgical books'	H. Gneuss, 'Liturgical books in Anglo-Saxon England', *Learning and Literature*, pp. 91–141.
Hart, *ECEE*	C. R. Hart, *The Early Charters of Eastern England* (Leicester, 1966).
Hart, *ECNENM*	C. R. Hart, *The Early Charters of Northern England and the North Midlands* (Leicester, 1975).
HBS	Henry Bradshaw Society Publications (London).
HCY	*The Historians of the Church of York and its Archbishops*, ed. J. Raine, 3 vols., RS (1879–94).
Heads	*The Heads of Religious Houses, England and Wales, 940–1216*, ed. D. Knowles, C. N. L. Brooke, and V. C. M. London (Cambridge, 1972).
Holschneider, *Organa*	A. Holschneider, *Die Organa von Winchester* (Hildesheim, 1968).
ICL	D. Schaller and E. Könsgen, *Initia Carminum Latinorum saeculo undecimo antiquiorum* (Göttingen, 1977).
KCD	J. M. Kemble, *Codex Diplomaticus Aevi Saxonici*, 6 vols. (London, 1839–48).
Ker, *Catalogue*	N. R. Ker, *Catalogue of Manuscripts Containing Anglo-Saxon* (Oxford, 1957).
Knowles, *MO*	D. Knowles, *The Monastic Order in England* (2nd edn., Cambridge, 1963).

LE	*Liber Eliensis*, ed. E. O. Blake, Camden Third Series, xcii (London, 1962).
Learning and Literature	*Learning and Literature in Anglo-Saxon England: Studies Presented to Peter Clemoes*, ed. M. Lapidge and H. Gneuss (Cambridge, 1985).
LVH	*Liber Vitae: Register and Martyrology of New Minster and Hyde Abbey Winchester*, ed. W. de G. Birch (London–Winchester, 1892).
Memorials	*Memorials of St Dunstan*, ed. W. Stubbs, RS (1874).
MGH	*Monumenta Germaniae Historica*.
Auct. antiq.	Auctores antiquissimi.
SS rer. Meroving.	Scriptores rerum Merovingicarum.
NMT	Nelson's Medieval Texts (London).
OMT	Oxford Medieval Texts (Oxford).
PL	*Patrologia Latina*, ed. J. P. Migne, 221 vols. (Paris, 1844–64).
Planchart, *Repertory*	A. E. Planchart, *The Repertory of Tropes at Winchester*, 2 vols. (Princeton, 1977).
Plummer, *Two Chronicles*	*Two of the Saxon Chronicles Parallel*, ed. C. Plummer, 2 vols. (Oxford, 1892–9, rev. D. Whitelock, 1952).
Plummer, *VBOH*	*Venerabilis Baedae Opera Historica*, ed. C. Plummer, 2 vols. (Oxford, 1896).
RB	*Revue bénédictine*.
Reg. conc.	*Regularis concordia*, ed. T. Symons, NMT (1953).
Rep. Hymn.	U. Chevalier, *Repertorium Hymnologicum*, 6 vols. (Louvain, 1892–1921).
Robertson, *AS Charters*	A. J. Robertson, *Anglo-Saxon Charters* (Cambridge, 1939).
Robinson, *Times*	J. A. Robinson, *The Times of St Dunstan* (Oxford, 1923).
RS	Rolls Series (London).
S	P. H. Sawyer, *Anglo-Saxon Charters: An Annotated List and Bibliography* (London, 1968).
Taylor and Taylor, *AS Architecture*	H. M. and J. Taylor, *Anglo-Saxon Architecture*, 3 vols. (Cambridge, 1965–78).
Temple, *AS Manuscripts*	E. Temple, *Anglo-Saxon Manuscripts, 900–1066* (London, 1976).
Tenth-Century Studies	*Tenth-Century Studies*, ed. D. Parsons (London–Chichester, 1975).
UL	University Library.

Winterbottom, *Three Lives*	*Three Lives of English Saints*, ed. M. Winterbottom (Toronto, 1972).
WS	*Winchester Studies*, ed. M. Biddle (Oxford, 1976–).

ADDENDVM (1996)

Very soon after the publication of this edition in 1991, Dr Rosalind Love drew our attention to a manuscript of Wulfstan's *Vita S. Æethelwoldi* which had previously escaped our notice: Lincoln, Cathedral Library, 150, a passional of mid-twelfth century date which seems once to have formed part of a three-volume set. Wulfstan's *uita* is on fos. 90r–97v. Collation suggests that the Lincoln manuscript has nothing to contribute to the reconstruction of the text: it lacks rubrics, the *praefatio*, and cc. 15–16. Where its text is preserved, it shows itself to belong to what we have called 'Stage 3' (p. clxxxv): with Tβ it omits the sentence *clausis diligenter. . . uideretur* from c. 12, and with Tβ has the bowdlerized version of Wulfstan's comment on the Northumbrians' drinking habits (*gaudentibus* for *inebriatis suatim*) also in c. 12. Of 'Stage 3' manuscripts, it agrees frequently with N (see, for example, pp. 60 n. d, and esp. 66 n. e), but never with T. It also has some individual errors, which shows that none of the later manuscripts could have been copied from it.

It may be helpful to draw attention to a few relevant publications which have appeared since 1991. The anonymous grammatical *Dialogus de .viii. partibus orationis* from Winchester mentioned on pp. lxxxvi–lxxxvii has now been edited by M. Bayless, '*Beatus quid est* and the study of grammar in late Anglo-Saxon England', in *History of Linguistic Thought in the Early Middle Ages*, ed. V. Law (Amsterdam, 1993), pp. 67–110. The eleventh-century prayer-book from the New Minster, Winchester (now London, British Library, Cotton Titus D. XXVI + XXVII), cited as the source of the *cursus* of prayers for the Virgin (pp. lxix–lxxv) has now been edited *in extenso* by Beate Günzel, *Ælfwine's Prayerbook*, HBS cviii (London, 1993). The production and reception of the *Regularis concordia*, a work almost certainly drafted by Æthelwold (pp. lviii–lxi), have been exhaustively studied by Lucia Kornexl, *Die Regularis Concordia und ihre altenglische Interlinearversion* (Munich, 1993).

INTRODUCTION

I. WULFSTAN OF WINCHESTER: LIFE AND WRITINGS

OF the life of Wulfstan, author of the *Vita S. Æthelwoldi*, very little is known.[1] He was a monk and priest at the Old Minster, Winchester, in the late tenth century; he rose there to become precentor, and hence is often referred to in contemporary sources as Wulfstan *Cantor*.[2] Thus in a list of monks of the Old Minster which was compiled during the bishopric of Ælfheah (984–1005) and which is preserved in the eleventh-century *Liber uitae* of Hyde Abbey (formerly the New Minster, Winchester), Wulfstan is listed among those who *specialiter se deuouerunt* in thirty-first place as follows: 'Wulfstan .i. Cantor. Sacerdos.'[3] Similarly, in the Old English translation of Chrodegang's *Regula canonicorum* which was made at Winchester *c.*1000, Wulfstan is included in a list of Old Minster monks which was added in the translation in order to illustrate Chrodegang's discussion of the hierarchy of ecclesiastical officers: 'þissum gemete, swylce man cweðe, Leofwine prauost, Wulfstan cantor, Byrhthelm diacon, Cynewerd cyrcwerd, Ælfnoð cild, and swa be eallum.'[4] Here it will be noticed that Wulfstan, as precentor (*cantor*), is listed after the prior, but before the deacon (*diacon*), the sexton (*cyrcwerd*), and an oblate (*cild*). Finally, in an Old English text known as the 'Vision of Eadwine', written by a monk of the New Minster, Winchester, in the time of

[1] See the accounts in T. Wright, *Biographia Britannica Literaria*, 2 vols. (London, 1842–6), i. 471–4; M. Bateson, *Dictionary of National Biography*, lxiii. 173–4; and M. Manitius, *Geschichte der lateinischen Literatur des Mittelalters*, 3 vols. (Munich, 1911–31), ii. 442–6.

[2] On the office of precentor or *cantor* at this time, see M. E. Fassler, 'The office of the Cantor in early western monastic rules and customaries: a preliminary investigation', *Early Music History*, v (1985), 29–51, esp. p. 51: 'The production of liturgical books was supervised by the cantor himself; he was the person who ordered and no doubt designed these books; he was the official who corrected mistakes and was responsible for changes in the traditional texts and music when they were made.'

[3] *LVH*, p. 25; Gerchow, *Gedenküberlieferung*, p. 323.

[4] A. S. Napier, *The Old English Version of the Enlarged Rule of Chrodegang*, EETS, os cl (London, 1916), p. 9.

Bishop Ælfsige (d. 1032), there is mention of various monks of the Old Minster who once accompanied Bishop Æthelwold (963–84) on a visitation of the New Minster, and these included *Wlstan cantor*.[5] There can be no doubt, then, that Wulfstan was monk and precentor at Winchester in the late tenth century; but beyond this scant information little is known. We do not know when Wulfstan was born, though from his *Narratio metrica de S. Swithuno* (see below) we learn that he was a child oblate at the Old Minster at the time of St Swithun's translation in 971: 'nos quoque nos pueri qua tempestate pusilli';[6] and that, during the few years following the translation, Wulfstan's studies in the monastic classroom were frequently interrupted by the miracles occurring at Swithun's tomb:

> Saepe etiam nobis pueris discentibus una
> quemlibet aut cantum seu qualemcumque libellum
> contigit, ut tota penitus nil discere luce
> possemus, signis pro crebrescentibus, omnes
> sed uice continua sacram repetiuimus aedem.[7]

These personal references, taken together, may suggest that Wulfstan was born *c.*960,[8] was given as oblate to the Old Minster, and spent his mature life there. We know the day, but not the year, when he died. His latest datable scholarly activity is his *Vita S. Æthelwoldi*, which was composed no earlier than 996.[9] He presumably died some time in the early eleventh century; the day of his death was 22 July, as we learn from an obit recorded against this date in a New Minster calendar of the early eleventh century.[10]

[5] F. E. Harmer, *Anglo-Saxon Writs* (Manchester, 1952), p. 401.

[6] *Narratio*, i. 899.

[7] *Narratio*, ii. 259–63: 'Often, too, while we young oblates were together in class learning either some chant or some particular text, it so happened that we were able to learn virtually nothing in the space of that day because of the burgeoning miracles, but rather we all went at once to the holy minster.'

[8] At one point in the *Vita S. Æthelwoldi* Wulfstan claims to have *seen* Ælfstan ordained abbot (c. 14), an event which probably took place in 964 (see below, p. 28 n. 1). If so, given that the minimum age for an oblate was 7, Wulfstan can have been born no later than 957.

[9] Note, however, the arguments of Planchart (*Repertory*, i. 32–3), who would see Wulfstan's scribal activity continuing into the first decade of the 11th c.; see also the suggestion (below, p. xxxviii) that Wulfstan may have accompanied Bishop Ælfheah when the latter was translated to Canterbury in 1005.

[10] The calendar is preserved in London, BL Cotton Titus D. XXVII (New Minster, Winchester, s. xi¹); Wulfstan's obit is ptd. *LVH*, p. 271, and Gerchow, *Gedenküberlieferung*, p. 333.

We are on slightly firmer ground with respect to Wulfstan's writings, though here too questions of attribution are invariably bedevilled by the fact that works probably or possibly by Wulfstan bear no indication of authorship; in such circumstances attributions to Wulfstan depend all too often on stylistic arguments.[11] Nevertheless there is a sizeable corpus of writings which can be attributed to Wulfstan with some confidence. It is best to begin by considering those attributions which may be regarded as certain, and then proceed to those which are less certain. We may begin with a statement by William of Malmesbury concerning the writings of Wulfstan. While discussing Bishop Æthelwold in the course of his *Gesta regum*, William makes the following observation concerning Wulfstan:

Huius [sc. Æthelwold's] uitam Wulstanus quidam, cantor Wintoniensis, discipulus eius scilicet et alumpnus, composuit stylo mediocri. Fecit et aliud opus De Tonorum Harmonia ualde utile, eruditi Angli indicium, homo uitae bonae et eloquentiae castigatae.[12]

Let us take these two works—*Vita S. Æthelwoldi* and *De tonorum harmonia*—in order.

1. *Vita S. Æthelwoldi*.[13] The five surviving manuscripts of this work bear no rubric ascribing it to Wulfstan. However, Wulfstan's authorship may be reliably ascertained on a number of grounds. First, William of Malmesbury knew of two *uitae* of Æthelwold, one of which he ascribed to Wulfstan, as quoted above, the other to Ælfric.[14] Two *uitae*—and only two—from the period earlier than William of Malmesbury have come down to us (see below): one anonymous, the other bearing Ælfric's dedication to Bishop Cenwulf of Winchester.[15] The obvious assumption, therefore, is

[11] A brief account of the writings attributable to Wulfstan is given by Gneuss, *Hymnar*, 246–8; see also the discussion in M. Lapidge, *The Cult of St Swithun*, *WS* iv (2) (Oxford, forthcoming).

[12] *Willelmi Malmesbiriensis monachi de gestis regum Anglorum*, ed. W. Stubbs, 2 vols., RS (1887–9), i. 166–7: 'A certain Wulfstan, the precentor at Winchester and Æthelwold's disciple and follower, composed his *uita* in the unadorned style. He also composed an extremely useful work *De tonorum harmonia*, a witness that he was a learned Englishman, a man of upright life and refined eloquence.'

[13] *BHL*, no. 2647.

[14] *Willelmi Malmesbiriensis monachi de gestis pontificum Anglorum*, ed. N. E. S. A. Hamilton, RS (1870), p. 406: 'reliquit [sc. Ælfric] aliquantos codices, non exigua ingenii monimenta uitam sancti Adelwoldi, antequam eam Wlstanus operiosius concinnaret.' On William's mistaken assumption about the priority of Ælfric's *uita*, see below, pp. cxlvi–clv.

[15] See below, pp. cxlvii and 71.

that the anonymous *uita* is that by Wulfstan; and this assumption is confirmed by various sorts of converging evidence (discussed more fully below, pp. cxlvi–clv): the important role played by Wulfstan in the translation of Æthelwold's remains, described modestly in the third person in the *Vita S. Æthelwoldi* (c. 42); the use of certain chapters of the *Vita S. Æthelwoldi* (cc. 42, 44) by Wulfstan in his *Narratio metrica de S. Swithuno*; and the use of certain phrases and tags in both works,[16] which betrays the workings of one mind. The *Vita S. Æthelwoldi* was composed after the translation of St Æthelwold, which took place on 10 September 996. It is not possible to state precisely how long afterwards: probably very soon, given that two chapters of the work were incorporated into the *Narratio metrica de S. Swithuno*, which is preserved in a manuscript written *c.*1000.[17] Indeed there are reasons for thinking that the *Vita S. Æthelwoldi* was composed to coincide with the translation itself (see below, p. c), which would imply a date of 996 for the work.

2. *De tonorum harmonia*. This work by Wulfstan has never been identified and is usually regarded as lost. If it is indeed lost, however, it was lost in comparatively recent times, for there is sound evidence that it was still extant in the fifteenth century. This evidence is provided by an unprinted, anonymous commentary on Boethius, *De musica*, which is preserved in two fifteenth-century manuscripts now in Oxford (Bodleian Library, Bodley 77; All Souls 90).[18] Among the large number of authorities on musical theory which are quoted in this commentary are four citations of a work by one *Wulstan* (surely our Wulfstan) entitled *Breuiloquium super musicam*. Because on two occasions the anonymous commentator quotes the very wording of Wulfstan, it is worth while reproducing these citations in the hope that they may ultimately be of use in identifying Wulfstan's treatise among the numerous anonymous treatises on music which have come down to us from the central Middle Ages. For the sake of convenience we quote these citations from Oxford, Bodleian Library, Bodley 77:

[16] Phrases such as *aula regia*, *nec mora* (Vergilian), the verb *perstringo*, and others, are mentioned in the notes below.

[17] See below, pp. xx–xxii.

[18] See A. White, 'Boethius in the medieval quadrivium', *Boethius: His Life, Thought and Influence*, ed. M. Gibson (Oxford, 1981), pp. 162–205, at 186.

(*a*) de quibus [sc. commendations of music] prout Dei gratia concesserit, ut habetur in breuiloquio Wulstani super musicam, in processu dicetur . . . (4^{v}).

(*b*) [on the harmony of the heavens]: Iob 38 ubi dicitur 'Quis enarrauit celorum racionem, et concentum celi quis dormire faciet?' [Job 38: 37]. Et hoc idem repetitur in breuiloquio Wulstani super musicam (5^{v}).

(*c*) Et Wulstanus in breuiloquio suo, 'Musica est', inquit, 'uirtus modorum uel troporum musice artis ut gaudentes plus gaudere faciat et plus dolere dolentes' (11^{v}).

(*d*) Et sciendum est quod habetur in breuiloquio Wulstani super musicam: 'est disposicio uocis quam metrici grece thesim appellant; econuerso acumen est eleuacio uocis, grece arsis uocata' (32^{r}).

Several points emerge from these citations: that the work was entitled *Breuiloquium super musicam*, not *De tonorum harmonia* (William's title was presumably a descriptive one);[19] that it was concerned with the theory rather than the practice of music;[20] and that it reflected to some degree Wulfstan's broad range of learning (note the Greek terms quoted from Isidore to illustrate the conception of *uox*). We may hope that this treatise will yet be identified: it would have unique value as the only work on music composed by an Anglo-Saxon.

In addition to these two works mentioned by William of Malmesbury, there is a lengthy poem which is transmitted under Wulfstan's name in manuscript and which has only recently come to light: the *Breuiloquium de omnibus sanctis*.[21] On the basis of the identifiable stylistic features of this poem, however, a larger corpus of poems written in similar style but which are transmitted anonymously in manuscript, may be attributed to Wulfstan with virtual certainty. We begin with the poem which bears Wulfstan's name.

3. *Breuiloquium de omnibus sanctis*. This newly discovered poem consists of 669 hexameters preceded by a prologue of 20 lines of

[19] The title *Breuiloquium* was also used by Wulfstan in his poem on All Saints; see below.

[20] Holschneider (*Organa*, pp. 79–80) conjectured that the work dealt with the theory of polyphony; but he did not have access to the Wulfstan quotations from the Boethius commentary. Note that Wulfstan's definitions of *thesis* and *arsis* derive from Isidore, *Etym.* i. 17. 21; cf. iii. 20. 9. For Wulfstan's knowledge of Isidore, see below, p. 6 n. 2.

[21] F. Dolbeau, 'Le *Breuiloquium de omnibus sanctis*: un poème inconnu de Wulfstan, chantre de Winchester', *AB* cvi (1988), 35–98.

epanaleptic (or paracteric) couplets and an epilogue of 27 hexameters having the acrostic NVNC ET IN AEVVM DEO GRATIAS AMEN and the telestich NVNC ET IN AEVVM SIT DEO LAVS AMEN. The poem proper is a metrical version of an anonymous Carolingian sermon on All Saints, which is known from its incipit as *Legimus in ecclesiasticis historiis*.[22] Briefly, the sermon begins (basing itself on Bede's *Historia ecclesiastica*) by describing the rededication by Pope Boniface IV of the Pantheon in Rome and then, apropos of the Pantheon (which in Greek means '(temple of) all the gods'), goes on to list the various categories of saints venerated by the Church and commemorated on All Saints Day (1 November): the nine orders of angels, patriarchs, prophets, John the Baptist, apostles, martyrs, doctors of the Church, confessors, and, finally, the Virgin Mary and various grades of female saints. The sermon enjoyed wide circulation and was certainly known in Anglo-Saxon England: Ælfric, for example, used it in several of his homilies.[23] As a result of its popularity it was frequently subjected to revision of one sort or another, and several different redactions are found in English manuscripts. The redaction followed by the poet of the *Breuiloquium* is like that found in a late eleventh-century English manuscript (now Durham, Cathedral Library, A. III. 29). The *Breuiloquium* itself is preserved uniquely in an eleventh-century continental legendary, now Brussels, Bibliothèque Royale II. 984 (Saint-Ghislain, s. xi²), fos. 30ᵛ–36ᵛ. Wulfstan's authorship of this poem is clear from the fact that his name—spelt VVLFSTANVS—is preserved in an acrostic in the hexameter lines of the verse prologue:

Vota serena tibi, Iesu bone, reddere uoui;
  Offero nunc eadem uota serena tibi.
Vita beata meis, rogo, crescat in actibus egris,
  Moribus ac uigeat uita beata meis.
Legis amore tue mihi da mala spernere certa;
  Da bona cuncta sequi legis amore tue.
Fulgida castra poli tecum letantur in astris
  Et mihi succurrant fulgida castra poli.

[22] Edited most recently (and discussed in the context of its influence in Anglo-Saxon England) by J. E. Cross, '*Legimus in ecclesiasticis historiis*: A sermon for All Saints and its use in Old English prose', *Traditio*, xxxiii (1977), 101–35. At the time this article was written, Cross was unaware of Wulfstan's *Breuiloquium*.

[23] Ibid., pp. 128–31.

Sint memores miseri, quibus est habitatio celi,
Quem peccata grauant, sint memores miseri.
Te mihi propitium faciant in tempore mortis
Iudiciique die te mihi propitium.
Auxiliare tuo peto, Christe benigne, misello
Seruoque in cunctis auxiliare tuo.
Nomen habere bonum lauacri cui in fonte dedisti,
Annue et in celo nomen habere bonum.
Versibus ecce cano, scriptis que tradita legi,
Et Dominum in sanctis, uersibus ecce cano.
Soluite uincla meae, sancti, rogo, tarda loquele,
Post mortemque anime soluite uincla mee.[24]

There can be no doubt that the VVLFSTANVS in question here is our Wulfstan *Cantor*, for a variety of reasons, which have been carefully set out by François Dolbeau and which may simply be summarized here:[25] the title of the poem includes the word *breuiloquium*, which was used by Wulfstan in his *Breuiloquium super musicam*; the *Breuiloquium de omnibus sanctis* includes a passage in praise of SS Peter and Paul (ll. 360–97) that has no correlate in the prose sermon *Legimus in ecclesiasticis historiis*, and this interpolation is best explained by assuming that the poet had a personal devotion to these saints and by recollecting that the Old Minster, Winchester, was dedicated to SS Peter and Paul; the manner of rendering prose into verse is exactly paralleled by that of the *Narratio metrica de S. Swithuno*, a poem which may plausibly be attributed to Wulfstan on independent grounds (see below); the *Breuiloquium de omnibus sanctis* shares a large number of phrases and lines with the *Narratio*

[24] Dolbeau, 'Le *Breuiloquium*', p. 63: 'I vowed to render joyous prayers to you, good Jesus; I now offer to you these same joyous prayers. I ask that my blessed life may grow strong through my feeble undertakings, and that my blessed life may flourish through my good behaviour. Grant to me through love of your law the ability to reject all certain evil [5]; grant to me the ability to pursue all good through love of your law. The gleaming citadels of heaven rejoice with you on high; and may these gleaming citadels of heaven come to my aid. May those whose dwelling is in heaven be mindful of the poor wretch whom sins oppress: may they be mindful of the wretch [10]. May they make you merciful to me at the time of death, and merciful to me on the Day of Judgement. I ask, O kindly Christ, that you assist your wretched follower, and that you assist your servant in every respect. You granted in the fountain of baptism that he should have a good name [15]; grant that he may also have a good name in heaven. Look: I sing in verses things which I have read handed down in writing, and in these verses I sing the Lord present in his saints. I ask, you saints, that you release the sluggish chains of my speech, and, after my death, that you release the chains of my soul [20].' Note the false quantities in *prŏpitium* (11) and *lauăcri* (15).

[25] Ibid., pp. 41–4, 49–59.

metrica de S. Swithuno (see below, pp. xxi–xxii) which cannot be explained as coincidence and which imply that the same poet was drawing in each case on a common, personal stock of hexametrical formulas; the same poetic models (principally Caelius Sedulius, Arator, and Venantius Fortunatus) are laid heavily under contribution in the two poems; the very same proficient metrical technique (use of nouns in *-amen* to fill the fifth foot of hexameters, elision, monosyllables in the final foot of hexameters, etc.) is found in both poems; the use of epanaleptic verses in the prologue to the *Breuiloquium* is paralleled in four epanaleptic hymns in honour of Winchester saints that may plausibly be attributed to Wulfstan (see below, pp. xxvii–xxix); and, finally, the structure and content of the *Breuiloquium de omnibus sanctis* are precisely paralleled in a further epanaleptic hymn on All Saints which has been attributed to Wulfstan on independent grounds (see below, p. xxix). In sum this evidence puts the attribution of the *Breuiloquium de omnibus sanctis* to Wulfstan Cantor beyond doubt. More importantly, it provides a firm basis for the analysis of Wulfstan's poetic style and technique, and this analysis in turn is decisive in the attribution to Wulfstan of other Anglo-Latin verse which has been transmitted anonymously in manuscript, and to which we may now direct our attention.

4. *Narratio metrica de S. Swithuno*.[26] This poem, a hexametrical version of the *Translatio et miracula S. Swithuni* by Lantfred of Winchester,[27] consists of some 3,386 lines and as such is the longest surviving Anglo-Latin poem. Lantfred's work was completed probably *c.*975 and dedicated to the monks of the Old Minster; it records the miracles which preceded the translation of St Swithun in 971, the translation itself, and the large number of miracles which followed the translation. After the fashion of the time this prose work was turned into hexameters so as to constitute a combined *opus geminatum* or 'twinned work' in both prose and

[26] *BHL*, no. 7947; *ICL*, nos. 3896, 7958; the poem is ed. M. Huber, *S. Swithunus: Miracula Metrica auctore Wulfstano monacho*, Beilage zum Jahresbericht des humanistischen Gymnasiums Metten (Metten, 1906); A. Campbell, *Frithegodi monachi Breuiloquium vitae beati Wilfredi et Wulfstani Cantoris Narratio metrica de sancto Swithuno* (Zürich, 1950), pp. 65–177. A new edition is forthcoming in Lapidge, *The Cult of St Swithun*.

[27] *BHL*, nos. 7944–6. There is an incomplete edition of this text by E. P. Sauvage in *AB* iv (1885), 367–410, complementing a fragmentary 18th-c. edition in the *Acta Sanctorum*. A complete edition, with translation and commentary, is forthcoming in Lapidge, *The Cult of St Swithun*.

verse.[28] From internal evidence it is certain that the author of the hexametrical version was a monk of the Old Minster. There are several clear indications that this monk was Wulfstan. Most important, in the individual dedication or *Epistola specialis* addressed to Bishop Ælfheah (984–1005), the monk describes himself as 'the least little servant of English hymn-singers' (*ultimus Anglorum seruulus hymnicinum*).[29] In order that the personal reference in this line should not be missed, the scribe of the earliest manuscript (London, BL Royal 15. C. VII)—a manuscript written at Winchester perhaps in 996 and in any case within a short time after the poem's completion—glossed the word *ymnicinum* as *cantorum* ('precentors');[30] and given that Wulfstan was consistently known in Winchester circles as Wulfstan *Cantor* (see above, p. xiii), the gloss would seem to be an explicit indication of the poem's authorship. This conclusion was first drawn by John Leland, who in the 1530s found the gloss *ymnicinum: cantorum* in a manuscript of the *Narratio metrica de S. Swithuno* at Sherborne and accordingly attributed the poem to Wulfstan.[31] Leland's attribution, which is entirely plausible, given the links between the poem and the prose *Vita S. Æthelwoldi*, can now be confirmed by the evidence of the *Breuiloquium de omnibus sanctis*, which, as we have seen, has come down to us attributed *nominatim* to Wulfstan. The most striking link between the two works is the fact that they share a number of hexametrical formulas:[32]

Breu. 9 . . . quibus est habitatio celi
NMSS II. 941 . . . quibus est habitatio caelum

Breu. 245 Ducentes uitam cum religione modestam
NMSS II. 822 quae duxit uitam cum religione modestam

[28] Dolbeau ('Le *Breuiloquium*', p. 45) rightly observes that 'depuis Aldhelm et Bède, les adaptations métriques sont un phénomène banal dans l'Angleterre médiévale'; see P. Godman, 'The Anglo-Latin *opus geminatum*: from Aldhelm to Alcuin', *Medium Ævum*, l (1981), 215–29; G. Wieland, '*Geminus stylus*: Studies in Anglo-Latin hagiography', *Insular Latin Studies*, ed. M. W. Herren (Toronto, 1981), pp. 113–33; M. Lapidge, 'Tenth-century Anglo-Latin verse hagiography', *Mittellateinisches Jahrbuch*, xxiv–xxv (1989–90).

[29] *Narratio*, Ep. spec. 12.

[30] London, BL Royal 15. C. VII, fo. 51r; see Campbell, *Frithegodi . . . et Wulfstani Cantoris Narratio metrica*, p. 65.

[31] J. Leland, *Commentarii de scriptoribus Britannicis*, ed. A. Hall (2 vols., Oxford, 1709), i. 165–6. The manuscript in question is Oxford, Bodleian Library, Auct. F. 2. 14. Leland's annotation on fo. 1r reads: 'Autor huius operis fuit Wolstanus praecentor Ventane ecclesie.'

[32] See Dolbeau, 'Le *Breuiloquium*', pp. 42–3.

Breu. 265 Hac eadem sexta ueniens aetate caduca
NMSS, ES 155 quam tulerat sexta ueniens aetate caduca

Breu. 266 Humano generi clemens succurreret omni
NMSS II. 1068 humano generi clemens succurrat ut omni

Breu. 340 . . . que nunc edicere longum est
NMSS II. 15 . . . que nunc edicere longum est

As Dolbeau remarks,[33] verbal similarities such as these (and many more can be adduced) cannot be a matter of coincidence, and imply that both poems are the product of one poet, an implication which is corroborated by the various sorts of stylistic and metrical evidence mentioned earlier.

Wulfstan probably composed his *Narratio metrica de S. Swithuno* in the years 992 × 994 during the archiepiscopate of Sigeric (990–4),[34] and put it in its final form shortly after the translation of St Æthelwold in 996, when two chapters of Wulfstan's prose *Vita S. Æthelwoldi* (cc. 42, 44) were turned into verse and incorporated into the poem.[35] (Although it bears no internal indication of date, the *Breuiloquium de omnibus sanctis* was probably composed shortly after the *Narratio metrica de S. Swithuno*, as Dolbeau has argued.[36]) Finally, it should be noted that the *Narratio metrica de S. Swithuno* is not only the longest surviving Anglo-Latin poem, but is also the most accomplished poem in terms of its metrical technique. Wulfstan here, as in his *Breuiloquium de omnibus sanctis*, shows an impressively wide knowledge of earlier verse (including that of Horace, which was not known in England before this time), and this knowledge has enabled him to master certain metrical techniques, such as the use of elision, the use of monosyllables in the sixth hexameter foot, and even the use of hypermetrical lines, which are all but unknown to other Anglo-Latin poets.[37] This unusual metrical expertise is another important criterion in the attribution of other poems to Wulfstan (see below).

[33] Dolbeau, 'Le *Breuiloquium*', p. 43: 'On m'accordera sans peine qu'il serait absurde de supposer l'existence de deux homonymes qui se recopieraient l'un l'autre. La seul position raisonnable consiste à interpréter ces parallèles comme des "autocitations" et à identifier le Wulfstan qui a signé le *Breuiloquium* avec l'auteur de la *Narratio metrica*.'

[34] *Narratio*, Ep. spec. 221–2.

[35] See below, pp. cxliv–cxlv. In any event a date of *c.*1000 as the outer limit for the poem's composition is suggested not only by the date of the manuscript but by the reference in *Narratio* i. 1077 to 'the turn of the millennium' (*saecli iam margine*).

[36] Dolbeau, 'Le *Breuiloquium*', p. 44.

[37] Ibid., pp. 52–9; see also Lapidge, *The Cult of St Swithun* (forthcoming), and below, p. xxxvii.

5. *Liturgical Materials relating to the Cult of St Æthelwold.* As we shall see (below, pp. c–ci), Wulfstan was active in promoting—and probably in initiating—the cult of Æthelwold; there is good reason to suspect that, as precentor, Wulfstan will have been responsible in the first instance for supplying the various prayers, tropes, and hymns needed for the liturgical celebration of the cult. However, by their very nature such liturgical pieces never carry any attribution of authorship; any deductions concerning Wulfstan's authorship of such *liturgica*, however plausible, must lack proof. Nevertheless it is interesting to remark that in the early twelfth century the Anglo-Norman historian Orderic Vitalis made for himself a copy of Wulfstan's *Vita S. Æthelwoldi*; this copy survives as Alençon, Bibl. mun. 14 (see below, pp. clvii, clxxx). To judge from the nature of its text and from other materials in the manuscript, Alençon 14 was evidently copied from a manuscript (now lost) which originated in the Old Minster, Winchester. What is striking is that the copy of the *Vita S. Æthelwoldi* on fos. 23ʳ–34ᵛ is followed immediately in the Alençon manuscript by a collection of liturgical materials all pertaining to the cult of St Æthelwold:[38]

(*a*) an epanaleptic, abecedarian hymn to St Æthelwold beginning 'Alma lucerna micat': 34ᵛ–35ʳ;

(*b*) a *hymnus uespertinalis* for St Æthelwold, in sapphic stanzas, beginning 'Inclitus pastor populique rector': 35ʳ⁻ᵛ;

(*c*) another hymn for St Æthelwold, this time in octosyllables (inc. 'Celi senator inclite'): 35ᵛ;

(*d*) a collect for St Æthelwold (with the rubric ORATIO) beginning 'Deus qui preclari sideris': 35ᵛ;

(*e*) a mass-set apparently intended for the feast of St Æthelwold's deposition on 1 August: 35ᵛ;

(*f*) a second collect for St Æthelwold beginning 'Gregem tuum pastor eterne': 35ᵛ;

(*g*) a second mass-set, this time specifically designated for the translation of St Æthelwold on 10 September (*.iiii. idus Septembris in translatione sancti Adeluuoldi*): 35ᵛ–36ʳ;

(*h*) a brief treatise entitled *De horis peculiaribus*, concerning various private devotional practices instituted by Æthelwold for his own *familia*: 36ʳ;

[38] The materials were printed from the Alençon manuscript by L. d'Achery and J. Mabillon, *Acta Sanctorum Ordinis S. Benedicti*, 9 vols. (Paris, 1668–1701), saec. v (1685), pp. 624–7, whence they were rptd. *PL* cxxxvii. 104–8.

(*i*) two *Introit* tropes (with chant-cues) for feasts of St Æthelwold, the first presumably for the deposition, the second for the translation: 36ʳ.

At this point the materials pertaining specifically to Æthelwold end, and are followed by various hymns in honour of two other Old Minster saints (Birinus and Swithun); this Winchester material ends on fo. 37ᵛ and the remainder of that folio is blank.

Let us consider these various liturgical pieces in the sequence set out above, asking in each case if there are any features of content or diction which could link them to Wulfstan.

(*a*) The epanaleptic, abecedarian hymn to St Æthelwold (inc. 'Alma lucerna micat').[39] This hymn is one of a group of five such hymns for Winchester saints and feasts; the five share so many features of style and diction that they are most economically to be considered as the work of one author (they are discussed more fully below, pp. xxvii–xxx). Several points may be mentioned here. This hymn shares certain phrases with Wulfstan's *Breuiloquium de omnibus sanctis* (cf., for example, *Breuiloquium* 392, 'Gentibus in cunctis spargunt que semina lucis', with l. 27 of the hymn: 'Omnibus inque locis sparsisti semina lucis') as well as with the *Narratio metrica de S. Swithuno*. Moreover, the metrical form is difficult and restrictive, and could only have been manipulated by a poet with considerable metrical skill. Most importantly, the hymn at two points refers to Æthelwold as the teacher who taught the poet while he was still a *puer*:

> Cuius ab ore sacro fluxerunt dogmata uitae,
> Hausimus omne bonum cuius ab ore sacro . . .
> Transfer ad alta poli pueros quos ipse nutristi,
> Nos prece continua transfer ad alta poli.[40]

Like Wulfstan, the author had been a student of Æthelwold at Winchester, and this creates a presumption in favour of Wulfstan's authorship, but it falls short of proof.

[39] *ICL*, no. 591; *Rep. Hymn.*, nos. 22794, 35139; ptd. *AH* xlviii. 9–12 (no. 1), *PL* cxxxvii. 104–5.

[40] *AH* xlviii. 10; *PL* cxxxvii. 104: 'From whose holy mouth flowed the doctrines of life; from whose holy mouth we absorbed all good . . . Take to the summits of heaven the boys whom you yourself nourished; take us to the summits of heaven with your ceaseless prayer.'

(*b*) The hymn for Vespers (inc. 'Inclitus pastor').[41] The rubric and text of the hymn in Alençon 14 are as follows: *hymnus uespertinalis saphico metro endecasillabo editus, adonium quarto continens in loco*. The hymn consists of five stanzas; thc feast for which it was intended is not specified, but—if considered alongside the following hymn in octosyllables—it was apparently intended for the feast of St Æthelwold's deposition. It is quoted and discussed below; for now, two points should be noted. First, we find here once again the specific statement that Æthelwold was the poet's teacher:

Qui pater noster fuit et magister
Exhibens sacre documenta uite
Et Deo semper satagens placere
Corde benigno.[42]

Secondly, note that the metrical form of the hymn is difficult and rather unusual among Anglo-Latin writings of this time.[43] It could only have been attempted by a poet of some metrical expertise.[44]

(*c*) The octosyllabic hymn for St Æthelwold (inc. 'Celi senator inclite') likewise consists of five stanzas;[45] it was presumably intended for use at Vespers on the vigil of the feast of St Æthelwold's translation. It is quoted and discussed below. The metrical form of this hymn, namely rhythmical octosyllables, is somewhat unusual for the period in which it was composed.[46] The

[41] *ICL*, no. 8011; *Rep. Hymn.*, no. 8849; ptd. *AH* xxiii. 126 (no. 209), xliii. 68 (no. 107), *PL* cxxxvii. 105, and below, pp. cxiii–cxiv.

[42] *AH* xxiii. 126, xliii. 68, *PL* cxxxvii. 105, and below, p. cxiv: 'He was our father and teacher, showing us the pattern of the holy life and always concerned to please God in his kindly heart.'

[43] Two hymns in sapphic metre addressed to St Oswald, bishop of Worcester and archbishop of York (inc. 'Rex angelorum dominator orbis' and 'Inclite pater super astra pollent'; neither listed in *ICL*) are preserved in the so-called 'Portiforium of St Wulstan', now Cambridge, Corpus Christi College 391 (Worcester, s. xi^{2}), p. 256, ptd. E. S. Dewick and W. H. Frere, *The Leofric Collectar II*, HBS lvi (1921), p. 607. However, note that these two Oswald hymns are in the rhythmical sapphic form widely practised in the Middle Ages; our hymn is genuinely quantitative, despite the error in *merĕremur*. On the sapphic form in general, see P. Stotz, *Sonderformen der sapphischen Dichtung: Ein Beitrag zur Erforschung der sapphischen Dichtung des lateinischen Mittelalters* (Munich, 1982).

[44] Note, however, that the form is discussed by Bede, *De arte metrica*, c. 18 (*CCSL* cxxiiiA. 132–3).

[45] *ICL*, no. 1793; *Rep. Hymn.* no. 3511; ed. *AH* xxiii. 127 (no. 210), *PL* cxxxvii. 105, and below, pp. cxiv–cxv.

[46] The only precise contemporary Anglo-Latin parallels for stanzaic hymns in rhythmic octosyllables (as distinct from continuous octosyllables, on which see below, n. 49) are those addressed to St Cuthbert in Cambridge, Corpus Christi College 183 (south-west England, s. x^{1}; provenance Durham) and Vatican City, Biblioteca

form is based ultimately on that of an Ambrosian hymn,[47] but unlike an Ambrosian hymn is in rhythmical rather than quantitative verse.[48] The Anglo-Latin antecedents for the use of rhythmic octosyllables are the poetry of Aldhelm, Æthilwald, and Boniface, and it is possible that the author of 'Celi senator inclite' was consciously writing in an ancient form rarely practised by his contemporaries.[49]

(*d*) The first collect (inc. 'Deus qui preclari sideris'), apparently intended for Vespers on the vigil of the feast of St Æthelwold's deposition. This collect is printed and discussed below (p. cxv); here it is sufficient to remark that it contains specific mention of Æthelwold's teaching: '. . . cuius magisterio totius religionis documenta cognouimus'. The statement that 'we came to know the doctrine of all holiness through his instruction' is most unusual and direct in a prayer of this sort, where one normally finds more generalized and less specific statements about the saint's powers of intercession. It is difficult to avoid the conclusion that these words were composed by a pupil of Æthelwold.

(*e*) The first collect of the first mass-set (printed and discussed below, pp. cxv–cxvi) also contains a reference to Æthelwold's learning, through which the author of the collect has been illuminated: 'cuius eruditione ueritatis tue luce perfundimur'.

(*h*) The brief treatise entitled *De horis peculiaribus* throws interesting light on Æthelwold's devotional practices at Winchester; it

Apostolica Vaticana, Reg. lat. 204 (St Augustine's, Canterbury, s. xi[in]), ed. C. Hohler, 'The Durham services in honour of St Cuthbert', *The Relics of St Cuthbert*, ed. C. F. Battiscombe (Oxford, 1956), pp. 155–91, at 169–76.

47 See P. Klopsch, *Einführung in die mittellateinische Verslehre* (Darmstadt, 1972), pp. 8–16.

48 As Klopsch notes (op. cit., p. 9), the second and fourth feet of the iambic dimeter of an Ambrosian hymn were invariably iambs (⏑ –); the first and third could be iambs, spondees (– –), or anapaests (⏑ ⏑ –). In the present poem, however, the second and fourth feet are frequently spondees (2: *pāstōr*; 4: *ēx āū-*) or even trochees (6: *-dēns sŭ-*). There is a hiatus in l. 18, a practice not tolerated in quantitative Ambrosian hymns. These features are enough to demonstrate that the poet was not attempting to write quantitative verse in this instance.

49 On the characteristics of earlier Anglo-Latin octosyllables (a very loose rhythmic structure, perhaps based simply on syllable-counting, tolerance of hiatus, with the final word of each line consisting of at least a trisyllable), see M. Lapidge and J. L. Rosier, *Aldhelm: The Poetic Works* (Cambridge, 1985), pp. 173–6, together with M. Herren, 'The stress systems in Insular Latin octosyllabic verse', *Cambridge Medieval Celtic Studies*, xv (Summer 1988), 63–84. For contemporary examples of continuous octosyllables, see Lantfred, *Translatio et miracula S. Swithuni*, cc. 26 (inc. 'Alme Deus munificens'), 34 ('Auctor o rerum prepotens').

is quoted and discussed below (pp. lxviii–lxxvii) and need only be briefly summarized here. It concerns the use of three supplementary offices to be said privately by those subject to Æthelwold's discipline (*quosque subiectos*). The offices consisted largely of psalmody; the first was dedicated to the Virgin Mary, the second to SS Peter and Paul (the saints to whom the Old Minster was dedicated), and the third to All Saints. Regrettably the author of the treatise (or the scribe of Orderic's exemplar) did not trouble to copy them out since they could be found *plerisque in locis*, and they have not yet been identified in a surviving Anglo-Saxon manuscript. However, the reference in the treatise to the 'approaching times of Antichrist' (*uicinis Antichristi temporibus*) may suggest that it was written before the turn of the millennium; it was in any case written by someone who had been a member of the *familia* of Æthelwold at the Old Minster.

(*i*) The two *Introit* tropes. There is no rubric in the manuscript (except the single word *tropi*), but the liturgical function of the two tropes can be determined from one of the 'Winchester Tropers' (see below, p. xxx), where they are given as *Introit* tropes without further specification.[50] These tropes are quoted and discussed below (pp. cxvii–cxviii), but here it may be noted that they have a striking resemblance to some hexameters in Wulfstan's *Narratio metrica de S. Swithuno*. Compare, for example, the line from the first trope:

inter apostolicos stola splendente *ierarchos*

with the following line from Wulfstan:

inter apostolicos sed lucet in axe *ierarchos*.[51]

It is difficult not to think that the one poet composed both lines.

These various sorts of converging evidence suggest, though they cannot prove, that Wulfstan was the author of some, perhaps all, of these liturgical pieces for the cult of St Æthelwold.

6. Five abecedarian, epanaleptic (paracteric) poems which are preserved in various manuscripts but which, because of a similarity in style and diction, are almost certainly the work of one author.

[50] Ed. W. H. Frere, *The Winchester Troper*, HBS viii (1894), pp. 32–3; *AH* xlix. 99 (nos. 209–10); Planchart, *Repertory* ii. 175 (nos. 170–1).

[51] *Narratio*, Ep. spec. 281. Note the false quantity *stōla*.

All five poems are transmitted anonymously in manuscript. It is essential to treat these epanaleptic poems individually, since they were apparently composed at different times (and since one of them exists in two distinct redactions). What is probably the earliest of them is a poem addressed to St Swithun and preserved in London, BL Royal 15. C. VII, fos. 49v–50r: 'Aurea lux patriae Wentana splendet in urbe.'[52] Given the origin and date of the Royal manuscript—Old Minster, Winchester, s. x/xi—and given the fact that the poem is there preserved alongside Wulfstan's *Narratio metrica de S. Swithuno*, there is some presumption that the poem was composed at Winchester in the last part of the tenth century. It is clear from the I-distich of the poem ('Illa uidere tuum meruit super aethra meatum / digna fuitque obitum ille uidere tuum') with its mention of Swithun's *obitus*, that the poem was intended in the first instance for the feast of St Swithun's deposition on 2 July; and this is confirmed by a rubric written against the I-distich in the margin of the manuscript (*in depositione .vi. non. Iulii*). However, by the late tenth century, three feasts of St Swithun were celebrated at Winchester: his deposition (2 July), translation (15 July), and ordination (29 October). The poet of 'Aurea lux patriae' evidently wished to give his poem some liturgical flexibility, so he composed two additional or alternative I-distichs, one pertaining to the translation on 15 July ('Iste dies rutilat tua quam translatio sacrat'), the other to the ordination on 29 October ('Ista dies renitet tua quam crismatio sacrat').[53] With these two additional distichs, then, the poem 'Aurea lux patriae' could be made to do service *ad libitum* for all the feast-days of St Swithun which were observed at Winchester.

The next epanaleptic poems to be considered are a group[54]

[52] *ICL*, no. 1444. This version of the poem is also contained in London, BL Cotton Nero E. I, pt. 2, fo. 52v–53r (the text of which, like that of Lantfred's *Translatio et miracula S. Swithuni* in the same manuscript, was demonstrably copied from Royal 15. C. VII), whence it is ptd. *AH* xix. 258–60 (no. 470). Another copy of the poem, with a few alterations, is contained in the aforementioned manuscript Alençon, Bibl. mun. 14. This manuscript was written by Orderic Vitalis, and the alterations are almost certainly his. The poem is ptd. from the Alençon manuscript by E. P. Sauvage, 'Hymni paracterici tres in laudem S. Swithuni', *AB* v (1886), 53–8, at pp. 57–8, and by C. Blume, 'Wolstan von Winchester und Vital von Saint-Évroult, Dichter der drei Lobgesänge auf die heiligen Athelwold, Birin und Swithun', *Sitzungsberichte der K. Akademie der Wissenschaften in Wien*, cxlvi (3) (Vienna, 1903), 9–12; cf. also Gneuss, *Hymnar*, p. 247.

[53] These two distichs are ptd. Gneuss, *Hymnar*, p. 118.

[54] The entire group is ptd. from the Rouen manuscript in *AH* xlviii. 9–18, and also by Blume, 'Wolstan von Winchester', pp. 3–12.

dedicated to Winchester saints and preserved in Rouen, Bibl. mun. 1385 (U. 107), a manuscript written at Winchester in the late tenth century (s. x^{ex}): two to St Swithun (inc. 'Aurea lux patrie', a redaction of the poem discussed above, and a second beginning 'Auxilium, Domine, qui te rogitantibus adfers'),[55] one to St Birinus, the apostle of Wessex (inc. 'Agmina sacra poli iubilent modulamine dulci'),[56] and the poem on St Æthelwold discussed earlier, beginning 'Alma lucerna micat sol aureus arua serenat'. Some of these poems have clear verbal links with the *Breuiloquium*: cf. l. 599 ('Organa dulcisonis agitet modulantia bombis' with 'Agmina sacra', l. 27: 'Organa clarisonis reboant tibi dulcia bombis'). It is unclear why the poem 'Aurea lux patriae' as preserved in the Royal manuscript should have undergone the drastic revision which results in the Rouen redaction; possibly the decision was taken to restrict 'Aurea lux patriae' exclusively to the feast of the deposition on 2 July,[57] and to compose an entirely new poem—'Auxilium, Domine'—for the feast of the translation.[58]

Finally there is an abecedarian, epanaleptic poem (inc. 'Aula superna poli reboet modulamine dulci') for the feast of All Saints (1 November).[59] The feast of All Saints was observed universally at this time, though it is worth recalling that Æthelwold included a special devotion for All Saints for his *familia* at the Old Minster, as we learn from the treatise *De horis peculiaribus* mentioned above. Furthermore, the structure of the poem (that is, the sequence of saints which is invoked) is paralleled precisely in the *Breuiloquium de omnibus sanctis*, equally a commemoration for All Saints. By the same token, there are various verbal links between 'Aula superna' and the *Breuiloquium*. With two lines of the *Breuiloquium* quoted above (6–7: 'Da bona cuncta sequi legis amore tue / Fulgida castra

[55] For 'Aurea lux patrie', see above, n. 52; for 'Auxilium Domine', see *ICL*, no. 1530. The two Swithun hymns are ptd. Sauvage, 'Hymni paracterici tres', pp. 53–8.

[56] *ICL*, no. 474; *Rep. Hymn.*, no. 729.

[57] In the Rouen manuscript there is a contemporary gloss against the line commemorating the feast (18: 'Haec benedicta dies astris arridet et aruis') as follows: *sexta nonas Iulii* (= 2 July, the feast of St Swithun's deposition).

[58] There is no rubric to the poem in the manuscript; but the mention of miracles performed by St Swithun in ll. 19–22 refers by implication to the translation, for it was only after the translation on 15 July 971 that Swithun's miraculous powers were publicly known.

[59] *ICL*, no. 1409a; ed. in P. Dronke, M. Lapidge, and P. Stotz, 'Die unveröffentlichten Gedichte der Cambridger Liederhandschrift (CUL Gg. 5. 35)', *Mittellateinisches Jahrbuch*, xvii (1982), 54–95, at pp. 59–65.

poli tecum letantur in astris') compare the following two lines of 'Aula superna':

7 Dat bona cuncta bonis Deus ille piusque bonusque
23 Milibus angelicis sursum letaris in astris.

Similarly there are unmistakeable verbal links between 'Aula superna' and the *Narratio metrica de S. Swithuno*. Consider, for example, the C-distich of 'Aula superna':

Cimbala psalmicinum modulant ibi dulciter ymnum
et feriunt iubilum cimbala psalmicinum.

The cadence of the hexameter recurs in *Narratio* i. 1318 ('curarentque Deo persoluere dulciter ymnum'), and the opening words of the pentameter are found in the *Epistola specialis* which prefaces the *Narratio* (161: 'et feriunt iubilum septem discrimina uocum'), where the poet is describing the mighty organ which was installed by Bishop Ælfheah at the Old Minster, Winchester.[60] The verbal links between these various poems, and the recognizable individuality of the poetic technique which they share, indicates beyond reasonable doubt that they are the work of one poet; and, thanks to the acrostic which prefaces the *Breuiloquium*, that poet may confidently be identified as Wulfstan Cantor.

The poem for All Saints, 'Aula superna', is preserved uniquely in the manuscript written at St Augustine's, Canterbury, near the middle of the eleventh century (Cambridge, UL Gg. 5. 35, fos. 362^{v}–363^{v}). The circumstances by which this poem came to be preserved in a Canterbury rather than a Winchester manuscript are not immediately clear; a possible explanation is given below (p. xxxviii).

7. Various hexametrical rubrics, tropes, and sequences in the so-called 'Winchester Tropers'. The term 'Winchester Tropers' is used to describe two musical manuscripts which preserve independent but related copies of a substantial collection of tropes, sequences, and organa originally intended for use in performance of the mass at Winchester in the late tenth century.[61]

[60] See discussion by Lapidge in 'Die unveröffentlichten Gedichte', p. 62. Note the false quantity *iŭbilum*.

[61] Ed. Frere, *The Winchester Troper*, pp. 3–68; the tropes in the two manuscripts are fully inventoried by Planchart, *Repertory*. See also J. Handschin, 'The two Winchester tropers', *Journal of Theological Studies*, xxxvii (1936), 34–49, 156–72, and Holschneider, *Organa*, esp. pp. 14–63.

The two manuscripts are: Cambridge, Corpus Christi College 473 (Old Minster, Winchester, s. xi^{in}) and Oxford, Bodleian Library, Bodley 775 (Old Minster, Winchester, s. xi^{med}). Although Bodley 775 is the later manuscript, it is evidently a copy of a (now lost) manuscript written at Winchester 978 × 985.[62] CCCC 473, on the other hand, was probably written 996 × 1005; its small format, together with the various additions and musical annotations, suggests that it was intended for the personal use of the precentor. In the case of the hexametrical rubrics, the simplest assumption is that they were composed *ad hoc* by whoever first assembled the collection.[63] In the case of both the tropes and sequences, however, what we have in these manuscripts is a collection of materials of Frankish origin (that is, pertaining in the first instance to Frankish saints and feasts) to which texts pertaining to English—and specifically Winchester—saints have been added. It is a reasonable assumption that these texts were composed at Winchester in the late tenth century; and since Wulfstan was the precentor at the Old Minster at that time, there is a consequent assumption that he is their author. Let us consider these tropes and sequences separately.

First, the tropes. The tropes in these two manuscripts have been comprehensively and accurately catalogued by Planchart, and the following list is based entirely on his catalogue. We give only those tropes which pertain to English saints and feasts, or which occur uniquely in one or both of the 'Winchester Tropers'.[64]

Proper Tropes. Holy Innocents (Planchart no. 5, 'Laudibus alternis'; 'O quam felix'; 'Eia nunc omnes pueri').

Introit Tropes. First Sunday in Advent (no. 9, 'Almifico quondam'); Feria .III. in Easter Week (no. 11, 'Aeterno populos'); St Michael (nos. 14, 'Coniuncti superis', and 20, 'Summi caelicolae'); Christmas (no. 41, 'Hymnidicis te, Christe'); St Andrew (nos. 43, 'Cum populis pietate sui', and 44, 'Intuitu placido'); Vigil of St John (no. 53, 'Hoc mihi donauerat'); St Justus (nos. 59, 'Cuius et in pueris', and 71, 'Ecce dies uenerandus adest'); St Denis (no. 73, 'En nunc martyribus'); Feria .II. in Easter Week (nos. 94, 'Conditor

62 Planchart, *Repertory*, i. 42.

63 The hexametrical rubrics are ptd. Frere, *The Winchester Troper*, pp. 47, 54, 67; see also Holschneider, *Organa*, pp. 88, 130.

64 See Planchart, *Repertory*, i. 145, 156; the numbers in the following list refer to Planchart's inventory.

almificus', and 95, 'Munere pro tali'); Annunciation (nos. 146, 'Contio uatidicis', 147, 'Germinis excelsi', 148, 'Hoc psalmista iubar', 149, 'Multiplici iubilo', and 150, 'Splendidus aduentum'); St Paul (no. 151, 'Caelica suspirans'); St Swithun (nos. 160, 'Aurea lux hodie rutilat', and 164, 'Ecce patronus adest'); the two tropes for St Æthelwold mentioned previously (nos. 170, 'Patris adest uotiua dies', and 171, 'Praesul Æðeluuoldus'; ptd. below, p. cxvii); Feria .IV. in Easter Week (nos. 184, 'Omnibus ecce piis', and 185, 'Quos mea perpetuo'); and Nativity of the Virgin (nos. 190, 'Cunctipotens Domine', and 192, 'Processisse paterno').

Offertory Tropes. Feria .II. in Easter Week (nos. 197, 'Morte triumphata', 198, 'Cernentes uacuum', 199, 'Cum sibi discipuli', 200, 'En ego saluator', and 248, 'Gentibus introitum'); Ascension (nos. 207, 'Laetetur cunctus', 208, 'Quaeque fidem rectam', 209, 'Excelsas, dignas Domino', and 210, 'Qui zabulum strauit'); St Swithun (nos. 249, 'Hos inter mea quos fecit', and 250, 'O dee uirtutum'); Feria .IV. in Easter Week (no. 265, 'Magnus et inmensus'); Pentecost (nos. 218, 'Victori mortis', 219, 'Hic ubi recta fides', and 220, 'Omnia quadrifidi'); Common of Apostles (nos. 226, 'Principium ex me principio', 227, 'Per quem uelle meum', and 228, 'Vt cunctis per me ueniat'); Purification of the Virgin (nos. 229, 'Cuncta quod ipse manes', 230, 'Ex me progenitum', and 231, 'Qui species superas'); Dedication of a Church (nos. 236, 'Qui caelum, terram, mare', and 237, 'Omnibus expletis fuerant'); Common of Virgins (nos. 243, 'Corporibus te delectant', and 244, 'Quod mecum mansit'); Common of Apostles again (nos. 246, 'Inspirante sacro', and 247, 'Humano generi'); St Paul (no. 259, 'Quos uirtute tui, rex caeli'); Common of Virgins again (nos. 245, 'Sustentans humiles', and 264, 'Maxima dona Deo'); St Michael (no. 278, 'Emundes mentem'); and Palm Sunday(?) (no. 281, 'Iudicium magno metuens').

Communion Tropes. Feria .IV. in Easter Week (no. 292, 'Vocis apostolicae'); Annunciation (no. 299, 'Virginis antiquae'); St Justus (no. 311, 'Iam miserens nobis Dominus'); Feria .III. in Easter Week (no. 316, 'Paschalis festi'); Feria .II. in Easter Week (no. 319, 'Confracta barathri'); St Paul (no. 290, 'Iesus tale suis'); Common of a Confessor (no. 295: 'Gloria celsa manet'); Common of Apostles (no. 300, 'Lucratis populis'); Ascension (no. 308, 'Plaudite corde, manu'); Common of a Martyr (no. 312, 'Haec meus accipiet');

Epiphany (no. 329, 'Stella duce Magi'); and St Peter (no. 318: 'Rex regum, Dominus').

Of course the fact that some of these tropes are not attested in earlier Continental repertories is no guarantee that they were composed at Winchester, let alone by Wulfstan. Perhaps only with tropes for saints venerated especially at Winchester—Swithun, Æthelwold, Justus—is it safe to assume a Winchester origin. However, all the tropes listed above are in the form of hexameters or groups of hexameters (although they clearly were not chanted as hexameters), and many of them have striking resemblances to hexameters in Wulfstan's other poetry. We mentioned earlier the verbal parallel between a line in the *Narratio metrica de S. Swithuno* and a trope for St Æthelwold (p. xxvii). There is also an indisputable parallel between one of the Introit tropes for St Justus (no. 71) and the *Breuiloquium de omnibus sanctis*. Compare the trope

> Ecce dies uenerandus adest, dicamus ouantes,
> Quem *statuere patres antiqui rite colendum*
> Et iubilant pariter mortales omne per aeuum

with ll. 49–50 of the *Breuiloquium*:

> *Antiqui statuere patres* hoc *rite* tenendum
> Hoc et in ecclesia generaliter esse *colendum*.[65]

Similarly, the phrasing of an Offertory trope for the Dedication of a Church (no. 237: '*Omnibus expletis* fuerant quae rite patranda') is reflected in Wulfstan's description of the dedication ceremony which took place at the Old Minster on 20 October 980: '*Omnibus expletis* tandem sollempniter hymnis.'[66] There are numerous such verbal correspondences between tropes in the Winchester repertory and Wulfstan's poetry—enough to suggest that Wulfstan may have been their author, a suggestion which in any case is likely enough, given Wulfstan's position as precentor at the Old Minster in the late tenth century. However, the matter requires closer investigation; the list of tropes given above would provide a starting-point for it, but in the present state of our knowledge cannot be regarded in any way as a list of tropes composed by Wulfstan.

65 See Dolbeau, 'Le *Breuiloquium*', p. 59.
66 *Narratio*, Ep. spec. 103.

A similar situation obtains with respect to the prose texts (proses) of the sequences in the 'Winchester Tropers'. Here, too, the two manuscripts preserve a substantial corpus of sequences, the core of which is of Continental origin but to which a number of sequences pertaining to English saints and feasts have been added. But whereas the tropes and organa from these two manuscripts have been systematically studied and catalogued, there has as yet been no systematic attempt to compare the repertory of sequences in the 'Winchester Tropers' with those in earlier Continental manuscripts.[67] The following list is therefore provisional. It consists of three parts: first, sequences pertaining to English (and specifically Winchester) saints; secondly, sequences preserved uniquely in one or both of the 'Winchester Tropers'; and thirdly, sequences whose earliest manuscript attestation is in one or both of the 'Winchester Tropers'.[68]

Sequences for English saints. St Birinus (no. 171, 'Caelum, mare, tellus / et, quae sunt, cuncta'); St Æthelwold (no. 205, 'Laude celebret / uox quoque Deum / dulcisona'); St Hæddi (no. 228, 'Aue, pontifice Hædde / rutilans in aula'); St Justus (no. 256, 'Fulget dies iucunda'); St Swithun (no. 337: 'Gaudens Christi / praesentia iucunda'); and SS Birinus and Swithun (no. 153: 'Laude resonet / te, Christe, deuote / supplex turma').[69]

Sequences preserved uniquely in one or both of the 'Winchester Tropers'. Holy Cross (nos. 12, 'Gaudeat / fidelis plebs uniuersa', and 13, 'Laus surgat / ubique Christo iucunda'); Easter Day (no. 22, 'Pange, turma, corde, uultu / Christo praeconia'); Sundays (*AH* xxxvii, nos. 41, 'Gloria / resonante cymbalarum', and 42, 'Consona caterua'; *AH* xl, nos. 41, 'Ad te pulchra', 42, 'Laude pulchra', 43, 'Alme Deus / cui seruiunt cuncta', 44, 'Angelicae / turmae pulcherrima', 45, 'Arce summa', 46, 'Aulae celsae lux summa', 47, 'Laus inclita / Domino reddatur', 48, 'Aulae plebs aethereae /

[67] The sequences in Bodley 775 are ptd. W. G. Henderson, *Missale ad usum insignis ecclesiae Eboracensis*, 2 vols., Surtees Society, lix–lx (Durham, 1872–4), ii. 218–318; see also *AH* xl. 21–342 *passim*.

[68] Unless otherwise specified, numbers in parentheses refer to the edition in *AH* xl. 21–342. We list only those sequences copied by the original scribes of the manuscripts, and omit those which were later additions.

[69] Note that we omit the sequences to St Æthelwold (no. 204: 'Dies sacra dies ista') and St Swithun (no. 306: 'Psallat ecclesia'), for these are later additions to the manuscripts and are stylistically distinct from those listed above; see also Holschneider, *Organa*, p. 79 n. 70.

cuncta iucunda', 49, 'Christicolarum sacrosancta', 50, 'Exultate Deo / agmina', 51, 'Laude canora / uox pulchra / sileat nulla', 52, 'Lyra pulchra / regem angelica', and 53, 'Laudent condita / omnia pulchra'); the Virgin Mary (no. 84, 'Salue, mater / Christi o inclita'); All Saints (no. 131, 'Gaudet clemens Dominus / super agmina sacra'); St Andrew (no. 140, 'Clara cantemus / sonoriter cantica'); St Augustine (no. 152: 'Aulae rutilae / micantem iubare / fratres, eia'); St John the Evangelist (no. 252, 'Laus harmoniae / resultet alleluia'); St Laurence (no. 272, 'Laurea clare laetantem'); St Martin (no. 289, 'Promere chorda / iam conetur intima'); St Peter in Chains (no. 314, 'Sollemnitate rutilans / apostolica'); Holy Martyrs (nos. 381, 'Arguta plectro syllaba / concrepante', and 382, 'Laudem dicite Deo / martyrum turba'); Holy Confessors (no. 390, 'Cantent / te Christe, nunc nostrae camenae'); Holy Virgins (no. 395, 'Alleluia / Deo promat / plebs nostra cantica pulchra'); and One Virgin (no. 399: 'Laude Christum / modulemus pulchra').[70]

Sequences attested first in one or both of the 'Winchester Tropers'. Resurrection of the Lord (nos. 21, 'Concinat orbis / cunctus Alleluia', and 23, 'Psalle lyrica / carmina'); Pentecost (no. 33, 'Gaude, mater ecclesia / filiorum'); All Saints (no. 95, 'Almae caelorum turmae'); Holy Innocents (no. 237, 'Pura Deum / laudet innocentia', and *AH* liii, no. 162, 'Celsa pueri concrepent melodia'); SS Peter and Paul (no. 315, 'Agmina laeta / plaudant caelica'); and St Bartholomew (*AH* liii, no. 129, 'Alle- cantabile sonet / chorus cantorum et / subiungat dulcibile / -luia').

Of these three groups of sequences, those in the first were evidently composed at the Old Minster, Winchester, in the late tenth century; and since Wulfstan as precentor will have been responsible for liturgical performance there, we have an a priori reason to suspect that he was their author. The suspicion could perhaps be confirmed by stylistic analysis of the sequences, but such analysis is hindered by the fact that the sequences are in prose, whereas the remainder of Wulfstan's poetic corpus (excepting only the poem in octosyllables: see above, p. xxv) is quantitative

[70] Note that we omit here a sequence which might on our own criteria otherwise be included, namely that for St Benedict (no. 165, 'Arce superna / cuncta qui gubernat / sidera'), since an internal reference to the church at Fleury where St Benedict's relics lay (*hac in sede*) suggests that the sequence was composed at Fleury, even though it is preserved solely in Winchester manuscripts. It provides in any case a further illustration of the links between Fleury and Winchester in the late 10th c.

verse, and verbal parallels are correspondingly infrequent. The problem is heightened for the sequences in the second and third groups, although here it might be possible to demonstrate stylistic links between them and the first group, thereby to confirm the supposition of Winchester origin. One of the sequences for St Swithun, for example—that beginning 'Gaudens Christi'—has a distinctive diction consisting of Graecisms (*ierarcha*, *malagmate*), Graecizing verbs in *-izo* (*sollemnizet*, *praeconizet*), and unusual compound adjectives (*multisona*, *caeliflua*); and some of these features, especially the compound adjectives, are found prominently in the various sequences composed for Sundays. Detailed stylistic analysis of the diction of all the sequences listed above might help to confirm the hypothesis of a Winchester origin for some of them. And if it could be established which sequences were composed at Winchester, there would be the same a priori case for considering Wulfstan as their author. But in the present state of our knowledge this can be no more than hypothesis.

Before we leave the 'Winchester Tropers', another possible aspect of Wulfstan's scholarly activity should be mentioned. Wulfstan was precentor at Winchester in the late tenth century, and of the two 'Winchester Tropers' one—CCCC 473—was written at the Old Minster in the early years of the eleventh century and was evidently designed as a precentor's personal chant-book. Now CCCC 473 is principally the work of two collaborating scribes; of these, Scribe I wrote the text for the troper and the prose texts or proses for the sequences (fos. 10–52, 55–78, 89–134); Scribe II, who—to judge from his scribal activity—was a specialist music scribe, copied the sequences (that is, the musical accompaniment of the proses) on fos. 81–8 and the *uox organalis* (that is, the second, accompanying voice) to the tropes on fos. 135–52, 163–89; the principal voice was not written down because it was evidently known from memory by the user of the book. (The remaining leaves, originally left blank by these two scribes, were filled in later by various eleventh-century hands.) It has been suggested, with some plausibility, that Wulfstan was the composer of the *uox organalis* in CCCC 473;[71] and, if so, there arises the tantalizing possibility that Scribe II is identical with Wulfstan himself.[72] Again, regrettably, this possibility cannot be proved.

[71] Holschneider, *Organa*, pp. 76–80.

[72] Planchart, *Repertory*, i. 25.

The sum of this evidence suggests that Wulfstan was a prolific and versatile author of Latin works, even if the precise limits of his activity can no longer (or not yet) be determined. Some progress in determining the corpus of his writings may yet be made by careful stylistic analysis of the works listed above; but it is important that the scope of this analysis not be limited to those works alone. One example of writings which also might merit attention is a group of three hymns[73] to St Augustine of Canterbury preserved uniquely in Durham, Cathedral Library, B. III. 32, fos. 29ʳ–30ʳ, an English manuscript datable to the first half of the eleventh century. It was formerly thought that the manuscript was written at Winchester, and hence Blume ascribed the group of hymns to Wulfstan, on no stronger grounds than those of the manuscript's supposed origin and the fact that one of the hymns (inc. 'Summa Dei bonitas') is in epanaleptic distichs, a form which, as we have seen, was practised by Wulfstan.[74] However, as Helmut Gneuss has pointed out,[75] there is no evidence that St Augustine of Canterbury was culted at Winchester, and it is now known that Durham B. III. 32 was written at Christ Church, Canterbury, not Winchester. These facts would seem to rule out the possibility of Wulfstan's authorship, for as far as we know he was associated only with the Old Minster in Winchester. Nevertheless the matter merits consideration. In the first place, the three hymns to St Augustine show surprising metrical versatility: the first (inc. 'Caelestis aulae nobiles')[76] is an Ambrosian hymn, a quantitative form not certainly practised elsewhere in eleventh-century England; the second (inc. 'Summa Dei bonitas')[77] is in epanaleptic distichs, which—although they are not abecedarian—have their closest English parallel in the poems of Wulfstan discussed above. Most interesting, however, is the third (inc. 'Aueto placidis praesul amabilis'),[78] which is in a stanzaic, quantitative verse-form practised by Horace[79] but, as far as we know, unique in Anglo-Saxon England and excessively rare in the Middle Ages as a whole. Each stanza consists of three lesser asclepiads (– –|– ∪ ∪ –|– ∪ ∪ –|∪ ⏓) followed by a glyconic (– –|– ∪ ∪ –|∪ ⏓).

[73] *AH* li. 164–6; also ptd. J. Stevenson, *The Latin Hymns of the Anglo-Saxon Church*, Surtees Society, xxiii (Durham, 1851), pp. 99–102.

[74] *AH* li. 165.

[75] Gneuss, *Hymnar*, p. 248.

[76] *ICL*, no. 1787; *Rep. Hymn.*, no. 3447.

[77] *ICL*, no. 15796; *Rep. Hymn.*, no. 19623.

[78] *ICL*, no. 1558; *Rep. Hymn.*, no. 2293.

[79] *Carm.* i. 6, 15, 24, 33; ii. 12; ii. 10, 16; iv. 5, 12.

Nobis ista dies sumptibus innuit
Quid tu, quis opibus florueris, situs
Cum terris redolens infima presseris,
Augustine placabilis.[80]

The excessive rarity of the verse-form in medieval Latin suggests that it could only have been attempted by a poet who was familiar with Horace and who was a thoroughly accomplished metrician. Our only evidence for the knowledge of Horace in late Anglo-Saxon England is from Winchester: a lively poem composed there during Æthelwold's bishopric (the author of this poem was possibly Lantfred)[81] and Wulfstan's own *Narratio metrica de S. Swithuno*.[82] And Wulfstan was beyond doubt an accomplished metrician. Let us assume, for the sake of argument, that Wulfstan did compose the three hymns to St Augustine. How then should we explain his devotion to the Canterbury saint? Planchart observed that the stint of Scribe II—possibly Wulfstan himself—in CCCC 473 had been inexplicably terminated, and he suggested that Wulfstan may have abandoned the copying of the manuscript in 1005 in order to follow his patron Ælfheah, who in that year was appointed archbishop of Canterbury.[83] This of course is pure hypothesis, and Planchart did not attempt to adduce any evidence in its favour. Yet there may be some, however tenuous. One of the epanaleptic hymns discussed above—that for All Saints, almost certainly composed by Wulfstan—is preserved uniquely in a mid-eleventh-century manuscript from St Augustine's, Canterbury (now Cambridge, UL Gg. 5. 35).[84] In this same manuscript is preserved a lengthy excerpt from Wulfstan's *Narratio metrica de S. Swithuno* (his hexametrical version of the 'Te Deum').[85] It may well be asked how these works were transmitted from Winchester to Canterbury. A move thither by Wulfstan would supply an explanation for this, and also a context for the composition of

[80] *AH* li. 166: 'This day signifies to us with its charges with what bounties you, gentle Augustine, when redolent on earth you were treading these lower regions, now flourish.' Note the false quantity *plăcabilis*.

[81] See M. Lapidge, 'Three Latin poems from Æthelwold's school at Winchester', *ASE* i (1972), 85–137, at p. 109.

[82] See A. Campbell, 'Some linguistic features of early Anglo-Latin verse and its use of classical models', *Transactions of the Philological Society*, 1953, 1–20, at p. 8; to this add Wulfstan, *Narratio*, Ep. spec. 91 (*foecundi calices*) = Horace, *Epist.* i. 5. 19.

[83] Planchart, *Repertory*, i. 33.

[84] See Dronke, Lapidge, and Stotz, 'Die unveröffentlichten Gedichte', pp. 59–65.

[85] Ibid., p. 55.

the three hymns to St Augustine of Canterbury. But it is unwise to write literary history on the basis of such tenuous evidence. It is enough to record that Wulfstan was one of the most accomplished Latin scholars of pre-Conquest England. We may now look more closely at the subject of his *Vita S. Æthelwoldi*, and the circumstances which led to its composition.

II. ÆTHELWOLD, WULFSTAN, AND THE *VITA S. ÆTHELWOLDI*

Wulfstan's *Vita S. Æthelwoldi* is the principal source for our knowledge of Æthelwold, but it is by no means the only one. Æthelwold was a very prominent personality in late tenth-century England, and it is not surprising that he should be mentioned in various contemporary sources such as the *Anglo-Saxon Chronicle*. These sources often corroborate or amplify the picture of Æthelwold which is drawn by Wulfstan, and it may be useful to set down briefly what may be known of this influential bishop from surviving Anglo-Saxon sources, including Wulfstan's *uita*.[1]

1. *The Chronology of Æthelwold's Life*

We may begin with the simple chronology of Æthelwold's life. Only on three occasions does Wulfstan give precise dates for events in Æthelwold's life: he gives the date on which he was elevated to the bishopric of Winchester (c. 16),[2] the date on which the rebuilt Old Minster was consecrated (c. 40), and the date on which Æthelwold died (c. 41).[3] For other events Wulfstan does not himself provide a date, but the date can be ascertained from other contemporary sources. Thus the translation of St Swithun, mentioned by Wulfstan in c. 26, can be dated precisely by reference to Lantfred's *Translatio et miracula S. Swithuni*.[4] Similarly, a

[1] For earlier accounts of Æthelwold, see Robinson, *Times*, pp. 104–22; E. S. Duckett, *Saint Dunstan of Canterbury* (London, 1955), pp. 111–36; and the various essays in *Bishop Æthelwold*.

[2] Also given in ASC 963 AE (Bately, *MS A*, p. 75; Plummer, *Two Chronicles*, i. 114–15).

[3] Also given in ASC 984 ACDE (Bately, *MS A*, p. 78; Plummer, *Two Chronicles*, i. 124–5).

[4] *Translatio*, praef.: 'post cuius [sc. Christi] ergo ineffabilem mirifice humationis adunationem, transcurso nongentorum curriculo annorum cum bis septeni reuolutione

number of events mentioned by Wulfstan may be dated precisely by reference to the *Anglo-Saxon Chronicle*: the deaths of Kings Athelstan (c. 10),[5] Edmund (c. 10),[6] and Eadred (c. 13),[7] or the refoundation of the Old and New Minsters in Winchester (cc. 18 and 20).[8] There is no doubt about the dates of events such as these; but other events, too, can probably be ascertained by reference to the *Anglo-Saxon Chronicle*. In c. 29, for example, we are told that Æthelwold once fed his people during a time of great famine by breaking up the church-plate, where the famine (*acerba fames*) in question is very probably that 'great famine' recorded in one version of the *Chronicle* s.a. 976: 'Her on þys geare wæs se miccla hungor on Angelcynne.'[9] By correlating the dating information given by Wulfstan himself with that obtained from other contemporary sources, therefore, it is possible to establish that Wulfstan followed a strictly chronological sequence in describing the events of Æthelwold's life; and our perception of this sequence in turn enables us to establish the *relative* chronology of those events for which Wulfstan and the contemporary sources do not assign precise dates. In the following table we set out the chronology of Æthelwold's life. Reading from left to right we give chapter-numbers of the *Vita S. Æthelwoldi* (omitting those chapters which do not refer to events in Æthelwold's life, such as cc. 3–5); the event in question; and the date assignable (conjectural dates are given in square brackets).

C.	*Event*	*Date*
1	Birth of Æthelwold in reign of K. Edward the Elder (899–924)	[904/5 × 909]
2	Æthelthryth, Æthelwold's nurse, in reign of K. Edward the Elder	[904/5 × 909]
6	Æthelwold's *pueritia* (aged 7–14)	[911/12 × 923/4]
7	Æthelwold's stay at K. Athelstan's household from the beginning of his *adolescentia*	[924 × 937/8]

lustri, quinetiam ferme annum Phoebo rotante medium'; the day is given in c. 3: 'Idus Iulii sanctae ac uenerabiles antistitis reliquiae sublatae sunt de monumento.'

5 ASC 940 A [*recte* 939] (Bately, *MS A*, p. 73; Plummer, *Two Chronicles*, i. 110).

6 ASC 946 A (Bately, *MS A*, p. 74; Plummer, *Two Chronicles*, i. 112).

7 ASC 955 A (Bately, *MS A*, p. 74; Plummer, *Two Chronicles*, i. 112).

8 ASC 964 A (Bately, *MS A*, p. 75; Plummer, *Two Chronicles*, i. 116).

9 ASC 976 C (Plummer, *Two Chronicles*, i. 122; ii. 164).

8	Bishop Ælfheah (934–51) ordains Æthelwold priest at some time before the death of K. Athelstan	934/5 × 27 Oct. 939
9	Æthelwold goes to Glastonbury at the command of K. Athelstan; becomes *decanus* at Glastonbury	*ante* 27 Oct. 939
10	K. Athelstan dies	27 Oct. 939
	Reign of K. Edmund	939–46
	Reign of K. Eadred	May 946–23 Nov. 955
	Æthelwold wishes to go overseas but is prevented by Queen Eadgifu (d. 966/7)	
11	Æthelwold becomes abbot of Abingdon in the reign of K. Eadred	*ante* 23 Nov. 955
12	K. Eadred visits Abingdon	*ante* 23 Nov. 955
13	K. Eadred dies	23 Nov. 955
	Beginning of K. Edgar's reign	957 (Mercia) 959 (Wessex)
	Æthelwold builds church at Abingdon	[957 × 963]
14	Dunstan becomes bishop of Worcester	957?
	Dunstan becomes archbishop of Canterbury	late 960
	Æthelwold sends Osgar to Fleury	[960 × 963]
	Æthelwold and Ælfstan at Abingdon	[960 × 963]
15	Æthelwold's accident	[960 × 963]
16	Æthelwold's election to Winchester	29 Nov. 963
17	Arrival at Winchester of monks from Abingdon	19 Feb. 964
18	Expulsion of secular clerics from the Old Minster by Wulfstan of Dalham	964
19	Æthelwold drinks poison	[964?]
20	Expulsion of clerics from New Minster	964
21	Osgar becomes abbot of Abingdon	[964 or later]
22	Æthelthryth becomes abbess of the Nunnaminster	[964 or later]
23	Refoundation of the monastery at Ely	[964 × 971]
24	Foundation of monasteries at Peterborough and Thorney	[964 × 971]
26	Translation of St Swithun	15 July 971
27	Construction of other monasteries with K. Edgar's consent	*ante* 8 July 975

C.	Event	Date
29	Severe famine in England	976
34	Renovation of the Old Minster	*ante* 980
40	Dedication of the renovated Old Minster	20 Oct. 980
41	Death of Æthelwold	1 Aug. 984
42	Vision of Ælfhelm	*ante* 10 Sept. 996
43	Translation of St Æthelwold	10 Sept. 996

It will be seen from this table that all the datable events have been arranged by Wulfstan in a strict chronological order. The recognition of this arrangement enables us to assign approximate dates to those events which are otherwise undated, and also to attempt a chronological reconstruction of Æthelwold's career.

2. *Æthelwold's* pueritia

Of the various phases of Æthelwold's life, that for which we have the least information is the earliest. For dating this earliest phase the information given by Wulfstan in cc. 8–10 is crucial. We there learn that Æthelwold and Dunstan were ordained priests by Bishop Ælfheah of Winchester (c. 8), who was not himself consecrated to that see until 934 or 935;[10] and the ordination of Æthelwold and Dunstan took place before Dunstan's departure for Glastonbury, which in turn took place before the death of King Athelstan on 27 October 939 (c. 8). The outer dating *termini* for Æthelwold's ordination are therefore 934/5 and 939; and on the assumption that he was ordained at the canonical age of 30, he will have been born 904/5 × 909. Furthermore, Wulfstan describes Æthelwold's *pueritia* in c. 6. We know from sources such as Isidore's *Etymologiae*—a text with which Wulfstan was certainly familiar—that *pueritia* was thought to last from the age of 7 to 14;[11] and on this reckoning, Æthelwold's *pueritia* will have fallen between the years 911/12 and 923/4 at the outside. Unfortunately, we have no further information on this period of Æthelwold's life.

[10] See M. A. O'Donovan, 'An interim revision of episcopal dates for the province of Canterbury, 850–950: part II', *ASE* ii (1973), 91–113, at pp. 111–12.

[11] *Etym.* xi. 2. 4; see A. Hofmeister, 'Puer, iuuenis, senex: Zum Verständnis der mittelalterlichen Altersbezeichnungen', *Papsttum und Kaisertum*, ed. A. Brackmann (Munich, 1926), pp. 287–316, esp. 289–96; cf. also J. A. Burrow, *The Ages of Man* (Oxford, 1986), pp. 34–40. Wulfstan quotes the *Etymologiae* in c. 3; see below, p. 6 n. 2.

3. *Æthelwold's* adolescentia

According to Wulfstan, Æthelwold went to King Æthelstan's court when he became an *adolescens* (c. 7). Again, from sources such as Isidore's *Etymologiae* we know that *adolescentia* lasted from the age of 14 to 28; and given that Æthelwold was born 904/5 × 909, his *adolescentia* will have fallen between 918/19 and 937/8. Furthermore, Wulfstan tells us that Æthelwold spent some considerable time in Athelstan's household (c. 7: *multum temporis agens in palatio*). The precise chronology is unattainable, but the most reasonable deduction is that Æthelwold was a member of the king's household in the late 920s and through most of the 930s. Following this deduction, it is possible that Æthelwold's presence at Athelstan's court is reflected in the witness-lists of charters issued during the 930s; the earliest surviving charter which may bear our Æthelwold's attestation is dated 932.[12] The implication of Wulfstan's narrative is that Æthelwold pursued a secular career at court until he was ordained by Bishop Ælfheah—at first to minor orders, then a few years later (*paucis labentibus annorum curriculis*) to the priesthood.[13]

At the command of King Athelstan (c. 9: *praecipiente rege*) and in order that he should be better educated (*quo melius imbueretur*), Æthelwold went to Glastonbury to study with Dunstan. While there he was professed (*monastici ordinis habitum ab ipso suscepit*) and subsequently became dean (*decanus*)[14] of the Glastonbury monks. While at Glastonbury Æthelwold studied grammar, metrics, and patristic literature (*diuinorum uoluminum*). It is not clear how long Æthelwold remained at Glastonbury: the next datable event mentioned by Wulfstan is Æthelwold's appointment as abbot of Abingdon in the reign of King Eadred (May 946–23 November 955). The date of the refoundation of Abingdon cannot be precisely determined; the date usually given is *c.*954, but it cannot be verified (see below). The implication is that Æthelwold spent a quite

[12] S 417 (= BCS 689); cf. also S 425 (= BCS 702) for 934; see also below, p. 11 n. 7.

[13] There is some stimulating discussion of Æthelwold's secular background and possible family connections by B. Yorke, in *Bishop Æthelwold*, pp. 68–74.

[14] On the meaning of the term *decanus*, see the *Regula S. Benedicti*, c. 21 ('. . . constituantur decani qui sollicitudinem gerant super decanias suas in omnibus secundum mandata Dei et praecepta abbatis sui. Qui decani tales eligantur, in quibus securus abbas partiat onera sua; et non eligantur per ordinem, sed secundum uitae meritum et sapientiae doctrinam'); cf. below, p. 16 n. 1.

considerable period of his life studying at Glastonbury: from the late 930s until, probably, the early 950s (when he himself was aged between his early thirties and his mid-forties). During these long years of study he acquired the very considerable learning which was to be reflected in his own writings and in those of his pupils.

4. *Æthelwold as Abbot of Abingdon*

With his appointment to Abingdon a new and more prominent phase of Æthelwold's career began:[15] that of monastic reformer. This aspect of his activity is well documented in contemporary sources, as we shall see, but from Wulfstan we learn several important facts: that Æthelwold took with him to Abingdon a number of monks from Glastonbury (c. 11), and that he enjoyed a close co-operation with King Eadred, who provided the endowment for the refoundation (cc. 11–12). Wulfstan further reports (c. 11) that the size of the endowment was 100 *cassati*—a fairly substantial amount—and that the grant was made from the royal fisc. Unfortunately no original charter recording this grant survives, and the various documents pertaining to the endowment which are preserved in the two twelfth-century Abingdon cartularies are untrustworthy in various ways.[16] Nevertheless there is no reason to doubt Wulfstan's report of the endowment. In a much later source the refoundation is said to have taken place in 954,[17] but it is not possible to verify this date from contemporary sources. Wulfstan also reports that a new church at Abingdon was begun under Eadred, and that it was subsequently brought to completion and dedicated in the reign of King Edgar (c. 13). From later sources[18] and from archaeology[19] we are able to form some notion of the splendid appearance of Æthelwold's church at Abingdon, which was still standing in the thirteenth century but was subsequently demolished. In any event, the relationship between

[15] See A. Thacker, 'Æthelwold and Abingdon', *Bishop Æthelwold*, pp. 43–64.

[16] S 567 (= BCS 906); *Chron. Abingdon*, i. 124–7; Gelling, *ECTV*, no. 64 ('charter thought to be a complete fabrication'). See also Thacker, in *Bishop Æthelwold*, pp. 51–2. For the two Abingdon cartularies, see Keynes, *The Diplomas*, pp. 10–13.

[17] The precise date is given by the 14th-c. chronicler John of Glastonbury (*The Chronicle of Glastonbury Abbey*, ed. J. P. Carley (Woodbridge, 1985), p. 124), but the source of John's information is unknown.

[18] Thirteenth-c. additions to the Abingdon Chronicle: *Chron. Abingdon*, ii. 277–8.

[19] M. Biddle, H. T. Lambrick, and J. N. L. Myres, 'The early history of Abingdon, Berkshire, and its abbey', *Medieval Archaeology*, xii (1968), 26–69, esp. pp. 63–5.

abbot and king which was responsible for the refoundation of Abingdon was to become a crucial factor in Æthelwold's programme of monastic renewal once he became bishop of Winchester.

5. *Æthelwold as Bishop of Winchester (963–984)*

The relationship between Æthelwold and the king was to become even closer with Eadred's successor, Edgar. We are told by Wulfstan that Æthelwold was on terms of intimate familiarity with the young king (c. 25), and Byrhtferth of Ramsey in his *Vita S. Oswaldi* adds the important detail that Æthelwold had been Edgar's tutor: 'instructus idem rex ad cognitionem ueri regis ab Æthelwoldo sanctissimo episcopo Wintoniensis ciuitatis.'[20] The intimacy of the relationship, and the royal support—financial and military—which it entailed, gave Æthelwold the basis for his vigorous programme of monastic renewal. Æthelwold's programme, referred to more generally as the 'Benedictine reform movement', is known to us chiefly through the writings of Benedictine monks such as Wulfstan, and it is inevitable that their perspective should have been biased in favour of the monks at the expense of the secular clergy who staffed cathedrals and parish minster churches; recent scholarly work has begun to focus more clearly on the secular clergy and to redress somewhat the monkish bias which informs tenth-century accounts of the movement and has inevitably influenced modern treatment of the political and institutional aspects of that movement.[21]

[20] *HCY* i. 426–7; the information is confirmed by Æthelwold's own remarks in the *prohemium* to the *Regularis concordia*: '. . . rex egregius [sc. Edgar], ab ineunte suae pueritiae aetate licet, uti ipsa solet aetas, diuersis uteretur moribus, attamen respectu diuino attactus, abbate quodam assiduo monente ac regiam catholicae fidei uiam demonstrante' (*Reg. conc.*, p. 1). Edgar was born in 943 (ASC 959 B); his *iniens pueritia* will therefore have fallen in 950 or shortly thereafter. We do not know certainly where Æthelwold was in 950, and hence cannot be certain about where the tutelage took place. Thacker (*Bishop Æthelwold*, p. 52), following Whitelock (*EHD*, p. 921), assumes Abingdon, and the assumption may gain some confirmation from Thacker's interesting argument that 'the church which Æthelwold came to rule and reform in 955 had only ten years before been a substantial minster associated with an important royal residence' (op. cit., p. 51): in other words, that the young atheling, resident *c.*950 at the royal estate at Abingdon, was attended there by Æthelwold, not yet an abbot, and—perhaps as a consequence of this attendance—Æthelwold was subsequently granted the monastery of Abingdon, which in so far as it was a royal estate may not have been so *neglectum* and *destitutum* as Wulfstan states (c. 11).

[21] On the political and institutional aspects of the reform, see J. Godfrey, *The Church in Anglo-Saxon England* (Cambridge, 1962), pp. 301–7; Knowles, *MO*, pp. 39–56; E. John,

Æthelwold was consecrated bishop of Winchester on 29 November 963 (c. 16). Winchester then—like all other cathedrals in England (and indeed Europe) at that time—was staffed with secular clergy or canons. Such canons might live more or less like monks depending, for example, on whether they adhered to the strict regulations of Chrodegang's *Regula canonicorum*; but in the opinion of Æthelwold (as implied by Wulfstan) those at Winchester were living sinfully—to the point that they had even stopped celebrating mass—and therefore deserved to be expelled and replaced with monks from Abingdon, who lived in strict accordance with the *Regula S. Benedicti*. Indeed, as Wulfstan remarks (c. 18), there were at that time no monks (properly speaking) anywhere in England, save at Glastonbury and Abingdon. The expulsion of the clerics was evidently plotted by the king and his advisers for some time. Edgar wrote to Rome seeking papal support for the move, and an apparently genuine letter from Pope John XII (955–64) survives which gives Edgar 'apostolic authority' (*auctoritate apostolica*) and which appears to have been sent some time in the autumn of 963.[22] The decision to expel the secular clergy and replace them with Benedictine monks had several important consequences. The secular clergy will have derived their living from the estates owned by Winchester, with the total endowment being (presumably) divided up into separate and individual livings. The expulsion of the canons entailed the forfeiture of these livings (which in some cases will have been very remunerative), with the church's endowment henceforth being owned corporately by the monks.[23] The canons can hardly have been expected to relinquish their livings cheerfully, and it is not surprising that their expulsion had to be effected through the force of a (no doubt

Orbis Britanniae and Other Studies (Leicester, 1966), pp. 154–80; id., in *Tenth-Century Studies*, pp. 10–36, 84–102; B. Yorke, in *Bishop Æthelwold*, esp. pp. 1–12, 65–88; and A. Gransden, 'Traditionalism and continuity during the last century of Anglo-Saxon monasticism', *Journal of Ecclesiastical History*, xl (1989), 159–207, esp. pp. 164–80. On secular clergy and parish minsters, see the brief remarks of S. D. Keynes in *ASE* xiv (1985), 298–301, as well as J. Blair, 'Secular minster churches in Domesday Book', *Domesday Book: A Reassessment*, ed. P. H. Sawyer (London, 1985), pp. 104–42, esp. 119–24, and P. H. Hase, 'The mother churches of Hampshire', *Minsters and Parish Churches: The Local Church in Transition 950–1200*, ed. J. Blair (Oxford, 1988), pp. 45–66, esp. 49–51, together with the remarks of Blair, ibid., pp. 1–7.

22 *Councils & Synods*, i. 109–13 (no. 29).

23 In accordance with the *Regula S. Benedicti*, c. 33: 'omniaque omnibus sint communia . . . ne quisquam suum aliquid dicat uel praesumat.'

armed) retinue sent by King Edgar and led by the royal reeve, Wulfstan of Dalham (c. 18), nor that the seething resentment created by these strong-arm tactics should have manifested itself first in an attempt on Æthelwold's life (c. 19) and should subsequently have erupted when, after the death of King Edgar in 975, there was an 'anti-monastic reaction' in certain parts of the country (notably Mercia) which sought to reclaim the estates confiscated by the monks.[24] Nevertheless, the establishment by Æthelwold of a monastic cathedral at Winchester provided a pattern which was soon to be followed by the principal English cathedrals,[25] notably Worcester,[26] Sherborne and Christ Church, Canterbury.[27]

After successfully expelling the canons and installing Benedictine monks in the Old Minster, Æthelwold followed the same procedure at the neighbouring New Minster (c. 20). Wulfstan does not give the precise dates of these expulsions, but we learn from the *Anglo-Saxon Chronicle* that both expulsions took place in 964: 'Her dræfde Eadgar cyng þa preostas on Ceastre of Ealdan mynstre ond of Niwan mynstre.'[28] The *Chronicle* adds that Æthelwold also refounded monasteries at Milton Abbas and Chertsey in that year, but Wulfstan is surprisingly silent on this subject.[29] In any case the establishment of Benedictine monks at the New Minster is recorded and commemorated in a splendidly produced document known as the 'New Minster Foundation Charter'.[30] This document is now London, BL Cotton Vespasian A. viii. Its text, lavishly written in gold lettering, is a charter in King Edgar's name recording the establishment of Benedictine monks at the New Minster and dated 966. The charter is preceded in the manuscript by an illumination showing King Edgar, flanked by the Virgin and St Peter, offering his charter to Christ seated on high,[31]

[24] The principal source is Byrhtferth, *Vita S. Oswaldi* iv. 12–14 (*HCY* i. 443–6); see D. J. V. Fisher, 'The anti-monastic reaction in the reign of Edward the Martyr', *Cambridge Historical Journal*, x (1950–2), 254–70.

[25] Knowles, *MO*, pp. 619–31, esp. 621.

[26] See P. H. Sawyer, 'Charters of the reform movement: the Worcester archive', *Tenth-Century Studies*, pp. 84–93, 228.

[27] N. Brooks, *The Early History of the Church of Canterbury* (Leicester, 1984), pp. 255–60.

[28] ASC 964 A (Bately, *MS A*, p. 75; Plummer, *Two Chronicles*, i. 116).

[29] Cf. below, p. l and n. 46.

[30] S 745 (= BCS 1190, KCD 527); also ptd. *Councils & Synods*, i. 119–33. A new edition by A. R. Rumble, with translation and commentary, is forthcoming in *WS* iv (3). On Æthelwold's possible authorship of this document, see below, p. lxxxix.

[31] See F. Wormald, *Collected Writings*, ed. J. J. G. Alexander, T. J. Brown, and J. Gibbs (London, 1984), pp. 105–10, esp. 108–10; Temple, *Anglo-Saxon Manuscripts*, p. 44 (no. 16).

and by an elegiac couplet describing Edgar's adoration of Christ (discussed below). The structure of the text roughly follows that of a tenth-century royal diploma, save that it includes a long section on the monks' need to observe the *Regula S. Benedicti*. There are several unusual features of this charter, especially its use of rhyming prose and Greek-based vocabulary, which suggest that it may have been drafted by Æthelwold himself, a suggestion which is confirmed by the unusual nature of Æthelwold's own attestation.[32]

Once Benedictine monasticism had been securely established in Winchester itself,[33] Æthelwold turned his attention farther afield. Wulfstan reports that he refounded monasteries at Ely (c. 23) and Peterborough (c. 24) and founded that at Thorney (c. 24). Wulfstan does not assign dates to these foundations, but from their place in the chronological scheme of his narrative we are permitted to infer that they all fell between 964, when the canons were expelled from the Old and New Minsters (cc. 18, 20), and 971, when the relics of St Swithun were translated into the Old Minster (c. 26).[34] Æthelwold's refoundation of Ely is amply documented in the so-called *Libellus Æthelwoldi*,[35] which is an extensive account, composed in Old English in the late tenth century, of Æthelwold's endowment of Ely. The original Old English version does not survive, but a Latin translation made at Ely between 1108 and 1131 is preserved in two twelfth-century English manuscripts, and this Latin translation in turn was incorporated in the better-known *Liber Eliensis* (1169 × 1174).[36] From the *Libellus* we learn the details concerning the many estates conferred on Ely by Æthelwold; we also learn, from the record of the many lawsuits involved, that in the service of his monks (and his patron saints) Æthelwold was an exceptionally hard-headed business-

[32] See M. Lapidge, 'Æthelwold as scholar and teacher', *Bishop Æthelwold*, pp. 89–117, at 95–6, and below, p. xc.

[33] In addition to the Old and New Minsters (cc. 18, 20), Wulfstan describes the refoundation of the Nunnaminster in c. 22.

[34] Various dates, all based on later sources, are given in *Heads*: Ely, 970 (p. 44), Peterborough, *c.*966 (p. 59) and Thorney, 972 or 973 (p. 73); see also below, pp. 39 n. 5, 40 n. 5, and 41 n. 8.

[35] Ed. T. Gale, *Rerum Anglicarum Scriptorum Veterum II: Historiae Britannicae, Saxonicae, Anglo-Danicae Scriptores XV* (Oxford, 1691), pp. 463–88. A new edition is in preparation by S. D. Keynes and A. Kennedy, *Anglo-Saxon Ely: Records of Ely Abbey and its Benefactors in the Tenth and Eleventh Centuries*; see Appendix B below, pp. 81–6.

[36] Material from the *Libellus Æthelwoldi* is in *LE*, pp. 75–117, 395–7.

man.[37] We are also well informed concerning Æthelwold's endowment of Peterborough.[38] In a twelfth-century Peterborough cartulary[39] there is a copy of a list of the gifts made by Æthelwold to his new foundation;[40] these include a substantial collection of ecclesiastical furniture and vestments, twenty-one books,[41] and a number of estates in Huntingdonshire and Northamptonshire with their berewicks and seed-tithes. As at Abingdon Æthelwold undertook to rebuild the church at Peterborough, and some remnants of his church were recovered by nineteenth-century excavations.[42] Concerning Æthelwold's endowment of Thorney we have less reliable evidence.[43] Various later sources (none earlier than the thirteenth century) preserve a document which is dated 973 and claims to be Æthelwold's foundation-charter but which, even if it may preserve some genuine elements, is in its present form a late and spurious confection.[44] Another charter, more authentic in form and preserved in the aforementioned Peterborough cartulary, records an exchange by Æthelwold of land in Sussex for an estate in Huntingdonshire which was given in turn to Thorney.[45] In any case there is no need to doubt Wulfstan's assertion that Æthelwold endowed Thorney *bonorum omnium possessione* (c. 24). Taken together, these various documents give us a clear impression of the scale of the munificence which Æthelwold lavished on his own foundations. Wulfstan mentions other monasteries founded by Æthelwold 'everywhere

[37] Cf. the remarks of D. Whitelock in *LE*, pp. xii–xvi, esp. xii ('the *Libellus* gives a clear, though not attractive, picture of Bishop Æthelwold'). For a list of estates in question, see Hart, *ECEE*, pp. 213–30, and discussion by E. Miller, *The Abbey and Bishopric of Ely* (Cambridge, 1951), pp. 16–21.

[38] See *The Chronicle of Hugh Candidus*, ed. W. T. Mellows (Oxford, 1949), pp. 27–30; see discussion by Hart, *ECEE*, pp. 243–7 and E. King, *Peterborough Abbey 1086–1310: A Study in the Land Market* (Cambridge, 1973), pp. 12–15.

[39] London, Society of Antiquaries 60 (Peterborough, s. xii[med]).

[40] S 1448 (= BCS 1128) and Robertson, *AS Charters*, pp. 72–5 (no. 39) and 325–30; see also discussion in King, *Peterborough Abbey*, p. 70.

[41] The booklist is ed. M. Lapidge, 'Surviving booklists from Anglo-Saxon England', *Learning and Literature*, pp. 33–89, at 52–5.

[42] J. T. Irvine, 'Account of the discovery of part of the Saxon abbey church of Peterborough', *Journal of the British Archaeological Association*, l (1894), 45–54; Taylor and Taylor, *AS Architecture*, ii. 491–4; and D. Mackreth, 'Recent work on monastic Peterborough', *Durobrivae*, ix (1984), 18–21.

[43] See Hart, *ECEE*, pp. 146–209, esp. 165–86, and S. Raban, *The Estates of Thorney and Crowland: A Study in Medieval Monastic Land Tenure* (Cambridge, 1977), p. 8.

[44] S 792 (= BCS 1297); Hart, *ECEE*, pp. 165–86.

[45] S 1377 (= BCS 1131); Robertson, *AS Charters*, pp. 322–4.

in England' (c. 27), but unfortunately does not specify where these were located.[46]

However, it was to the Old Minster in Winchester that Æthelwold devoted his especial attention. This attention is reflected in two great events, both mentioned—rather cursorily—by Wulfstan: namely, the translation of St Swithun on 15 July 971 (c. 26) and the rebuilding of the monastic precincts and the Old Minster itself (c. 34), which was consecrated on 20 October 980 (c. 40). On the translation of St Swithun we are well informed by Lantfred, who was a Continental monk living at the Old Minster in the early 970s. Lantfred's *Translatio et miracula S. Swithuni*, written probably *c.*975, is an extensive account of the miracles and revelations which preceded the translation, of the translation itself, and of the countless miracles which followed it.[47] Æthelwold's principal role in the translation is stressed throughout, and there are grounds for thinking that one of Æthelwold's motives in undertaking the translation was to effect a reconciliation with Eadsige, one of the canons who had been expelled from the Old Minster and who was a relative of Æthelwold: for after the translation Eadsige was professed as monk and became the sacristan of St Swithun's shrine. The principal purpose of the translation, however, was the simple one of increasing the prestige of the Old Minster. The success of the translation was reflected in the spread of Swithun's cult, and this spread entailed a huge increase in the numbers of pilgrims who sought his shrine. In order to accommodate these pilgrims, and to provide St Swithun with a shrine appropriate to his new-found prestige, Æthelwold undertook to rebuild the Old Minster. An accurate notion of the massive building-works undertaken by Æthelwold is conveyed by Wulfstan in the dedicatory epistle (or *epistola specialis*)

[46] As we have seen, ASC 964 A (Bately, *MS A*, p. 76; Plummer, *Two Chronicles*, i. 116) states that Æthelwold expelled clerics from Chertsey (Surrey) and Milton Abbas (Dorset) and replaced them with monks. To these two foundations one may safely add St Neots (Hunts.), for there is sound evidence in the *Liber Eliensis* that it was Æthelwold's initiative which led to the founding of the priory at Eynesbury (later St Neots): *LE* ii. 29 (ed. Blake, pp. 102–3); Hart, *ECEE*, pp. 27–9; and M. Lapidge, *The Annals of St Neots with Vita Prima Sancti Neoti*, ed. D. Dumville and M. Lapidge (Cambridge, 1985), pp. lxxxvii–lxxxviii, where the foundation is dated to *c.*980. Knowles (*MO*, pp. 51–2) would add St Albans and Crowland to the list of Æthelwold's foundations; but for the first there is no evidence linking its (re)foundation with Æthelwold, and for the second, good evidence that the refoundation was the personal undertaking of the layman Thurkytel (see D. Whitelock, 'The conversion of the Eastern Danelaw', *Saga-Book of the Viking Society*, xii (1941), 159–76, at 174–5).

[47] Ed. Lapidge in *The Cult of St Swithun*.

of his *Narratio metrica de S. Swithuno*;[48] and the notion conveyed by Wulfstan has been brilliantly confirmed by the excavations carried out at Winchester by Martin Biddle during the 1960s.[49] From these excavations it is clear that Æthelwold's rebuilt Old Minster was one of the largest and most magnificent churches in the Europe of his day.

When Æthelwold died, aged nearly 80, on 1 August 984, his rebuilt Old Minster will have been a suitably lavish monument to the energy and resources which he contributed to the renewal of Benedictine monasticism in tenth-century England.

6. *Æthelwold and Benedictine Monasticism*

We have seen that Æthelwold was the first English bishop to institute a monastic cathedral, and that he was instrumental in founding or refounding those monasteries which were among the most rich and powerful in late Anglo-Saxon England. Taken in combination these two facts explain why Æthelwold is to be regarded as the principal proponent of the tenth-century Benedictine reform in England.[50] But although certain aspects of this reform are relatively well understood[51]—its implications for land tenure, for example, or the importance of royal patronage—there are many others still to be explored: to name but one aspect, the written sources which inspired and guided Æthelwold and his colleagues have yet to be properly assessed. This is not the place to attempt such an assessment, but a few points may be mentioned in so far as they throw light on Æthelwold's reforming activities.

The primary intellectual source of Benedictine monasticism in tenth-century England was the *Regula S. Benedicti*.[52] This statement

[48] *Narratio*, Ep. spec. 35–124.

[49] The full account of these excavations will appear in M. Biddle and B. Kjølbye-Biddle, *The Anglo-Saxon Minsters at Winchester*, *WS* iv (1) (Oxford, forthcoming); for now see M. Biddle, '*Felix urbs Winthonia*: Winchester in the age of monastic reform', *Tenth-Century Studies*, pp. 123–40, and 'Archaeology, architecture, and the cult of saints in Anglo-Saxon England', *The Anglo-Saxon Church*, ed. L. A. S. Butler and R. K. Morris (London, 1986), pp. 1–31, at 22–5.

[50] Cf. John, *Orbis Britanniae*, p. 160.

[51] On royal patronage and land tenure, see especially E. John, *Orbis Britanniae*, pp. 154–80, 181–209, and id., 'The church of Winchester and the tenth-century reformation', *Bulletin of the John Rylands Library*, xlvii (1965), 404–29.

[52] Ed. R. Hanslik, *Benedicti Regula* (*CSEL* lxxv; 2nd edn., 1977); A. de Vogüé and J. Neufville, *La Règle de saint Benoît* (7 vols., *Sources chrétiennes*, clxxxi–clxxxvi; Paris, 1971–7).

is an apparent truism, but it is essential nevertheless to take cognizance of the large number of copies of this text which were produced in England from the second half of the tenth century onwards.[53] The *Regula S. Benedicti* has come down to us in three distinct recensions:[54] the *textus purus*, deriving from St Benedict's original (thus preserving Benedict's vulgar Latin) and extant in a single manuscript; the *textus interpolatus*, a version produced probably at Rome *c.*600 in which Benedict's vulgarisms have been normalized; and the *textus receptus* or 'mixed' recension, which emerged from Carolingian circles in the early ninth century when, as a result of the reforms of Benedict of Aniane (see below), readings from the *textus purus* were incorporated into the *textus interpolatus*. There is no evidence that the *textus purus* was ever known in Anglo-Saxon England. There is one surviving manuscript of the *textus interpolatus* (now Oxford, Bodleian Library, Hatton 48) which was written somewhere in Mercia *c.*700 and later owned by Worcester and hence was, in theory at least, available in the tenth century for copying.[55] However, of the eleven surviving manuscripts of the *Regula* which were written in England between *c.*950 and *c.*1100, all belong to the *textus receptus* tradition.[56] The implication is that all these copies derive from Carolingian exemplars, rather than from exemplars available in England at that time such as Hatton 48. Furthermore, given that there is substantial contamination in these manuscripts which prevents them from being satisfactorily classified, one must reckon with a far larger number of copies than the mere eleven which have survived.[57] Unfortunately, however, none of the extant manuscripts can have

[53] Conveniently listed by M. Gretsch, 'Æthelwold's translation of the *Regula Sancti Benedicti* and its Latin exemplar', *ASE* iii (1974), 125–51, at pp. 126–7; see also id., *Die Regula Sancti Benedicti in England* (Munich, 1973), pp. 19–48.

[54] There is a convenient summary of the textual tradition by P. Meyvaert, 'Towards a history of the textual transmission of the *Regula S. Benedicti*', *Scriptorium*, xvii (1963), 83–110; see also the earlier studies by L. Traube, 'Textgeschichte der *Regula S. Benedicti*', *Abhandlungen der Königlich Bayerischen Akademie der Wissenschaften*, phil.-hist. Klasse, xxi (1898), 601–731, and H. Plenkers, *Untersuchungen zur Überlieferungsgeschichte der ältesten Mönchsregeln* (Munich, 1906), pp. 29–52.

[55] *The Rule of St Benedict*, ed. D. H. Farmer, *Early English Manuscripts in Facsimile*, xv (Copenhagen, 1968).

[56] Gretsch, 'Æthelwold's translation', p. 129; *Die Regula Sancti Benedicti in England*, p. 63.

[57] Cf. Gretsch, 'Æthelwold's translation', p. 131: '. . . *RSB* must have been extant fairly early in at least one copy in each of the approximately forty-six monasteries which existed in England after the Benedictine reform and before the Norman Conquest'.

been written at Abingdon during the period of Æthelwold's abbacy or at Winchester during his episcopacy, so we have no certain evidence regarding the text of the *Regula* used by him (save to remark that it was almost certainly a copy of the *textus receptus* based on a Carolingian exemplar).[58] Note that, among the surviving manuscripts from Anglo-Saxon England, there is one manuscript which was written at Abingdon in the late tenth century (Cambridge, Corpus Christi College 57)[59] and another written probably at Winchester in the mid-eleventh century (London, BL Cotton Titus A. IV).

With the multiplication of copies of the *Regula S. Benedicti* went the closer study of its text; and this closer study was much facilitated by use of the early ninth-century commentary by the Carolingian scholar Smaragdus of Saint-Mihiel,[60] the *Expositio in Regulam S. Benedicti*.[61] Of the forty-four surviving manuscripts of this work,[62] only two are known certainly to have been written in Anglo-Saxon England, but one of these may bear directly on our study of Æthelwold: Cambridge, UL Ee. 2. 4. The script of the principal scribe of Ee. 2. 4 is a very early and primitive form of Anglo-Caroline script which is known as 'Bishop Style II' and which is datable to the mid-tenth century, that is, to the earliest period in which Caroline script was being attempted by English scribes.[63] Certain features of the script are evidently indebted to the Insular minuscule written in ninth-century Wales and Cornwall, which seems to suggest that it was written at a south-western centre. Furthermore, the text *per se* suggests that that

[58] There is the interesting report in the 13th-c. addition to the Chronicle of Abingdon to the effect that Æthelwold 'fecit etiam uenire [sc. to Abingdon] regulam Sancti Benedicti a Floriaco monasterio' (*Chron. Abingdon*, ii. 278); on relations between Æthelwold, Winchester, and Fleury, see below, p. 27 n. 4.

[59] CCCC 57 is ed. J. Chamberlin, *The Rule of St Benedict: The Abingdon Copy* (Toronto, 1982).

[60] See F. Rädle, *Studien zu Smaragd von Saint-Mihiel* (Munich, 1974).

[61] *Expositio in Regulam S. Benedicti*, ed. A. Spannagel and P. Engelbert, *CCM* viii (1974).

[62] See W. Witters, 'Smaragde au moyen âge: La diffusion de ses écrits d'après la tradition manuscrite', *Études ligériennes d'histoire et d'archéologie médiévales*, ed. R. Louis (Auxerre, 1975), pp. 361–76, at 365, 370–1.

[63] See T. A. M. Bishop, 'An early example of Insular-Caroline', *Transactions of the Cambridge Bibliographical Society*, iv (1964–8), 396–400, where the suggestion is made that the corrector of CUL Ee. 2. 4 may have been Dunstan himself, and id., *English Caroline Minuscule* (Oxford, 1971), p. 2 (no. 3). The manuscript is incomplete, lacking the first six quires; *membra disiecta* now exist as Oxford, Bodleian Library, lat. theol. c. 3, fos. 1, 1*, 2.

centre was a Benedictine monastery; and, as we know from Wulfstan (c. 18), the only Benedictine monastery in south-western England at that time was Glastonbury.[64] CUL Ee. 2. 4 also contains corrections and additions in a recognizable hand that recurs *inter alia* in 'St Dunstan's Classbook' (Oxford, Bodleian Library, Auct. F. 4. 32) and has been conjecturally identified as Dunstan's own. We know that Æthelwold was familiar with Smaragdus' *Expositio* (see below), and there is therefore some reason to suspect that Ee. 2. 4 is a manuscript which was seen and studied by Æthelwold while he was at Glastonbury during the 940s. But the matter cannot be proved.

In any event Æthelwold's interest in the text and circulation of the *Regula S. Benedicti* later manifested itself in his preparation of an English translation of it. We know from the aforementioned *Libellus Æthelwoldi* (as it is preserved in the twelfth-century *Liber Eliensis*) that King Edgar and Queen Ælfthryth commissioned from Æthelwold an English translation of the *Regula S. Benedicti* in exchange for an estate at Sudbourne.[65] In some eight manuscripts and fragments there survives an Old English translation of the *Regula*, and although in all of them the work is transmitted anonymously, there is scholarly agreement that the translation must be Æthelwold's.[66] In so far as it was commissioned by Edgar and Ælfthryth, the translation will have been produced in the decade between the date of their marriage in 964 and that of Edgar's death in 975, in other words, when Æthelwold was bishop of Winchester. Æthelwold's translation is extremely accurate and follows the Latin text closely, only departing from it occasionally in order to incorporate materials from Smaragdus' *Expositio in Regulam S. Benedicti*.[67] Æthelwold's purpose in undertaking the translation appears simply to have been that of making the work widely accessible to interested laymen such as the king and queen

[64] Cf. the statement in the Old English tract entitled 'King Edgar's Establishment of Monasteries', a work almost certainly by Æthelwold (see below), where it is stated that before Edgar's reign 'there were only a few monks in a few places in so large a kingdom who lived by the right rule. This was in no more places than one, which is called Glastonbury' (*Councils & Synods*, i. 148–9).

[65] *LE*, p. 111.

[66] *Die angelsächsischen Prosabearbeitungen der Benediktinerregel*, ed. A. Schröer (2nd edn., rev. H. Gneuss, Darmstadt, 1964); on Æthelwold's authorship, see pp. xiii–xviii, 269–72.

[67] See Gretsch, 'Æthelwold's translation', pp. 144–6; id., *Die Regula Sancti Benedicti in England*, pp. 257–62.

themselves, and to others who might be drawn by it to the monastic life. This much seems clear from a short treatise in Old English known as 'King Edgar's Establishment of Monasteries', which was almost certainly composed by Æthelwold to serve as the preface to his translation of the *Regula*.[68] The treatise is preserved in a single manuscript (London, BL Cotton Faustina A. x, fos. 148^{r}–161^{v}) of early twelfth-century date and unknown origin. It contains an account of the establishment of Christianity in England through Pope Gregory's mission, and the subsequent establishment of monasteries; then after a statement on the decline of monasticism during the ninth century the treatise goes on to a lengthy and fulsome account of King Edgar's establishment of monasteries and his pious interest in the religious life. In this connection it mentions Edgar's commissioning of the translation of the *Regula S. Benedicti* and explains that 'although keen-witted scholars . . . do not require this English translation, it is nevertheless necessary for unlearned laymen. . . . Therefore let the unlearned natives have the knowledge of this holy rule by the exposition of their own language, that they may the more zealously serve God . . .'.[69] Here is unambiguous evidence that the propagation of Benedictine monasticism in tenth-century England was chiefly due to Æthelwold.

The *Regula S. Benedicti* itself was the primary basis for the reformed monasticism: it provided the general guidelines according to which a monk's life was to be ordered and, as we have seen, was thought—by Æthelwold at least—to be of potential benefit to interested laymen. However, the practice of Benedictine monasticism had developed considerably since the days of its founder, and the *Regula*, couched often in terms of general admonition and exhortation, was not by itself sufficiently detailed to serve as a guide for all aspects of the daily monastic routine. It required, in other words, to be supplemented.

The problems of supplementing the *Regula S. Benedicti*—and thereby facilitating its widespread adoption—had already been faced by Carolingian ecclesiastics in the early years of the ninth

[68] *Councils & Synods*, i. 142–54 (no. 33); on Æthelwold's authorship, see D. Whitelock, 'The authorship of the account of King Edgar's establishment of monasteries', *Philological Essays: Studies in Old and Middle English Language and Literature in Honour of Herbert Dean Meritt*, ed. J. L. Rosier (The Hague, 1970), pp. 125–36.

[69] *Councils & Synods*, i. 152–3.

century. Although monastic reform (and the widespread adoption of the *Regula*) had been mooted during Charlemagne's lifetime,[70] it was particularly during the reign of Louis the Pious (814–40), and at the instigation of his principal ecclesiastical adviser, Benedict of Aniane,[71] that a concerted programme of reform was initiated.[72] This programme principally included promulgation of the following *acta*: first, some so-called *acta praeliminaria* issued perhaps in 816;[73] next, the decrees of a synod held in July 816;[74] then those of a second synod held in July 817 pertaining to the life of monks;[75] and finally a compilation based on the decrees of these two synods, made perhaps in 818 or 819, which is known as the *Regula S. Benedicti abbatis Anianensis siue Collectio capitularis*.[76] The first purpose of this legislation was to encourage uniformity of observance by urging the adoption of the *Regula S. Benedicti* specifically in the recension known as *textus purus*; but it also encouraged circulation of a text known as the 'Memoriale qualiter', a work intended as a supplement to the *Regula S. Benedicti* and providing detailed guidance on the conduct of the monks' daily routine.[77] The 'Memoriale qualiter' was probably composed in the late eighth century, perhaps by Benedict of Aniane himself; in any case it owed its wide circulation to Benedict of Aniane's reforms. One aspect of these reforms, and one which is well attested in the 'Memoriale qualiter', was the introduction of more formal ritual into the life of the monk. Whereas the *Regula S.*

[70] J. Semmler, 'Karl der Große und das fränkische Mönchtum', *Karl der Große: Lebenswerk und Nachleben*, ed. W. Braunfels, 4 vols. (Düsseldorf, 1965–8), ii. 255–89.

[71] P. Schmitz, 'L'influence de saint Benoît d'Aniane dans l'histoire de l'ordre de Saint-Benoît', *Settimane di studio del Centro italiano di studi sull'alto medioevo*, iv (1957), 401–15; R. Grégoire, 'Il monachesimo carolingio dopo Benedetto d'Aniane', *Studia monastica*, xxiv (1982), 349–88; id., 'Benedetto di Aniane nella riforma monastica carolingia', *Studi medievali*, xxvi (1985), 573–610; J. Semmler, 'Benedictus II: *una regula, una consuetudo*', *Benedictine Culture, 750–1050*, ed. W. Lourdaux and D. Verhelst, *Mediaevalia Lovanensia*, xi (Louvain, 1983), pp. 1–49.

[72] See J. Semmler, 'Zur Überlieferung der monastischen Gesetzgebung Ludwigs des Frommen', *Deutsches Archiv*, xvi (1960), 310–88, and his briefer remarks in *CCM* i. 425–32, as well as Grégoire, 'Benedetto di Aniane', pp. 590–2.

[73] *CCM* i. 433–6; see also Semmler, 'Zur Überlieferung', pp. 321–32.

[74] *CCM* i. 451–68; see J. Semmler, 'Die Beschlüsse des Aachener Konzils im Jahre 816', *Zeitschrift für Kirchengeschichte*, lxxiv (1963), 15–82.

[75] *CCM* i. 469–81.

[76] *CCM* i. 501–36.

[77] *CCM* i. 177–82; see also C. Morgand, 'Le "Memoriale monachorum": Nouveau témoin de l'"ordo qualiter",' *Jumièges: Congrès scientifique au XIIIe centenaire*, 2 vols. (Rouen, 1955), ii. 765–74.

Benedicti had allowed the monk a certain freedom to pursue private prayer, reading, and meditation, Benedict of Aniane's legislation sought to occupy much of the monk's time with communal prayer and psalmody. The increased emphasis on formal ritual and communal prayer is characteristic of the reformed Benedictine monasticism of tenth-century England, as we shall see.

The extent to which the reforms advocated by Benedict of Aniane were adopted throughout the Carolingian kingdom is not our concern here. What is important to note is that all the conciliar legislation promulgated by the Carolingian synods of 816 and 817 circulated widely in tenth-century England and exercised a decisive influence on the thinking of the English reformers, Æthelwold among them. Thus the *Acta praeliminaria* of the Council of Aachen of 816 survive uniquely in a manuscript written at Winchester *c.*1000.[78] The *Regula S. Benedicti abbatis Anianensis siue Collectio capitularis* survives in some thirty-five manuscripts, of which five are English of tenth- or eleventh-century date; of these, one is from Abingdon and one from Winchester.[79] The same five English manuscripts which preserve the *Collectio capitularis* also contain copies of the 'Memoriale qualiter'; in addition, a copy of the 'Memoriale qualiter' is contained in the aforementioned manuscript from Winchester which contains the *Acta praeliminaria*.[80] That this work was carefully studied in Anglo-Saxon England is clear from the Old English glossing which it received.[81] These various texts, then, served as the inspiration and guidelines

[78] Rouen, Bibl. mun. 1385, fos. 24ᵛ–26ʳ; see *CCM* i. 433–6.

[79] Listed by Semmler, *CCM* i. 503–9; see also 'Zur Überlieferung', pp. 341–4. The Anglo-Saxon manuscripts are: Cambridge, UL Ll. I. 14 (s. xi²), fos. 105ᵛ–108ᵛ; Cambridge, Corpus Christi College 57 (Abingdon, s. x²), fos. 37ᵛ–40ᵛ; London, BL Cotton Tiberius A. III, fos. 2–173 (Christ Church, Canterbury, s. xi^med, but copied from a Winchester exemplar), fos. 169ʳ–173ʳ; Titus A. IV (Winchester, s. xi^med), fos. 107ʳ–111ʳ, and Harley 5431, fos. 4–126 (? Frankish origin, s. x²; provenance St Augustine's, Canterbury), fos. 107ʳ–114ʳ. See also M. Bateson, 'Rules for monks and secular canons under Edgar', *EHR* ix (1894), 690–708, and the brief remarks by P. Wormald, in *Bishop Æthelwold*, p. 31.

[80] The thirty surviving manuscripts of 'Memoriale qualiter' are listed by Semmler, *CCM* i. 179–94. The Anglo-Saxon manuscripts are: Cambridge, UL Ll. I. 14, fos. 100ᵛ–104ᵛ; CCCC 57, fos. 33ʳ–37ʳ; BL Cotton Tiberius A. III, fos. 164ʳ–168ᵛ; Titus A. IV. fos. 111ʳ–117ᵛ; Harley 5431, fos. 114ʳ–126ᵛ; and Rouen 1385, fos. 20ʳ–24ᵛ.

[81] Ed. A. S. Napier, EETS, os cl (1916), pp. 119–28 (the text wrongly called by Napier the 'Epitome of Benedict of Aniane' is in fact the 'Memoriale qualiter'; it is ptd. from London, BL Cotton Tiberius A. III); see also H. Sauer, 'Die Ermahnung des pseudo-Fulgentius zur Benediktinerregel und ihre altenglische Glossierung', *Anglia*, cii (1984), 419–25.

for the reformed Benedictine monasticism; and given the Winchester origin of some of the manuscripts which preserve them, it is not fanciful to think that Æthelwold himself played an active role in their dissemination.

In any case all these Carolingian texts—the decrees of the councils of 816 and 817 and the 'Memoriale qualiter'—were laid heavily under contribution in the compilation of the monastic customary which was the epitome of the reformed Benedictine monasticism in England, namely the *Regularis concordia*.[82] This important and influential customary was compiled in the wake of a synod held in Winchester some time between 970 and 973 by none other than Æthelwold himself. That Æthelwold was the author of the *Regularis concordia* is stated explicitly by Ælfric—who had been a pupil of Æthelwold at the time—in the preface to the abbreviation of that work which he made for his own monks of Eynsham (hence normally referred to as the 'Letter to the Monks of Eynsham'): 'ideoque haec pauca de libro consuetudinum [sc. the *Regularis concordia*] quem sanctus Æthelwoldus Wintoniensis episcopus cum coepiscopis et abbatibus tempore Eadgari felicissimi regis Anglorum undique collegit'.[83] In compiling the work Æthelwold drew principally on the *textus receptus* of the *Regula S. Benedicti* (see above) and the 'Memoriale qualiter', but he also used the conciliar decrees of the councils of Aachen.[84] However, the *Regularis concordia* also stipulates certain observances which appear to derive from the customs of contemporary Continental houses; indeed Æthelwold notes in the *prohemium* that he drew on the advice of monks from Fleury and Ghent: 'accitis Flor⟨iac⟩ensis

[82] Ed. T. Symons (NMT, London, 1953); Symons's edition, revised by S. Spath, is rptd. *CCM* vii (3) (1984), 61–147.

[83] 'Aelfrici abbatis Epistula ad monachos Egneshamnenses directa', ed. H. Nocent, *CCM* vii (3) (1984), pp. 151–85, at 155. For reasons which are now difficult to grasp, Symons found this statement to be unclear: 'Ælfric is not clear; but his words are commonly quoted as evidence that Ethelwold was the "author" of the Concordia' (*Reg. conc.*, p. li). Symons was labouring under the view, first mooted by Edmund Bishop and promoted by J. A. Robinson (*Times*, p. 155), that Dunstan was the inspiration behind the *Regularis concordia*, Æthelwold merely his amanuensis ('Dunstan the mind, Ethelwold the pen'). But if Ælfric's words are read without prejudice, his explicit statement that Æthelwold compiled the work (and it *is* a compilation, drawn *inter alia* from the 'Memoriale qualiter') is incontestable; and the verbal links with other writings attributable to Æthelwold put the matter beyond doubt (see Lapidge, in *Bishop Æthelwold*, pp. 98–100).

[84] See Robinson, *Times*, pp. 150–5; Symons, *Reg. conc.*, pp. xlviii–xlix, and the *apparatus fontium* to the Symons–Spath edition in *CCM* vii (3); see also T. Symons, 'The sources of the *Regularis Concordia*', *Downside Review*, lix (1941), 14–36, 143–70, 264–89.

beati Benedicti necnon praecipui coenobii quod celebri Gent nuncupatur uocabulo monachis'.[85] One may perhaps surmise the identity of these advisers. We know that Æthelwold was in immediate contact with his disciple Osgar, who had studied at Fleury (see Wulfstan, c. 14), as well as with Lantfred, a Frankish monk who had probably come to Winchester from Fleury and who subsequently returned there; he will also have been in touch with Bishop Oswald of Worcester and Germanus, sometime abbot of Winchcombe, both of whom had studied at Fleury.[86] Of advisers from Ghent, we know that Womar, an abbot of St Peter's in Ghent, spent time among Æthelwold's *familia* at the Old Minster, where he was later remembered with special affection;[87] and of course Archbishop Dunstan, who is named in the *prohemium* of the *Regularis concordia*, had spent some years of exile at St Peter's in Ghent. Æthelwold will therefore have been well placed to learn about the monastic customs of Fleury and Ghent. Until recently it was thought that the customs of reformed Lotharingian monasteries such as Gorze, which were in observance in Ghent, had exercised a decisive influence on the *Regularis concordia*.[88] However, the balance has recently been redressed somewhat with the discovery and publication of a monastic customary composed in the late tenth century by one Theodoric (Thierry) and known to editors as the *Consuetudines Floriacenses antiquiores*.[89] Theodoric had been a monk at Fleury before moving to Amorbach in 1002, and it is thought that his *Consuetudines* preserve details of tenth-century

[85] *Reg. conc.*, p. 3; *CCM* vii (3), 72.

[86] For Lantfred, see below, p. xciv; for Oswald and Germanus, see Byrhtferth, *Vita S. Oswaldi* ii. 4–9, iii. 7 (*HCY* i. 413–18, 422–3) and Hart, *ECNENM*, pp. 337–8, 356.

[87] Womar is listed among those who 'devoted themselves particularly' to the Old Minster, as follows: 'Domnus abba Womarus qui olim cenobio Gent prelatus hanc deuotus adiit gentem huiusque se familie precibus humillime commendauit' (*LVH*, p. 24; Gerchow, *Gedenküberlieferung*, p. 323). Womar's death is recorded in ASC 981 C (Plummer, *Two Chronicles*, i. 124). Womar was abbot of Ghent from 953 onwards: see P. Grierson, *Les Annales de Saint-Pierre de Gand et de Saint-Amand* (Brussels, 1937), pp. xvi, 19 and 21. A metrical epitaph of Womar is ptd. *MGH*, Poetae Latini Aevi Carolini, v. 300.

[88] See H. Dauphin, 'Le renouveau monastique en Angleterre au xe siècle et ses rapports avec la réforme de S. Gérard de Brogne', *RB* lxx (1960), 177–96, and T. Symons, '*Regularis Concordia*: history and derivation', *Tenth-Century Studies*, pp. 37–59.

[89] See A. Davril, 'Un coutumier de Fleury du début du XIe siècle', *RB* lxxvi (1966), 351–4; 'Un moine de Fleury aux environs de l'an mil: Thierry, dit d'Amorbach', *Études ligériennes*, ed. Louis, pp. 97–104. The *Consuetudines Floriacenses antiquiores* are now ed. A. Davril and L. Donnat, *CCM* vii (3), 3–60.

Fleury observance; in any case, many details in Theodoric's *Consuetudines*—such as the duties of the monastic *circator*—are precisely paralleled in the *Regularis concordia*. The close relationship is best explained on the assumption that Æthelwold's Fleury informants described to him customs which were subsequently recorded by Theodoric, perhaps some twenty or thirty years after the compilation of the *Regularis concordia* in the early 970s.

Although the *Regularis concordia* is largely a work of compilation, it contains many customs which are not found either in the Carolingian texts or in contemporary Continental customaries. The repeated prayers for the royal house, for example, have no parallel in other customaries, and may be a reflection of Æthelwold's close relationship with King Edgar. Several liturgical ceremonies stipulated in the *Regularis concordia*, such as the three prayers for the veneration of the Cross on Good Friday, are apparently of English origin, and are discussed below. There are also numerous details of observance for which no parallel has been found, and which are probably native customs.[90]

The *Regularis concordia* provided the model for reformed Benedictine monasticism in England, and as such was widely known and widely influential, even though the number of surviving manuscripts is surprisingly small. Wulfstan in his *Vita S. Æthelwoldi* quotes verbatim from it in referring to provisions of the winter *horarium* (c. 35); Ælfric, as we have seen, produced an abbreviated version of it for his own use at Eynsham. A complete Old English interlinear gloss to the text was produced, perhaps at Canterbury, and another manuscript preserves a fragment of an English translation.[91] There could be no more explicit testimony to the central role played by Æthelwold in the tenth-century monastic reform movement.

7. *Æthelwold and the Liturgy*

We have seen that, in compiling the *Regularis concordia*, Æthelwold was concerned to regulate the daily observances of English Benedictine monks. Since much of a monk's day was taken up with the

[90] See Symons, *Reg. conc.*, p. xlvi.

[91] Ed. H. Logeman, 'De consuetudine monachorum', *Anglia*, xiii (1891), 365–448, xv (1893), 20–40 (a new edition by L. Kornexl is in preparation); see also J. Zupitza, 'Ein weiteres Bruchstück der Regularis Concordia in altenglischer Sprache', *Archiv*, lxxxiv (1890), 2–16, from CCCC 201 (s. xi[in]).

liturgy of mass and office, we may be sure that Æthelwold will also have given his attention to the correct performance of the liturgy in the attempt to ensure that English ceremony was in keeping with Continental practice. By the same token, as bishop of a large diocese it will have been his responsibility to see that pontifical ceremonies were conducted correctly, again in keeping with Continental practice. It is clear that, from the early tenth century onwards, the English church was open to the influence of Continental practice, for it is from this time that we see the importation not only of liturgical service-books but also of the various Carolingian treatises which were concerned with the meaning and standardization of the liturgy, such as the *Expositio Libri Comitis* of Smaragdus of Saint-Mihiel or the *De ecclesiasticis officiis* of Amalarius of Metz.[92] We may surmise that Æthelwold was familiar with Continental texts such as these, as well as with the forms of Continental liturgical practice. However, it is easier to state such a surmise than to document the influence of Æthelwold on the liturgy of the Anglo-Saxon church.[93] The reason is that very few liturgical manuscripts written in England during the period *c*.960 × *c*.1000 have survived;[94] and of these, none can be attributed to Abingdon during the period of Æthelwold's abbacy and only a few at most are attributable to that of his episcopate at Winchester. It is true that the *Regularis concordia* often contains precious information especially pertaining to the form of the Divine Office; but in the absence of surviving office-books it is not easy to determine how and if the stipulations in the *Regularis concordia* were

[92] Of some fifty surviving manuscripts of Smaragdus' *Expositio Libri Comitis*, two were written in England: Oxford, Bodleian Library, Barlow 4 (Worcester, s. xi^{in}) and Worcester, Cathedral Library, F. 91 (Worcester, s. x^{2}). The following manuscripts of Amalarius' *De ecclesiasticis officiis* were written or owned in Anglo-Saxon England: Boulogne, Bibl. mun. 82 (s. x^{2}); Cambridge, Corpus Christi College 192 (Brittany, s. x; provenance Canterbury); Trinity College B. 11. 2 (St Augustine's, Canterbury, s. x^{2}); Copenhagen, Det kongelige Bibliotek, Gl. kgl. Saml. 1595 (Worcester or York, s. xi^{in}); and London, BL Cotton Vespasian D. xv, fos. 102–21 (s. x/xi). In addition, two manuscripts contain excerpts from this work of Amalarius (CCCC 190 and 265) and a third contains a fragmentary English translation of iii. 1 (CCCC 44, fos. 1–2: Canterbury, s. xi^{1}).

[93] There is very little direct testimony to Æthelwold's liturgical practice; note however Ælfric's observation in his pastoral letter to Archbishop Wulfstan that Æthelwold maintained the strict habit of celebrating mass no more than once a day (*Councils & Synods*, i. 251–2). The Abingdon Chronicle gives a lengthy list of ecclesiastical furniture provided by Æthelwold during his abbacy (*Chron. Abingdon*, i. 344–5).

[94] Anglo-Saxon liturgical manuscripts are conveniently listed by Gneuss, 'Liturgical books'.

implemented. And although there are substantial numbers of service-books dating from the eleventh century, these must be used with great caution as evidence for practices of the tenth. It is convenient to survey the evidence, such as it is, under five headings: (*a*) the mass; (*b*) the Divine Office; (*c*) pontifical ceremonies; (*d*) chant; and (*e*) private prayer.

(*a*) *The mass.* The central part of the mass, the *canon missae*, was fixed and invariable. However, various prayers which were pronounced by the celebrant were combined with the *canon*; these prayers (*collecta*, *secreta*, *praefatio*, and *postcommunio*) were variable, or 'proper', depending on which Sunday or saint's day the mass was being performed. So, too, the parts of the mass which were sung (Introit, gradual, offertory, and communion) were variable in this way, as was the lesson. Before the tenth century, the variable prayers said by the celebrant were collected in a book for his use called a sacramentary; those parts of the mass which were sung were similarly collected together, for the use of the precentor, into a book called the gradual; and the lessons which were read by the deacon were either collected in a gospel-lectionary (also called evangeliary or evangelistary) or simply marked up in a gospel-book for the deacon's use. From the late tenth century onwards, all these functions were combined in the one book, called a plenary missal (or simply missal), which contained the celebrant's prayers, chant-cues for the sung parts of the mass, and incipits of the lessons. From this it will be clear that, in order to form a clear notion of how mass was performed at Æthelwold's Winchester, we should need either a plenary missal of that date (if such a thing was in existence by then) or else the three individual books used by celebrant, precentor, and deacon respectively. Unfortunately, although some fragments survive (to be discussed below), there is no complete surviving mass-book from tenth-century Winchester. Nor is the *Regularis concordia* very informative on the structure of the mass, since its principal concern is with the Divine Office. It does contain certain instructions for the performance of mass at Easter; and several prayers there stipulated (for the ceremony of the Sepulture of the Cross) have an interesting reflex in mass-books of the late tenth and early eleventh centuries.[95] But for specific

[95] See *Reg. conc.*, pp. 39–40, 43–6; the mass-books which reflect these practices are the fragmentary Oslo, Riksarkivet, Mi. 1 (discussed below) and the so-called 'Missal of

information on the mass we are obliged to turn to the fragmentary mass-books.

The first of these is a sacramentary consisting now of twenty-six leaves which had formerly been pasted together so as to constitute the boards of the famous 'Winton Domesday' (London, Society of Antiquaries 154).[96] These leaves, which have now been mounted separately as MS 154*, were originally thirteen bifolios of a tenth-century manuscript which was broken up in the twelfth century when the 'Winton Domesday' was bound. To judge from the evidence of script alone, the leaves were probably written in Brittany some time in the tenth century.[97] We know that a substantial number of manuscripts, many of them liturgical, were imported from Brittany into England during the tenth century. It is possible, but not provable, that the sacramentary was already at Winchester in Æthelwold's day; it was certainly there when it was broken up to form the binding of the 'Winton Domesday' some time in the twelfth century.

The text is a Gregorian sacramentary of the type called *Hadrianum ex autentico*, that is, it is a descendant of the copy sent on request by Pope Hadrian to Charlemagne.[98] In sacramentaries of this type, the masses for Sundays (the *temporale*) and those for saints' days (the *sanctorale*) are given in a single sequence. However, the exemplar sent by Hadrian was a mass-book intended for use at Roman stational masses (that is, masses said on specified days at the various churches in Rome) by the pope, and accordingly it did not contain the characteristic prayers (called 'prefaces' or *praefationes*) which were then in use in the Gallican rite; in other words, the *Hadrianum* had to be supplemented. A supplement was produced, probably by Benedict of Aniane and hence called the *Supplementum Anianense*, in the early ninth century; this supplement included *praefationes* drawn from mass-books of the type called

Robert of Jumièges', now Rouen, Bibl. mun. 274 (Y. 6), of early 11th-c. date but unknown English origin.

[96] On the manuscript, see F. Wormald, 'Fragments of a tenth-century sacramentary from the binding of the Winton Domesday', *Winchester in the Early Middle Ages*, ed. M. Biddle, *WS* i. 541–9, and N. R. Ker, *Medieval Manuscripts in British Libraries I: London* (Oxford, 1969), pp. 307–8.

[97] See *WS* i, pl. XI.

[98] Ed. J. Deshusses, *Le Sacramentaire grégorien: Ses principales formes d'après les plus anciens manuscrits*, Spicilegium Friburgense, xvi (2nd edn., Fribourg, 1979). See also K. Gamber, *Sakramentartypen* (Beuron, 1958), pp. 137–8, 159–65, where a list of criteria is given for classification. According to these criteria, our sacramentary belongs to Gamber's H-type.

'Eighth-Century Gelasian'.[99] But in time the need continually to supplement the *Hadrianum* was found to be inconvenient, and from the third quarter of the ninth century onwards the *praefationes* from the supplement were interpolated into their appropriate places in the main body of the *Hadrianum*, so as to produce what are called 'fused' Gregorian sacramentaries.[100] The sacramentary in Society of Antiquaries 154* is of this sort: it includes, in one sequence, masses for Sundays and saints' days from Holy Innocents (28 December) to Easter (the remainder of the liturgical year has been lost), and into these masses have been interpolated various prayers from the *Supplementum Anianense*.[101]

Repeated use soon brought to light another inconvenient aspect of the Gregorian sacramentaries of the *Hadrianum* type, namely the fact that the masses of both the *temporale* and the *sanctorale* were set out in a single sequence. This arrangement is inconvenient *inter alia* because the sequence alters from year to year with the changes in date of the movable feasts such as Easter (and therefore the Sundays which are keyed to Easter, such as Pentecost, etc.). The result was that, by the early tenth century, it became usual in sacramentaries for the *temporale* to be separate from the *sanctorale*.[102] Similarly, as time went on, it became increasingly clear that the saints' days provided with masses in the *Hadrianum* (which, after all, reflected the usage of eighth-century Rome, not tenth-century Europe) were an inadequate reflection of local saints' cults, and henceforth it became normal to include in the *sanctorale* masses for local patron saints, so that, for example, a tenth-century sacramentary from a church in northern France will almost invariably include masses for northern French saints. Seen against these two parallel developments, the tenth-century sacramentary which is Society of Antiquaries 154* is distinctly archaic. In this sacramentary, as in the early ninth-century sacramentaries of the *Hadrianum* type, the *temporale* and the *sanctorale* are arranged in a single sequence. This feature sets it apart from all other surviving Anglo-Saxon sacramentaries of tenth-century or later date.[103] Further-

[99] See J. Deshusses, 'Le "Supplément" au Sacramentaire grégorien: Alcuin ou saint Benoît d'Aniane', *Archiv für Liturgiewissenschaft*, ix (1965), 47–71.

[100] See, for example, *CLitLA*, nos. 755, 770.

[101] The contents of the sacramentary are fully listed by Wormald, art. cit. (n. 96).

[102] The earliest example of the new arrangement is apparently *CLitLA*, no. 910: Paris, BN lat. 9432 (Amiens, s. x).

[103] Note that the early 10th-c. missal known as 'Leofric A', the earliest stratum of

more, it does not include a mass for any saint that is not found in the *Hadrianum ex autentico*. This feature, too, sets it apart from all other Anglo-Saxon sacramentaries, which, from the late tenth century onwards, invariably include masses not only for local northern Frankish saints (reflecting in this the origin of their exemplars) but local English saints as well.[104] These features imply that Society of Antiquaries 154* is a tenth-century copy of a ninth-century *Hadrianum*-type sacramentary. The importation of such a book seems to go hand in hand with the importation of Carolingian books on monastic rule and liturgical ceremony (see above), and throws interesting light on the liturgy during the earliest phase of the English Benedictine reform movement.

Another witness—again, regrettably in fragmentary form—to the structure of the mass at Winchester in Æthelwold's time is a collection of leaves from a now dismembered missal preserved (mostly) in Riksarkivet in Oslo and referred to for the sake of convenience as Mi. 1.[105] Although it bears no mark of origin or medieval provenance, there are various reasons for associating this fragmentary missal with Winchester. It is written throughout in the elegant Anglo-Caroline script written principally at Winchester and Winchester dependencies, and designated as Style I by T. A. M. Bishop; indeed, Bishop has given his opinion that the script of the missal resembles that written at Winchester *c.*1000 (s. x/xi).[106] It is thus somewhat later than the period of Æthelwold's bishopric, and substantially later than Society of Antiquaries 154*. What are the grounds for associating it with Æthelwold's Winchester?

Mi. 1 is a missal rather than a sacramentary: for each mass it includes, alongside prayers said by the celebrant, cues for the

the 'Leofric Missal' (Oxford, Bodleian Library, Bodley 579: ed. F. E. Warren, *The Leofric Missal* (Oxford, 1883)), has separate *temporale* and *sanctorale*. 'Leofric A' was written in either northern France or England (the question of origin has never been satisfactorily resolved) *c.*900, but was at Glastonbury *c.*970, when the texts comprising 'Leofric B' were added.

[104] The principal northern Frankish saints in question are Audoenus (Ouen), Audomarus (Omer), Bertinus (Bertin), and Vedastus (Vaast).

[105] The fragments are listed by L. Gjerløw, *Adoratio Crucis* (Oslo, 1961), pp. 29–32.

[106] As reported by Gjerløw, *Adoratio Crucis*, p. 35. Bishop compared the script (illustrated by Gjerløw, p. 53) with that of Copenhagen, Det kongelige Bibliotek, Gl. kgl. Saml. 10 (? Winchester, s. x^{ex}); one might also compare the script of the 'Benedictional of Archbishop Robert', now Rouen, Bibl. mun. 369 (Y. 7) (New Minster, Winchester, s. x^{2}); illustrated *The Benedictional of Archbishop Robert*, ed. H. A. Wilson, HBS xxiv (1903), pls. III–IV.

various chants and tracts and incipits for the lessons. It is thus a much more 'modern' book than Society of Antiquaries 154*, a forerunner of the plenary missals which began to appear during the course of the eleventh century. By the same token, the *temporale* in Mi. 1 is separate from the *sanctorale*. The much-truncated *sanctorale* contains mass-sets for three saints only: Agatha, Vedastus, and Valentinus. The first and third of these are found in Gregorian sacramentaries of the *Hadrianum*-type (including Society of Antiquaries 154*); but Vedastus, who is the patron saint of Saint-Vaast in Arras, must represent an addition made in a northern French copy anterior to Mi. 1.[107] As we shall see, Æthelwold imported monks from Corbie to teach plain-chant to his Abingdon monks, and the veneration of northern French saints, especially Vedastus, is a characteristic feature of liturgical books from the Winchester of his episcopacy.[108] Another feature of Mi. 1 links it to Æthelwold: uniquely among Anglo-Saxon mass-books, Mi. 1 contains three prayers which are prescribed by the *Regularis concordia* to be said as part of the service for the veneration of the Cross on Good Friday.[109] This various evidence, which does not amount to proof, may suggest that Mi. 1 is a slightly later copy of a mass-book which was in use in Æthelwold's Winchester at the time the *Regularis concordia* was promulgated in *c.*973.[110]

A number of mass-books written at Winchester in the eleventh century survives; but in so far as these are in some cases as much as a century later than Æthelwold's episcopacy, they offer at best

[107] The Vedastus masses are found in Cambrai, Bibl. mun. 162 + 163 (N. France, s. ix¹), on which see *CLitLA*, no. 761; the masses are ptd. from this manuscript by Deshusses, *Le Sacramentaire grégorien*, pp. 690–1.

[108] Vedastus is especially commemorated in the 'Benedictional of St Æthelwold' (see below, p. lxxxi) and the Claudius Pontifical I (see below, p. lxxix). There are also masses for Vedastus in the 'Missal of Robert of Jumièges' (ed. H. A. Wilson, HBS xi (1896), p. 161), a manuscript with undoubted Winchester connections, if it was not written there, and the 'Missal of the New Minster' (ed. D. H. Turner, HBS xciii (1962), p. 73).

[109] *Reg. conc.*, pp. 42–4 (cc. 44–5). Note that these prayers are paraliturgical and hence it is not surprising that they are not found in mass-books (with the curious exception of Mi. 1); they are, however, found in a mid 11th-c. prayer-book perhaps from Winchester, now London, BL Cotton Galba A. xiv (ed. B. J. Muir, *A Pre-Conquest English Prayerbook*, HBS ciii (1988), pp. 143–6, no. 68) and in the 'Portiforium of St Wulstan', now CCCC 391 (ed. A. Hughes, 2 vols., HBS lxxxix–xc (1958–60), ii. 608–10), a manuscript of Worcester origin but based in many respects on Winchester materials.

[110] Cf. Gjerløw, *Adoratio crucis*, p. 50: '. . . it is quite possible that the sacramentary underlying *Mi 1* represents the sacramentary in use at Old Minster in St Æthelwold's Winchester.'

indirect evidence for the shape of the mass in his day.[111] Unless new evidence should come to light, our knowledge of the mass as it was performed by Æthelwold must remain fragmentary.

(*b*) *The Divine Office*. We have seen that the *Regularis concordia* was drafted by Æthelwold, acting on the advice of various advisers familiar with Continental customs, and that its principal concern was to regulate the daily activities of English Benedictine monks. Accordingly, much of the *Regularis concordia* is taken up with instructions about the performance of the Divine Office at various liturgical seasons. However, with few exceptions (such as the insistence upon prayers for the royal house, mentioned above),[112] these instructions have been adapted from earlier Continental customaries, and scarcely represent Æthelwold's personal contribution to English monastic observance.[113] Furthermore, it is very difficult to estimate how widely the stipulations of the *Regularis concordia* were adopted in English monasteries, because there are so few surviving office-books. Occasionally a later office-book will contain prayers stipulated by the *Regularis concordia*: for example, a late eleventh-century breviary from Worcester, the so-called 'Portiforium of St Wulstan' (Cambridge Corpus Christi College 391) records certain stipulations concerning Maundy Thursday which are evidently indebted to the *Concordia*.[114] But this book is the only breviary which has survived from Anglo-Saxon England. In other words, it is exceedingly difficult to estimate Æthelwold's impact on the performance of the Divine Office in England at large.

[111] The mass-books in question are: CCCC 41 (s. xi¹; ed. R. J. S. Grant, *Cambridge, Corpus Christi College 41: The Loricas and the Missal* (Amsterdam, 1979), pp. 56–112); CCCC 422, the so-called 'Red Book of Darley' (s. xi^{med}, unptd.; but see C. Hohler, 'The Red Book of Darley', *Nordiskt kollokvium II i latinsk liturgiforskning* (Stockholm, 1972), pp. 39–47); Le Havre, Bibl. mun. 330 (s. xi²; ed. D. H. Turner, *The Missal of the New Minster*, HBS xciii (1962)); Worcester, Cathedral Library, F. 173 (s. xi^{med}; unptd.); and the fragmentary missal in Stockholm, Kammararkivet, Mi. 1 (s. x/xi; see T. Schmid, 'Smärre liturgiska bidrag', *Nordisk tidskrift för bok- och biblioteksväsen*, xxxi (1944), 25–34). One might also consider the aforementioned 'Missal of Robert of Jumièges', which certainly has Winchester connections, even if its precise origin cannot be determined; see C. Hohler, 'Les saints insulaires dans le missel de l'archevêque Robert', *Jumièges*, ii. 293–303.

[112] When we recall the role played by King Edgar in Æthelwold's reform of monasteries, and the fact that Æthelwold had been Edgar's tutor, we may well suspect that the presence of prayers for the royal house in the *Regularis concordia* is the personal contribution of Æthelwold; but there is no way of verifying this suspicion.

[113] See Symons, *Reg. conc.*, p. xlvi.

[114] Ibid., pp. 38 n. 17, 39 n. 11.

Interestingly, however, there is evidence of Æthelwold's influence on the performance of private, supplementary offices by his own monks at the Old Minster, Winchester. Our knowledge of these offices derives from a brief note entitled *De horis peculiaribus*, which is found among the materials pertaining to the cult of St Æthelwold in Alençon, Bibl. mun. 14 (a manuscript copied by Orderic Vitalis from materials originally assembled at Winchester). As we have seen (above, p. xxiii), there are grounds for thinking that Wulfstan himself may have composed these materials. For this reason, *De horis peculiaribus* deserves to be quoted in full:

Preterea beatus pater Adeluuoldus horas regulares et peculiares sibi ad singulare seruitium instituit quas in tribus cursibus ordinauit, humillima diligentia quosque subiectos ammonens ut hoc secreto famulatu ignitis sathane temptamentis uigilanter resisterent et ea per Dei gratiam resistendo superarent, et ut fides que per nostri creatoris et piissimi redemptoris incarnationem luce clarius enituit, instante future persecutionis tempore que iam uicinis Antichristi temporibus ingruit nullo modo (quod absit!) titubando uacillet, sed his diuinis roborata preconiis integra iugiter et inuiolata permaneat. Est enim prima psalmodie cantilena ad laudem beate Dei genitricis semperque uirginis Mariae procurata; secunda autem ad honorem beatorum apostolorum Petri et Pauli omniumque nostri saluatoris humanitati presentialiter famulantium; tercia uero ad suffragia Omnium Sanctorum postulanda, ut eorum pia intercessione protecti multiformem uersipellis Antichristi et membrorum eius fallaciam expugnare et Christo remunerante celestium premiorum palmam mereamur accipere. Que uidelicet hore plerisque in locis habentur adscripte et ideo in hoc codicello sunt pretermisse.[115]

[115] Alençon, Bibl. mun. 14, fo. 36^{r}; ptd. *PL* cxxxvii. 107–8: 'Moreover, our blessed father Æthelwold instituted regular (supplementary) offices, unique to himself, for individual observance, and he arranged these offices in three *cursus*, and with the most modest insistence he urged those subject to him that, with this private observance, they should vigilantly resist the fiery temptations of Satan and, through God's grace, could overcome them by active resistance, and that the faith, which shone more brightly than light through the incarnation of our Creator and merciful Redeemer, should in no wise waver in uncertainty (which Heaven forbid!) at the approaching time of our future persecution, which launches its attack as the times of Antichrist draw near, but rather, strengthened by these praises of God, remain perpetually whole and inviolate. The first chant of psalmody is devoted to praise of the blessed mother of God ever-virgin Mary; the second is to the glory of the blessed apostles Peter and Paul and to all those who assisted the humanity of our Saviour by their presence; the third is a petition for the assistance of All Saints, so that, protected by their merciful intercession, we may be found worthy to conquer the manifold trickery of the shape-shifting Antichrist and his associates, and to receive the palm of heavenly reward through Christ's bounty. These

It is a pity that the author of the brief treatise (or the scribe of the manuscript) did not see fit to copy out the three *cursus* in question. But there can be no doubt that they were intended as supplementary offices (*horas . . . peculiares*) for private devotion and not merely as a set of prayers, and that it was Æthelwold himself who devised and instituted them (*ad singulare seruitium instituit*). If they could be identified, these offices would be an immensely valuable index to Æthelwold's spirituality.

Unfortunately the search to identify these offices in Anglo-Saxon liturgical manuscripts is not straightforward. We are hampered here as elsewhere by the paucity of surviving office-books, and by the fact that, by their very nature, offices of this sort never bear a mark of authorship. Of the three offices in question, that for SS Peter and Paul (the patron saints of the Old Minster) is the most problematical: to our knowledge, no such office is preserved in any surviving Anglo-Saxon manuscript. For the other two offices, however, an attempt at identification is worthwhile.

First, the office for the Virgin. That Æthelwold should himself have instituted such an observance is potentially of great significance, in view of the widespread use at a later time of the *Horae de Beata Maria Virgine*. On present evidence the *Horae BMV* do not seem to have originated earlier than the late tenth century,[116] and they are first attested in England in two manuscripts of the second half of the eleventh century.[117] By this time, however, they have become fully developed offices for all of the canonical hours, and it is impossible to conjecture what, if anything, they might owe to liturgical practice instituted by Æthelwold a century earlier. Evidence that is more reliable and closer in time to Æthelwold is provided by a prayer-book written at the New Minster, Winchester, in the third decade of the eleventh century, now London, BL Cotton Titus D. XXVI + XXVII.[118] The second part of this book

offices are available in writing in a number of places, and accordingly they have been omitted from this manuscript.'

[116] See E. Bishop, *Liturgica Historica* (Oxford, 1918), pp. 225–7; Gneuss, *Hymnar*, pp. 110–12; and M. Clayton, *The Cult of the Virgin Mary in Anglo-Saxon England*, *Cambridge Studies in Anglo-Saxon England*, ii (Cambridge, 1990), pp. 65–81.

[117] See E. S. Dewick, *Facsimiles of Horae BMV*, *HBS* xxi (1902); the manuscripts in question are London, BL Cotton Tiberius A. III, fos. 107^{v}–115^{v}, and Royal 2. B. V, fos. 1^{r}–6^{r}.

[118] See Ker, *Catalogue*, pp. 264–6 (no. 202); Temple, *Anglo-Saxon Manuscripts*, pp. 94–5 (no. 77), as well as the earlier studies by W. de G. Birch, 'On two Anglo-Saxon

(Titus D. XXVII) contains, on fos. 81ᵛ–85ʳ, an office in honour of the Virgin bearing the rubric *In honore sanctae Mariae*. This office has never been printed in full,[119] and is worth reproducing here; as will be seen, it consists in the recitation of various antiphons, the *Quicumque uult*, a hymn, more antiphons, the *Pater noster*, the *Credo*, three collects, and then a sequence of four prayers (one of them lengthy) addressed to the Virgin, and finally five brief *preces* to end with.

/81ᵛ/ Deus in adiutorium meum intende. Domine. Gloria. Sicut erat. A Aue Maria. ⟨PS⟩ Deus in nomine tuo. Confitemini Domino. Beati inmaculati *usque in finem*. Quicumque uult. A Aue Maria, gratia plena. Dominus tecum, benedicta tu in mulieribus. Alleluia.
CAPITVLVM Ab initio ante secula creata sum et usque ad futurum seculum non desinam et in habitatione sancta coram ipso ministraui. ℟ Beata es Maria que omnium portasti creatorem. Deum genuisti qui te fecit et in eternum permanes uirgo. ℣ Aue Maria, gratia plena. Dominus tecum, genuisti.
HYMNVS Aue mari⟨s⟩ stella.[120]
℣ Post partum uirgo. A Succurre sancta. Magnificat. A Succurre, sancta genetrix Christi, miseris ad te confugientibus, adiuua et refoue omnes qui in te confidunt, /82ʳ/ ora pro totius mundi piaculis, interueni pro clero, intercede pro monachorum choro, exora pro sexu femineo.

Kyrrie leyson. Christe leyson. Kyrrie leyson. Pater noster. Et ne nos inducas. Credo in Deum. Carnis resurrectionem. Beata mater. Post partum uirgo. Aue Maria. Specie tua. Domine exaudi.
COLLECTA Auerte, quesumus Domine, iram tuam.
ALIA Famulorum tuorum, quesumus Domine, delictis ignosce.
ITEM Supplicationes seruorum tuorum.

ORATIO DE SANCTA MARIA. Singularis gratia, sola sine exemplo mater et uirgo Maria, quam Dominus ita mente et corpore castam inuiolatamque custodiuit ut digna existeres, ex qua sibi nostre redemptionis pretium Dei filius corpus aptarit: obsecro te, misericordissima, per cuius partum totus saluatus est mundus, intercede pro me misero spurcissimo,

manuscripts in the British Museum', *Transactions of the Royal Society of Literature*, 2nd ser., xi (1878), 463–612, and *LVH*, pp. 251–83.

[119] It is partially ptd. (as far as 'ITEM. Supplicationes seruorum tuorum') by J. Leclercq, 'Formes anciennes de l'Office mariale', *Ephemerides Liturgicae*, lxxiv (1960), 89–102, at pp. 101–2. Since the office proper consists of incipits of psalms, versicles, and responds, it has not been translated here.

[120] This hymn (*ICL*, no. 1545) and the prayers which follow (as far as *exora pro sexu femineo*) are found in a Vespers office for the BVM in BL Royal 2. B. v (ed. Dewick, *Facsimiles of Horae BMV*, cols. 15–16).

/82v/ cunctis iniquitatibus fedo, ut qui ex meis actibus nihil aliud dignus sum quam eternum subire supplicium; sed tuis, uirgo splendidissima, saluatus meritis et intercessionibus, perenne celorum consequar regnum, annuente Iesu Christo filio tuo Domino nostro, qui cum Deo coeterno patre et spiritu sancto uiuit.[121]

ORATIO AD DEI GENITRICEM. Sancta et intemerata uirgo Maria, solamen et refocillatio omnium credentium, ex qua auctor nostre salutis incarnari dignatus est, submissis te interpello suspiriis et deuotissima exoro interuentione ut ⟨ad⟩ proprium pro me intercedas misero et probroso filium, quatinus quicquid in meis actibus prauum ac anime sospitati est contrarium deleat et abstergat, quicquid utile proficuumque hoc plantet consolidetque, ne humani generis callidissimus aduersator de meo /83r/ letetur interitu, sed tuo iuuamine expulsus tristetur, meque per tua [perpetua *MS*] sancta suffragia taliter Christi componat gratia, ut mente pariter et corpore perseuerem incorrupta, humilis et mansueta, fidei spei caritatisque donis fulcita prefulgidis, omnibusque Christi ita obtemperans iussis, ut cum mihi dies sorsque uenerit suprema in collegio beatorum spirituum tibi iugiter suppeditantium merear annumerari, te mitissima mundi polique regina interueniente et Christo filio tuo annuente, qui cum coeterno patre et almo pneumate uiuit et gloriatur, unus omnipotens Deus per cuncta climata secli. AMEN.[122]

[121] This prayer is found in various Carolingian prayer-books, such as the so-called 'Fleury Prayer-Book' (*PL* ci. 1400) and the prayer-books of Troyes and Tours (ed. A. Wilmart, *Precum libelli quattuor aeui karolini* (Rome, 1944), pp. 16 and 140 respectively); it is also found in later English prayerbooks, such as the Arundel Psalter (London, BL Arundel 60, fo. 136r): see H. Barré, *Prières anciennes de l'Occident à la mère du Sauveur* (Paris, 1963), pp. 135–6, and Clayton, *The Cult of the Virgin Mary in Anglo-Saxon England*, p. 111. 'PRAYER CONCERNING ST MARY. Individual distinction [other manuscripts read *meriti* or *gratiae* in the genitive], unique and unparalleled mother and virgin, Mary, whom the Lord preserved chaste and inviolate in mind and body so that you should be worthy that the Son of God should fit to himself a human body out of you as the price of our redemption: I beseech you, most merciful one, through whose offspring the entire world gains salvation, intercede for me, a filthy wretch, loathsome with every kind of guilt, seeing that through my deeds I am not worthy to undergo anything but eternal punishment; but, O radiant Virgin, redeemed by your merit and intercession may I attain the eternal realm of heaven with the permission of your Son, Jesus Christ our Lord, who lives with God the coeternal Father and Holy Spirit.'

[122] This prayer occurs uniquely here; it is ptd. Barré, *Prières anciennes*, pp. 136–7, and Clayton, *The Cult of the Virgin Mary*, pp. 111–12. 'PRAYER TO THE MOTHER OF GOD. Holy and undefiled Virgin Mary, solace and sustenance of all believers, from whom the author of our salvation deigned to receive incarnation, I beseech you with humble sighs and pray that with your most holy intervention you may intercede with your Son on behalf of me, a wretch and reprobate, so that he may destroy and extinguish whatsoever in my deeds is awry and contrary to the health of my soul, but may implant and consolidate whatever is useful and advantageous, so that the very crafty adversary of the human race may not rejoice at my death, but, expelled through your assistance, may be saddened, and

ORATIO AD SANCTAM MARIAM. Sancta et gloriosa Dei genetrix semperque uirgo Maria, tu mundo meruisti generare saluatorem: exaudi me et miserere mei nunc /83ᵛ/ et semper propter honorem sancte et excellentissime uirginitatis tue; te deprecor humiliter, esto mihi, queso, saluatrix et adiutrix, apud Deum omnipotentem, ut ipse me pius pastor et princeps pacis a peccatorum meorum maculis emundet, et ab inferni tenebris eripiat et ad uitam perducat aeternam. Et qui per te, castissima uirgo, uenit in hunc mundum et humanum genus suo sanguine lauauit et inferni claustra destruxit et celestis regni ianuas aperuit, ille me per misericordiam suam in hoc saeculo saluare et conseruare dignetur, et post finem huius uitae labentis aliquam partem aeterne beatitudinis in sanctorum societate concedat. AMEN.[123] /84ʳ/

O VIRGO VIRGINVM DEI GENETRIX MARIA, mater Domini nostri Iesu Christi, regina angelorum et totius mundi, oraculum aeterne uitae, claritas [claritatis *MS*] celorum, que nec primam similem uisa est habere ⟨nec⟩ sequentem, per pretiosum sanguinem filii tui unigeniti Domini nostri Iesu Christi, quem in pretium nostrae salutis effudit, et per

through your holy support may Christ's grace so sustain me that I may continue incorrupt in mind as well as in body, humble and mild, sustained by the resplendent gifts of faith, hope, and charity and obeying all the commands of Christ, so that when the final day of my lot has come upon me, I may deserve to be numbered among the company of the blessed spirits perpetually attending you, through your intercession, most merciful queen of heaven and earth, and with the permission of Christ your Son, who lives and exults with the coeternal Father and Holy Spirit, one omnipotent God throughout all regions of the world. AMEN.' Note that the feminine grammatical forms from *incorrupta* to *fulcita* show this prayer to have been spoken by a woman.

[123] This prayer is known only from two earlier English prayerbooks (see Barré, *Prières anciennes*, pp. 68–70, and Clayton, *The Cult of the Virgin Mary*, pp. 98–104): the 'Book of Nunnaminster', now London, BL, Harley 2965 (southern England, s. viii/ix), ed. W. de G. Birch, *An Ancient Manuscript of the Eighth or Ninth Century Formerly Belonging to St Mary's Abbey or Nunnaminster, Winchester* (London/Winchester, 1889), p. 88; and the 'Book of Cerne', now Cambridge, UL Ll. 1. 10 (? Mercia, s. ix¹), ed. A. B. Kuypers, *The Prayer Book of Aedeluald the Bishop commonly called the Book of Cerne* (Cambridge, 1902), pp. 155–6 (no. 58). In the 'Book of Cerne' the prayer is attributed to one Alchfrith, who is known to us from other 9th-c. sources, notably the poem *De abbatibus* by Aediluulf: see W. Levison, *England and the Continent in the Eighth Century* (Oxford, 1946), pp. 295–302, and M. Lapidge, 'Aediluulf and the school of York', *Lateinische Kultur im VIII. Jahrhundert*, ed. A. Lehner and W. Berschin (St. Ottilien, 1989), pp. 161–78. 'PRAYER TO ST MARY. Holy and glorious mother of God, ever-virgin Mary, you were found worthy to give birth to the Saviour of the world: hear me and have mercy on me now and for ever, through the honour of your holy and most excellent virginity; and I humbly beseech you, be for me, I beg, my saviour and supporter before Almighty God, so that he, the kindly Shepherd and Prince of Peace, may cleanse me from the stains of my sins and snatch me from the shadows of hell and lead me to eternal life. And may he who came into this world through you, chaste virgin, and washed the human race with his blood and burst the gates of hell and opened the doors of the heavenly realm, deign in his mercy to save and preserve me in this world and after the end of this transient life grant me some part of eternal blessedness in the company of saints. AMEN.'

sanctam et uenerabilem et salubrem crucem eius in qua adfixus stare dignatus est pro salute generis humani, qui est fabricator mundi, et inter mortis supplicium quod ipse Dei filius sponte pro nobis in cruce pati uoluit, te suo discipulo sancto Iohanni commendauit dicens, 'Ecce mater tua': adiuua nos, et per gloriosam resurrectionem eius adiuua me miserum et peccatorem sanctis meritis tuis et gloriosis precibus tuis in infirmitate /84^{v}/ corporis mei et anime meae nunc laborantem et in hora exitus mei ex hac presenti uita et in omnibus tribulationibus et angustiis meis et in omnibus necessitatibus meis in hoc seculo et in futuro, illius [illi *MS*] ad laudem et gloriam et honorem qui me miserum creauit, quem tu, sacratissima et castissima et sanctissima et beatissima omnium feminarum uirgo Dei genetrix Maria, mundi saluatorem et redemptorem de tuo sancto et intemerato uirginali utero edidisti; et per illius amabile nomen et maiestatis suae nomen quod Deus omnium seculorum a cunctis Christianis fidelibus uocatur et creditur, et per ipsius sanctissimum amorem intercede pro nobis et pro rege nostro et pro famulo tuo et pro fratribus quoque et sororibus nostris, qui se in meis orationibus se commendauerunt, et /85^{r}/ pro omnibus qui in tribulatione et captiuitate sunt, et pro omni populo Christiano et pro animabus omnium fidelium defunctorum apud Deum, quia ipse est seculi uita et redemptio nostra et salus nostra et omne gaudium nostrum et refugium nostrum in omni tribulatione et angustia que circumdederunt nos, et omnis consolatio nostra, qui ex te nasci dignatus est unigenitus summi patris filius Dominus noster Iesus Christus: sit crucifixo Domino Deo nostro decus et imperium, honor et potestas et gloria et gratiarum actio in secula sempiterna. AMEN.[124]

[124] There is no known source of this prayer, which is ptd. Barré, *Prières anciennes*, pp. 137–8, and Clayton, *The Cult of the Virgin Mary*, pp. 112–13. Barré notes (ibid., pp. 135–6) that a similar prayer is found in an 11th-c. psalter from Nonantola, which implies that it and the Winchester prayer may have a common source. The Winchester version of the prayer is also found in the Arundel Psalter (BL Arundel 60, fo. 142^{r-v}). 'O VIRGIN OF VIRGINS, MARY, MOTHER OF GOD, mother of our Lord Jesus Christ, queen of the angels and of all the world, prophet of eternal life, brilliance of the heavens, who have never been seen to have a precedent or a successor: through the precious blood of your only begotten Son our Lord Jesus Christ, which he shed as the price of our salvation; and through his holy and venerable and life-giving Cross, on which he deigned to stand fastened for the salvation of human kind, who is the creator of the world, and during the torment of dying which this same Son of God willingly endured for us on the Cross, commended you to St John, his disciple, saying, "Behold your mother": help us, and through his glorious resurrection help me, a wretch and a sinner, by means of your holy merits and your glorious prayers, now while I struggle in the weakness of my body and my soul, at the hour of my departure from this present life, and in all my tribulations and anxieties and in all my needs in this world and the next, to the praise and glory and honour of him who created my wretched self, him whom you, most venerable and chaste and holy and blessed of all women, Mary, virgin mother of God, brought forth from your holy and undefiled virginal womb as the Saviour and Redeemer of the world; and

PRECES SANCTE. Sancta mater Christi, Maria, esto mihi adiutor famulo tuo, ut per tua sacra suffragia celestia adipisci merear gaudia. per.
ITEM. Fili Dei uiui et fili sancte Mariae uirginis, /85^{v}/ sicut uis et sicut tu scis et sicut potes, sic miserere mei indigno misero peccatori.
ALIA. Qui cognoscis omnia occulta, a peccatis meis munda me et per sacram tuae intemerate matris semper uirginis Marie interuentionem tempus mihi concede ut repenitens plangam quod peccaui; miserere mei, Christe saluator mundi.
ITEM ALIA. Multa et innumerabilia sunt, Domine, peccata mea; intercedente sancta Maria cum omnibus sanctis, indulge et miserere mei, quia peccaui tibi nimis.
ORATIO. Domine Iesu Christe, tibi flecto genua mea, tibi corde credo, tibi confiteor omnia peccata mea: miserere mihi miserrimo peccatori. AMEN.[125]

The prefatory material of this *cursus* is derived from known antiphons and hymns, and of the longer prayers, two are known from earlier sources. To some extent, therefore, the *cursus* is a work of compilation rather than original composition, and in such circumstances it is not possible to mount arguments for authorship on stylistic grounds. Nevertheless certain details in the two longer

through his lovable name and the name of his majesty, by which he is called and believed to be God of all ages by all the Christian faithful, and through his holy love intercede for us and for our king and for your servant and also for our brothers and for our sisters, who have commended themselves to my prayers, and for all those who are in travail and in captivity, and for all the Christian people, and for the souls of all the faithful dead who are with God, because he is the life of this world and our redemption and our salvation and all our joy and our refuge in all travail and anguish which oppress us, and all our consolation, he who deigned to be born through you, the only-begotten Son of the highest Father, our Lord Jesus Christ: distinction and authority, honour and power and glory and thanksgiving be to our crucified Lord God, for ever and ever. AMEN.'

[125] These brief prayers are not apparently found elsewhere. 'HOLY PRAYERS. Holy mother of Christ, Mary, be a helper to me your servant, that through your holy support I may deserve to attain celestial bliss.

DITTO. O son of the living God and Son of the holy virgin Mary, have mercy on me, a wretch and unworthy sinner, just as you will and as you best know how and as you are able.

ANOTHER PRAYER. You who know all secrets, cleanse me from my sins and through the holy intervention of your undefiled mother, the ever-virgin Mary, grant me time that in penitence I may lament the fact that I have sinned; have mercy on me, O Christ, Saviour of the world.

LIKEWISE ANOTHER. Many and countless are my sins, O Lord; be kind and have mercy on me through the intercession of Mary and all the saints, for I have sinned greatly against you.

A PRAYER. O Lord Jesus Christ, I bend my knees before you, I believe in you with my heart, I confess to you all my sins: have mercy on me, a most wretched sinner. AMEN.'

prayers for which no source has been identified may point to Æthelwold. In the second of these ('Oratio ad Dei genitricem'), the usual simple formulas of the doxology have been replaced with Graecisms (*almo pneumate*, *per cuncta climata*), and we know the use of ostentatious Graecisms to be characteristic of the Latin literature composed at Winchester under Æthelwold. In the fourth and longest of the prayers ('O uirgo uirginum') there is a petition on behalf of the king (*intercede pro nobis et pro rege*), and we have seen that prayers for the king were a novel feature incorporated by Æthelwold into the *Regularis concordia*. These slight indications help to confirm the suspicion that the supplementary office for the Virgin in Titus D. XXVII is identical with that mentioned by the author of *De horis peculiaribus*; but absolute proof of Æthelwold's authorship is lacking.

The supplementary office for All Saints mentioned in *De horis peculiaribus* is also of considerable interest in the context of Æthelwold's Winchester, in view of the fact that the *Regularis concordia* mentions two such offices, one intended for Matins (c. 19) and one for Vespers (c. 56).[126] Unfortunately the *Regularis concordia* does not quote either of these offices, and it is not clear whether either of them can be identified with that mentioned in *De horis peculiaribus*. The matter is clarified by an unprinted office bearing the rubric DE OMNIBVS SANCTIS AD VESPERAM in London, BL Cotton Tiberius A. III (written at Christ Church, Canterbury, in the mid eleventh century, but quite clearly copied from a Winchester exemplar),[127] fo. 57r-v. The structure of this office is broadly similar to that for the Virgin discussed above: it begins with various antiphons, a hymn, the *Pater noster*, and then a sequence for various saints, set out like a litany and including several English confessors.

Deus in adiutorium. Gloria patri. A In consilio iustorum et congregatione magna opera Domini. PS Confitebor tibi Domine in toto corde. In consilio. A Pretiosa est in conspectu Domini mors sanctorum eius. PS Credidi. A Euntes ibant et flebant mittentes semina sua. PS In

[126] See T. Symons, 'Monastic observance in the tenth century', *Downside Review*, xxxi (1932), 449–64, at pp. 451–6; xxxii (1933) 137–52. On the veneration of All Saints and Æthelwold's Winchester, and Wulfstan's contribution to this veneration, see above, p. xxix; note also that Ælfric in his *Colloquium* describes the day of an oblate which includes an Office for All Saints: 'deinde cantauimus de omnibus sanctis et matutinales laudes' (ed. G. N. Garmonsway, *Ælfric's Colloquy* (2nd edn., London, 1947), p. 47).

[127] Ker, *Catalogue*, p. 244 (no. 186, item 10*a*); Temple, *AS Manuscripts*, pp. 118–19 (no. 100).

conuertendo. A Iusti confitebuntur nomini tuo Domine et habitabunt recti cum uultu tuo. PS Eripe me Domine. CAPIT Scimus quoniam diligentibus Deum omnia cooperantur in bonum his qui secundum propositum uocati sunt sancti. Deo gratias. ℟ Exultent iusti in conspectu Dei. Et delectentur in letitia. In conspectu. Gloria patri. YMNVS. Christi redemptor omnium, conserua tuos famulos.[128]
℣ Iusti autem in perpetuo uiuent. A Dabo sanctis meis locum nominatum in regno patris mei. PS Magnificat anima. Gloria patri. Kyrieleyson. Christe eleyson. Pater noster. Et ne nos. Aue Maria gratia. A Beata mater et innupta uirgo gloriosa regina mundi, intercede pro nobis ad Dominum. ℣ Post partum uirgo inuiolata.

Sancte Michahel archangele, defende nos in prelio ut non pereamus in tremendo iudicio. 'In conspectu angelorum psallam tibi.'

Inter natos mulierum fuit homo missus a Deo cui nomen 'Tu es Petrus et super hanc petram'.

Sancte Paule apostole, 'predicator ueritatis et doctor gentium', intercede pro nobis ad Deum qui te elegit.

Andreas, Christi famulus, dignus Deo apostolus, germanus Petri et in passione socius. 'In omnem terram exiuit sonus eorum.'

Sacerdos Dei Martine, pastor egregie, ora pro nobis Deum.

Ora pro nobis, beate Benedicte, ut digni efficiamur pro missione Christi.

Sancte Cuthberte, confessor Christi uenerande, adesto nostris precibus pius et propitius.

Beate Birine, predicator egregie, succurre nobis tua sancta intercessione.

Sancte Suuithune, gloriose con/57v/fessor Christi, ora pro peccatis nostris ad Dominum.

O beate Iudoce, magna fide tua intercede pro nobis ad Deum qui te elegit.

Beate Æþelðryð, uirgo Dei electa, intercede pro peccatis nostris omniumque populorum.[129]

[128] *ICL*, no. 2220.

[129] 'St Michael the Archangel, defend us in the struggle so that we do not perish at the terrible Judgement. "I will sing praise to thee in the sight of the angels" (Ps. 137 (138): 1).

'Among the sons of women there was sent a man from God whose name was "Thou art Peter and upon this rock" (Matt. 16: 18).

'St Paul the Apostle, "preacher of the truth and teacher of the Gentiles" (1 Tim. 2: 7), intercede on our behalf with God, who chose you.

'Andrew, servant of Christ, apostle worthy of God, brother of Peter and companion in his suffering. "Their sound hath gone forth into all the earth" (Ps. 18: 4 (19: 4); Rom. 10: 18).

Offerentur regi uirgines. Exultent iusti. Letamini in Domino et exultate iusti.
OREMVS. Tribue, quesumus, Domine, omnes sanctos tuos iugiter orare pro nobis et semper eos clementer audire. Per.
Deus in adiutorium. Gloria patri. **PS** Deus misereatur nostri. **A** Post partum uirgo inuiolata permansisti, Dei genetrix, intercede pro nobis. **PS** Dominus regnauit decorem. **A** Laudemus Dominum quem laudant angeli, quem Cherubin et Seraphim 'Sanctus Sanctus Sanctus' proclamant. **PS** Iubilate Deo. **A** Vos amici mei estis si feceritis que precipio uobis dicit Dominus. **PS** Deus Deus meus. **A** Ora pro nobis, beate Benedicte, ut digne efficiamus pro missione Christi. **PS** Benedicite. **A** Omnium sanctorum chori laudate Dominum de celis. **PS** Laudate Dominum. **CAPIT** Sancti per fidem uicerunt regna, operati sunt iustitiam, adepti sunt repromissiones. In Christo Iesu Domino nostro. ℟ Iusti autem. ℣ Et apud Dominum est.
YMNVS. Iesu salus.[130]
℣ Exultent iusti. **A** Iusti fulgebunt sicut sol in regno patris eorum. Benedictus Dominus Deus Israel. Kyrieleyson. Vt supra.

Of the confessors invoked in this *cursus* for All Saints, Martin, Benedict, and Cuthbert were universally culted, and do not point to a local observance. However, Birinus and Swithun were specifically culted at the Old Minster, Winchester, Iudoc at the New Minster, Winchester, and Æthelthryth at Ely, a Winchester dependency which had been refounded by Æthelwold, as Wulfstan tells us (c. 23). The petitions to these saints point unmistakably to Winchester as the origin of the *cursus*. Furthermore, the fact that Swithun (who was translated in 971) is included but Æthelwold is omitted, suggests that the *cursus* was composed between 971 and 996 at the outside, and may well date from the period of Æthelwold's episcopacy. There are good grounds, then, for thinking that this *cursus* for All Saints is identical with that instituted by Æthelwold for the private observance of his monks at Winchester and referred to in the *Regularis concordia*.

'Martin, priest of God, excellent shepherd, pray to God on our behalf.
'Pray for us, St Benedict, that we may be made worthy for Christ's mission.
'St Cuthbert, venerable confessor of Christ, attend kindly and mercifully to our prayers.
'St Birinus, excellent preacher, assist us through your holy intercession.
'St Swithun, glorious confessor of Christ, pray to the Lord for our sins.
'O St Iudoc, intercede on our behalf with your great faith to God, who chose you.
'St Æthelthryth, chosen virgin of God, intercede for our sins and those of all peoples.'

130 *ICL*, no. 7665 (where the hymn is dated to the early 10th c.); *AH* li. 227 (no. 197).

(*c*) *Pontifical ceremonies.* There are various ecclesiastical ceremonies which can only be performed by a bishop, such as the consecration of a church or cemetery, the coronation of a king, the blessing of an abbot, or the ordination of a priest or deacon or cleric in minor orders. The instructions for the performance of these various ceremonies are called an *ordo*. From the eighth century onwards, booklets containing various *ordines* survive, and in due course *ordines* were collected together so as to constitute a bishop's handbook or pontifical. There is considerable variety in content between pontificals from the period before the late tenth century, when the massive and thorough collection of pontifical *ordines*, known as the Romano-German Pontifical, was assembled probably at Mainz. The Romano-German Pontifical does not appear to have been used in England before the mid eleventh century.[131] A number of Anglo-Saxon pontificals survives from the period before the introduction of the Romano-German Pontifical, and of these, there is one which may have been written at Winchester during Æthelwold's episcopacy: Cambridge, Sidney Sussex College Δ. 5. 15 (100).[132] A Winchester origin for this manuscript seems probable on palaeographical grounds, since its principal scribe is found in other Winchester manuscripts of the late tenth century; it subsequently migrated to Durham during the course of the eleventh century.[133] Sidney Sussex Δ. 5. 15 is not a complete pontifical; rather, it is a booklet consisting of two quires (14 folios) and containing nothing but *ordines* for the ordination of priests, deacons, and clerics in minor orders.[134] There is no localizable feature in the *ordines* themselves. However, they are textually related to those in a definable group of Anglo-Saxon pontificals;[135]

131 See M. Lapidge, 'The origin of CCCC 163', *Transactions of the Cambridge Bibliographical Society*, viii (1981), 18–28; 'Ealdred of York and MS. Cotton Vitellius E. xii', *Yorkshire Archaeological Journal*, lv (1983), 11–25.

132 The Sidney Sussex Pontifical is ed. H. M. J. Banting, *Two Anglo-Saxon Pontificals*, HBS civ (1989), pp. 157–70.

133 See T. A. M. Bishop, *English Caroline Minuscule* (Oxford, 1971), p. 14 (no. 16) and pl. xiv.

134 On early services of ordination in Anglo-Saxon England, see G. Ellard, *Ordination Anointings in the Western Church before 1000* (Cambridge, Mass., 1933), esp. pp. 14–50, 78–87; A. Snijders, '*Acolythus cum ordinatur*: Eine historische Studie', *Sacris erudiri*, ix (1957), 163–98, at 174–5; B. Kleinheyer, *Die Priesterweihe im römischen Ritus: Eine liturgiehistorische Studie* (Trier, 1962), pp. 85–114; and H. B. Porter, *The Ordination Prayers of the Ancient Western Churches* (London, 1967), esp. pp. 72–7.

135 The group includes the 'Dunstan Pontifical', Paris, BN, lat. 943; unptd.; the 'Egbert Pontifical', ed. Banting, *Two Anglo-Saxon Pontificals*, pp. 3–153; the 'Benedic-

and of this group, the *ordines* in Sidney Sussex Δ. 5. 15 correspond nearly verbatim to those in a pontifical written *c.*1000 at either Worcester or York, now preserved as part of London, BL Cotton Claudius A. III.[136] The relationship is relevant, because the pontifical in Claudius A. III appears to derive ultimately from a northern French exemplar, inasmuch as it contains benedictions for St Vedastus. Prayers for this saint are found in other service-books from Æthelwold's Winchester, as we have seen.[137] Sidney Sussex Δ. 5. 15, then, is a Winchester book which could have been used by Æthelwold.

We are on firmer ground with a service-book which was certainly used by Æthelwold, the famous 'Benedictional of St Æthelwold', now London, BL Add. 49598.[138] The various pontifical ceremonies mentioned above, such as the ordination of a priest or deacon, could only be performed by a bishop. Similarly, only a bishop could pronounce an episcopal benediction during mass (if mass was performed by a priest, the benediction was omitted). The episcopal benediction was a tripartite prayer pronounced by the bishop after the *Pater noster* and immediately before communion. The use of pre-communion episcopal benedictions was in origin an eastern practice, but it became fully developed in Visigothic Spain and Francia by the seventh century (it was never adopted by Rome, however, with the result that there were various papal attempts to suppress it), and was a salient feature of the Gallican rite. The result is that various collections of benedictions for Sundays and saints' days were assembled in Francia no later than the eighth century.[139] One of the earliest collections, the so-called 'Long' or 'Gallican' benedictional (consisting of some 75 benedictions) was probably compiled in the

tional of Archbishop Robert', ed. H. A. Wilson, HBS xxiv (1903); and the first of the three pontificals bound together in BL Cotton Claudius A. III, known as 'Claudius I', ed. D. H. Turner, *The Claudius Pontificals*, HBS xcvii (1971), pp. 1–88.

[136] Cf. Turner, *The Claudius Pontificals*, pp. 31–41, and Banting, *Two Anglo-Saxon Pontificals*, pp. 157–67. It is curious that Turner makes no mention of the Sidney Sussex manuscript.

[137] See above, n. 108.

[138] G. F. Warner and H. A. Wilson, *The Benedictional of St Æthelwold* (Oxford, 1910).

[139] On the origin and forms of the benedictional, see R. Amiet, *The Benedictionals of Freising*, HBS lxxviii (1974), pp. 3–22; *CPB* iii, pp. vi–lxv; A. Prescott, 'The structure of English pre-Conquest benedictionals', *British Library Journal*, xiii (1987), 118–58, at pp. 119–21; and id., 'The text of the Benedictional of St Æthelwold', *Bishop Æthelwold*, pp. 119–47, esp. 121–7.

diocese of Autun in the late seventh century,[140] and is preserved variously in the sacramentaries of Angoulême and Gellone, and in a manuscript from Freising now in Munich.[141] Another collection, known as the 'Gregorian' benedictional, was probably assembled in the early ninth century, possibly by Benedict of Aniane, as part of the supplement to the Gregorian sacramentary known as the *Hadrianum ex autentico*.[142] These are the two principal collections; however, because such collections were particularly susceptible to adaptation and interpolation (so as to incorporate benedictions for locally celebrated feasts and saints), manuscript benedictionals vary enormously one from the other, with the result that it is difficult to trace relationships except in broad outline.

The Benedictional of St Æthelwold is perhaps the most lavishly produced manuscript which has survived from Anglo-Saxon England.[143] According to the prefatory poem written by its principal scribe, who names himself as Godemann, the manuscript was commissioned by Æthelwold himself.[144] Since it includes benedictions for St Swithun, whose cult only gained prominence after the translation in 971, the manuscript must have been written between 971 and 984, the date of Æthelwold's death; in fact there are convincing reasons for thinking that it was written in 973, the year of Edgar's coronation.[145] The illuminations in the manuscript have long occupied the attention of art historians, but only recently has the text of the benedictional itself been the subject of detailed analysis.[146] It is now clear that the 'Benedictional of St Æthelwold' is a piece of liturgical scholarship in its own right, for it presents a systematic attempt to combine, for each Sunday and each feast, the

[140] J. Deshusses, 'Le bénédictionnaire gallican du VIIIe siècle', *Ephemerides Liturgicae*, lxxvii (1963), 169–87.

[141] Sacramentary of Angoulême, ed. P. Saint-Roch, *Liber sacramentorum Engolismensis*, *CCSL* clixC (1987); sacramentary of Gellone, ed. A. Dumas and J. Deshusses, *Liber sacramentorum Gellonensis*, 2 vols., *CCSL* clix–clixA (1981). The second benedictional of Freising (Munich, Staatsbibl., Clm. 6430) is ed. Amiet, *The Benedictionals of Freising*, pp. 76–120.

[142] Ed. Deshusses, *Le Sacramentaire grégorien*, pp. 576–98.

[143] Temple, *AS Manuscripts*, pp. 49–53 (no. 23); see also J. J. G. Alexander, 'The Benedictional of St Æthelwold and Anglo-Saxon illumination of the reform period', *Tenth-Century Studies*, pp. 169–83, as well as the forthcoming full-length study by Deshman (below, n. 145).

[144] The poem is ptd. M. Lapidge, 'The hermeneutic style in tenth-century Anglo-Latin literature', *ASE* iv (1975), 67–111, at pp. 105–6.

[145] R. E. Deshman, *The Benedictional of St Æthelwold* (Princeton, forthcoming).

[146] Prescott, in *Bishop Æthelwold*, pp. 119–47.

benedictions of the 'Gallican' or 'Long' benedictional with those of the 'Gregorian'. Usually the Gregorian benediction is given first, followed by the Gallican (marked *item alia* or the like).[147] Because of this systematic arrangement, the sources of the 'Benedictional of St Æthelwold' can be identified with some confidence. The 'Gregorian' benedictions evidently derive from a Gregorian sacramentary of the *Hadrianum* type and containing the *Supplementum Anianense*. The 'Gallican' benedictions apparently derive from a benedictional written somewhere in northern France, because they include benedictions for one localizable saint: Vedastus. However, the 'Benedictional of St Æthelwold' also contains various benedictions not found in earlier benedictionals, and there is reason to suspect that these were composed in England.[148] Principal among these are benedictions for two Winchester saints, Swithun and Æthelthryth. The presumption must be that these benedictions were composed at Winchester for Æthelwold's personal use—if not by Æthelwold himself, at least under his supervision. It is therefore worth quoting these benedictions:

Swithun[149]

a. Deus qui praesentis diei festiuitatem in beati antistitis Suuithuni celebritate uenerabilem sanxisti, tribue nobis tanti patroni interuentu practicae uitae subsidium ac aeternae theoricae lucrum. Amen.

b. Quique illum nouissimis ferme mundi temporibus multiplici ac pene ineffabili miraculorum copia ut fidei faculam identidem succenderet

[147] Ibid., pp. 128–32 (table 1).

[148] Ibid., nos. 35 (St Vincent), 100, 102, 110, 112, 116, 118, 120, 122, 124, 126, 130, 132, 134, 136 (all for Sundays after Pentecost), 140 (St Æthelthryth), 145 (St Swithun), 146 (St Benedict), 147 (St Laurence), 152–3 (Nativity BVM), 156 ('sabbato mense septimi' [*sic*]), 157–8 (Michaelmas), 159–60 (All Saints), 163 (St Cecilia), 164 (St Clement), 165–7 (St Andrew), and 168 (St Thomas): in all, some thirty-two benedictions which have a claim to be considered as English compositions.

[149] *CPB*, no. 1088. 'a. God, who have blessed the venerable feast of this present day for the celebration of St Swithun, grant us through the intercession of so great a patron assistance in this active life and the bounty of the eternal contemplative life. Amen.

'b. And may he who wished in almost the last days of the world to reveal him as most holy through an abundant and all but inexpressible supply of miracles so that he should constantly ignite the torch of faith, grant that you may, flourishing in the fertility of all virtues and suffused with the dew of faith, hope, and charity, persevere in the sacred task with good works. Amen.

'c. So that, illuminated by the teaching of this merciful supporter and strengthened by his manifold assistance, you may deserve to be joined in the celestial realm with him who on this day joyfully entered the recesses of heaven. Amen.

'*Quod ipse praestare*.'

sanctissimum manifestare uoluit, uos uirtutum omnium fecunditate floridos, fidei spei caritatisque rore perfusos, in sancto proposito cum bonis operibus perseuerare concedat. Amen.

c. Qui pii suffragatoris doctrina irradiati et multiplici suffragio corroborati, illi in caelesti regione mereamini adiungi, qui hodierna die tripudians caeli secreta penetrauit. Amen.

Quod ipse praestare.

Æthelthryth[150]

a. Omnipotens unus et aeternus Deus, pater et filius et spiritus sanctus, qui beatae Æðelðryðe animum septiformis gratiae ubertate ita succensum solidauit, ut duorum coniugum thalamis asscita immunis euaderet castamque sibi piissimus sponsam perpetim adoptaret, uos ab incentiua libidinum concupiscentia muniendo submoueat et sui amoris igne succendat. Amen.

b. Et qui eius integritatem per imputribile corpus post obitum manifeste designauit signisque miraculorum ineffabiliter ostendit, uos in sanctis operibus castos fideliter usque ad uitae terminum perseuerare concedat. Amen.

c. Quatinus ab huius recidiui saeculi cupiditate remoti, uirtutum omnium lampadibus adornati, eius in caelis mereamini habere consortium quae terreni regis caritatiue contempsit thalamum, spretaque lata terrenae cupiditatis uia artam monasticae conuersationis eligere uoluit uitam, ac hodierna die uoti compos caelestem aeterni regis intrare promeruit aulam. Amen.

Quod ipse praestare dignetur.

The 'Benedictional of St Æthelwold' is a service-book decorated on a scale of magnificence previously unknown in a book of this

[150] *CPB*, no. 1805. 'a. May almighty God, one and eternal, Father and Son and Holy Ghost, who set alight and strengthened the conviction of St Æthelthryth with the bounty of sevenfold grace so that, summoned to the bridal chambers of two husbands, she was able to escape scot-free and that the Holy Bridegroom was able to adopt her as his chaste spouse in perpetuity, remove you from the provocative concupiscence of lust and ignite you with the fire of his love. Amen.

'b. And may he who clearly revealed her purity through her incorruptible body after death and who revealed her ineffably through miracles grant you the ability to persevere committedly chaste in good works until the end of your life. Amen.

'c. So that, remote from desire for this transient world, adorned with the lamps of all virtues, you may deserve to have in heaven the fellowship of her who through divine love scorned the bridal bed of an earthly king and, having rejected the wide highway of earthly lust, wished to choose the narrow way of monastic life, and on this day, obtaining her wish, deserved to enter the celestial hall of the eternal king. Amen.

'*Quod ipse praestare dignetur*'.

sort,[151] and it is difficult not to see Æthelwold, with his well-attested taste for lavish display, as the inspiration behind the book's design. By the same token, the scholarly combination of the two kinds of benedictional which the book represents may well be the personal contribution of Æthelwold himself, as may the composition of the benedictions for Swithun and Æthelthryth. Here, if anywhere, the personal influence of Æthelwold on the liturgy of the Anglo-Saxon church may be felt.[152]

(*d*) *Chant.* There is a celebrated passage in the twelfth-century *Chronicon monasterii de Abingdon* where it is stated that Æthelwold wished his Abingdon monks—who, having been trained at various places, had different customs in plainchant (*differenti more legendo canendique instituti*)—to hymn God in a uniform manner, and accordingly he summoned some experienced monks from Corbie to train his own *familia* in chanting: '... ex Corbiensi coenobio, quod in Francia situm est, ecclesiastica ea tempestate disciplina opinatissimo uiros accersiit solertissimos, quos in legendo psallendoque sui imitarentur.'[153] This is a precious testimony, but unfortunately it cannot be tested, because there is no surviving music-book of any sort—gradual, antiphoner, or troper—from tenth-century Abingdon. Fortunately there is much better evidence for Winchester, for we have two music-books—the so-called 'Winchester Tropers'[154] which provide a clear picture of at least one aspect of the chant (that is, the trope repertory) at late tenth-century Winchester. One of these books, now Oxford, Bodleian

[151] There are few examples of illuminated benedictionals earlier than the Benedictional of St Æthelwold; cf., however, *CLitLA*, no. 287. The (wrongly named) 'Ramsey Benedictional' (Paris, BN lat. 987) and the 'Benedictional of Archbishop Robert' (Rouen, Bibl. mun. 369 (Y. 7)) are both lavishly illuminated; but both are late 10th-c. Winchester products.

[152] Prescott has shown convincingly that the Benedictional of St Æthelwold and the 'Ramsey Benedictional' (which he proves to be a Winchester product probably compiled at Winchester as the first essay at a truly English benedictional: *Bishop Æthelwold*, pp. 133–5) together constitute what may be called the 'Winchester Benedictional', and that the influence of this 'Winchester Benedictional' was felt on all later English benedictionals: 'of the many liturgical reforms made by Æthelwold at Winchester, the new form of benedictional introduced by him appears to have been among the most influential. This makes the Benedictional of St Æthelwold doubly significant: it emerges as not only a magnificent book used by Æthelwold himself, but also as a text representing one of Æthelwold's most enduring achievements. Indeed, the benedictional tradition to which it gave rise may be seen as one of the major literary products of the English ecclesiastical revival' ('The structure of English pre-Conquest benedictionals', p. 134).

[153] *Chron. Abingdon*, i. 129.

[154] Ed. Frere, *The Winchester Troper*.

Library, Bodley 775, was copied in the mid eleventh century from a lost exemplar which had been written, to all appearances, at Winchester during the years 978 × 986, perhaps in Æthelwold's lifetime; the other, now Cambridge, Corpus Christi College 473, was written at Winchester *c.*1000. As we have seen (above, p. xxxvi), CCCC 473 was written as a precentor's handbook, and may possibly have been owned, used, and written in by Wulfstan himself. The tropes contained in these 'Winchester Tropers' have been the subject of a comprehensive study by Alejandro Planchart.[155] On the basis of Planchart's research, it is clear that much of the Winchester trope repertory has its closest parallel in music manuscripts from northern France;[156] interestingly, one such book, now Cambrai, Bibl. mun. 75, is a mid-eleventh-century manuscript from Saint-Vaast in Arras, whose patron saint was St Vedastus. Here as elsewhere the links between Æthelwold's Winchester and northern France are manifest.

Other aspects of the chant at Winchester at this time are less well known, since the manuscript evidence in question is all much later. It has been suggested, nevertheless, that the antiphonary which lies behind the 'New Minster Missal' (Le Havre, Bibl. mun. 330), a plenary missal from the New Minster dating from the second half of the eleventh century, may have derived from Corbie via Abingdon.[157] Unfortunately there is no means of proving such conjectures. Nor is there any reason to suspect that Æthelwold himself had a proficient knowledge of plainchant. Yet here, too, as a result of his contacts with northern France, Æthelwold exercised a decisive influence on the Anglo-Saxon liturgy, even if the precise limits of that influence cannot be defined in this case.

(*e*) *Private prayer.* As with other liturgical forms, private prayers were seldom transmitted with any indication of authorship, but usually passed anonymously into prayer-books, where they were collected for the use of their owners. In other words, if Æthelwold had composed prayers for the purposes of his private meditation, we should not expect these to be transmitted under his name in prayer-books of the period. In any event, there is no surviving prayer-book which was written at Winchester during the period of

155 Planchart, *Repertory*.
156 Ibid., i. 173–7.
157 Turner, *The Missal of the New Minster*, p. xxvi.

his episcopacy; and the few surviving prayer-books from eleventh-century Winchester contain no prayers attributable to him. However, there is some late (that is, twelfth-century) evidence that Æthelwold on one occasion at least composed a prayer. The *Chronicon monasterii de Abingdon* preserves a prayer for the protection of Abingdon said to have been composed there by Æthelwold before his departure for Winchester in 963.[158] This prayer is as follows:

Deus aeterne, ante cuius conspectum assistunt angeli, et cuius nutu reguntur uniuersa, protege, Domine, quaeso, locum istum qui in nomine tuo et beatae Mariae constructus est, et per uirtutem nominis tui recedat ab eo uirtus inimicorum umbraque phantasmatum et incursio turbinum, percussio fulminum, laesio tonitruum, calamitas tempestatuum, omnisque spiritus procellarum. Praeterea quaeso, Domine, ut non ignis domum istam consumat, nec homo inimicus per superbiam eam destruat; sed tu, piissime Deus, conserua eam et guberna; multiplicique fructuum ubertate pinguescat, ut omnes habitantes in ea uoce et corde te hymnizent et suaui modulatione nomen tuum magnificent, et super eos descendat benedictio tua et super locum istum maneatque semper. Per Dominum nostrum.[159]

This prayer does not occur in any earlier source, and the attribution to Æthelwold may well derive from genuine tradition. It bears no marks of Æthelwold's characteristic inclination towards ostentatious (especially Greek-based) vocabulary, yet it has a fine rhetorical sentence-structure, implying that its author was a Latinist of some competence. The question is best left open.

[158] *Chron. Abingdon*, i. 347: 'orauit etiam pro domo ista, antequam ad episcopatum Wintoniensem uocatus esset, orationem.' Note also that this prayer of Æthelwold is preserved in the so-called Abingdon Breviary of 1528 (Cambridge, Emmanuel College, S 1. 4. 6), fo. 354^{r-v}; see below, p. cxxxvii n. 63.

[159] *Chron. Abingdon*, i. 347–8: 'Eternal God, before whose sight the angels are present, and through whose command all things are governed, protect, Lord, I beseech you, this place which was built in your name and the Virgin Mary's, and through the might of your name may the force of enemies and the shadow of phantoms and the assault of winds, the bolt of lightning, the damaging clap of thunder, the disaster of tempests and every blast of storms—may these all pass us by. Moreover, Lord, I beseech you that fire not consume this house, nor a spiteful man destroy it through arrogance; but rather, O merciful God, protect and govern it; and may it grow fat in the manifold abundance of its fruits, so that all those dwelling in it may hymn you in voice and heart, and may magnify your name in sweet harmony; and may your blessing descend upon them and upon this place and remain there forever. Through our Lord etc.'

8. *Æthelwold as Scholar*

Æthelwold had a very considerable reputation for learning.[160] He apparently acquired this learning during his years of study at Glastonbury. Wulfstan (c. 9) tells us specifically that Æthelwold learned there 'skill in the liberal art of grammar and the honey-sweet system of metrics' (*liberalem grammaticae artis peritiam atque mellifluam metricae rationis dulcedinem*) and also read the best-known of Christian patristic authors (*catholicos quoque et nominatos studiose legebat auctores*). It is not easy to test these assertions, however.

We may begin with the question of Æthelwold's skill in grammar. No treatise on grammar has come down to us under Æthelwold's name. It is possible that when the various unprinted and anonymous Latin grammatical works which survive in manuscript from the late Anglo-Saxon period are better understood, it may be possible to assign one or more of them to Æthelwold's Winchester. One example may be mentioned: in London, BL Harley 3271 (unknown English origin, s. xi^{1}), there is a grammar entitled *Dialogus de .viii. partibus orationis* (fos. 93^{r}–113^{v}). This dialogue bears no unambiguous mark of its origin, but it is noteworthy that at one point it cites, as examples of first-declension proper nouns, the three English cities *Wintonia*, *Londonia*, *Eboraca* (fo. 98^{r}). The fact that Winchester is named first among the three cities might suggest an origin there. Other evidence points in the same direction. The *Dialogus* draws substantially on Priscian's *Institutiones grammaticae*, a work which was certainly known in Winchester circles—and not certainly elsewhere in England in the late tenth century—since it was quoted by Lantfred and Ælfric; furthermore, the *Excerptiones de Prisciano*, a work possibly compiled in England that draws on the *Institutiones grammaticae*, served as the basis of Ælfric's Grammar.[161] Another significant feature of the

[160] See Lapidge, in *Bishop Æthelwold*, pp. 89–117.

[161] In the prefatory *Epistola* to his *Translatio et miracula S. Swithuni*, Lantfred quotes a sentence from the preface to Priscian's *Institutiones grammaticae* (ed. M. J. Hertz in *Grammatici Latini*, ed. H. Keil, 8 vols. (Leipzig, 1857–80), ii. 1–2); and this same sentence is quoted by Ælfric in the prologue to his *Vita S. Æthelwoldi* (below, p. cl n. 26). Ælfric's own Grammar (ed. J. Zupitza, *Ælfrics Grammatik und Glossar* (2nd edn, rev. H. Gneuss, Berlin–Zürich–Dublin, 1966) is based on the *Excerptiones de Prisciano*, an unprinted compendium of Priscian's massive work that is preserved in three 11th-c. manuscripts (two of them English): see V. Law, 'Anglo-Saxon England: Ælfric's *Excerptiones de arte grammatica anglice*', *Histoire, épistémologie, langage*, ix (1987), 47–71, at pp. 51–4.

Dialogus is that, in giving examples of nouns of various declensions, it frequently cites entire hexameters from Caelius Sedulius' *Carmen Paschale*.[162] This poem was read universally as a school-text, of course, but it may be worth remembering that Wulfstan—who presumably learnt his proficiency in metrics from Æthelwold—models his own hexameters on those of Caelius Sedulius more than any other poet's.[163] None of this amounts to proof; but we know from Wulfstan that Æthelwold 'taught the rules of grammar' to his students (c. 31) and hence it is possible that, when unprinted grammars such as the *Dialogus* have been properly studied alongside Ælfric's Grammar, some light may be thrown on Æthelwold's own knowledge of that discipline. For the time being we remain in the dark.

Nor do we have any evidence to illustrate Wulfstan's statement that Æthelwold mastered the 'honey-sweet system of metrics'. No metrical treatise in Æthelwold's name has survived; no verse composed by him has yet been identified. Again, we know from Wulfstan (c. 31) that Æthelwold was concerned to instruct his students in the rules of metrics (*regulas . . . metricae rationis tradere*), and it is worth remarking in this connection that Wulfstan himself was perhaps the most skilled metrician produced in Anglo-Saxon England. This skill is evident in his handling of the hexameter—in his variety of rhythms, manipulation of elisions, use of monosyllabic and pentasyllabic words to vary the pace of the final two feet, avoidance of end-stopped lines, and so on—as well as in his unusual proficiency in a number of demanding metrical forms, such as epanaleptic couplets, abecedarian hymns, and sapphic stanzas, none of which have any parallel in other tenth-century Anglo-Latin verse.[164] That Wulfstan's proficiency (if not his virtuosity) was learnt from Æthelwold seems to be confirmed by the verse of another of Æthelwold's students, the Godemann who wrote the 'Benedictional of St Æthelwold' and composed the poem of thirty-eight hexameters which serves as its preface. This

[162] e.g. fo. 98v: 'De genetiuo singulari, secundae declinationis: "Peruia diuisi patuerunt cerula ponti" [= *CP* i. 136]; de datiuo singulari qui in *-o* desinit, ut "Cantemus socii Domino cantemus honorem" [= *Hymn.* i. 1]; de ablatiuo eiusdem declinationis: "Plenus et ille Deo postquam miracula terris" [= *CP* i. 176]; de accusatiuo eiusdem declinationis: "Nectaris aeria populum dulcedine pastum" [= *CP* i. 150]; de uocatiuo eiusdem ab *-us* in *-e* correptam, "Omnipotens aeterne Deus spes unica mundi" [= *CP* i. 60].'

[163] See Dolbeau, 'Le *Breuiloquium*', p. 52.

[164] See Dolbeau, op. cit., pp. 52–8, and further discussion in Lapidge, *The Cult of St Swithun*.

poem, too, shows technical mastery of the hexameter (variety in rhythm, use of elision, use of monosyllables in the sixth foot, avoidance of end-stopped lines).[165] Quite possibly it was Æthelwold who taught this metrical proficiency to his two students.

Wulfstan's statement concerning the extent of Æthelwold's reading in patristic literature could only be reliably documented if Æthelwold had left a sizeable corpus of Latin writing; but such is not the case. There is only one substantial Latin work which can confidently be attributed to Æthelwold, namely the *Regularis concordia*, and this work, by its very utilitarian nature, is scarcely a vehicle for ostentatious display of the fruits of reading in patristic literature. The main body of the *Regularis concordia* reveals Æthelwold's thorough familiarity with the *Regula S. Benedicti*, the 'Memoriale qualiter', the papal *ordo* known as *Ordo Romanus Primus*, and possibly other customaries brought to his notice by his advisers.[166] However, the *Regularis concordia* is prefaced by a brief *prohemium*, and here Æthelwold took the opportunity of writing more flamboyantly than was appropriate elsewhere in the work. From the *prohemium* we can see that Æthelwold's prose style was much indebted to his study of Aldhelm's prose *De uirginitate*, especially in its use of arcane vocabulary and alliteration. Æthelwold frequently reproduces Aldhelm's turn of phrase.[167] At various points Æthelwold's prose also embodies reminiscences of Latin hexametrical verse, in particular that of Juvencus, Venantius Fortunatus, and Aldhelm; but this is as we should expect of a scholar who had learned the *mellifluam metricae rationis dulcedinem*.[168] To these few Latin works may be added Bede's *Historia ecclesiastica*, which is alluded to in the *Regularis concordia*

[165] Cf. Lapidge, in *Bishop Æthelwold*, pp. 106–7.

[166] See Symons, *Reg. conc.*, pp. xlv–l. For the *Regula S. Benedicti* and 'Memoriale qualiter', see above, pp. liv and lvi respectively; for the *Ordo Romanus primus*, see E. G. C. F. Atchley, *Ordo Romanus Primus* (London, 1905), and M. Andrieu, *Les Ordines Romani du haut moyen âge*, 5 vols. (Louvain, 1931–61), ii. 1–108. For other customaries possibly known to Æthelwold, see Symons, *Tenth-Century Studies*, pp. 37–59, and above, p. lviii.

[167] Cf. Lapidge in *Bishop Æthelwold*, p. 99 n. 71, where it is noted that the following phrases are from Aldhelm's prose *De uirginitate* (ed. R. Ehwald, *MGH*, Auct. antiq. xv (Berlin, 1919)): *Christi opitulante gratia* (*Reg. conc.*, p. 1; Ehwald, p. 282); *erectis ad aethera palmis inmensas* . . . *grates* (*Reg. conc.*, p. 3; Ehwald, p. 229); *praesago afflatus spiritu* (*Reg. conc.*, p. 4; Ehwald, p. 268); and *tyrannidem potentatus* (*Reg. conc.*, p. 4; Ehwald, p. 251).

[168] The phrase *iusto moderamine* (*Reg. conc.*, p. 11) is from either Juvencus, *Euang.* ii. 575 or Aldhelm, *CdV* 831, and *sors inreuocabilis orae* (*Reg. conc.*, p. 66) is from Venantius Fortunatus, *Carm.* ix. 2. 1.

and laid heavily under contribution in the Old English account of King Edgar's establishment of monasteries which, as we have seen, was probably intended by Æthelwold to serve as the preface to his translation of the *Regula S. Benedicti*.[169] But in sum these few titles do not fully bear out Wulfstan's assertion that Æthelwold carefully studied (*studiose legebat*) the best-known patristic authors.

A slightly fuller picture of Æthelwold's Latin scholarship emerges from consideration of various anonymous writings which can reliably be attributed to him. Reasons for attribution have been set out more fully elsewhere;[170] it is sufficient here simply to list and describe the writings in question. It is probable in the first instance that Æthelwold may have been personally responsible for drafting a number of Anglo-Saxon charters, including one of King Edgar's charters dated 960 and bearing the subscription *ego Aþelwold abbas depinxi*,[171] where *depinxi* may refer to the act of drafting or copying,[172] and a later charter of 966 bearing the subscription *ego Æþelwold episcopus karessi*,[173] where the unique verb of attestation, *karessi* (a Graecism from χαράσσω), seems to be in keeping with Æthelwold's inclination to flamboyant, hermeneutic vocabulary.[174] More interesting is the question of whether Æthelwold may have been responsible for drafting the so-called 'New Minster Foundation Charter'.[175] This lavishly written and illuminated charter survives as a small book of thirty-two leaves in London, BL Cotton Vespasian A. VIII.[176] The text is preceded by an illumination showing King Edgar, flanked by the Virgin and St Peter, offering the charter to Christ; the illumination is accompanied by the following elegiac couplet which was presumably composed by the author of the charter (and hence is arguably the sole surviving specimen of Æthelwold's Latin verse):

Sic celso residet solio qui condidit astra;
  Rex uenerans Eadgar pronus adorat eum. (3r.)

[169] *Reg. conc.*, p. 3 (Bede, *HE* i. 27); 'King Edgar's Establishment of Monasteries', *Councils & Synods*, i. 143 (Bede, *HE* i. 23–6, 33, ii. 1).

[170] Lapidge, in *Bishop Æthelwold*, pp. 93–101.

[171] S 687 (= BCS 1055, KCD 481), an original single-sheet charter (now London, BL Cotton Aug. ii. 40) whose genuineness is not suspect in any way.

[172] Cf. Lapidge, in *Bishop Æthelwold*, pp. 92–3 and n. 28.

[173] S 739 (= BCS 1175) and *Burton*, p. 34 (no. 21).

[174] Lapidge, 'The hermeneutic style', pp. 85–90.

[175] S 745 (= BCS 1190); *Councils & Synods*, i. 119–33 (no. 31).

[176] F. Wormald, *Collected Writings I*, pp. 108–10 and pls. 96–8.

The charter, which is dated 966, bears a peculiar attestation by Æthelwold himself ('ego Aðelwold, ecclesie Wintoniensis episcopus, regis gloriosissimi beneuolentiam abbatem mea altum mediocritate et alumnos quos educaui illi commendans crucis signaculo benedixi'). This and other features suggest that the charter, as well as the prefatory elegiac couplet, may have been composed by Æthelwold. The most striking of these features is the language of the charter, which is unusually ornate (even by the standards of tenth-century English diplomatic) and includes a number of Graecisms, some of them exceptionally rare, such as *macrobius* (μακρόβιος, 'long-lived') or *policrates* (πολυκρατής, 'very mighty'). The use of this vocabulary links this charter with another text which must be considered in this connection, namely a letter (preserved in the late tenth-century Anglo-Latin letter-collection in Cotton Tiberius A. xv) addressed by an unnamed English bishop to a foreign duke or count concerning the theft of a gospel-book.[177] There are various reasons, historical and stylistic, for thinking that the unnamed bishop is Æthelwold.[178] The historical reasons include the fact that the bishop describes himself as primate of a see whose patron saint is a confessor; at the date of the letter (and letter-collection) the only English see which could be so described was Winchester with its patron saint the confessor Swithun. The stylistic reasons are that the author of the letter uses occasional alliteration and phrasing indebted to Aldhelm, features which we have already seen in the *Regularis concordia*; and in fact there is one clear verbal link between the letter and the *Regularis concordia*.[179] Similarly, there is a verbal link between the letter and the 'New Minster Foundation Charter', in that the author of the letter employs the extremely rare Graecism *policrates* in precisely the way it had been used in the charter. All these links combine to suggest that Æthelwold, author of the *Regularis concordia*, was also the author of the 'New Minster Foundation Charter' and the anonymous letter to a Continental duke. These works, together with perhaps one or two Anglo-Saxon charters, make up the exiguous corpus of Æthelwold's Latin writing.

From this corpus we can learn something of Æthelwold's Latin training, even if—regrettably—we remain poorly informed on the

[177] *Memorials*, pp. 361–2.
[178] See Lapidge, in *Bishop Æthelwold*, pp. 96–8.
[179] Cf. *Memorials*, p. 62, and *Reg. conc.*, p. 1 (the phrase *coenobia . . . diruta*).

question of what books he had studied. It is clear that Æthelwold had a pronounced taste for flamboyant language: alliteration, rhyming prose (such as is found throughout the 'New Minster Foundation Charter'), exotic vocabulary, especially Graecisms. Most of these features could have been learnt directly from the study of Aldhelm's prose. Can we surmise that Aldhelm was one of the *nominatos . . . auctores* studied by Æthelwold at Glastonbury? And was it Æthelwold who was responsible in turn for placing Aldhelm's Latin prose at the centre of the late Anglo-Saxon curriculum?[180] Such questions cannot yet be answered.

Æthelwold may have expressed himself ostentatiously in Latin, but there can be no doubt about the soundness of his training in Latin grammar. This much is clear from his English translation of the *Regula S. Benedicti*. The studies of Mechthild Gretsch have demonstrated the nature and quality of Æthelwold's technique of translation.[181] As she has shown, Æthelwold stayed very close throughout to the Latin text of the *Regula*, only making occasional departures in order to stress the importance of the *opus Dei* or to clarify an ambiguity in the original or to incorporate a comment from the *Expositio in Regulam S. Benedicti* of Smaragdus of Saint-Mihiel.[182] The most striking feature of the translation is its impeccable accuracy: in a text of some 100 printed pages' length, there are apparently only two places where Æthelwold has misunderstood the Latin.[183] This is a creditable performance in an age which lacked the full apparatus of dictionaries, concordances, grammars, and commentaries of which a modern translator may avail himself.

The evidence of the translation of the *Regula S. Benedicti*, then, confirms the view that Æthelwold was a proficient Latinist, but it does not advance the question of what books he may have studied. A final piece of evidence may be mentioned in this connection, namely a list of some twenty-one books which were sent as a gift by Æthelwold to Peterborough on the occasion (probably) of the

[180] Cf. Lapidge, 'The hermeneutic style', pp. 74–5.

[181] Gretsch, 'Æthelwold's translation', pp. 143–8; *Die Regula Sancti Benedicti in England*, pp. 236–306.

[182] 'Æthelwold's translation', pp. 143–4; *Die Regula Sancti Benedicti in England*, pp. 241–62. Recall that Smaragdus' *Expositio in Regulam S. Benedicti* is preserved in a manuscript (Cambridge, UL Ee. 2. 4) which may have been written at Glastonbury during the period when Æthelwold was there.

[183] 'Æthelwold's translation', p. 147; *Die Regula Sancti Benedicti in England*, pp. 279–83.

refoundation of that house in *c.*970.[184] The list is a mildly eccentric one. Among the patristic authors it includes Cyprian's *Epistulae*, Augustine's *Contra Academicos*, and Julian of Toledo's *Prognosticum*, but omits the standard biblical commentaries of Jerome and the best-known theological writings by Ambrose, Augustine, and Gregory. It includes several poetic texts: the *Carmina* of Paulinus of Nola; an anonymous *Passio S. Eustachii*;[185] and Abbo of Saint-Germain's *Bella Parisiacae urbis*. Several of the works listed might be described as lexicological: Jerome's treatise on Hebrew names, Isidore's *Synonyma* and *De differentiis uerborum*, and an unidentifiable work *De litteris Grecorum*, probably a Greek–Latin glossary. The last item reminds us of Æthelwold's taste for Graecisms, and this taste would also have been fostered by study of Abbo's *Bella Parisiacae urbis*.[186] The rather eccentric nature of the list, and its bias towards poetry and lexicology (especially the Greek lexicon) allows the suspicion that it might represent a collection of books assembled personally by Æthelwold, and hence might serve as an index to the nature of his reading; but this is no more than a suspicion.

The sum of this evidence endorses in broad outline the picture drawn by Wulfstan of Æthelwold's scholarly achievement, even though it is not possible, in the present state of our knowledge, to confirm the picture in every detail. Yet the fact that Æthelwold could number among his students two of the most prolific and learned authors of the late tenth century—Ælfric and Wulfstan—confirms our impression that he was a reputable scholar in his own right, and it is to the achievements of his students, therefore, that we must now turn.

9. *Æthelwold and his Students*

At one point of the *Vita S. Æthelwoldi* Wulfstan gives us a memorable portrait of Æthelwold in his role of teacher: 'It was always agreeable to him to teach young men and mature students, translating Latin texts into English for them, passing on the rules of

184 'Surviving booklists from Anglo-Saxon England', *Learning and Literature*, pp. 33–89, at 52–5.

185 See M. Lapidge, 'Æthelwold and the *Vita S. Eustachii*', *Scire litteras: zum Geistesleben des Mittelalters*, ed. S. Krämer and M. Bernhard (Munich, 1988), pp. 255–65.

186 See P. Lendinara, 'The third book of the *Bella Parisiacae Urbis* by Abbo of Saint-Germain-des-Prés and its Old English gloss', *ASE* xv (1986), 73–89.

grammar and metric, and encouraging them to do better by cheerful words' (c. 31). The general tenor of this statement is borne out by remarks made by Æthelwold's student Godemann in the poem which is prefixed to the 'Benedictional of St Æthelwold'.[187] There Æthelwold's pupils are described as the 'children' (*pueri*) for whose well-being 'father' Æthelwold is responsible, and Godemann places in Æthelwold's mouth the fervent wish that he not lose one 'little lamb' (*agniculum*) from the flock entrusted to him. Æthelwold's relationship to his students was clearly a paternal one.

Various evidence helps to illustrate Wulfstan's statement that Æthelwold translated Latin texts into English for his students. We have seen that he translated the *Regula S. Benedicti* into English, probably for the benefit of a lay audience; but it might also have served as a useful tool to enable young monks to master the *Regula* before they were professed (after which time they would regularly hear the Latin text of the *Regula* read aloud to them at daily chapter). In any case Æthelwold's translation of the *Regula* provides an interesting link with a variety of other texts in Old English which, in their turn, cast light on Æthelwold's educational practices at Winchester. One striking feature of his technique of translation is seen in his consistent preference, when various alternative choices were available, of one Old English word to render a single Latin word. Thus, for example, in rendering Latin *praesumere* Æthelwold invariably chose the word *gedyrstlæcan* ('to presume', 'dare') rather than its close synonym *geþristlæcan*.[188] A consistent set of lexical preferences such as this is a feature which distinguishes not only Æthelwold's own translation, but also a number of Old English texts which, for various reasons, can be associated with Winchester, and makes probable the supposition that the lexical preferences which they display are the direct outcome of Æthelwold's teaching. It has become conventional to speak in this context of the 'Winchester School' of Late Old English.[189] The Old English writings which belong to this school

[187] Lapidge, 'The hermeneutic style', pp. 105–6.

[188] See Gretsch, *Die Regula Sancti Benedicti in England*, pp. 332–3, 371–2, and W. Hofstetter, *Winchester und der spätaltenglische Sprachgebrauch* (Munich, 1987), pp. 30–1.

[189] See H. Gneuss, 'The origin of Standard Old English and Æthelwold's school at Winchester', *ASE* i (1972), 63–83; Hofstetter, *Winchester*, *passim*; and id., 'Winchester and the standardization of Old English vocabulary', *ASE* xvii (1988), 139–61.

are the following:[190] the writings of Ælfric; interlinear glosses in several psalters; interlinear glosses to copies of what are called the 'monastic' canticles, usually also included in psalters; interlinear glosses to copies of the monastic hymnal and to the *Expositio hymnorum* (a teaching text in which the hymns of the monastic office are set out in plain prose); the fragmentary Old English translation of the *Regularis concordia*; and the Old English translation of Chrodegang's *Regula canonicorum*. It is not possible, of course, to say that each of these works was produced under Æthelwold's personal supervision, or even to be entirely certain that each of them was written by someone who had been trained by him. Nevertheless they share enough lexical similarities fairly to warrant the term 'school', and it is noteworthy that the range of texts in question reflects the interests of Æthelwold as we have seen them in other contexts: the psalter, monastic canticles, and hymnal pertain to performance of the Divine Office, and the *Regularis concordia* and Chrodegang's *Regula canonicorum* are pertinent to the regulation of monastic life. These are the interests which lay closest to Æthelwold's heart.

On the evidence of texts of the 'Winchester School' we may surmise that Æthelwold encouraged and supervised the translation of Latin texts pertinent to monastic life; but there was other scholarly activity at late tenth-century Winchester as well. Under Æthelwold's patronage a number of important Latin writings were produced. Foremost among these was the *Translatio et miracula S. Swithuni* by one Lantfred,[191] a foreign scholar, probably from Fleury,[192] who was a member of Æthelwold's *familia* at the Old Minster.[193] The *Translatio* is an extensive account, in the hagiographical form which became current during the tenth century,[194] of the events leading up to, and the miracles which followed,

[190] Thirteen such texts are listed by Hofstetter, *Winchester*, pp. 29–116; see also 'Winchester and the standardization', pp. 152–4.

[191] Ed. Lapidge, *The Cult of St Swithun* (forthcoming).

[192] The evidence that Lantfred was from Fleury is set out by Lapidge (ibid.). It is, briefly, that there is a surviving letter addressed to Dunstan by a monk of Fleury who gives his name in abbreviated form as .L. (*Memorials*, pp. 376–7), and who claims to have spent time in England and seeks to have returned to him certain books now in the possession of Æthelwold's disciple Osgar (on the books, see J. Carley, 'Two pre-Conquest manuscripts from Glastonbury Abbey', *ASE* xvi (1987), 197–212, esp. 209–10); and that the rhyming prose and various individual phrases in the letter by .L. are found in Lantfred's *Translatio*.

[193] *LVH*, p. 25; Gerchow, *Gedenküberlieferung*, p. 323.

[194] See below, pp. civ–cvi.

Æthelwold's translation of the remains of St Swithun in 971; on internal grounds, the work is to be dated to *c.*975. It is dedicated to the *familia* of monks at the Old Minster, and although the dedication does not mention Æthelwold by name, there is not much doubt that Æthelwold and Lantfred were closely associated and that Æthelwold was its real patron. The *Translatio* is a substantial work, consisting of forty chapters, some of them lengthy, and written in accomplished Latin prose whose principal characteristics are rhyming clauses and a high proportion of Greek vocabulary. Lantfred shows himself to have been familiar with a wide range of authors, some of them (such as Martianus Capella) not otherwise known in England at this time. The *Translatio* was one of the most imposing Anglo-Latin works of the late tenth century: through it, the cult of St Swithun was publicized widely throughout England. Wulfstan clearly worked under the shadow of this work. His own *Narratio metrica de S. Swithuno* is a hexametrical contrafactum of Lantfred's text, and, as we shall see, his account of the translation of St Æthelwold in 996 is heavily indebted to Lantfred's account of the translation of St Swithun.

Another Winchester scholar of this time who is known to us by name is the Godemann who was the scribe of the 'Benedictional of St Æthelwold' and who composed the thirty-eight-line Latin poem which prefaces it.[195] The poem shows Godemann to have been a proficient poet, as we have seen, and one who affected the use of Greek vocabulary. It is likely that both these features were the result of Æthelwold's teaching.

Also to be associated with Æthelwold's Winchester are three poems preserved anonymously in Cambridge, UL Kk. 5. 34, a manuscript written at Winchester in the late tenth century.[196] The poems are: a debate, in hexameters, between a master named Ioruert and an insolent student on the nature and content of the school curriculum (*Altercatio magistri et discipuli*); a reply by the student in continuous adonics (*Responsio discipuli*); and a poem in elegiacs on the nature of free will and providence based largely on Boethius (*Carmen de libero arbitrio*). The fact that the unique manuscript in which they are preserved was written at Winchester, and that Wulfstan of Winchester recycles various lines from these

[195] Lapidge, 'The hermeneutic style', pp. 85–6, 105–6.

[196] M. Lapidge, 'Three Latin poems from Æthelwold's school at Winchester', *ASE* i (1972), 85–137.

poems in his own verse,[197] suggests strongly that the poems were composed at Winchester. The *Carmen de libero arbitrio* includes in its closing lines a prayer for an unnamed bishop who chastised evil practices like a father and who welcomed foreigners to his *familia*:[198]

> Gentes Anglorum felices praesule tanto
> ritus qui prauos corrigit ut genitor,
> extorresque superuenientes uosque beati:
> cunctis his tribuit quicquid opus fuerit.
> Quis numerare queat bona nobis quae bonus ille
> contulit hanc postquam uenimus ad patriam?
> Idcirco Dominum rogitemus corde fideli
> praebeat ut famulo gaudia pro merito. (179–86.)

The statement that his bishop corrected evil practices like a father reminds us forcibly of Wulfstan's description of Æthelwold in the *Vita S. Æthelwoldi*: 'circumiuitque famulus Christi Ætheluuoldus singula monasteria, mores instituens ... et stultos ut a malo discederent uerberibus corrigendo' (c. 27). We have seen that Æthelwold was affectionately described as a 'father' by his monks, and that he welcomed foreign clerics, such as Womar and Lantfred, into his *familia* at the Old Minster. Other verbal links, especially with Lantfred's *Translatio*, suggest that the unnamed bishop is indeed Æthelwold, and these three poems all stem from the period of his bishopric at Winchester. That their author might have been Lantfred himself is suggested by the manuscript rubric to the first of the poems: 'Versus .L. de quodam superbo'. That .L. here may refer to Lantfred receives some support from the fact that a letter addressed to Dunstan and apparently written by Lantfred after his return to Fleury, bears the signature '.L. uestrorum infimus dulorum', suggesting that, in Winchester circles at least, it was sufficient to refer to Lantfred as .L.. The poems share various unusual phrases—such as *caelica Tempe* for 'heavenly vales'—with

[197] See *ASE* i (1972), 89 (the phrase *foedum iam claude labellum*: *Narratio* i. 1105 = *Altercatio* 68); to this can be added the phrase *reserat qui limen Olimphi* (*Narratio*, Ep. spec. 4 = *De libero arbitrio* 163).

[198] Ibid., p. 136: 'Happy the English with such a bishop, who corrects the depraved practices of the church like a father; and you foreigners lately arriving are blessed as well: to all these he has granted whatsoever was necessary. Who could count all the bounties which that good man has conferred on us since we came to this land? For that reason let us beseech the Lord with faithful heart that he grant happiness to his servant as he well deserves.'

Lantfred's *Translatio*, and like that work they draw on various authors, especially Martianus Capella, which were evidently first studied in England at this time. Lantfred could have been the author of these three Winchester poems, therefore. In any case the poems clarify an implication drawn earlier, namely that the school of oblates or *pueri* was conducted by a lay master, in this case the Welshman Ioruert, whereas Æthelwold concerned himself with the monks at a later stage of their education.

Whether or not it was Lantfred who composed these poems, they show that scholarly activity at Æthelwold's Winchester was a vital, corporate enterprise, and not merely the domain of one or two isolated individuals. It is possible that, as our knowledge of late tenth-century England advances, other anonymous writings may be attributed to this school. Mention has already been made of the grammatical *Dialogus de .viii. partibus orationis*. It is also worth mentioning an unprinted computus which is preserved in several Winchester manuscripts and which evidently dates from this period. The manuscripts in question are: Cambridge, Trinity College R. 15. 32 (945) (New Minster, s. xi^{in}); London, BL Arundel 60 (New Minster, s. xi^{2}), Cotton Tiberius C. VI (Old Minster, s. xi^{med}), Titus D. XXVI (New Minster, s. xi^{1}) and Vitellius E. XVIII (New Minster, s. xi^{med}). The calendars contained in these manuscripts are very closely related,[199] and the computistical materials accompanying the calendars are similarly related. These include (variously, as is always the case with computistical manuscripts: no two ever have precisely the same contents) the brief tract entitled *Ratio calculandi de duodecim mensibus*, a sequence of tables (for computing ferial regulars and concurrents, lunar and zodiacal tables, and a table of termini for the moveable feasts), various brief tracts on epacts and concurrents, and finally an Easter table for the years 978–1097. The whole collection is extremely concise, pared down to the bare essentials of computistical science. As Peter Baker has demonstrated, the work was apparently 'assembled by a single, intelligent worker at Winchester around the year 978.'[200] Whether this computus was compiled under Æthelwold's supervision or with his knowledge is impossible to say: nothing in our sources implies that Æthelwold was a skilled computist.

[199] F. Wormald, *English Kalendars before* A.D. *1100*, HBS lxxii (1934), nos. 9–12.

[200] In the introduction to the forthcoming edition, with M. Lapidge, of Byrhtferth's *Enchiridion*, EETS (London).

Nevertheless, this 'Winchester Computus', as it has been called, is a further piece of evidence for the vitality of scholarship at Winchester during his episcopacy.

However, the most distinguished *alumni* of Æthelwold's school at Winchester were Ælfric and Wulfstan, who were the most voluminous authors in Old English and Latin respectively in the late Anglo-Saxon period. Ælfric describes himself in general as *Wintoniensis alumnus*[201] and specifically as Æthelwold's pupil. We know from Wulfstan's *Vita S. Æthelwoldi* (c. 37) that Æthelwold took delight in handing on the 'rules of grammar' to the young men of his *familia*, and Ælfric in his own Grammar claims to be passing on an account of Latin grammar *sicut didicimus in schola Aðelwoldi*.[202] There is one obvious respect in which the pupil embodied the teaching of the master: the concern for clarity and accuracy which we have seen to be characteristic of Æthelwold's translation of the *Regula S. Benedicti* is also the salient characteristic of Ælfric's English prose (though it should also be mentioned that in his few Latin writings Ælfric vigorously rejected the ostentatious, hermeneutic diction which Æthelwold apparently fostered).[203] The lexical preferences which are found in Æthelwold's English prose and which characterize the 'Winchester School', are found preeminently in Ælfric's prose.[204] This is not the place to survey the corpus of Ælfric's English writings; suffice it to say that these embrace computus, grammar, biblical exegesis, liturgy, ecclesiastical law, and regulation of the monastic life.[205] In sum they reveal a respectably wide range of reading in patristic, Insular, and Carolingian sources, and there is a presumption that some of these sources may have been studied under Æthelwold's supervision. In this respect it is interesting to note that among the twenty-one books which Æthelwold donated to Peterborough there are four works—Bede's commentary on Mark, Julian of Toledo's *Prognosticum*, the Hiberno-Latin treatise *De duodecim abusiuis saeculi* and (probably) Ratramnus of Corbie's *De corpore et sanguine Domini*—

[201] *Vita S. Æthelwoldi*, c. 1 (below, p. 71).

[202] *Grammar*, ed. Zupitza, p. 1.

[203] On the clarity of Ælfric's English prose, see for example P. Clemoes, 'Ælfric', *Continuations and Beginnings*, ed. E. G. Stanley (London, 1966), pp. 176–209, esp. 196–201.

[204] Hofstetter, *Winchester*, pp. 38–66.

[205] For the canon of his writing, see P. Clemoes, 'The chronology of Ælfric's works', *The Anglo-Saxons: Studies in some Aspects of their History and Culture presented to Bruce Dickins*, ed. P. Clemoes (London, 1959), pp. 212–47.

which were certainly known to Ælfric.[206] It is tempting to think, but impossible to prove, that Ælfric had studied these four works under Æthelwold's personal supervision; in any event they give some idea of the sort of theological works which were studied and discussed in Æthelwold's school.

It may also be the case that the very considerable learning of Wulfstan (discussed below, pp. cv–cxi) is to some extent a reflection of his study under Æthelwold's supervision. Just as Æthelwold's concern to pass on the rules of grammar is reflected in Ælfric's Grammar, so his concern to pass on the rules of metric may be reflected in the substantial corpus of Wulfstan's surviving poetry. As has been mentioned, Wulfstan was an extremely competent metrician, expert in a variety of difficult and exacting metres. He was thoroughly familiar with the Christian Latin poets who constituted the core of the early medieval curriculum: Juvencus, Caelius Sedulius, Arator, Venantius Fortunatus, and Aldhelm. Of these, we have seen that Æthelwold himself was certainly familiar with the poetry of Venantius Fortunatus, and Aldhelm, and possibly Juvencus as well; and recall that the *Dialogus de .viii. partibus orationis*, arguably a product of Æthelwold's Winchester, contained extensive quotations from Caelius Sedulius. Once again, it is tempting to think that Wulfstan studied these poets under Æthelwold's personal supervision. In any case Wulfstan clearly felt a deep personal debt to Æthelwold's teaching, and to some extent this debt is reflected in his *Vita S. Æthelwoldi*.

10. *Æthelwold and Wulfstan*

It is abundantly clear from Wulfstan's *Vita S. Æthelwoldi* that it was primarily Wulfstan himself who was instrumental in effecting the translation of Æthelwold's remains on 10 September 996. According to c. 42, the train of events leading up to the translation were initiated by the appearance of St Æthelwold in a dream to a blind man named Ælfhelm. In the dream Ælfhelm is instructed to go to Winchester and to make himself known to Wulfstan:

Cum festinus Wintoniam perueneris et Veteris Coenobii ecclesiam intraueris, accersiri fac ad te monachum quendam Wulfstanum, cognomento Cantorem. Hic cum ex ore tuo uerba meae legationis audierit, te

[206] Lapidge, in *Bishop Æthelwold*, p. 110.

mox indubitanter ad meum perducet tumulum, ibique recipies lumen oculorum tuorum.

It is significant that Wulfstan was singled out as the monk best placed to set the translation proceedings in motion: as the precentor at the Old Minster, he will have been well informed about the procedures involved in the canonization of a saint. In the train of Æthelwold's appearance, Ælfhelm does go to the Old Minster and conveys his message to Wulfstan, who, being torn between hope and fear (*admirans inter spem et timorem*), took the blind man to Æthelwold's tomb, where he was cured. Æthelwold subsequently appeared in dreams to other people, including Wulfstan himself (c. 43), and the translation was undertaken in due course. Once the translation had been completed—at Wulfstan's instigation—the promotion of the cult of St Æthelwold would thereafter have depended on the publication of Æthelwold's sanctity and intercessory powers through a suitable *uita* and the provision of the necessary hymns and prayers for the liturgical commemoration of the saint on his feast-day. As we shall see (below, pp. cxiii–cxviii), it was very probably Wulfstan, in his role as precentor, who supplied the necessary liturgical materials for celebrating the cult of St Æthelwold at the Old Minster. In a word, the translation of Æthelwold and the promotion of his cult seems to have been the personal achievement of Wulfstan.

Wulfstan would have undertaken this task as an act of *pietas* to his former abbot and master, no doubt. But there are certain passages in the *Vita S. Æthelwoldi* which feed the suspicion that Wulfstan, in promoting the translation and cult of St Æthelwold, was fulfilling a promise made to his abbot during his lifetime. Consider, for instance, the passage (c. 4) where Wulfstan records a miracle which happened to Æthelwold's mother when she was pregnant with the future saint:

Quadam namque die cum mater eius stipata ciuibus staret in ecclesia, sacrae missae celebrationi interesse desiderans, sensit animam pueri quem gerebat in utero uenisse et in eum Dei nutu cuncta moderantis intrasse, sicut postea ipse sanctus qui nasciturus erat, iam episcopus, nobis gaudendo referebat.

To the question, 'how did Wulfstan know of this miracle?' the answer is that Æthelwold told him (*nobis* here presumably refers to the authorial 'we' rather than to an audience of well-wishers: the subject is a matter of some intimacy, not of public boasting). But in what circumstances would Æthelwold have wished to convey such information to Wulfstan? It would seem that Æthelwold was consciously supplying Wulfstan with materials that could be used in an eventual *uita*; and this would imply in turn that Æthelwold had foreseen the possibility of his own canonization and entrusted Wulfstan with the task of carrying it out. There are other passages in the *Vita S. Æthelwoldi* which are capable of a similar interpretation. Thus in c. 41 Wulfstan records that Æthelwold had once told him of a vision in which the exact place of Æthelwold's burial had been revealed to him: '. . . sepultus est in cripta ad australem plagam sancti altaris, ubi eum requiescere debere, sicut ipse nobis retulit, olim sibi caelitus ostensum est.' Such visions are a common hagiographical topos, and it might seem that Æthelwold, in relating it to Wulfstan, was supplying his future hagiographer with the materials for his *uita*. The suspicion is intriguing, but cannot be more than that. Whatever the case, Wulfstan undertook his duties as Æthelwold's hagiographer proficiently, and showed himself thoroughly familiar with the conventions of hagiography. We may now turn to that hagiography.

III. WULFSTAN AS HAGIOGRAPHER

During the early Middle Ages the saint's *uita* was one of the most widely practised forms of Latin literature.[1] It has been estimated that some 600 *uitae* survive from the period up to the ninth century,[2] and the tenth century, too, was prolific in this regard.[3] The purpose of any *uita* was to manifest the individual *uirtus*, or miraculous power, of the saint in question: to show that, through

[1] See H. Delehaye, *Cinq Leçons sur la méthode hagiographique* (Brussels, 1934), pp. 7–41; R. Aigrain, *L'Hagiographie, ses sources, ses méthodes, son histoire* (Paris, 1953), esp. 156–70; and R. Grégoire, *Manuale di agiologia: Introduzione alla letteratura agiografica* (Fabriano, 1987), esp. 144–75. There is nothing in English of comparable utility; see, however, the annotated bibliography in *Saints and their Cults*, ed. S. Wilson (Cambridge, 1983), pp. 309–417.

[2] The estimate is that of C. W. Jones, *Saints' Lives and Chronicles in Early England* (Ithaca, NY, 1947), p. 211. Jones's estimate is based on *BHL*, in which all medieval saints' *uitae* are listed.

[3] See L. Zoepf, *Das Heiligen-Leben im 10. Jahrhundert* (Leipzig–Berlin, 1908).

his miracles on earth the saint was a vessel of divine *uirtus* who could be appealed to, successfully, to intercede with God on a suppliant's behalf. The suppliant needed to be assured that the saint to whom he was appealing was a member in good standing of the community of saints dwelling with God, and hence was in an advantageous position to intercede. It was the hagiographer's responsibility to portray his subject as an undoubted member of that community who possessed the same *uirtus* as other saints. Accordingly all saints' *uitae* have a similar form: the saints perform similar miracles; they are born, live, and die in the same way. The similarity of saintly lives is not therefore a testimony to the impoverished imagination of medieval hagiographers; on the contrary, the similarity was born of necessity, for no suppliant would wish to think that the saint to whom he was appealing was an eccentric who had nothing in common with other saints. The more the saint was seen to have in common with other saints, the more likely the suppliant would be assured of the success of his petition. That is why saints' *uitae* share the same form and conventions.

The form and conventions of medieval hagiography were established through the widespread popularity of a few early saints' *uitae*: that of St Anthony by Athanasius, composed in Greek but translated into Latin by one Evagrius;[4] Jerome's three *uitae* of Malchus, Hilarion, and Paul of Thebes;[5] and, above all, Sulpicius Severus' *uita* of St Martin.[6] It was works such as these which established the pattern for the *uita* of that class of saint known as a confessor, that is, a distinctively saintly man but one who—unlike a martyr—did not die for his faith (a different form and conventions existed for the *passio* of a martyr). The pattern for a confessor's *uita* is normally as follows: the saint is born of noble stock, his birth being portended or accompanied by miraculous occurrences; during his early youth the saint displays outstanding aptitude for

[4] *BHL*, no. 609; ptd. *PL* lxxiii. 125–70.

[5] *BHL*, no. 5190, 3879, 6596 respectively; ptd. *PL* xxiii. 55–60, 29–54, 17–28 respectively. On Jerome as hagiographer, see E. Hendrikx, 'Saint Jérôme en tant qu'hagiographe', *Ciudad de Dios*, clxxxi (1968), 661–7.

[6] *BHL*, no. 5610; ed. C. Halm, *CSEL* i (1866), pp. 109–37, and J. Fontaine (3 vols., Sources chrétiennes, cxxxiii–cxxxv; Paris, 1967); see also A. Loyen, 'Les miracles de saint Martin et les débuts de l'hagiographie en Occident', *Bulletin de littérature ecclésiastique*, lxxiii (1972), 147–57; and C. Stancliffe, *St Martin and his Hagiographer: History and Miracle in Sulpicius Severus* (Oxford, 1983).

Christian learning (rapid mastery of the psalter is the normal manifestation of this aptitude) and reveals that he is destined for the religious life; he turns from the secular world to the Church, is tonsured in minor orders and then proceeds upwards through the various ecclesiastical grades—deacon, priest, bishop; during the course of his ecclesiastical career he reveals that he is a vessel of divine *uirtus* by performing various miracles, which are usually recorded at some length; eventually the saint foresees the end of his earthly life approaching, gathers his disciples around him and exhorts them to good works, and dies peacefully; after his death miracles occur at his tomb, indicating that the saint has found favour with God and his saints. Of course variations are possible within this broad framework: the *uita* of a reclusive monk who retreated to the desert in order to pursue a contemplative life would inevitably have a somewhat different focus from that of an active bishop; but the overall pattern, established by the Late Latin *uitae* mentioned above, was invariable. Accordingly, when in the late seventh and early eighth centuries English authors began to compose *uitae* of native English saints, they adhered closely to the hagiographical pattern established by their late-antique models, sometimes going so far as to incorporate verbatim lengthy passages from those models in their own *uitae*. And the early Anglo-Latin *uitae*[7]—Stephen of Ripon's *uita* of St Wilfrid, Felix's *uita* of St Guthlac, the anonymous *uitae* of Cuthbert and Ceolfrith, Bede's own *uita* of St Cuthbert—served in their turn as models for later hagiographers.[8]

By the late tenth century the prospective hagiographer will have had before him a wealth of literary models. By then every principal saint culted by the western Church was the subject of one or more *uitae*. From the late eighth century onwards these *uitae* had begun to be gathered together into increasingly larger

[7] B. P. Kurtz, *From St Antony to St Guthlac: A Study in Biography* (Berkeley, Calif., 1926); B. Colgrave, 'The earliest saints' lives written in England', *Proceedings of the British Academy*, xliv (1958), 35–60.

[8] Stephen of Ripon, *Vita S. Wilfridi* (*BHL*, no. 8889), ed. B. Colgrave, *The Life of Bishop Wilfrid by Eddius Stephanus* (Cambridge, 1927); Felix, *Vita S. Guthlaci* (*BHL*, no. 3723), ed. B. Colgrave, *Felix's Life of St Guthlac* (Cambridge, 1956); the anonymous *Vita S. Ceolfrithi* (*BHL*, no. 1726), ed. Plummer, *VBOH* i. 388–404; and the anonymous *Vita S. Cuthberti* (*BHL*, no. 2019) and that of Bede (*BHL*, no. 2021), both ed. B. Colgrave, *Two Lives of St Cuthbert* (Cambridge, 1940). All these early Anglo-Latin *uitae* were circulating in manuscript in late 10th-c. England, in some cases as part of the 'Cotton–Corpus Legendary' (see below).

manuscript collections known as passionals or legendaries.[9] At first the *uitae* in these collections were arranged more or less randomly: this is the case with the earliest surviving Anglo-Saxon passional, now Paris, BN lat. 10861 (?Christ Church, Canterbury, s. ix^{in}), which contains eighteen *passiones* of martyrs universally venerated, in no apparent order.[10] Subsequently, however, collections of this sort were arranged according to the liturgical year. One such legendary was that known as the 'Cotton–Corpus Legendary', a compilation which originated in north-eastern Francia or Flanders in the late ninth century and which is preserved uniquely in English manuscripts.[11] This important legendary, which consists of some 165 saints' *uitae*, was widely influential in Anglo-Saxon England,[12] and was a forerunner of the massive legendaries, such as that now preserved (fragmentarily) in London, BL Arundel 169,[13] which were assembled in post-Conquest England. A late tenth-century hagiographer such as Wulfstan will have been familiar with legendaries such as the 'Cotton–Corpus Legendary', and will therefore have had before him numerous saints' *uitae* on which to model his own.

Winchester in the late tenth century was an active centre of hagiography. The initial impulse was given by Lantfred, whose *Translatio et miracula S. Swithuni*, completed *c.*975, was composed at Winchester and dedicated to the *familia* of the Old Minster. As we have seen, Lantfred was a monk of Fleury, and may be presumed to have been in touch with developments in hagiography then taking place on the Continent, particularly in respect of translations of saints' relics. Wulfstan was much influenced by the form and diction of Lantfred's *Translatio*, as we shall see. Another hagiographer, who was trained at Winchester under Æthelwold and who was apparently a contemporary of Wulfstan, was Ælfric. Ælfric is known as the author of an extensive collection of *Lives of*

[9] See Aigrain, *L'Hagiographie*, pp. 178–85, and G. Philippart, *Les Légendiers latins et autres manuscrits hagiographiques* (Turnhout, 1977), esp. pp. 27–36.

[10] See M. P. Brown, 'Paris, Bibliothèque Nationale, lat. 10861 and the scriptorium of Christ Church Canterbury', *ASE* xv (1986), 119–37.

[11] See W. Levison, SS rer. Meroving. vii. 545–6, and the works by P. Zettel cited below, n. 12.

[12] P. H. Zettel, 'Ælfric's hagiographic sources and the Latin legendary preserved in BL MS Cotton Nero E.i + CCCC MS 9 and other manuscripts' (D.Phil. thesis, Oxford, 1979), and 'Saints' lives in Old English: Latin manuscripts and vernacular accounts: Ælfric', *Peritia* i (1982), 17–37.

[13] See below, pp. clxviii–clxxi.

Saints[14] containing some 27 items, all in English and mostly in the form of saints' *uitae*, intended as reading material for various feasts of the *sanctorale*; in addition, various items in his two series of *Catholic Homilies* are in the form of saints' *uitae* and pertain to the *sanctorale*.[15] In sum, Ælfric composed some sixty-two items for the *sanctorale*, most of which are in the form of saints' *uitae*. For the *uitae* of non-English saints, Ælfric apparently drew on a copy of the 'Cotton–Corpus Legendary', as Patrick Zettel has shown.[16] For the English saints, in particular Cuthbert, Edmund, Oswald, Birinus, Swithun, and Æthelthryth, there is evidence that Ælfric assembled a hagiographical commonplace-book, drawn from various sources (principally Bede's *Historia ecclesiastica*, but also including such works as Abbo's *Passio S. Eadmundi*) and then based his English *uitae* on materials contained in the commonplace-book.[17] The point is simply that Ælfric was a hagiographer familiar with a wide range of hagiographical materials; and there is no reason to doubt that his Winchester colleague Wulfstan had a similar familiarity.

From the *Vita S. Æthelwoldi* it is clear that Wulfstan was indeed familiar with earlier hagiography. He certainly knew Sulpicius Severus' *Vita S. Martini*, for example, for he models his account of the poisoning attempt on Æthelwold's life (c. 19) on a similar incident in Sulpicius (c. 6).[18] His account of Æthelwold's generosity to the poor (c. 29) is modelled on a similar incident in the anonymous *Passio S. Laurentii*.[19] Both the *Vita S. Martini* and the *Passio S. Laurentii* are contained in the 'Cotton–Corpus Legendary', and since both were used by Ælfric,[20] there is no need to doubt that Wulfstan had read them in this source as well. Another earlier *uita* which arguably served Wulfstan as model was Bede's prose *Vita S. Cuthberti*. The *uitae* of Bede and Wulfstan share one

[14] W. W. Skeat, *Ælfric's Lives of Saints*, EETS, os lxxvi, lxxxii, xciv, civ (1881–1900).

[15] Both series are ed. B. Thorpe, *The Homilies of the Anglo-Saxon Church: The First Part, containing the Sermones Catholici or Homilies of Ælfric* (2 vols., London, 1844–6); the Second Series is ed. M. Godden, *Ælfric's Catholic Homilies: The Second Series. Text*, EETS, ss v (1979).

[16] See above, n. 12.

[17] See below, pp. cxlviii–cxlix.

[18] See below, p. 35 n. 3.

[19] *BHL*, no. 1754; for the incident, see H. Delehaye, 'Recherches sur le légendier romain', *AB* li (1933), 34–98, at 83, and below, p. 46 n. 1.

[20] For Ælfric's use of the *Vita S. Martini*, see Zettel, 'Saints' lives in Old English', pp. 24–7.

striking structural feature, namely that they each contain forty-six chapters. The number is apparently not a random one. It has been pointed out by Walter Berschin[21] that the number 46 has a symbolical significance derived both from the numerical value of the name Adam (in Greek numerical notation, α = 1, δ = 4, α = 1 again, and μ = 40: hence 46 in all) and from the forty-six years which it took to build the Temple (John 2: 20). Various commentators from Augustine onwards took the number 46 to represent the *perfectio dominici corporis*, and Bede (in Berschin's view) was attempting to represent this *perfectio* when he organized his *Vita S. Cuthberti* in forty-six chapters. That Wulfstan should likewise have arranged his *Vita S. Æthelwoldi* in forty-six chapters suggests that he was following the example of Bede and that he understood the significance of the number 46.

Wulfstan was also much influenced by the form of his Winchester colleague Lantfred's *Translatio et miracula S. Swithuni*. In describing the translation of St Swithun's remains from a prominent grave outside the Old Minster into the Old Minster itself, an event which took place on 15 July 971, Lantfred showed himself thoroughly familiar with the literary form in which such *translationes* were cast from the ninth century onwards.[22] The most famous translations were those of St Dionysius at Paris and of St Benedict at Fleury (Lantfred's mother house); but during the tenth century such translations became common, and one may suspect that in translating St Swithun's remains at Winchester Æthelwold was simply attempting to keep up with contemporary Continental fashion. From this time onwards the the literary account of a translation achieved a conventional form:[23] characteristically, the saint whose remains required translation would appear in a vision to someone in a position to effect that translation and give instructions as to how it was to be effected; one or two miracles would occur to show that the vision was not a figment of the visionary's imagination; the translation would in due course be effected with much ceremony; and further miracles would then occur to reveal

[21] W. Berschin, '*Opus deliberatum ac perfectum*: Why did the Venerable Bede write a second prose life of St Cuthbert?', *St Cuthbert, his Cult and Community to AD 1200*, ed. G. Bonner, D. Rollason, and C. Stancliffe (Woodbridge, 1989), pp. 95–102, at 99–101.

[22] See discussion in M. Lapidge, *The Cult of St Swithun*, *WS* iv (2) (forthcoming).

[23] See *DACL* xv (2) (1953), cols. 2695–9, s.v. 'Translations'; Delehaye, *Cinq leçons*, pp. 75–116; Aigrain, *L'Hagiographie*, pp. 186–92; and M. Heinzelmann, *Translationsberichte und andere Quellen des Reliquienkultes* (Turnhout, 1979), esp. pp. 94–9.

the saint's renewed *uirtus*. Lantfred's *Translatio* of St Swithun adheres closely to this form: Swithun first appears in a dream vision to a certain smith and instructs him to go to Eadsige, a secular cleric and relative of Æthelwold who had been expelled from the Old Minster by Æthelwold but who subsequently became a monk and was made sacristan of St Swithun's shrine (c. 1); Eadsige in due course reports this matter to Æthelwold, and the truth of the report is confirmed by various miracles (cc. 2–3); St Swithun is duly translated (c. 3), and the remainder of the work is devoted to miracles performed at St Swithun's shrine. Now at the end of his *Vita S. Æthelwoldi* Wulfstan has occasion to describe the translation of St Æthelwold which took place in 996, and it is clear that he modelled his account on that of Lantfred. Thus St Æthelwold appears in a vision to a certain citizen of Wallingford named Ælfhelm; he instructs Ælfhelm to go to the Old Minster and report the vision to Wulfstan (c. 42); the man goes to Winchester and is miraculously cured of his blindness, thereby confirming the veracity of his vision (c. 42); St Æthelwold is duly translated on 10 September 996 (c. 43); various miracles occur which show that St Æthelwold has been received into heaven and now has the divine *uirtus* to release us from our sins (cc. 44–6). There is no doubt that Wulfstan knew Lantfred's *Translatio*, for he rendered it in hexameters in his *Narratio metrica de S. Swithuno*; but that he was following its structure in his account of the translation of St Æthelwold is clear from various unambiguous verbal reminiscences of Lantfred which occur in that account.[24]

Numerous other features of Wulfstan's *Vita S. Æthelwoldi* betray his familiarity with earlier hagiography, even when they are not traceable to specific sources. Thus Wulfstan adheres to the conventional pattern of a saintly life in describing Æthelwold's descent from noble stock (c. 1); the miracles which attended his birth (cc. 2 and 4); his early aptitude for Christian learning (c. 6); his turning to the monastic life, consecration, and procession through the various ecclesiastical grades; and so on. When describing the monk Ælfstan's unflinching obedience to Æthelwold (Ælfstan had been ordered by Æthelwold to plunge his hand into a boiling cauldron: c. 14), the abbot enjoined the monk not to mention the episode to anyone. The injunction is based ultimately

[24] See below, p. 67 n. 4.

on Christ's command to the two blind men not to reveal who had healed them (Matt. 9: 30), but it occurs frequently in hagiography (for example, in Bede's prose *Vita S. Cuthberti*, c. 10, where Cuthbert enjoins the monk who had seen him bless the sea-otters not to repeat the incident to anyone). In details such as this Wulfstan's *uita* is entirely conventional.

Nevertheless, there are many respects in which Wulfstan departed from his models. Although the beginning of Æthelwold's life adheres closely to hagiographical convention, as we have said, the end more nearly resembles a chronicle entry, with its reference to *anno Domini* and regnal dating: '... spiritum caelo reddidit in Kalendis Augusti, anno dominicae incarnationis nongentesimo octogesimo quarto, episcopatus autem sui uicesimo secundo, regni moderamina gubernante Æthelredo rege Anglorum' (c. 41). In Wulfstan's account, Æthelwold has no premonition of his death; there is no gathering of disciples and no death-bed exhortation to Christian virtue by the dying bishop. Whereas the greater part of most saints' *uitae* is taken up with miracles, Wulfstan devotes a mere five chapters to miracles performed by Æthelwold (cc. 32–6). One has the sense that, as Wulfstan's narrative approached the times which he had himself experienced, he became more concerned to provide an accurate record of his mentor's achievements; he therefore followed the chronological framework of a chronicle rather than the pattern of earlier saints' *uitae*. From c. 10 onwards, Wulfstan seems to have been basing his chronology on a version of the Anglo-Saxon Chronicle, possibly the A-version (or Parker Chronicle) which was very probably at Winchester in the late tenth century.[25] Thus in c. 10 he gives precise dates for the 'great carnage' of pagans (presumably the Battle of *Brunanburh*), the death of King Athelstan, the succession and death of King Edmund, and the succession of King Eadred, all of which apparently derive from the Anglo-Saxon Chronicle.[26] In any event, such chronological precision is alien to the spirit of hagiography, and sets Wulfstan's work apart from the *uitae* which were its model.

The *Vita S. Æthelwoldi* is composed throughout in clear, articulate prose which William of Malmesbury rightly described as *mediocris*, 'unadorned'.[27] Wulfstan's sentences are sometimes

[25] See Bately, *MSA*, pp. xiii–xiv.
[26] See below, pp. 17 nn. 6, 8, 18 n. 1.
[27] *Gesta regum*, ed. Stubbs, i. 167; quoted above, p. xv.

long, but their structure is always clear. They sometimes tend to verbosity—the unfortunate effect of too much study of Aldhelm, no doubt—and Wulfstan frequently uses several words where one would do. Wulfstan's verbosity stands out in clear relief if one of his long sentences is compared to the abbreviation which Ælfric subsequently made of it. For example, in describing Æthelwold's treatment of the monk who had committed a minor theft (c. 33), Wulfstan writes:

Transactis itaque tribus diebus et tribus noctibus, cum res furata minime esset inuenta, locutus est uir sanctus in capitulo coram omni multitudine fratrum, terribili indignatione et comminatione inquiens . . .

Ælfric pared this sentence drastically:

Iterum transactis tribus diebus, non inuenta pecunia, locutus est episcopus omnibus fratribus dicens . . . (c. 22).

From Ælfric's point of view, it was otiose to specify 'three nights' alongside the three days, or to state, 'in the chapter-house with the entire multitude of monks' when 'all the monks' would do, or to embellish the bishop's words with the statement that they were delivered with 'terrible indignation and commination'. But as a Latin stylist Ælfric was excessively severe. From Wulfstan's point of view, the verbal parallelism of 'three days and three nights' and the rhyme of the polysyllabic substantives *indignatione/ comminatione* impart to the episode a certain dignity. Wulfstan certainly preferred the long word to the short one,[28] and he had a particular love of agentive nouns ending in *-or*.[29] He often modelled his sentences on Aldhelm. Yet in comparison with other Winchester products of the late tenth century Wulfstan's language is remarkably restrained. The so-called 'hermeneutic' style which characterizes much Anglo-Latin writing of that time, most evident in the use of archaisms, neologisms, and Graecisms,[30] is remarkably absent from Wulfstan. In the *Vita S. Æthelwoldi* there is no example of archaism or neologism. A very few Graecisms occur: *basileus* (c. 16), *carisma* (c. 8), *discolus* (c. 28), and *mandra* (c. 22). Of these, however, *basileus* ('king') is current in royal diplomas issued

[28] Cf. Winterbottom, *Three Lives*, p. 3.

[29] e.g. pref. (*saluator, fundator, institutor*) or c. 28 (*protector, consolator, susceptor, defensor, corrector, recreator, adiutor*).

[30] Lapidge, 'The hermeneutic style', pp. 69–76, 87.

by King Edgar, *carisma* ('gift') is common in Christian Latin from the fourth century onwards, *discolus* ('malefactor') is biblical (1 Pet. 2: 18), and *mandra* ('sheepfold', hence 'monastery') is used by classical as well as Christian authors. In this respect, Wulfstan's prose is indeed 'unadorned'.

In another important respect Wulfstan reveals himself as a conscious, but unostentatious, stylist, namely in the employment of rhythmical *cursus*. Latin prose writers from Cicero onwards had taken care to embellish their prose by the use of certain *clausulae*, that is, various recurrent patterns of alternating long and short syllables at the end of a clause or sentence. During Late Antiquity rhythmical cadences or *cursus* based on the natural stress of words began to replace the quantitative *clausulae*.[31] In order to record and analyse *cursus* a notational system has been devised which may be described briefly. The intention of the system is to record the rhythm or stress-pattern of the final two words of any sentence. Accordingly, 'p' refers to stress on the penultimate syllable, where 'pp' refers to stress on the antepenultimate syllable. The system records: (*a*) the stress of the second-last word, whether p or pp; and (*b*) the number of syllables and the stress—again, p or pp—of the final word. Thus pp 4p denotes a cadence in which the second-last word is stressed on the antepenultimate syllable, and the last word consists of four syllables and is stressed on the penultimate syllable: *uerbéribus corrigéndo*. During the early Middle Ages the four most common *cursus* were the following (the illustrations are taken from Wulfstan); p 3p or *cursus planus* (c. 8: *uítam finíuit*; c. 23: *adgregáre curáuit*); p 4p or *cursus trispondaicus* (c. 1: *aetérnae claritátis*; c. 4: *gaudéndo referébat*); p 4pp or *cursus tardus* (pref.: *migráuit caeléstia*; c. 6: *mererétur exístere*); and pp 4p or *cursus uelox* (c. 3: *órdinem redeámus*; c. 23: *Dómino commendáuit*). Now of the nearly 200 cadences in the *Vita S. Æthelwoldi*, it is noteworthy that nearly 60% end with one of these four *cursus*: p 3p, 18%, pp 4p, 16%; p 4pp, 13%; and p 4p, 11%. These figures agree very closely, especially in the order of the four preferred cadences, with those of two ninth-century authors who are known to have practised *cursus*, namely Hincmar of Rheims and Anastasius Bibliothecarius;[32] they also

[31] T. Janson, *Prose Rhythm in Medieval Latin from the 9th to the 13th Century* (Stockholm, 1975).

[32] Ibid., pp. 36–40. For Hincmar, the figures are: p 3p, 23%; p 4pp, 15%; pp 4p, 12%; for Anastasius, p 3p, 17%; pp 4p, 12%; p 4pp, 11%; and p 4p, 7% (note that for Anastasius the order of preferred *cursus* is identical to that of Wulfstan).

agree remarkably well with those of two well-known prose stylists of the tenth century, Liutprand of Cremona and Atto of Vercelli.[33] In his use of *cursus*, then, Wulfstan reveals himself as a skilful but unostentatious stylist who belongs in the company of the best ninth- and tenth-century authors.

One final aspect of Wulfstan's style deserves mention, namely his knowledge and quotation of earlier literature. For some authors the saint's *uita* was a flexible vehicle for showing off a wide range of reading. Byrhtferth of Ramsey, for example, fills his *uitae* of Oswald and Ecgwine with quotations from earlier authors, always introduced ostentatiously with phrases such as *illud scholastici dicentis*, *ut quidam ait rhetor in suis*, or the like. There is no quotation of this sort in Wulfstan's *uita* of Æthelwold. This is not to imply that the range of Wulfstan's reading was narrow; on the contrary, the hexameters of his *Narratio metrica de S. Swithuno* are filled with reminiscences of earlier poets—of Vergil and Horace, for example, and of numerous Christian Latin poets such as Juvencus, Caelius Sedulius, Arator, and Venantius Fortunatus.[34] The fact that Wulfstan never quotes directly from any of these authors is a token of his stylistic restraint. Furthermore, the fact that there are very few poeticisms in his prose may suggest that he was consciously avoiding them. Only occasionally does a Vergilian expression invade his prose: thus his *pennarum remigiis* (c. 2) is indebted to Vergil's *remigio alarum* (*Aen.* i. 301, vi. 19), or his *inter spem et timorem* (c. 42) to Vergil's *spemque metumque inter* (*Aen.* i. 218); but such reminiscences are rare. Instead, Wulfstan's prose contains reminiscences of those prose works closest in spirit to his subject: the *Regula S. Benedicti* and the *Regularis concordia*.[35]

In an age when most Latin prose was characterized by ostentatious, hermeneutic vocabulary, Wulfstan's prose stands out for its modesty and sobriety. Wulfstan was not as severe a stylist as Ælfric, who in his redaction of the *Vita S. Æthelwoldi* found much to excise; but in comparison (say) with the Aldhelmian pomposity of Byrhtferth, Wulfstan is a master of restraint. Perhaps it was this feature which commended itself to later generations of readers; in

[33] Ibid., pp. 40–2. For Liutprand the figures are: p 3p, 21%; p 4pp, 15%; pp 4p, 14%; and p 4p, 8%. No percentage figures are given for Atto, but his usage 'shows only small variations' from the pattern of Liutprand. The pattern of these two Italian authors closely resembles Wulfstan's.

[34] See Dolbeau, 'Le *Breuiloquium*', p. 52; Lapidge, *The Cult of St Swithun*.

[35] See below, pp. 16 n. 1, 52 n. 3.

any event, as we shall see, Wulfstan's *Vita S. Æthelwoldi* enjoyed an enormously wide circulation, and it was his *uita* above all which spread the fame and cult of St Æthelwold.

IV. THE CULT OF ST ÆTHELWOLD

In the late tenth century, the process of canonization of a saint was a much less formal affair than it was to become in later centuries. Such canonization did not then require papal approval, or even archiepiscopal or episcopal approval; it required simply the earnest conviction that while on earth a holy man or woman had been a vessel of God's power, hence that he or she was empowered—after entering the heavenly kingdom—to intercede with God on behalf of mortal men, and the consequent liturgical celebration of the saint's intercessory powers on an appointed day. If the saint was known only locally, or was only recently deceased, he or she could be satisfactorily commemorated by use of the generalized prayers found in mass and Office books and designated for use (say) *in natali unius confessoris* or *in natali unius uirginis*. However, if it were thought appropriate to commemorate the saint in more specific terms—to appeal to him or her by name, as it were—then specific prayers naming the saint were required. And it follows that if the saint were recently deceased, or his miraculous powers had only recently come to light, such prayers would need to be composed afresh, for use on the day appointed for the saint's commemoration (this would normally be the day on which he died and was born into the eternal life—his *dies natalis*—or the day on which his remains were translated to a more appropriate shrine; but of course other days were possible as well). Within a monastic community, the saint would be commemorated in both mass and office on the appointed day, or feast day. In order to commemorate the saint at mass, a mass-set (that is, the set of four 'proper' or variable prayers which were pronounced by the celebrant on that particular day: *collecta*, *secreta*, *praefatio*, and *postcommunio*) was needed; and if the introit was to be troped, a proper trope was needed as well. The commemoration of a saint in the Office would normally begin—at least in the case of important saints—at vespers on the vigil or day before the feast itself (the office in question is called the 'First Vespers' of the saint), and for vespers a collect and a hymn were needed. And on the feast day itself, beginning at matins, lections concerning the saint (usually excerpted from the saint's *uita*) were needed.

After the translation of St Æthelwold on 10 September 996, the decision was taken—within his former *familia* at the Old Minster—to commemorate him liturgically. And since Æthelwold had manifested his intercessory powers through the miracles which preceded the translation of his remains, it would have seemed appropriate to commemorate him both on the feast of his deposition (1 August) and of his translation (10 September). For such commemoration, the following liturgical pieces were needed, therefore: collects and hymns for First Vespers for each of the two feasts; lections for matins for each of the two feasts; and, for the mass itself, tropes and mass-sets for each of the two feasts. Now it is interesting that there is a collection of precisely such pieces (omitting only the lections), all in Æthelwold's name, in Alençon, Bibl. mun. 14, fos. 34^{v}–36^{r}, a manuscript which, as we have seen (pp. xxiii–xxvii), was copied in the early twelfth century by Orderic Vitalis from a lost exemplar which apparently originated in the Old Minster. The pieces follow immediately Orderic's copy of Wulfstan's *Vita S. Æthelwoldi*, and there is good reason to associate them with Wulfstan himself: as the precentor at the Old Minster, he would have been responsible for liturgical performance there, and as Æthelwold's devoted *alumnus* he may well have taken the initiative in composing whatever liturgical pieces were needed for his commemoration. For these reasons the collection of liturgical pieces in Alençon 14 deserves detailed consideration; it is set out below as it occurs in the manuscript (with the omission of the brief treatise *De horis peculiaribus*, which did not itself form part of the liturgy).[1]

1. A hymn, designated specifically as a hymn for Vespers (*hymnus uespertinalis*), but without any specification of feast day, consisting of five sapphic stanzas:[2]

1 Inclitus pastor populique rector,
Cuius insignem colimus triumphum,

[1] The treatise *De horis peculiaribus* is ptd. and discussed above, pp. lxviii–lxxvii.

[2] *ICL*, no. 8011; *Rep. Hymn.*, no. 8849; ptd. *AH* xxiii. 126 (no. 209), xliii. 68 (no. 107); *PL* cxxxvii. 105: '(1) Æthelwold, the excellent shepherd and ruler of the people, whose

Nunc Adeluuoldus sine fine letus
Regnat in astris.

2 Qui pater noster fuit et magister
Exhibens sacre documenta uite,
Et Deo semper satagens placere
Corde benigno.

3 O diem sanctum, celebrem, choruscum
Quem Dei nobis pietas sacrauit,
Vt patri tanto mereremur almum
Promere tantum.

4 Nunc eum nisu rogitemus omni
Abluat nostrum pius ⟨u⟩t reatum
Et sua sancta prece nos ad altum
Ducat Olimpum.

5 Sit Deo soli decus et potestas,
Laus in excelsis honor ac perennis
Qui suis totum moderans gubernat
Legibus orbem.

2. A second hymn, without specification of Office and again without specification of feast day, consisting of five octosyllabic stanzas:[3]

1 Celi senator inclite
Sancte pastor ecclesie:
O Adeluuolde supplices[4]
Tuos exaudi seruulos!

glorious triumph we celebrate, now rules joyous in heaven without end. (2) He was our father and teacher, showing us the pattern of the holy life, and always concerned to please God in his kindly heart. (3) O holy day, renowned, resplendent, which God's mercy hallowed for us, that we should be found worthy to celebrate so great a day for so great a father. (4) Now let us beseech him with every effort that (reading *ut* for MS *et*) he may mercifully wipe away our guilt and with his holy prayer lead us to heaven on high. (5) Let power and glory and praise on high and everlasting honour be to God alone, who governs the entire world with his laws.'

[3] *ICL*, no. 1793; *Rep. Hymn.*, no. 3511; ptd. *AH* xxiii. 127 (no. 210); *PL* cxxxvii. 105: '(1) Distinguished senator of heaven, shepherd of Holy Church, O Æthelwold, hear your suppliant servants. (2) Now, o star resplendent on high among the stars, procure for us, kindly one, the gifts of the Holy Spirit. (3) We beseech you with prostrate hearts here in the presence of your limbs: attend, calmly and propitiously, to our prayers, (4) so that, protected by your indispensable patronage we may arrive at the perpetual joys of heaven. (5) May the Inborn and Only-begotten, Three-and-One God, Holy Spirit of both, grant this to us!'

[4] The line as transmitted has no end-rhyme for *seruulos* and should perhaps be emended to *Adeluuolde supplices nos*, or (more radically) to *O Adeluuolde seruulos / exaudi supplices tuos*.

2 Iam sidus inter sidera
Resplendens super ethera,
Nobis benignus impetra
Paracliti karismata.

3 ⟨P⟩ronis[5] rogamus mentibus
Hic coram tuis artubus:
Nostris adesto precibus
Serenus ac propitius,

4 Vt tuis necessariis
Protecti patrociniis,
Ad celorum perpetua
Perueniamus gaudia.

5 Prestet nobis Ingenitus
Hoc atque Vnigenitus
Sanctus amborum Spiritus
Trinus et unus Dominus!

3. A collect (with the rubric ORATIO), as follows:[6]

Deus qui preclari sideris sancti pontificis Adeluuoldi illustratione nouam populis Anglorum tribuisti lucem hodierna die clarescere . tuam supplicite implorамus clementiam ut cuius magisterio totius religionis documenta cognouimus illius et exemplis informemur et patrociniis adiuuemur. Per.

4. A mass-set (with the rubric AD MISSAM), as follows:[7]

Deus qui hodiernam diem beati confessoris tui Adeluuoldi episcopi transitu nobis honorabilem dedicasti . concede propicius ut cuius

[5] MS *ronis* (the rubricator of Orderic's exemplar omitted to supply the initial *P*).

[6] 'O God, who with the illumination of the bright star of St Æthelwold the bishop have bestowed a new light to shine this day on the English people, we humbly beseech Your mercy that we may be instructed by the example and supported by the patronage of him through whose teaching we learned the pattern of all religious observance.'

[7] 'O God, who consecrated this day as glorious through the passing away of Bishop Æthelwold, your blessed confessor, grant kindly that we may achieve the joys of heavenly life through the intercession of him through whose learning we are imbued with the light of your truth. *Per.*

SECRETA O Lord, we beseech you that the annual celebration of our holy father Bishop Æthelwold may make acceptable and commend to you the proffered services of our subjection, so that, strengthened by his holy supplication we may be found worthy to obtain the remission of all our sins and the company of eternal bliss. *Per.*

PREFATIO *Vere dignum et aeterne . . . Deus*. Because the blessed and longed-for joy of the present day is upon us, which, glorious with the distinction of the apostolic honour [i.e. St Peter *ad uincula*] and solemnized by the rose-red blood of martyrs [i.e. the Maccabees], you consecrated with the more recent renown of the glorious bishop eruditione ueritatis tue luce perfundimur . eius intercessione celestis uite gaudia consequamur. Per.

SECRETA Oblata seruitutis nostre munera tibi Domine quesumus annua sancti patris nostri Adeluuoldi episcopi sollemnitas commendet accepta . ut eius pia supplicatione muniti . cunctorum nostrorum remissionem peccaminum et beatitudinis sempiterne mereamur optinere consortium. Per.

PREFATIO VD aeterne Deus. Quoniam adest nobis iocunda et uotiua presentis diei leticia . quam apostolici culminis honore sublimem roseoque martirii cruore sollempnem . gloriosi pontificis Adeluuoldi moderna celebritate consecrasti . et spem nobis tante fiducie contulisti . ut nos paternis eius suffragiis et a peccatorum nostrorum nexibus soluas et ad celestia regna perducas. Per Christum.

POSTCOMMVNIO Refectos Domine uitalis alimonie sacramentis sancti confessoris tui Adeluuoldi intercessione gloriosa nos protege et ad eternum celestis mense conuiuium peruenire concede. Per.

5. A second collect, this time with the simple rubic ALIA.[8]

Gregem tuum, pastor eterne, pii suffragatoris Adeluuoldi patris nostri defensione guberna quesumus Domine, ut cuius beniuolentia prouocante superni amoris dulcedine pascimur . eius interueniente patrocinio et a temporalis uite perturbationibus eruamur et mansuris supernorum ciuium gaudiis inseramur. Per.

6. A second mass-set, this time specifically designated for the feast of the translation on 10 September (*.iiii. idus Septembris in translatione sancti Adeluuoldi*).[9]

Æthelwold, and because you thereby gave us hope of such great security, may you release us from the bonds of our sins through his paternal intercession and lead us to the kingdom of heaven. *Per Christum*.

POSTCOMMVNIO O Lord, protect us now that we are nourished with the sacraments of life-giving sustenance through the glorious intercession of Æthelwold, your holy confessor, and grant that we may arrive at the eternal banquet of the celestial table. *Per*.'

[8] 'O Lord our eternal Shepherd, we beseech you, guide your flock through the protection of our holy patron, father Æthelwold, so that we may be snatched from the turmoil of earthly life and enrolled in the lasting delights of the heavenly citizens through the intercession of him through whose appealing benevolence we are fed on the sweetness of heavenly love. *Per*.'

[9] 'O God, who bestowed on us your holy bishop Æthelwold as a teacher of eternal salvation, kindly grant that we may always be assisted by the merits and prayers of him whose annual feast of translation we are celebrating. *Per*.

SVPER OBLATVM O Lord, we pray that the prayer of our holy father, Bishop Æthelwold, may commend our sacrifice to you so that, with his intercession, the mercy of your holy majesty and the longed-for remission of our sins may come about for us. *Per*.

PREFATIO *Vere dignum aeterne . . . Deus*. Celebrating the longed-for translation of the

Deus qui nobis sanctum pontificem tuum Adeluuoldum salutis eterne doctorem tribuisti . concede propicius ut cuius annua translationis sollemnia colimus eius semper meritis adiuuemur et precibus. Per.

SVPER OBLATVM Sacrificium nostrum tibi Domine quesumus sancti patris nostri Adeluuoldi episcopi commendet oratio ut nobis eo suffragante fiat sanctae maiestatis tuae propiciatio et peccatorum nostrorum exoptata remissio. Per.

PREFATIO VD aeterne Deus. Votiuam beati pontificis Adeluuoldi translationem pia ueneratione celebrantes teque cernua deuotione exorantes ⟨quaesumus⟩ ut ipsum nos apud clementiam tuam sentiamus habere patronum quem tua gratia largiente salutis eterne meruimus suscipere magistrum. Per Christum.

POSTCOMMVNIO Vt hec communio nos Domine tibi dignos efficiat beatus pater noster Adeluuoldus suffragio quesumus pie intercessionis optineat. Per.

7. Two Introit tropes for St Æthelwold, with the simple rubric TROPI, accompanied by chant-cues, but not specified for any particular feast.

Patris adest uotiua dies, cantemus ouantes. *Statuit ei.*
Pontificem templo sibi quem sacrauit in isto. *Et principem.*
Inter apostolicos stola splendente ierarchos. *Vt sit illi.*
Adeluuolde pia prece nos defende misellos. *In eternum.*[10]

Presul Adeluuoldus quia fulsit in ordine magnus. *Statuit ei.*
Constituens illum hodie super ethra polorum. *Et principem.*
Gloria splendor honor decus et ueneratio perpes. *In eternum.*[11]

blessed bishop Æthelwold with devout reverence and beseeching you with prostrate devotion, we pray that we may perceive that we have him as patron with your clemency whom we were found worthy to have as the teacher of eternal salvation through your bountiful grace. *Per Christum.*

POSTCOMMVNIO We pray, Lord, that our blessed father Æthelwold may bring it about with the help of his devout intercession that this communion may make us worthy of you. *Per.*'

[10] Planchart, *Repertory* ii. 175 (no. 170); *AH* xlix. 99 (no. 209); Frere, *The Winchester Troper*, p. 32; *PL* cxxxvii. 107–8: 'The longed-for day of our father is here: let us sing rejoicing. *Statuit ei.* Whom he ordained as his bishop in this church. *Et principem.* With gleaming stole among the apostolic priests. *Vt sit illi.* Æthelwold, defend us poor little wretches with your merciful prayer. *In eternum.*'

[11] Planchart, *Repertory* ii. 175 (no. 171); *AH* xlix. 99 (no. 210); Frere, *The Winchester Troper*, p. 33; *PL* cxxxvii. 107–8: 'Bishop Æthelwold, because he shone greatly in the assembly. *Statuit ei.* Establishing him today beyond the ethereal realms. *Et principem.* Glory, excellence, distinction, grace, and perpetual devotion. *In eternum.*'

Although the tropes are supplied with chant-cues, there is no accompanying neumatic notation.

It will be seen that the various liturgical pieces in Alençon 14, if properly sorted, are those which are proper to commemoration of the deposition and translation of St Æthelwold: namely, for the deposition, the hymn (no. 1) specified for (First) Vespers and the accompanying collect (no. 3), together with an Introit trope ('Patris adest') and a mass-set (no. 4) for the feast-day itself; and, for the translation, a second hymn (no. 2) and accompanying collect (no. 5) for (First) Vespers together with an Introit trope ('Presul Adeluuoldus') and mass-set (no. 6) for the feast-day itself. The only proper pieces which are lacking from this collection are the lections for matins on each of the two feast-days; and these could conveniently have been supplied from a copy of Wulfstan's *Vita S. Æthelwoldi*.

The fact that all these liturgical pieces—hymns, collects, tropes, and mass-sets—are preserved together as an undifferentiated collection confirms the suspicion that they are the product of one author and that they represent a literary rather than a liturgical compilation, in so far as they are not differentiated with respect to their various liturgical functions. That is to say, if they were to be used for liturgical purposes, they would need to be differentiated and distributed into the various liturgical books used for various liturgical functions: hymns and collects into a book for the celebration of the office (a hymnal and a collectar respectively; or, perhaps alternatively at this period, a primitive breviary which contained both hymns and collects for the Office); tropes into a troper; and mass-sets into a sacramentary or missal. In fact most of the liturgical pieces contained in the undifferentiated collection in Alençon 14 are found independently in liturgical manuscripts; and consideration of these various manuscripts illuminates the growth and spread of the cult of St Æthelwold.

We may begin with the two hymns, since these are *not* found in a liturgical manuscript—hymnal or otherwise—independently of the collection in Alençon 14. But, given the state of the surviving manuscript evidence, the absence of the two Æthelwold hymns from any extant Anglo-Saxon hymnal is not surprising.[12] In his

[12] Gneuss, 'Liturgical books', p. 119.

thorough study of surviving Anglo-Saxon hymnals, Helmut Gneuss has identified two broadly defined Anglo-Saxon families of the so-called 'New Hymnal':[13] one (moderately well attested) from Canterbury, the other (poorly attested) from Winchester. The 'Canterbury-type' of New Hymnal is attested in three fully preserved hymnals of late tenth- and early eleventh-century date; and it is noteworthy that none of these contains either of the hymns for St Æthelwold.[14] The 'Winchester-type' of New Hymnal is less well attested: its outlines are known from the list of hymns prescribed by Ælfric in his 'Letter to the Monks of Eynsham',[15] and by the hymnal contained in Cambridge, Corpus Christi College 391 (the 'Portiforium of St Wulstan'), pp. 227–78, which is in broad outline a 'Winchester-type' hymnal, but one which has been adapted to Worcester use by the suppression of hymns for Winchester saints and the substitution of hymns for Worcester saints such as St Oswald.[16] In these circumstances, it is not perhaps surprising that neither of the witnesses to the 'Winchester-type' hymnal contains either of the hymns for St Æthelwold. As far as the evidence of hymnals is concerned, therefore, we may be fairly sure that hymns for St Æthelwold had been definitely excluded from Canterbury use, and that the uneven nature of the surviving evidence for Winchester use makes it difficult to determine whether or not hymns for St Æthelwold formed part of that use. In any event, it is worth remarking that, in the late eleventh century in the aftermath of the Norman Conquest, an entirely new type of New Hymnal replaced the 'Canterbury' and 'Winchester' types, and hence that later medieval English hymnals throw no further light on the question of hymns in honour of St Æthelwold.[17]

A slightly clearer picture emerges from consideration of Anglo-Saxon collectars. Four collectars have survived from Anglo-Saxon England.[18] Of these, one was written before the translation of St Æthelwold in 996, and understandably omits any collect for that saint.[19] Another such collectar (now London, BL, Harley 2961) was

[13] Gneuss, *Hymnar*, pp. 67–74.

[14] The manuscripts in question are London, BL Add. 37517 (Canterbury, s. x^ex); Cotton Vespasian D. XII (? Canterbury, s. xi^med); and Durham, Cathedral Library, B. III. 32 (Canterbury, s. xi^1).

[15] Ed. Spath, *CCM* vii (3), 158–9.

[16] Dewick and Frere, *The Leofric Collectar*, ii. 605–7.

[17] Gneuss, *Hymnar*, pp. 71, 75–83.

[18] Gneuss, 'Liturgical books', p. 113.

[19] The so-called 'Durham Ritual', now Durham, Cathedral Library, A. IV. 19 (s. x^in).

written for the use of secular canons of Exeter cathedral in the mid-eleventh century, and omits any collect for St Æthelwold.[20] The collectar in London, BL Cotton Titus D. XXVI, fos. 20r–50v, is part of a private prayer-book, and includes a very peculiar selection of collects, few of them specified for any particular saint's feast, but mostly for generalized feasts, such as those for 'one martyr' or 'one confessor', and so on; in short, the collectar in Titus D. XXVI contains no collect for St Æthelwold. However, the aforementioned 'Portiforium of St Wulstan', CCCC 391, contains a full collectar intended for institutional use at Worcester; from internal evidence it is clear that this manuscript was written at Worcester in 1065.[21] As has been mentioned earlier, this manuscript was based substantially on a Winchester exemplar: this much is clear from the preponderance of Winchester saints who receive specific commemoration. Among these Winchester saints is St Æthelwold, for whose commemoration CCCC 391 includes collects for both the deposition and translation. For the deposition, CCCC 391 gives the first of the collects printed above as no. 3 (inc. 'Deus qui preclari');[22] and this is followed with another collect under the rubric *alia oratio*, which is in fact the *collecta* from the first mass-set printed above as no. 4 (inc. 'Deus qui hodiernam diem').[23] The inclusion of this latter collect implies that the compiler of CCCC 391 was unconcerned that it was originally intended for use at mass. For the feast of the translation, CCCC 391 curiously omits the collect composed specifically for the occasion and given above as no. 5 (inc. 'Gregem tuum pastor'); in its place is given the collect (inc. 'Deus qui nobis sanctum pontificem') from the second mass-set quoted above (no. 6).[24] Again, it would appear that the compiler of CCCC 391 was unaware of the original function of the collects which he was copying. More interesting is the fact that he added to the collect for the translation two more collects, neither of which is found in the collection in Alençon 14; either or both may have been transmitted from Winchester or may have been composed *ad hoc* at Worcester:

COLLECTA VT SVPRA Deus qui nos iocunda pretiosi confessoris tui Aþeluuoldi festiuitate letificas, presta quesumus ut grex deuotus

[20] Ed. Dewick and Frere, *The Leofric Collectar*, i.

[21] Ed. A. Hughes, *The Portiforium of St Wulstan*, 2 vols., HBS lxxxix–xc (1958–60).

[22] Ibid. ii. 136 (no. 1882).

[23] Ibid. (no. 1883).

[24] Ibid. 142 (no. 1920).

ascendat quo pastor apostolicus et sydus aureum glorianter precessit. Per.[25]

ITEM ALIA Concede quesumus omnipotens Deus . ut illuc deuotionis nostrae tendat affectus . quo tecum sydus aureum et gloriosus exultat presul Aþeluuoldus.[26]

These collects are good evidence that St Æthelwold was being culted in the cathedral Office at Worcester in the second half of the eleventh century.

Collects which were used institutionally (as in CCCC 391) for First Vespers could of course also be used in private devotions. Accordingly, we might expect to find such collects in private prayer-books, if a representative number of such books had survived from late Anglo-Saxon England. But we have very few such books.[27] As we have seen, the collects in one such book—Cotton Titus D. XXVI—are mostly generalized in their application. It is interesting to note, therefore, that in another such prayer-book, which was very possibly compiled in one of the Winchester houses, namely London, BL Cotton Galba A. XIV, there is a prayer for St Æthelwold (fo. 125^r) which is simply the collect for Vespers printed above as no. 3, beginning 'Deus qui preclari sideris'.[28] But further evidence for the cult of St Æthelwold in Anglo-Saxon private devotion is lacking.

So far we have seen that it was especially at Winchester (and at places indebted to Winchester use, such as Worcester) that St Æthelwold was culted. A similar picture results from the analysis of the mass-sets for St Æthelwold in Anglo-Saxon sacramentaries and missals.[29] We may begin with the so-called 'Missal of Robert

[25] Ibid. (no. 1921) 'COLLECTA VT SVPRA. O God, who bring us bliss through the joyous feast of your precious confessor Æthelwold, grant, we beseech you, that the devout flock may ascend where the apostolic shepherd and golden star has gone before in glory. *Per.*'

[26] Ibid. (no. 1922): 'ITEM ALIA. Grant, we beseech you, omnipotent God, that the devotion of our love may proceed to where the golden star and glorious bishop Æthelwold rejoices with you.'

[27] Gneuss, 'Liturgical books', p. 138.

[28] B. J. Muir, *A Pre-Conquest English Prayer-Book*, HBS ciii (1988), p. 159 (no. 77).

[29] For a list, see Gneuss, 'Liturgical books', pp. 101–2. We omit from discussion Worcester, Cathedral Library, F. 173 (New Minster, Winchester, s. xi^1, provenance Worcester), since it is fragmentary, consisting of only 30 leaves and two parts of leaves, and nothing of the *sanctorale* remains: see F. E. Warren, 'An Anglo-Saxon missal at Worcester', *The Academy*, xxviii (1885), 394–5. However, the part that remains contains a service for the Burial of the Dead, and one of the prayers in that service is addressed *inter alios* to St Æthelwold: 'Deus cuius misericordie nullus est numerus, suscipe preces

of Jumièges' (which is properly a sacramentary, not a missal) now in Rouen, Bibl. mun. 274 (Y. 6).[30] The manuscript is so named because it came into the possession of Robert, sometime archbishop of Canterbury (1044–51), and was given by him to Jumièges; however, the manuscript was evidently written somewhat earlier than Robert's lifetime, probably in the early eleventh century. There is no scholarly consensus on where it was written: arguments have been advanced in favour of Canterbury, Winchester, Ely, and Peterborough.[31] In view of the prominence given to St Æthelwold in the sanctoral, an origin in Canterbury can be safely ruled out; an origin in Ely or Peterborough (both of which were refounded by Æthelwold) as well as in Winchester itself would fit well with other evidence for the liturgical celebration of his cult, as we shall see. The important point is that this sacramentary contains a large number of proper masses for saints culted specifically at Winchester, and among these is St Æthelwold, whose deposition and translation are both fully commemorated. For the deposition, the first of the mass-sets given above (no. 4) is given;[32] curiously this mass-set is preceded by the collect for first vespers (no. 3), which, as we have seen, was intended for performance in the office. The implication is that these prayers were copied from an undifferentiated collection such as that found in Alençon 14. The same is true of the prayers for St Æthelwold's translation: here the mass-set printed above (no. 6) is followed by the collect for first vespers found in the Alençon collection (above, no. 5: 'Gregem tuum').[33] This collect is designated with the rubric AD VESPERAM; the fact that it is positioned *after* the mass-set implies once again that the compiler of the 'Missal of Robert of Jumièges'

nostras, et intercedentibus sanctis confessoribus tuis BYRINO et SVVITHVNO atque ATHELVVOLDO omnibusque sanctis quorum reliquie in hoc continentur monasterio [sc. the New Minster, Winchester], anime famuli tui lucis letitiam concede, atque in regione uiuorum sanctorum tuorum tribue societatem. per eum' (ed. C. H. Turner, 'The churches at Winchester in the early eleventh century', *Journal of Theological Studies*, xvii (1916), 65–8, at p. 67).

30 Ed. H. A. Wilson, *The Missal of Robert of Jumièges*, HBS xi (1896).

31 See bibliography in Temple, *AS Manuscripts*, pp. 89–91 (no. 72), and esp. F. E. Warren, *The Leofric Missal* (Oxford, 1883), pp. 275–93; J. B. L. Tolhurst, 'Le missel de Robert de Jumièges, sacramentaire d'Ely', *Jumièges: Congrès scientifique du XIIIe centenaire*, 2 vols. (Rouen, 1955), i. 287–93; C. E. Hohler, 'Les saints insulaires dans le missel de l'archevêque Robert', ibid. 293–303.

32 Wilson, *The Missal of Robert of Jumièges*, pp. 193–4.

33 Ibid., p. 194.

was, in this instance at least, copying unthinkingly from an exemplar containing a collection of prayers such as that in Alençon 14, and that he did not know (or care) whether the collect was for First or Second Vespers. Similar uncertainty about the function of the collects and mass-sets in the Alençon 14 collection is characteristic of English missals from the eleventh century onwards.

Another Winchester witness to the full cult of St Æthelwold is the 'New Minster Missal', now in Le Havre, Bibl. mun. 330.[34] This book is the only plenary missal to have survived from Anglo-Saxon England; it was written, almost certainly at the New Minster Winchester, in the later eleventh century. Its sanctoral contains mass-sets for both the deposition and translation of St Æthelwold. For the deposition, the first mass-set printed above (no. 4) is given; however, this is preceded—inappropriately—by the collect for vespers (no. 3), and the inappropriateness is made all the more striking by the rubric AD VESPERAS; furthermore, the mass-set is followed by another collect, that given as no. 5 above, which (as we have seen) was intended for first vespers on the feast of the translation, *not* for mass on that of the deposition.[35] The inclusion of these two collects—both intended for the office of vespers, but for different feasts—suggests once again that the compiler of this missal was drawing on a collection of prayers for St Æthelwold like that in Alençon 14, and simply did not realize that the two additional collects had no rightful place in a missal.[36] For the feast of the translation the 'New Minster Missal' merely (and rightly) gives the mass-set printed above as no. 6.

There is only one other surviving sacramentary from the Anglo-Saxon period which preserves the mass-sets for the deposition and translation of St Æthelwold, namely London, BL Cotton Vitellius A. XVIII.[37] This manuscript once belonged to Bishop Giso of Wells (1061–88), and was probably written for his personal use at Wells. To judge from the large number of Winchester saints whose feasts are commemorated in the sanctoral (Æthelthryth, Eadburg, Swithun, Grimbald, and Birinus), it would seem that Giso's sacramentary was copied from a Winchester exemplar; and this fact

[34] Ed. D. H. Turner, *The Missal of the New Minster, Winchester*, HBS xciii (1962).

[35] Ibid., pp. 132–3.

[36] The oddity is remarked by Turner, ibid., p. xxiv n. 5.

[37] Giso's sacramentary has not been printed integrally; but the mass-sets for English saints are ptd. Warren, *The Leofric Missal*, pp. 303–7.

would explain the presence of the two mass-sets for St Æthelwold. For the deposition of St Æthelwold Giso's sacramentary has on fo. 122^{r-v} the mass-set printed above as no. 4;[38] for the translation—which is wrongly placed before the feast of the deposition—it has on fo. 119^{v} the mass-set printed above as no. 6.[39] Giso's sacramentary, therefore, proves that St Æthelwold was being culted in at least one south-western house in the late eleventh century, and *ipso facto* that the cult was not restricted to Winchester alone.

On the other hand, Anglo-Saxon sacramentaries provide no evidence that St Æthelwold was widely culted in the eleventh century. There are no mass-sets for St Æthelwold in the following sacramentaries: the 'Leofric Missal' (Oxford, Bodleian Library, Bodley 579), a Continental manuscript (= Leofric A) which has substantial additions made at Glastonbury *c*.970 (= Leofric B) and further additions made at Exeter in the mid eleventh century (= Leofric C), but neither set contains any liturgical prayers for St Æthelwold;[40] Cambridge, Corpus Christi College 41, a copy of the Old English Bede which has copied in its margins parts of a sacramentary, including a fragmentary sanctoral, but no mass-set for St Æthelwold;[41] Cambridge, Corpus Christi College 422 (the 'Red Book of Darley'), a manuscript apparently written at Winchester in the mid eleventh century for use at Sherborne but which surprisingly omits any prayer or mass-set for St Æthelwold;[42] and Cambridge, Corpus Christi College 270, a late eleventh-century sacramentary from St Augustine's, Canterbury, which has no mass-sets for any Winchester saint.[43] To judge from the evidence of surviving Anglo-Saxon sacramentaries, therefore, it was principally at Winchester—and churches which derived liturgical materials directly from Winchester—where St Æthelwold was commemorated with proper masses. But it is always well to bear in mind the partial picture which surviving manuscript evidence may portray, in particular that there is no surviving sacramentary from Abingdon, and none certainly from Ely, Peterborough, or Thorney, from the period before 1100.

[38] Warren, *The Leofric Missal*, p. 306.

[39] Ibid.

[40] Ibid., pp. 251–69.

[41] The fragmentary *sanctorale* has only four feasts: see R. J. S. Grant, *Cambridge, Corpus Christi College 41: The Loricas and Missal* (Amsterdam, 1979), p. 30.

[42] See C. Hohler, 'The Red Book of Darley', *Nordiskt kollokvium II i latinsk liturgiforskning* (Stockholm, 1972), pp. 39–47, esp. p. 44 on the Winchester content of the book.

[43] Ed. M. Rule, *The Missal of St Augustine's Abbey, Canterbury* (Cambridge, 1896).

From the period after 1100 a greater number of missals survives, but the picture of the extent of the cult of St Æthelwold which emerges from these missals is not substantially different from that which the pre-1100 sacramentaries portrayed.[44] Once again it is principally in churches affiliated in some way with Winchester that St Æthelwold was commemorated. Thus the twelfth-century Bury Missal (Laon, Bibl. mun. 238) has the mass-set for St Æthelwold's translation printed above as no. 6, but has entered it against the feast of the deposition.[45] On the other hand, a thirteenth-century missal from Ely (Cambridge, University Library, Ii. 4. 20) has a mass-set for the deposition, but not for the translation, and the same is true of a late fourteenth-century missal from Peterborough (Oxford, Bodleian Library, Gough Lit. 17). Mass-sets for St Æthelwold occur sporadically in other late medieval missals, such as the Sherborne Missal[46] (1396 × 1407) and the Westminster Missal of Nicholas Lytlington;[47] but generally speaking it was only at houses which had some special affiliation with Æthelwold that he was commemorated with proper masses.[48]

Finally, we may turn to the two Introit tropes which are given among the Æthelwold materials in Alençon 14. These two Introit tropes are preserved in one other manuscript, namely one of the two aforementioned 'Winchester Tropers', now Cambridge, Corpus Christi College 473, fo. 43^r, where they are given, following immediately on tropes for the Assumption, with this rubric: 'Tropi in festiuitate sancti Adeluuoldi episcopi et confessoris.'[49] It will be recalled that CCCC 473 was very probably written as a precentor's book for use at the Old Minster, and may well have been Wulfstan's own personal troper. We need not doubt, therefore,

[44] The contents of sanctorals in post-Conquest missals are set out helpfully by J. W. Legg, *Missale Westmonasteriense*, 3 vols., HBS i, v, xii (1891–7), iii. 1406–1628; on mass-sets for St Æthelwold, see iii. 1575–6.

[45] See V. Leroquais, *Les Sacramentaires et les missels manuscrits des bibliothèques publiques de France*, 3 vols. (Paris, 1924), i. 219–20.

[46] In the private ownership of the Duke of Northumberland, but now on loan in the BL; see J. W. Legg, 'Liturgical notes on the Sherborne Missal, a manuscript in the possession of the Duke of Northumberland at Alnwick Castle', *Transactions of the St Paul's Ecclesiological Society*, iv (1896), 1–31.

[47] Legg, *Missale Westmonasteriense*, ii. 891–2.

[48] Note that there are no proper masses for St Æthelwold either in *The Sarum Missal*, ed. J. W. Legg (Oxford, 1916) or in the *Missale ad usum percelebris ecclesiae Herefordensis*, ed. W. G. Henderson (Leeds, 1874).

[49] Frere, *The Winchester Troper*, pp. 32–3; see Planchart, *Repertory*, ii. 99 (nos. 209–10).

that the two Introit tropes for St Æthelwold were sung at Winchester in Wulfstan's time; what is not clear is whether they were ever sung elsewhere. They are not found in the other 'Winchester Troper' (Oxford, Bodleian Library, Bodley 775).[50] Nor are they found in the only other troper surviving from Anglo-Saxon England: London, BL Cotton Caligula A. XIV, a mid-eleventh-century manuscript perhaps from Christ Church, Canterbury.[51] On the evidence of tropers, therefore, one would be obliged to conclude that it was only under Wulfstan's personal supervision that the feast of St Æthelwold was commemorated with proper tropes.

The collection of liturgical materials in Alençon 14 represents the nucleus of texts needed for the commemoration of St Æthelwold at mass and office. However, there are a few other liturgical forms not found in Alençon 14 which would find a place in the full commemoration of St Æthelwold, such as sequences for mass, lections for the night office, and pontifical benedictions. Consideration of liturgical forms such as these helpfully supplements the picture of the cult of St Æthelwold which emerges from study of the manuscript transmission of the various pieces in Alençon 14.

We may best begin with the evidence of sequences. The sequence was a particular sort of trope which was interpolated into the Alleluia of the mass. Sequences were usually collected separately from tropes (the collection of sequences was called a sequentiary), although for sake of convenience the troper was often bound up with the sequentiary. Thus both of the 'Winchester Tropers' contain sequentiaries; and these in turn contain sequences for St Æthelwold. The first of these is found uniquely in Bodley 775, a manuscript which was written at the Old Minster in the mid-eleventh century, and is as follows:[52]

[50] A curious omission, given that the sequentiary in Bodley 775 contains two sequences for St Æthelwold, whereas one of these is omitted from the sequentiary in CCCC 473. It is Planchart's view (*Repertory*, i. 31) that Bodley 775 was copied from an Old Minster exemplar dating from before 985.

[51] See Planchart, *Repertory*, i. 43–50. The only English saints with proper tropes are Ælfheah, Dunstan, and Edmund (ibid. 47).

[52] *ICL*, no. 8710; ed. *AH* xl. 181–2 (no. 205): '(1) Let also the voice celebrate God with sweet-sounding praise; (2*a*) who is wondrous in his saints, providing great miracles through their merits; (2*b*) saints who are wonderfully resplendent throughout all time, just like gleaming stars. (3*a*) Among them shines brightly a distinguished jewel of the Lord, Æthelwold, in the star-studded court; (3*b*) whom the English land honours and praises, and the beloved Church of God adores, and the heavenly citizens as well. (4*a*) As bishop he taught the English to ascend the lofty palaces of heaven through his

1. Laude celebret
uox quoque Deum
dulcisona;

2*a*. Qui in suis
mirabilis est sanctis,
eorum dans meritis
magna mirabilia;

2*b*. Qui per tota
splendificant saecula
astrea mirifice
uelut luminaria.

3*a*. Perspicua
inter quos emicat
inclita
Domini gemma
stelligera
Atheluuoldus curia;

3*b*. Quem Anglica
honorat patria,
laudat et
Dei dilecta
ecclesia
amat et plebs caelica.

4*a*. Qui praesul excelsa
docuit Anglos
caeli scandere palatia
sua per exempla lucida.

4*b*. Modo et immensa
gaudia habet,
quae semper optauit in ista
uersans mortali tristitia.

5*a*. Hinc tibi sit
Christe, gloria,
uia, lux, ueritas
paxque tuorum,
omnia per tempora,
caelica
per quem pollet
Atheluuoldus
in aula;

5*b*. Pro meritis
cuius nunc nostras
preces et munera
hac domo sacra
suscipe per saecula
praemia
et fulgida nos reuoca

ad alta,

shining example. (4*b*) Now he possesses those great joys which he always hoped to achieve while he was living in this mortal state of sadness. (5*a*) Hence, O Christ, may there be glory to you, and the way, the light, the truth, and peace to all your followers forever—you through whom Æthelwold flourishes in the heavenly citadel. (5*b*) Through whose merits please now receive our prayers and gifts in this sacred house, receive rewards for ever and call us to the gleaming heavens, (6*a*) where he shines forth, adorned with golden stole and glorious crown. (6*b*) This resplendent shepherd, distinguished lamp of the holy church, (7*a*) now gleaming among the stars above in sight of the Lord, a star golden through the distinction of all virtues, (7*b*) who wisely dispensed his holy talents and redoubled them with his learned speech, on behalf of his future palm on high. (8*a*) And because our merits cannot achieve rewards such as these, (8*b*) may your mercy alone, O Lord, assist us, we beseech you; (9*a*) may it always strengthen us; absolve our sins through all the holy prayers of St Æthelwold, and give us times of peace, (9*b*) and always grant prosperous realms and holy tabernacles in the blessed glory of the saints, where the golden father whom our (10*a*) verse now sings, a canticle resounding with beautiful harmony, (10*b*) enjoys your venerable presence without end, (11*a*) because he loved you alone as Lord above all things, (11*b*) faithfully fulfilling your heavenly commands without end. (12*a*) Through his holy assistance (12*b*) purify our hearts, (13) you who reign forever.'

6*a*. Quo stola aurea
corona et gloriosa
comptus promicat.

6*b*. Pastor hic rutilans,
lampas ecclesiae sanctae
satis inclita,

7*a*. Iam inter superna
coruscans sidera
in conspectu
Domini sidus nunc
aureum omni
uirtutum gloria,

7*b*. Sacra qui talenta
prudenter dispersit,
duplicauit
lingua doctiloqua
pro sibi palma
futura supera.

8*a*. Et quia nostra
merita non ualent
obtinere talia,

8*b*. Tua nos sola,
Domine, adiuuet,
petimus, clementia;

9*a*. Quae nos semper muniat;
et piis precibus almi
omnibus Atheluuoldi
relaxa peccamina,
nobis pacis tempora
et praesta

9*b*. Semperque prosperrima
regna concede beata
sanctorum in gloria
et sancta tabernacla;
ubi pater aureus,
quem nostra

10*a*. Cantat nunc camena
consono concentu resultans
cantica,

10*b*. Tua perfruitur
sine fine ueneranda
praesentia;

11*a*. Quia te solum
dilexit Dominum
super omnia,

11*b*. Tua iugiter
complens fideliter
iussa caelica.

12*a*. Cuius per sacra
suffragia

12*b*. Nostra emunda
praecordia,

13. Qui regnas per saecula.

The second of the sequences for St Æthelwold occurs in both 'Winchester Tropers'. In CCCC 473, however, it occurs as an addition made by a hand of the later eleventh century (fo. 157^{r}), and is as follows:[53]

[53] *ICL*, no. 3682; ed. *AH* xl. 180–1 (no. 204); see also Planchart, *Repertory*, i. 31: '(1) This sacred day, this very glorious day, (2*a*) on which the holy soul of our father St Æthelwold, (2*b*) having shed the soil of the body, sought the joyous heavens. (3*a*) For this boy born to a noble and orthodox stock (3*b*) gave many signs of future sanctity even from his holy infancy. (4*a*) Called to God's service, he excelled everyone through the merit and distinction of his character. (4*b*) He was kindly, with mental honesty, taming the flesh with vigils and much fasting; (5*a*) he abounded with the grace of charity and the sweetness of mercy more than all other men; (5*b*) filled with wisdom he enjoyed the divine gift of prudent discretion. (6*a*) Trained in monastic discipline, educated in holy ways, he practised heavenly exercise. (6*b*) Outstanding in obedience, because of the clear distinction of his life he deserved to become father and abbot of

1. Dies sacra, dies ista,
dies ualde gloriosa,

2*a*. Qua beati patris sancta
Ætheluuoldi anima

2*b*. Exuta corporis gleba,
laeta petit aethera.

3*a*. Hic itaque ex prosapia
puer editus orthodoxa
et ingenua,

3*b*. Ab ipsa sacra infantia
multa futurae sanctitatis
dat insignia.

4*a*. Ad Dei promptus obsequia,
uniuersos morum praecellit
merito et gratia,

4*b*. Benignus ac mente sincera,
uigiliis carnem edomans
et multa inedia.

5*a*. Caritatis gratia
ac pietatis dulcedine
prae omnibus adfluebat,

5*b*. Plenus sapientia
discretionis fruebatur
diuinitus prudentia.

6*a*. Monachorum disciplina
eruditus, sanctimonia
informatus, caelestia
meditatur exercitia.

6*b*. Summus oboedientia,
propter clara uitae merita
monachorum promeruit
fieri pater atque abba.

7*a*. Arbor fecunda
tanta uirtutum
floruit gratia

7*b*. Vrbe Wentana
ut praesulari
functus sit infula.

8*a*. Clericos, quorum peruersa
erat uita,
pellit ab ecclesia;

8*b*. Monachos, quorum sanctitas
magna erat,
seruituros adgregat.

9*a*. Fide fortis hausta
ueneni pocula superat.

9*b*. Et de templi alta
ruentem monachum liberat.

10*a*. Multa struit coenobia,
thesauros euacuat,
de famis angustia
egenorum
eripit millia;

10*b*. Furem solo uerbo ligat,
confitentem absoluit,
semiplenum olei
uas perditum
reddit et accumulat.

monks. (7*a*) A fruit-bearing tree, he flourished with such grace of virtue (7*b*) that he was installed in episcopal office in Winchester. (8*a*) He expelled from the church those clerics whose life was sinful; (8*b*) he assembled there obedient monks, whose sanctity was great. (9*a*) Strong in his faith, he overcame the effects of a draught of poison. (9*b*) And he freed from injury a monk who fell from the top of the church. (10*a*) He built many monasteries; he emptied out his treasures; he freed thousands of needy folk from the straits of hunger. (10*b*) He bound a thief by his word alone and released him when he confessed; he restored a lost flask half-full of oil and increased its contents. (11*a*) Bright jewel among confessors, devoutly obtain forgiveness for us, (11*b*) so that we may be found worthy to reign with you in that eternal land, (12) in which blessedly you perform your holy office for ever and ever.'

11*a*. Clara confessorum gemma,
ueniam
pie nobis impetra,

11*b*. Vt nos tecum in sempiterna
regnare
mereamur patria,

12. In qua felix sollemnizas
per aeterna saecula.

There is no way of knowing when precisely these sequences were composed (the mid-eleventh-century date of Bodley 775 provides the outer dating-limit), nor how they were used. It is possible that one was intended for the deposition, the other for the translation, but they bear no rubrics to that effect. The second sequence is evidently based on Wulfstan's *Vita S. Æthelwoldi* (thus stanza 9a is from Wulfstan's c. 19, 9b from c. 34, 10a from c. 29, and 10b from cc. 33 and 32), but this is no indication of its date. These two sequences, therefore, show that the cult of St Æthelwold was fully elaborated at the Old Minster, but there is no evidence for thinking that it was elaborated on a similar scale elsewhere.

Let us turn to the evidence of lections for the night office. We have seen that Alençon 14 contained all the liturgical materials needed for commemorating St Æthelwold in the office, with one exception, namely the lections to be read at the night office at the three nocturns of matins; and we surmised that this need could have been filled by using a manuscript copy of Wulfstan's *Vita S. Æthelwoldi* suitably annotated. Such annotation would be needed to indicate the beginning and end of each of the nine (or twelve) lections, for otherwise, in the case of a relatively long saint's *uita* such as Wulfstan's, the lector would not know where to begin and where to stop. It was normal at this period to mark up saints' *uitae* with a roman numeral in the margin to denote the beginning of each lection, and *tu autem* (for *Tu autem*, *Domine*, *miserere nobis*, the words said by the lector to signal the end of each lection, to which the congregation replies *Deo gratias*) at the end. Thus an early copy of Lantfred's *Translatio et miracula S. Swithuni*—a work in many ways unsuitable for reading at office—is marked in this way for eight lections (London, BL Royal 15. C. vii (Old Minster, s. x/xi), fos. 1–7). In view of this practice, it is rather surprising that none of the manuscripts of Wulfstan's *Vita S. Æthelwoldi* has been so marked, for the work must almost certainly have been used in this way. This rather unsatisfactory situation regarding office lections—which in the early Middle Ages were apparently supplied *ad hoc* from available saints' *uitae*—was rectified in the later Middle Ages, from the thirteenth century onwards, by the compilation of lections of a standard length and content, which were then incorporated into breviaries. Normally earlier saints' *uitae* were laid under contribution for these breviary lections.

It is not surprising, therefore, that Wulfstan's *Vita S. Æthelwoldi* should have been drawn on by compilers of breviary lections. Two examples will illustrate the process of compilation. The first is the thirteenth-century Ely breviary (Cambridge, UL Ii. 4. 20), which contains two sets of lections.[54] The dates of the feasts in question are not specified, but it would seem that the first set was intended for the deposition on 1 August, and the second probably for the translation on 10 September. The first set is drawn principally from the early chapters of Wulfstan's work (cc. 1, 6–7, 9–11, 16) but concludes with the account of Æthelwold's death in c. 41; it is preceded and followed by a collect, and is as follows:

LECTIO .i. Preclarus et Deo dignus Etheluuoldus ex ingenua Christianorum propagine oriundus in ipsa mox puericia sacris litterarum studiis est traditus. Qui agilis natura, acutus ingenio, studebat teneros puericie annos morum honestate et uirtutum maturitate uincere et ad Dei implendam uoluntatem totam mentis sue intencionem dirigere. [cc. 1, 6.]

LECTIO .ii. Cumque florentis adolescencie contigisset etatem iubente Ethelstano rege, ab Elfego Wintoniensi episcopo prius ad clericatus officium tonsoratus, deinde in gradum sacerdotalem consecratus est. [c. 7.]

LECTIO .iii. Etheluuoldus igitur Christi famulus apud predictum presulem Elfegum quo melius imbueretur aliquandiu commoratus est, ac postmodum Glestoniam perueniens a magnifico uiro Dunstano eiusdem monasterii abbate monastici ordinis habitum suscepit. [c. 9.]

LECTIO .iiii. Qui cum pro merito sanctitatis ab omnibus amaretur et monasterii decanus ab abbate suo constitueretur, nullum elacionis incurrit periculum sed tante subiectis prebuit humilitatis exemplum ut cotidiano manuum opere ortum excoleret et fratribus ad prandium poma ac diuersi generis legumina prepararet. [c. 9.]

LECTIO .v. Contigit itaque regem Ethelstanum obisse et fratrem eius Edmundum regni gubernacula suscepisse. Cui post modicum temporis crudeliter interempto, successit in regnum frater eius Edredus. [c. 10.]

[54] The manuscript consists of a missal (fos. 1–207) bound up with a breviary (fos. 208–318); it is unprinted. The lections are on fos. 252^{v}–253^{r}, and are preceded by the collect 'Deus qui beatum Æthelwoldum' and followed by that beginning 'Deus qui hodiernam diem' (see above, pp. cxvii, cxv).

LECTIO .vi. Placuit ergo regi Edredo dare sancto Ethylwoldo quendam locum Abbanduna uocabulo in quo modicum antiquitus habebatur monasterium, sed erat tunc neglectum ac destitutum, quatinus in eo monachos Deo seruituros ordinaret. [c. 11.]

LECTIO. vii. Congregauit igitur uir Dei in eodem loco in breui gregem monachorum quibus ipse abbas ordinatus est. Deinde ab Edgaro Anglorum basileo ad episcopatum Wintoniensis ecclesie electus a beato Dunstano Dorobernensis sedis antistites consecratur. Qui clericorum irreligiosam uitam non ferens, eos de Veteri Monasterio expulit et adducens de Abbanduna monachos illic regia auctoritate locauit. [cc. 11, 16.]

LECTIO .viii. Eo tempore quo sanctus Etheluuoldus de hac uita erat exiturus uenit ad quandam uillam sexaginta milibus ab urbe Wintonia distantem. Ibi ergo cum aliquandiu moraretur, acri cepit infirmitate grauari et sacrati olei liquore perunctus diuina corporis et sanguinis perceptione exitum suum muniuit, sicque ualefaciens et dans pacem filiis suis inter uerba oracionis spiritum celo reddidit. [c. 41.]

The rather eccentric nature of the compiler's choice is clear: the first seven lections concentrate on Æthelwold's youth and abbacy at Abingdon, but omit any mention of his activities as bishop of Winchester. Nor do they contain any example of his miraculous power, and one can only wonder whether a thirteenth-century monastic congregation at Ely found any spiritual edification in the Anglo-Saxon history-lesson contained in lection v.

The second set, which in fact is made up of two groups of three lections each, focuses on Æthelwold's refoundation of the East Anglian monasteries (Wulfstan, cc. 23–4), beginning with Ely, where the breviary was compiled, and continues with the miracle of Godus, who fell from the scaffolding during building-works at the Old Minster (c. 34).[55]

LECTIO .i. Est quedam regio famosa Ely uocitata in prouincia Orientalium Anglorum sita. In qua regione locus omni ueneracione dignus habetur magnificatus nimium reliquiis et miraculis sancte Etheldrede, regine et perpetue uirginis, ac sororum eius; sed in ipso tempore erat destitutus et regali fisco deditus. [c. 23.]

LECTIO .ii. Hunc ergo locum famulus Christi Etheluuoldus dato precio emit a rege Edgaro, constituens in eo gregem monachorum non minimum et eiusdem loci situm monasterialibus edificiis decentissime renouauit eumque terrarum possessionibus affluentissime locupletatum et eterne

[55] fos. 254^{v}–255^{r}; no collects are included. The rubric ('in .iiii. N. agatur de S. Ethelwoldo') points to commemoration on 2 Aug. (see below, p. cxli).

libertatis priuilegio confirmatum omnipotenti Domino commendauit. [c. 23.]

LECTIO .iii. Alterum quoque locum in regione Giruorum beatus Etheluuoldus precio obtinuit a rege et nobilibus terre, positum in loco supra ripam fluminis Nen qui consuete Burch apellatur. Cuius loci basilicam congruis domorum structuris ornatam et terris adiacentibus copiose ditatam in honorem beati Petri consecrauit ibique cateruam monachorum coadunauit. [c. 24.]

The second group concerns the monk Godus:

LECTIO .i. Cum uir Dei Etheluuoldus Veterem renouare decreuisset Ecclesiam, iussit fratres laboribus una cum operariis insistere. Contigit autem quodam die dum fratres starent ad summum culmen templi cum cementariis, ut unus illorum Godus nomine caderet a summis usque ad terram. [c. 34.]

LECTIO .ii. Qui mox ut terram attigit incolumis surgens stetit nil mali passus de tanta ruina, seque crucis signaculo benedixit, admirans quid illic ageret aut quomodo illuc ueniret; et cunctis qui aderant uidentibus, ascendit ad locum ubi antea steterat et accipiens trullam operi quod inchoabat diligentius insistebat. [c. 34.]

LECTIO .iii. Cui ergo hoc miraculum asscribendum est ni illi cuius iussu ad opus obediencie exiuit? Qui iccirco ledi non potuit quia hunc in casu suo uiri Dei meritum portauit et a periculo ruine incolumem protexit. [c. 34.]

Given that the breviary was compiled for use at Ely, the choice of the first group seems entirely reasonable. On the other hand, it is not clear what interest or relevance the miracle concerning the unfortunate Godus could have had to a thirteenth-century Ely congregation. In sum, the choice of lections made by the Ely compiler leaves much to be desired.

A more rational choice of lections was made somewhat later, and independently, by the compiler of the breviary of Hyde Abbey (formerly the New Minster), Winchester, which is preserved in two manuscripts (both dated *c.*1300) now in the Bodleian Library: Rawlinson, Liturg. e. 1* and Gough Liturg. 8.[56] There are two sets of lections in the Hyde breviary, one for the deposition, the other for the translation. The compiler thoughtfully chose his readings

[56] Ed. J. B. L. Tolhurst, *The Monastic Breviary of Hyde Abbey Winchester*, 6 vols., HBS lxix–lxxi, lxxvi, lxxviii, lxxx (1932–42).

for the deposition from cc. 1–41 of Wulfstan's *uita* so that they would pertain to Æthelwold's life and death; they are as follows:[57]

LECTIO .i. Erant parentes sancti pontificis Athelwoldi ex ingenua Christianorum propagine oriundi, Wentane ciuitatis urbani temporibus senioris Edwardi regis Anglorum, florentes in mandatis et iustificationibus Domini, sine querela fideliter incedentes. [c. 1.]

LECTIO .ii. Qui dum cotidianis bonorum operum pollerent incrementis, eximio Dei munere decorati sunt, quo talem mererentur gignere, cuius eruditione et exemplis non solum populi presentis eui, set eciam futuri peruenirent ad noticiam ueri luminis, ut exusti caligine tenebrosi erroris gloria fruerentur eterna claritatis. [c. 1.]

LECTIO .iii. Natus igitur puer Athelwoldus, in ipsa mox puericia sacris litterarum studiis est traditus, ut cui aliis uiam salutis erat ostensurus, ipse prius cum Maria secus pedes Domini sederet et uerbum ex ore illius salubriter audiret. [c. 6.]

LECTIO .iiii. Erat enim agilis natura et subtilis ingenio, ita ut quicquid maiorum tradicione didicerat, non segniter obliuioni traderet, set tenaci potius memorie commendaret. Studebat eciam lubricos puericie annos morum honestate et uirtutum maturitate uincere, diuinis semper obsequiis omnia membra sua mancipare, et ad implendam Dei uoluntatem totam mentis sue intencionem dirigere conabatur. [c. 6.]

LECTIO .v. Cumque beatus Æthelwoldus pro merito sanctitatis sue ab omnibus amaretur et monasterii decanus ab abbate suo constitueretur, et nullum elationis incurrit periculum, set tante subiectis prebuit humilitatis exemplum, ut cotidiano manuum opere ortum excolendo laboraret et fratribus ad prandium poma ac diuersi generis legumina prepararet. [c. 9.]

LECTIO .vi. Et post spiritualem animarum refectionem corporum quoque necessaria ministraret, in corde semper retinens illud dominicum preceptum: Quicumque uoluerit inter uos maior fieri, sit uester minister; et qui uoluerit inter uos primus essse, erit uester seruus. [c. 9.]

LECTIO .vii. Rex igitur Eadmundus qui fratri suo Athelstano successit in regnum magnam circa Dei famulum cepit habere dilectionem, ita ut eius uoluntati abbate Dunstano consentiente monasterii quod Abendonia dicitur abbas preficeretur. [cc. 10–11.]

LECTIO .viii. Circa hec tempora eligitur abbas Dunstanus in episcopum Wigorniensis ecclesie, et post aliquot annorum curricula factus est archiepiscopus Dorobernie, doctrina et actione precipuus. [c. 14.]

[57] Ed. Tolhurst, *The Monastic Breviary of Hyde Abbey Winchester*, iv. 309^{r-v}; preceded by the collect 'Deus qui hodiernam diem'.

LECTIO .ix. Cuius consilio Edgarus rex Anglorum felicissimus beatum Athelwoldum ecclesie Wintoniensi prefecit episcopum, quem iubente rege idem archiepiscopus sollempniter consecrauit. [c. 16.]

LECTIO .x. Erat autem uir Dei Athelwoldus a secretis Edgari incliti regis Anglorum, sermone et opere magnifice pollens, in plerisque locis ecclesias construens et ubique Christi euangelium annuncians. [c. 25.]

LECTIO .xi. Pater erat uir sanctus et pastor monachorum, peruigil sanctimonialium protector et uirginum, uiduarum consolator, peregrinorum susceptor, ecclesiarum defensor, errantium corrector, pauperum recreator, pupillorum et orphanorum adiutor, qui plus impleuit opere quam lingua nostra sermone possit euoluere. [c. 28.]

LECTIO .xii. Cum igitur tot uirtutum redoleret aromatibus, tempore quo de hac mortali uita erat exiturus et laborum premia a Deo percepturus, acri cepit infirmitate grauari et sacrati olei liquore perunctus dominici corporis et sanguinis perceptione exitum suum muniuit, et sic ualefaciens et dans pacem filiis suis inter uerba orationis spiritum celo reddidit. [c. 41.]

As will be seen, the compiler chose his readings carefully, so that the first four pertain to Æthelwold's family origins and childhood, the next few to his novitiate and abbacy at Abingdon, while the remaining ones contain general statements on his episcopate at Winchester and his death. The lections for the translation in the Hyde breviary are drawn entirely from cc. 42–3 of Wulfstan's *uita*, and appropriately pertain to the miraculous appearances of Æthelwold in dreams which led to the translation of his body.[58]

LECTIO .i. Anno duodecimo post obitum gloriosi pontificis Athelwoldi, placuit superne dispensationi illum per celestia signa reuelari, eiusque ossa de sepulchro leuari, ut lucerna que ad tempus sub modio latebat, super candelabrum poneretur quatinus luceret omnibus qui in domo Dei sunt. [c. 42.]

LECTIO .ii. Est enim ciuitas modica que Walinkeforda nominatur, in qua uir quidam morabatur cui nomen erat Alfelmus, qui casu lumen oculorum amittens, cecitatem multis perpessus est annis. [c. 42.]

LECTIO .iii. Apparuit igitur predicto in sompnis sanctus antistes Athelwoldus, eumque ut maturius Wintoniam pergeret et ad eius tumbam gracia recuperandi uisus accederet, admonuit dicens: Idcirco te uisito, et que uentura sunt tibi prenuncio, ut per tue salutis signum manifestetur, quia me oportet leuari de tumulo in quo iaceo. [c. 42.]

[58] Ibid. 341^{v}–342^{r}; preceded by the collect 'Deus qui nobis sanctum pontificem tuum Athelwoldum'.

LECTIO .iiii. Predictus uir uocem secum loquentis agnoscens, sancto patri gracias egit quod eum uisitare dignaretur, et quia ubi sepultus esset penitus ignorauit, qualiter sepulchrum eius scire et adire potuisset diligenter inquisiuit. [c. 42.]

LECTIO .v. Cui uir Dei nomen alumpni et monachi sui innotuit, cuius hactenus homo ille nescius extitit, dixitque ei: Cum Wintoniam perueneris et Veteris Cenobii ecclesiam ingressus fueris, accersiri fac ad te monachum quemdam Wlstanum cognomento Cantorem. Hic cum mee legationis audierit uerba, te mox ad meum perducet tumulum ibique recipies lumen oculorum tuorum. [c. 42.]

LECTIO .vi. Credulus uir prefatus uerbis et promissionibus sacris pontificis, Wyntoniam adiit, ecclesiam intrauit, predictum accersiuit, accersitumque postulauit ut missatica beati patris impleret, narrans eidem et cunctis astantibus ordinem uisionis. [c. 42.]

LECTIO .vii. Ille uero frater admirans, inter spem et timorem se medium posuit et uicino obediencie pede iussis sancti pontificis humiliter obtemperans, ad antrum sarcofagi cecum perduxit. Qui pernox ibidem in oratione permansit, et mane facto iam amplius ductore non indigens ad propria cum gaudio reuersus est uidens, corde et animo benedicens Dominum. [c. 42.]

LECTIO .viii. Hec reuelatio longe lateque diuulgata est, que tam euidenti miraculo fuerat comprobata. Exinde famulus Christi predicto fratri Wlstano et plerisque aliis per nocturnam uisionem manifestus apparuit, illisque per hec et hec indicia manifestius aperuit, quia superne complaceret uoluntati eum de tumulo transferri et digne in ecclesia collocari. [c. 43.]

Taken together, the breviaries of Ely and Hyde give a clear notion of how Wulfstan's *Vita S. Æthelwoldi* could be used as a source of lections for the night office. None of the sets of lections is entirely satisfactory, and part of the fault is Wulfstan's *uita* itself: that is to say, it is a work which does not easily lend itself to excerpting and anthologizing. So awkwardly does it yield up short lections that one must ask if Wulfstan had the needs of the night office uppermost in his mind as he was writing it. In any case it is fitting in some sense that the last four lections for the translation in the Hyde breviary should be entirely concerned with the role of Wulfstan in Æthelwold's translation, for it was he who supplied the material for the lections themselves.

As in the case of the other liturgical forms we have considered, so in the case of breviaries there is reason to think that it was only at Winchester, and in churches once affiliated to Winchester, that St Æthelwold was culted. This impression is confirmed by the negative evidence of breviaries of other late medieval English uses: no lections for St Æthelwold are found in the breviaries of Sarum,[59] York,[60] Hereford,[61] or Exeter.[62] The map might perhaps be drawn in greater detail if, for example, we had surviving breviaries from centres such as Abingdon;[63] but in broad outline the evidence of breviaries confirms that of the other liturgical forms examined above.

One type of service book which has not yet been considered, and which might be thought to yield information on the extent of the cult of St Æthelwold, is the benedictional. We have seen that when mass was celebrated by a bishop, a tripartite benediction proper to the feast in question was pronounced by the bishop after the *Pater noster*. A number of eleventh-century English benedictionals survive,[64] but surprisingly few of these contain benedictions for St Æthelwold. More surprising, especially in view of the evidence considered above, is the fact that it is only in benedictionals from Canterbury that St Æthelwold is commemorated. In one such benedictional, now London, BL Harley 2892 (Christ Church, Canterbury, s. xi^{1}),[65] Æthelwold's name has simply been interpolated into an existing benediction for 1 August. This day was the feast of St Peter in Chains and of the Maccabees; and the simplest way of commemorating St Æthelwold was merely to add his name

[59] Ed. F. Procter and C. Wordsworth, *Breviarium in usum insignis ecclesiae Sarum*, 3 vols. (Cambridge, 1879–86). But note that the use of Sarum is *not* monastic.

[60] Ed. S. W. Lawley, *Breviarium ad usum insignis ecclesie Eboracensis*, 2 vols., Surtees Society, lxxi, lxxv (London, 1880–3).

[61] *The Hereford Breviary*, ed. W. H. Frere and L. E. G. Brown, 3 vols., HBS xxvi, xl, xlvi (1904–11).

[62] H. E. Reynolds, *Legenda Sanctorum: The Proper Lessons for Saints' Days according to the Use of Exeter* (London, 1880).

[63] Although no manuscript breviary from Abingdon survives, there is an early printed breviary, *Portiforium ad usum nigrorum monachorum Abendoniae in monasterio Abendonensi per Iohannem Scolarem* (1528). This book is scarce, and we have consulted the copy in Cambridge, Emmanuel College, S. 1. 4. 6. Æthelwold is commemorated in the litany (fo. 145^{v}) with a repetition; the book also includes a series of eight lections (fo. 274^{r}–275^{r}) for St Æthelwold, of which the first seven are drawn almost verbatim from Wulfstan's *Vita S. Æthelwoldi*, as follows: *lectio* i (c. 1), ii (c. 4), iii (c. 5), iv (c. 5), v (c. 7), vi (c. 9), and vii (c. 11). It will be seen that these lections from the Abingdon breviary concern the early part of Æthelwold's life, up to and including his abbacy of Abingdon.

[64] Gneuss, 'Liturgical books', pp. 133–4.

[65] Ed. R. M. Woolley, *The Canterbury Benedictional*, HBS li (1917).

to those of the other saints being commemorated, and this is what has happened in Harley 2892:[66]

a. Exaudi preces supplicum tuorum omnipotens rerum conditor . qui es gloria sanctorum . remuneratio fidelium . purificatio gentium . recuperatio confitentium. Amen.

b. Sic huic familie ad hodiernam beati apostoli tui Petri ac sancti antistitis Aþeluuoldi atque sanctorum Machabeorum confluenti sollempnitatem des dona salutis adquirere . ut tue maiestati mereatur uota offerre et te placabilem sibi cum exultantibus animis obtinere. Amen.

c. Et intercessione sancti Petri apostolorum principis et almi presulis Aþeluuoldi atque Machabeorum martyrum . quorum hodierna die celebramus triumphum . illuc tibi deuoti occurramus per ueniam . quo idem celestis clauiger per crucis suspendia ac beatus pontifex Aþeluuoldus per gloriosam confessionem . ac sancti martyres meruerunt ascendere per tormenta. Amen.

Quod ipse prestare dignetur.

Such a joint commemoration must have seemed cumbersome especially where it was felt that St Æthelwold merited individual attention. Accordingly, at some point early in the eleventh century a tripartite benediction solely in Æthelwold's name was composed. There is only one surviving manuscript which preserves this benediction: Paris, BN lat. 987, a manuscript written at Winchester by the scribe Godemann, probably during Æthelwold's lifetime (see above, p. lxxxiii), but which had been taken to Christ Church, Canterbury, by the early eleventh century, where a number of supplementary benedictions were added, among them the following benedictions for St Æthelwold (the benedictions are intended for the feast of the translation on 10 September):[67]

[66] Ed. Woolley, *The Canterbury Benedictional*, p. 103; listed *CPB*, no. 1347: 'a. Hear the prayers of your suppliants, omnipotent creator of the world, who are the glory of your saints, the recompense of the faithful, the purification of the peoples and the restoration of those who confess. Amen.

b. 'Grant that this *familia* may attain the gifts of salvation, flocking to you in today's solemn feast of your apostle St Peter and the holy bishop Æthelwold and the holy Maccabees, so that it may deserve to offer prayers to your majesty and with rejoicing spirits to find you responsive to its needs.

c. 'And through the intercession of St Peter, prince of the apostles, and the holy bishop Æthelwold and the martyred Maccabees, whose triumph we are celebrating today, let us by your forgiveness devoutly come to meet you in the place to which this same heavenly key-bearer through the torture of the cross, and the blessed bishop Æthelwold through his glorious confession, and the holy martyrs through their sufferings were found worthy to ascend. Amen.'

[67] F. 100^{v} (unptd.); listed *CPB*, no. 1218 (note that these benedictions have been adapted from a set intended for St Dunstan):

a. Deus sacerdotum gloria et confessorum corona . uos interuentu sancti patris uestri Ætheluuoldi episcopi . cuius uos uoluit translationis sollemnitatem celebrare . ab omni malo dignetur liberare et uirtutum ornamentis decorare. Amen.

b. Praestetque misericors . ut qui uobis doctor honestus fulsit in terris . pro uobis etiam interuentor assiduus sit in caelis . et quae eius exemplo didicistis et praedicatione . uos faciat implere digna conuersatione. Amen.

c. Et dum communis resurrectio uenerit, hic patronus uester cum ceteris sanctis doctoribus uestris . uos non ad iudicium sed ad misericordiam Dei perducat . et tremendo examine peracto . illorum comitante suffragio . oues suas pastor bonus ad caelestia pascua introducat. Amen.

Quod ipse prestare dignetur.

We have seen that other types of liturgical book from Canterbury contain no commemoration of Æthelwold. The occurrence of pontifical benedictions in two early eleventh-century benedictionals is therefore striking, and the most reasonable explanation is that they owe their presence there to Ælfheah, who was Æthelwold's successor as bishop of Winchester (984–1005), but was subsequently elevated to the archbishopric (1005–12). As archbishop of Canterbury, Ælfheah was head of the Christ Church *familia*, and it is plausible that liturgical books written for his use would reflect his devotion to his illustrious predecessor at Winchester. To this limited extent, therefore, the cult of Æthelwold was observed at Canterbury; but the fact that no other Canterbury service-books contain any commemoration of Æthelwold of any sort suggests strongly that the pontifical benedictions for Æthelwold reflect the personal devotion of Ælfheah, and did not long outlive him.

The evidence of the liturgical forms themselves needs to be correlated with that of calendars: it was the record of a saint's day

'a. May God, the glory of priests and the crown of confessors, through the intercession of your holy father Bishop Æthelwold, the feast of whose translation he wished you to celebrate, deign to release you from all evil and to adorn you with the ornaments of virtue. Amen.

'b. And may he mercifully arrange it that he who shone on earth as your virtuous teacher may also be your attentive intercessor in heaven, and may he make you achieve through worthy behaviour the things which you learned from his example and preaching. Amen.

'c. And when the universal resurrection shall come, may this your patron saint, together with all your other holy teachers, lead you not to judgement but to God's mercy, and when the terrifying doom is past, may that good shepherd lead his sheep to the heavenly pastures by the help of those saints. Amen.'

in a liturgical calendar which reminded the ecclesiastic in charge of a particular church's liturgy that such-and-such a saint was to be commemorated on such-and-such a day. If the evidence surveyed earlier indicates that the church in question possessed service books containing prayers for St Æthelwold, then we may be doubly sure that he was commemorated there; but if his feasts are recorded in the calendar of a particular church and there is no corroborating evidence of prayers in service-books, it may simply be that he was commemorated by means of one of the generalized mass-sets *in natale unius confessoris* or the like. As we might expect, the feasts of both the deposition and translation of St Æthelwold are recorded in pre-Conquest calendars from Winchester (five such calendars survive);[68] and we have seen evidence that service-books containing prayers for St Æthelwold survive from the early eleventh century onwards. The two feasts are also recorded in the calendars in Cambridge, Corpus Christi College 422 (written at Winchester for Sherborne, s. xi^{med}), Oxford, Bodleian Library, Douce 296 (Crowland, s. xi^{med}), and Vatican City, Biblioteca Apostolica Vaticana 12 (written at Canterbury (?) for Bury St Edmunds, s. xi^{1}).[69] In each of these three cases Winchester influence may either be seen or suspected; but in the absence of surviving pre-Conquest service books from these churches containing prayers for the saint, there can be no certainty that he was fully commemorated. A similar conclusion may be drawn from the pre-Conquest calendars from churches elsewhere in England, for these show less concern to commemorate St Æthelwold fully: thus a calendar from Worcester has the deposition only,[70] whereas two West Country calendars have the feast of the translation only.[71] The evidence of pre-Conquest calendars is only partial, however, inasmuch as there are no surviving calendars from Abingdon or—

[68] F. Wormald, *English Kalendars before AD 1100*, HBS lxxii (1934), nos. 9 (London, BL Cotton Titus D. XXVII: New Minster, Winchester, s. xi^{1}), 10 (Cambridge, Trinity College, R. 15. 32: New Minster, Winchester, s. xi^{in}), 11 (London, BL Arundel 60: New Minster, Winchester, s. xi^{2}), 12 (BL Cotton Vitellius E. XVIII: New Minster, Winchester, s. xi^{med}); the commemoration is also found in the calendar in the *Missal of Robert of Jumièges*, ed. Wilson, p. 16.

[69] Wormald, op. cit., nos. 14, 20, and 19 respectively.

[70] Oxford, Bodleian Library, Hatton 113 (Worcester, s. xi^{2}): Wormald, op. cit., no. 16. The omission of the translation is not surprising, since the feast of Æthelwold's translation—10 Sept.—happens also to be that of St Ecgwine, a bishop and patron saint of Worcester.

[71] Wormald, op. cit., nos. 6 (Cambridge, UL Kk. 5. 32) and 7 (London, BL Cotton Vitellius A. XII).

excepting those from Crowland and Bury St Edmunds already mentioned—from any of the fenland monasteries such as Ely, Thorney, and Peterborough.

A broadly similar pattern is found in post-Conquest calendars,[72] although it is noticeable that certain changes were made in the dates on which St Æthelwold was commemorated. We have seen that 1 August, the day of Æthelwold's deposition, was also the feast of St Peter in Chains and of the Maccabees; in order to relieve this crowding, the feast of St Æthelwold's deposition was postponed in certain churches to 2 August. Another development was that, in churches which had a historical link with Æthelwold, more feasts in his name were added to the calendar. Thus at Abingdon, his deposition was celebrated on the traditional date of 1 August, an additional feast was added on the following day (*in crastino S. Adelwoldi*) and the octave was celebrated on 8 August; the traditional feast of the translation on 10 September, however, is not recorded in the Abingdon calendar.[73] At Ely St Æthelwold was commemorated on 2 August and again on 8 October.[74] At Deeping in Lincolnshire (a cell of Thorney founded in 1139 whose calendar almost certainly reflects that of Thorney) the deposition was celebrated on 2 August, and an *exceptio S. Adelwoldi* was celebrated on 23 October, but, once again, the feast of the translation on 10 September is not recorded.[75] A few churches continued to commemorate St Æthelwold on 2 August and 10 September, such as Abbotsbury and Chertsey. But in a great many of the principal English churches, he was not commemorated at all. The calendars from the following churches contain no notice of Æthelwold whatsoever:[76] St Albans (surprisingly, perhaps, in view of Æthelwold's alleged role in refounding that house),[77] St Augustine's and Christ Church, Canterbury, Chester, Crowland, Dunster (Somerset), Durham, Gloucester, Muchelney, Ramsey, St Neots, Salisbury, and Westminster.

[72] F. Wormald, *English Benedictine Kalendars after AD 1100*, 2 vols., HBS lxxvii, lxxxi (1939–46). These two volumes include calendars arranged alphabetically from Abbotsbury to St Neots; the third volume was never printed but is in preparation by Nigel Morgan.

[73] Ibid., no. 2. [74] Ibid., no. 12. [75] Ibid., no. 9.

[76] All these calendars are ptd. ibid., excepting Ramsey, for which we have consulted the unptd. calendar in London, BL Cotton Galba E. x, and Salisbury, for which we consulted Legg, *The Sarum Missal*.

[77] See above, p. l n. 46.

Another liturgical form which may help to illuminate the way in which Æthelwold was commemorated is the litany of saints.[78] Litanies were used in both public and private devotions; but it is clear that the mention of one saint's name—usually among dozens of others—need not (indeed cannot) imply commemoration in any other form. Nevertheless, it is surprising how few pre-Conquest litanies contain petitions to St Æthelwold: he is petitioned in four litanies from Winchester (as we should expect), in one each from Worcester, Crowland and Bury St Edmunds, and—oddly, perhaps, in view of other sorts of liturgical evidence—in three litanies from Exeter.[79] These ten litanies account for fewer than one-fifth of the surviving Anglo-Saxon litanies. Whether the same situation obtains with respect to post-Conquest litanies is impossible to say in the present state of knowledge.

Two final kinds of evidence require mention. The first is that of relics.[80] If a saint was being actively culted at a particular church it would be normal for that church to try to obtain relics of the saint: in the case of St Æthelwold, from the Old Minster in Winchester. On the other hand, the possession of a saint's relics by a church might well imply that that saint was specifically culted there, even in the absence of other sorts of liturgical evidence. It is interesting to note, therefore, that the following churches claimed to possess relics of St Æthelwold: Abingdon,[81] Bath,[82] Glastonbury,[83] Peterborough,[84] Shrewsbury,[85] Salisbury,[86] Thorney,[87] and Westminster.[88] Note once again that several of these churches (Abingdon, Glastonbury, Peterborough, and

[78] For the pre-Conquest period, see M. Lapidge, 'Litanies of the saints in Anglo-Saxon manuscripts: a preliminary list', *Scriptorium*, xl (1986), 264–77.

[79] Ibid., nos. 6, 8, 9, 12, 16, 22, 23, 32, 45, 46.

[80] The indispensable (but unfortunately unprinted) source for the study of English relic-lists is I. G. Thomas, 'The cult of saints' relics in medieval England' (Ph.D. thesis, London, 1974).

[81] *Chron. Abingdon*, ii. 155–8.

[82] *Two Cartularies of the Priory of S. Peter at Bath*, ed. W. Hunt, Somerset Record Society, vii (1893), pp. lxxv–lxxvi.

[83] *The Chronicle of Glastonbury Abbey*, ed. J. P. Carley (Woodbridge, 1985), p. 26.

[84] *The Chronicle of Hugh Candidus*, ed. W. T. Mellows (Oxford, 1949), pp. 54–6.

[85] H. Owen and J. B. Blakeway, *A History of Shrewsbury*, 2 vols. (London, 1825), ii. 42–3, at 43.

[86] C. Wordsworth, *Ceremonies and Processions of the Cathedral Church of Salisbury* (Cambridge, 1901), pp. 33–40, at 37; note that Salisbury was not monastic.

[87] Wormald, *English Benedictine Kalendars after AD 1100*, i. 129–30.

[88] *History of Westminster Abbey by John Flete*, ed. J. A. Robinson (Cambridge, 1909), pp. 68–73, at 72.

Thorney) could claim a personal link with the saint during his lifetime. Finally, the evidence of church dedications, especially of parish churches, provides a sound index to the popularity of a saint's cult. In the case of St Æthelwold that evidence is entirely negative. Only one pre-Reformation church appears to have been dedicated in his name:[89] Alvingham in Lincolnshire.[90] We know from the Abingdon Chronicle that a chapel built at Abingdon in the time of Abbot Ingulf (1130–59) was dedicated to St Æthelwold,[91] but this dedication did not survive to modern times.

The sum of liturgical evidence indicates that the cult of St Æthelwold was initiated at the Old Minster at the time of his translation in 996, that it spread in Anglo-Saxon times to the other Winchester houses and to churches which had had some personal link with the saint, such as Abingdon and the fenland monasteries of Ely, Thorney, and Peterborough, but that he was only culted rarely and sporadically outside these churches, and certainly not outside England. This is to say that, in spite of the energetic efforts by Æthelwold's own followers—Wulfstan at Winchester and (perhaps) Ælfheah at Canterbury—the cult was extremely limited in extent and duration, was restricted almost entirely to monastic foundations, and never achieved any degree of popularity outside these foundations.

V. LATER USES AND KNOWLEDGE OF THE *VITA S. ÆTHELWOLDI*

Æthelwold was an ecclesiastic of immense importance in the late tenth century, and this importance was properly recognized both by contemporaries and by succeeding generations. Furthermore, as we have seen, the cult of St Æthelwold was established at Winchester in the late tenth century and spread thereafter to other ecclesiastical centres, particularly those affiliated in some way with Æthelwold during his lifetime, such as Abingdon and the fenland

[89] See F. Arnold-Foster, *Studies in Church Dedications or England's Patron Saints*, 3 vols. (London, 1899), iii. 361; see also F. Bond, *Dedications and Patron Saints of English Churches* (Oxford, 1914), p. 23 (no. 230).

[90] Given the remoteness of Alvingham from places where Æthelwold was certainly culted, there must be considerable doubt about the identity, particularly since other saints named Æthelwald (such as the bishop of Lindisfarne, d. 721) were culted in Northumbria.

[91] *Chron. Abingdon*, ii. 291.

monasteries which he either founded or refounded. In view of the spread of the cult of St Æthelwold, it is not surprising that Wulfstan's *Vita S. Æthelwoldi*, the earliest work to contain an account of the saint's activities, should also have enjoyed a wide circulation. But in fact it enjoyed wider circulation than might be surmised from the relatively restricted diffusion of the cult and by the relatively small number of surviving manuscripts of the *uita* (five).[1] This much is evident from the numerous later authors who made use of the work in one way or another. It is essential, therefore, briefly to sketch the history of the reception of the *Vita S. Æthelwoldi*, for this reception throws light in turn on the manuscript transmission of the work. We shall treat the various later users of the *Vita S. Æthelwoldi* in approximate chronological order.

(a) *Wulfstan,* Narratio metrica de S. Swithuno

The earliest author to make use of the *Vita S. Æthelwoldi* was Wulfstan himself. In the dedicatory letter, or *Epistola specialis*, of his *Narratio metrica de S. Swithuno*, Wulfstan had occasion to mention the saints who were venerated at the Old Minster, and among these saints he included an account of St Æthelwold, who is eulogized as follows:

> Summus et antistes, patrie decus, altor egentum,
> spes peregrinorum, splendor honorque patrum,
> noster Aðelwoldus pastor, pater atque magister.[2]

There is a eulogy of Æthelwold very similar to this in the *Vita S. Æthelwoldi*, c. 28. Of course the sentiments expressed in these lines are common enough in medieval Latin hagiography,[3] but the phrase *pastor, pater atque magister* is strikingly like that in c. 28, where Wulfstan describes Æthelwold as *pater . . . et pastor monachorum*. After this eulogy, Wulfstan goes on in the poem to describe two miracles performed through Æthelwold's intercession:

> Comperit hoc nuper quidam uir nobilis Ælfhelm
> in somnis tumbam iussus adire sacram.

[1] See below, pp. clxviii–clxxix.

[2] Ep. spec. 271–3: 'And there too is the greatest of bishops, the glory of his country, the sustainer of the poor, the hope of pilgrims, a celebrity and eminence among the fathers, Æthelwold, our own shepherd, father and teacher.'

[3] In particular, Wulfstan's lines are indebted to Venantius Fortunatus, *Carm.* iii. 22a. 7–8: 'lumen dulce meum, *patriae* uigor, *altor egentum*, / *spes peregrinorum*, ductor *honorque patrum*.'

Cuius erant oculi nimio glaucomate clausi,
nec ualuit Phoebum cernere nec radium.
Qui mox huc ueniens, sanctus mandauit ut idem,
percepit clarum luminis intuitum;
et nullo ducente redit, miratur et in se
qualis erat ueniens, qualis et hinc rediens.
Sic etiam quaedam nimis infirmata puella
ducitur ad tumulum matre gemente sacrum.
Protinus obdormit: uigilans sanissima surgit,
incolomisque domum cum genetrice redit.[4]

The first of these miracles—that concerning Ælfhelm—is told in *Vita S. Æthelwoldi*, c. 42; the second, concerning the blind girl, is told in c. 44. The greater part of the *Epistola specialis* was evidently composed during the archbishopric of Sigeric (990–4), for he is spoken of as alive in ll. 221–2 ([Sigeric] '. . . quem Deus e caelis tueatur ubique supernis / Anglorum populis seruet et incolumem'); the metrical accounts of the two miracles, however, must have been incorporated into the poem some time after 10 September 996, the date of Æthelwold's translation. The verse follows the wording of the prose closely: thus, for example, the prose *cum genitrice domum rediit* is simply recast as part of the final pentameter quoted above (*domum cum genetrice redit*). The most economical explanation of the relationship between the prose and verse accounts is that Wulfstan, after completing his *Vita S. Æthelwoldi* for the occasion of Æthelwold's translation (see above, pp. c–ci), decided to incorporate the accounts of the two posthumous miracles into his poem.

(b) *Byrhtferth of Ramsey*, Vita S. Oswaldi

At one point in his *Vita S. Oswaldi* (iii. 11), Byrhtferth has occasion to discuss the saintly behaviour of King Edgar, which he attributes to Æthelwold's tuition and guidance:

Instructus ⟨namque eṛat⟩ idem rex ad cognitionem ueri regis ab Æþeluuoldo sanctissimo episcopo Wintoniensis ciuitatis. Iste enimuero

[4] Ep. spec. 289–300: 'A certain nobleman, Ælfhelm, who was ordered in a dream to approach the sacred tomb, recently discovered this. His eyes were sealed with excessive glaucoma, nor was he able to see the sun or its light. As soon as he came here—as the saint had commanded—he regained a clear perception of the light; and he returned without a guide, amazed at how he had been when he arrived and how he was when returning. Similarly a certain very sick girl is brought to the holy tomb by her grieving mother. Straightway she falls asleep; when she awakens she gets up fully cured and returns home in good health with her mother.'

ipsum regem ad hoc maxime prouocauit, ut clericos a monasteriis expulit et ut nostris ordinibus contulit, quia eius erat eximius consiliarius. Relinquam ergo sua beata gesta suis, que satis lucide descripta sunt; nos uero cepta persequamur.[5]

Byrhtferth is here proposing to leave the hagiography of St Æthelwold to Æthelwold's own followers (*suis*), for they have already been 'recorded clearly enough'.[6] Byrhtferth's *Vita S. Oswaldi* was written during the decade 995 × 1005, while Ælfric was archbishop of Canterbury.[7] Byrhtferth, therefore, can only be referring to Wulfstan's *Vita S. Æthelwoldi*, completed in 996 or shortly thereafter, for Ælfric of Cerne's abbreviation of the work (see below) was not completed until 1006. In any case, Ælfric's abbreviated *vita* scarcely circulated—it survives in but one copy—whereas Wulfstan's work enjoyed very wide circulation, as we shall see. The evidence of Byrhtferth indicates that it had reached Ramsey by 1005 at the latest.[8]

(c) *Ælfric,* Vita S. Æthelwoldi

Ælfric, a monk of Winchester and Cerne, and subsequently abbot of a new monastic foundation at Eynsham (d. *c.*1010), was a former student of Æthelwold who subsequently became the most prolific and most widely read vernacular author of the Anglo-Saxon period.[9] He is best known today for his writings in Old English—

[5] *Vita S. Oswaldi* iii. 11 (*HCY* i. 426–7): 'For this same king had been instructed in the knowledge of the True King by Æthelwold, the holy bishop of the town of Winchester. Æthelwold urged the king above all to expel the clerics from the monasteries and to bestow them on our order, being his principal adviser. I shall leave Æthelwold's saintly accomplishments, which have been recorded clearly enough, to his own followers; let me continue what I have started.'

[6] Cf. the remarks of D. J. V. Fisher, 'The early biographers of St Ethelwold', *EHR* lxvii (1952), 381–91, at pp. 388–90.

[7] *Vita S. Oswaldi* iv. 21 (*HCY* i. 452), where Archbishop Ælfric is spoken of in the present tense: 'est huius rei testis Ælfricus archiepiscopus ciuitatis Cantiae.'

[8] The suggestion has been raised (by M. Winterbottom, 'Three lives of St Ethelwold', *Medium Ævum*, xli (1972), 191–201, at p. 193) that the phrase *quae satis lucide descripta sunt* 'looks uncomfortably like a later addition', on the grounds that the syntax of the sentence is disjointed. Against this it must be said: that there is no evidence of interpolation elsewhere in the *Vita S. Oswaldi*; that this sort of 'disjointed' syntax is the hallmark of Byrhtferth's style (cf. *Vita S. Ecgwini* i. 11: 'quoniam superius aliqua perstrinximus aliorum que apta uidebantur'); and that elsewhere in the *Vita S. Oswaldi* Byrhtferth makes a similar statement concerning the *uita* of St Dunstan (v. 6; *HCY* i. 457): 'liber eiusdem uitae descriptus luce clarius demonstrat.'

[9] See P. A. M. Clemoes, 'The chronology of Ælfric's works', *The Anglo-Saxons: Studies in Some Aspects of their History and Culture Presented to Bruce Dickins*, ed. P. Clemoes (London, 1959), pp. 212–47, and, more generally, J. Hurt, *Ælfric* (New York, 1972).

including two series of *Sermones catholici* or 'Catholic Homilies' for the liturgical year, a series of 'Lives of Saints', various occasional homilies, pastoral letters, and the earliest Latin grammar to be composed in any European vernacular. But he was also the author of a number of Latin writings, and among these is a *Vita S. Æthelwoldi*.[10] Ælfric's authorship is clear from the dedication of the work: 'Ælfricus abbas, Wintoniensis alumnus, honorabili episcopo Cenulfo et fratribus Wintoniensibus salutem in Christo.' Cenwulf was bishop of Winchester only for a short period during the year 1006, and Ælfric's *Vita S. Æthelwoldi* can therefore be dated precisely to that year.[11] Now there is a very close verbal relationship between the *vitae* of Wulfstan and Ælfric, and it is clear that one of them must be derived from the other. If the arguments advanced earlier for dating Wulfstan's *vita* to 996 are sound, then Ælfric's work, which was completed a decade later in 1006, must be the debtor. However, the question of the priority of these two works has been the subject of a considerable amount of scholarly discussion, and it is worth while to review once again, and thoroughly, the evidence for Ælfric's dependence on Wulfstan.[12]

Before we proceed to a close analysis of the two works, several aspects of Ælfric's scholarly working habits need to be borne in mind. Ælfric was by nature an abbreviator. His normal procedure when producing a homily or saint's life seems to have been first to produce a Latin abbreviation of the text in question, and thereupon to produce an Old English translation of his abbreviation. This process can be illustrated by several examples. Boulogne-sur-mer, Bibl. mun. 63, fos. 1–34, is an English manuscript of the first half of the eleventh century; its contents reveal it as a later copy of a commonplace-book assembled by Ælfric himself.[13] These contents include: (*a*) abbreviated excerpts from Julian of Toledo, *Prognosticon* (1^{r}–10^{r}), which were used by Ælfric in two Old English homilies in his First Series of 'Catholic Homilies' and in an occasional homily for the Octave of Pentecost;[14] (*b*) Ælfric's

[10] See below, pp. 70–80 (Appendix A).

[11] Note in any case that Ælfric claims to be writing *uiginti annis post eius* [sc. Æthelwold's] *migrationem*, hence in 1004 or thereafter.

[12] Previous reviews of the evidence include Robinson, *Times*, pp. 168–70; Fisher, 'The early biographers', and Winterbottom, 'Three lives of Saint Ethelwold'.

[13] See E. M. Raynes, 'MS Boulogne-sur-Mer 63 and Ælfric', *Medium Ævum*, xxvi (1957), 65–73.

[14] The excerpts are ptd. M. McC. Gatch, *Preaching and Theology in Anglo-Saxon England: Ælfric and Wulfstan* (Toronto, 1977), pp. 134–46.

Pastoral Letter to Archbishop Wulfstan; (*c*) a *Sermo in natale Domini et de ratione animi* (13ʳ–18ʳ) consisting of abbreviated excerpts from Alcuin's *De animae ratione* that were used by Ælfric in the first of his 'Lives of Saints' (*De natiuitate Christi*);[15] (*d*) excerpts from Isidore and other authors entitled *De septem gradibus ecclesiasticis* (22ʳ–23ʳ) that were used by Ælfric in several of his pastoral letters; (*e*) excerpts from a pseudo-Augustinian sermon *De his qui auguria adtendunt* (29ʳ–31ʳ) that were used by Ælfric for his homily *De auguriis*; and a number of shorter excerpts that were variously used by Ælfric in other of his writings. It will be seen from this summary of the contents of Boulogne-sur-mer 63 that Ælfric's working-methods involved first the excerpting of works pertinent to his interests, and then the reworking of these excerpts into writings intended for publication. Similar light is thrown on Ælfric's working methods by consideration of the contents of another manuscript which is arguably a later copy of a hagiographical commonplace-book compiled by Ælfric himself, namely Paris, BN lat. 5362,[16] written *c.*1100 by a Norman scribe, in England or possibly in Normandy (the later provenance is Fécamp). This manuscript preserves the unique copy of Ælfric's *Vita S. Æthelwoldi* (fos. 74ʳ–81ʳ), but its other contents all have close links with Ælfric, and may be listed briefly. Note that we are concerned only with the contents of fos. 1–84, the first ten quires, for these were evidently copied from one exemplar and are concerned solely with English saints; the remainder of the book (fos. 85–128) contains *uitae* of various saints venerated in Normandy. The contents of the first ten quires include Bede's *Vita S. Cuthberti* (1ʳ–51ᵛ), various excerpts from Bede's *Historia ecclesiastica* pertaining to St Cuthbert (51ᵛ–52ᵛ); excerpts from the *Historia de S. Cuthberto* (53ᵛ–54ʳ); Abbo's *Passio S. Eadmundi* (54ᵛ–68ʳ); excerpts from Bede's *Historia ecclesiastica* pertaining to Oswald, king and martyr (68ᵛ–70ʳ) and to St Birinus (70ʳ⁻ᵛ); the *Epitome miraculorum et translationis S. Swithuni* (70ᵛ–74ʳ),[17] an abbreviation of Lantfred's *Translatio et miracula*

[15] See the remarks of M. R. Godden, 'Anglo-Saxons on the mind', *Learning and Literature*, pp. 271–98, at 278–85, 298; an edition of these Alcuin excerpts by T. H. Leinbaugh is forthcoming.

[16] See the Bollandists' *Catalogus codicum hagiographicorum latinorum . . . qui asseruantur in Bibliotheca Nationali Parisiensi*, 4 vols. (Brussels, 1889–93), ii. 354–66. There is a full discussion of the contents of this manuscript, and the use made of them by Ælfric, in Lapidge, *The Cult of St Swithun* (forthcoming).

[17] *BHL*, no. 7948; ptd. *PL* clv. 61–6 and Lapidge, *The Cult of St Swithun*.

S. Swithuni; Ælfric's *Vita S. Æthelwoldi* (74r–81r); and excerpts from Bede's *Historia ecclesiastica* pertaining to St Æthelthryth (81r–84v); the last part of fo. 84v is blank, and is the last leaf of the tenth quire (signed K). Nearly all these contents were used in some way by Ælfric in other of his writings although, as in the case of Boulogne-sur-mer 63, only one of them bears his name. Thus Bede's prose *Vita S. Cuthberti* forms the basis of 'Catholic Homilies' II, no. x, and a further borrowing from this work is interpolated into Ælfric's 'Life of Oswald'.[18] Abbo's *Passio S. Eadmundi* was the basis for Ælfric's 'Life of Edmund, king and martyr'.[19] The Oswald excerpts formed the basis of Ælfric's 'Life of Oswald king and martyr';[20] furthermore, the Birinus excerpts in the Paris manuscript correspond exactly to the material on St Birinus which was interpolated by Ælfric into his 'Life of Oswald'.[21] The *Epitome* of Lantfred's *Translatio et miracula S. Swithuni* served as the source of Ælfric's 'Life of Swithun';[22] and the excerpts on St Æthelthryth served as the basis for his 'Life of Æthelthryth'.[23] In other words, many of the contents of BN lat. 5362—a number of them consisting of excerpts—were used in some way by Ælfric in his vernacular hagiographical writings. When seen in its manuscript context, the *Vita S. Æthelwoldi* too stands out clearly as an abbreviation, and we may perhaps be permitted to wonder whether Ælfric intended at some point to use his *Vita S. Æthelwoldi* as the basis for a vernacular life of St Æthelwold, but never accomplished the task.

The contents of the Boulogne and Paris manuscripts give a clear impression of Ælfric's work as an abbreviator; but this same propensity is also to be seen in others of his writings. His so-called 'Letter to the Monks of Eynsham'[24] is a simple abbreviation of Æthelwold's *Regularis concordia* with additions from the liturgical writings of Amalarius.[25] An unprinted compilation known as the

[18] Ed. M. Godden, *Ælfric's Catholic Homilies. The Second Series: Text*, EETS, ss v (1979), pp. 81–91. The Cuthbert episode in the 'Life of Oswald' is in *Ælfric's Lives of Saints*, ed. W. W. Skeat, 2 vols., EETS, os 76, 82, 94, 114 (1881–1900), ii. 142.

[19] Skeat, *Ælfric's Lives of Saints*, ii. 314–34 (no. xxxii).

[20] Ibid. 129–42 (no. xxvi).

[21] Ibid. 132–4.

[22] Ibid. i. 440–70 (no. xxi); cf. discussion by Lapidge, *The Cult of St Swithun* (forthcoming).

[23] Ibid. 432–40 (no. xx).

[24] Ed. H. Nocent, *CCM* vii (3). 149–85.

[25] Ibid., p. 155: '. . . ideoque haec pauca de libro consuetudinum, quem sanctus Aðeluuoldus Wintoniensis episcopus . . . undique collegit . . . scriptitando demonstro . . . addens etiam aliqua de libro Amalarii presbiteri'; on the additions from Amalarius, see J. R. Hall, 'Some liturgical notes on Ælfric's "Letter to the Monks of Eynsham",' *Downside Review*, xciii (1975), 297–303.

Excerptiones de Prisciano, which is preserved anonymously in three manuscripts,[26] is arguably the work of Ælfric, for it served as the basis for his Grammar.[27] Finally, William of Malmesbury noted that Ælfric had compiled an 'abbreviatio Passionis S. Edmundi';[28] but this work has apparently not survived (or has not yet been identified).

Ælfric's work as abbreviator was not merely functional. His prose—both in Latin and Old English—is marked by its terseness and clarity, and by its avoidance of pompous and unnecessary verbosity. He writes in the preface to the Second Series of his 'Catholic Homilies' that he was concerned 'plus prodesse auditoribus simplici locutione quam laudari artificiosi sermonis compositione'.[29] His concern with clarity goes hand in hand with his inclination to abbreviation, as is clear from the preface to his 'Lives of Saints':

> Hoc sciendum etiam quod prolixiores passiones breuiamus uerbis, non adeo sensu, ne fastidiosis ingeratur tedium si tanta prolixitas erit in propria lingua quanta est in Latina: et non semper breuitas sermonem deturpat sed multotiens honestiorem reddit.[30]

The final clause—'brevity does not always disfigure speech but very frequently renders it more attractive'—might well be taken as Ælfric's stylistic keynote. In the light of these stylistic predilections we can easily imagine—without prejudice to the question of priority—that Ælfric, being faced with Wulfstan's *Vita S. Æthelwoldi*, would have deplored its prolixity. Ælfric, by contrast, describes his own *Vita S. Æthelwoldi* characteristically as *hec breuitas*: 'this brief account.'[31]

With these considerations in mind, let us examine the two *vitae*

[26] Ker, *Catalogue*, nos. 2 (Antwerp, Plantin–Moretus Museum M. 16. 2 [*olim* 47] + London, BL Add. 32246) and 371 (Paris, BN nouv. acq. lat. 586), both early 11th-c.; to these Vivien Law has added Chartres, Bibl. mun. 56 (83), fos. 1–88: see her 'Anglo-Saxon England: Ælfric's *Excerptiones de arte grammatica anglice*', *Histoire, épistémologie, langage*, ix (1987), 47–71, at pp. 51–2, and above, p. lxxxvi.

[27] Law, op. cit., pp. 51–4.

[28] *Gesta pontificum*, ed. Hamilton, pp. 406–7.

[29] Godden, *Ælfric's Catholic Homilies. The Second Series: Text*, p. 1.

[30] Skeat, *Ælfric's Lives of Saints*, i. 4: 'It is further to be noted that I abridge the more extensive lives, not in sense but in wording, so that boredom will not be inflicted on weary readers if the vernacular version should end up as lengthy as the Latin original: brevity does not always disfigure speech but very frequently renders it more attractive.'

[31] Below, p. 79.

of Æthelwold. Ælfric's is by far the shorter, and many chapters in Wulfstan's work have no correlate in Ælfric.[32] The relationship may best be seen from two parallel passages:

Wulfstan, c. 19

*De*inde cum praedicti fratres in Veteri Coenobio regularis uitae normam seruare coepissent et multi illuc ad Dei famulatum senes conuersi, iuuenes adducti et paruuli oblati confluerent, *ex inuidia clericorum datum est episcopo uenenum bibere in aula sua cum hospitibus prande*nti omnemque eis humanitatem exhibenti, quatinus *illo extincto* seruos Dei expellerent, rursumque in unum congregati *libere pristinis frui* potu*issent flagitiis. Erat namque ei moris* statim *post tres aut quattuor offulas modicum quid bibere*; *bibitque nesciens adportatum sibi uenenum* totum quod erat in calice, *et statim in pallorem facies eius inmutata est et uiscera* ill*ius nimium ui* grassantis *ueneni cruciabantur. Surrexit* autem *uix a mensa exiens ad lectulum, serpsitque uenenum per omnia membra eius*, iam instantem *minitans sibi mortem. At ille tandem* recogitans *coepit exprobrare semet ipsum, dix*itque *ad animum suum*: '*Vbi est modo fides tua? Vbi sunt* cogitationes sensus tui? Nonne *uerba Christi* uera sunt et fidelia, *quibus* in euangelio pollicetur *dic*ens, "*Et si mortiferum quid biberint* credentes, *non eis nocebit*?" Nonne ipse qui haec loquitur praesens est diuinitate, licet absens sit corpore? Ipse procul dubio, ipse hoc ueneni uirus in te euacuare potest qui semper omnia potest.'

Ælfric, c. 15

Dehinc denique, ex inuidia clericorum, datum est episcopo uenenum bibere in sua aula, in qua cum hospitibus prandebat, ut illo extincto libere pristinis quiuissent frui flagitiis. Erat namque ei moris mox post tres aut quattuor offulas propter infirmitatem quid modicum bibere; bibitque nesciens adportatum sibi uenenum omne quod anaphus habebat, et statim in pallorem facies eius immutata est et uiscera eius nimium ui ueneni cruciabantur. Surrexit tunc uix a mensa exiens ad lectulum, serpsitque uenenum per omnia membra eius, mortem minitans sibi. At ille tandem coepit exprobrare semet ipso, dicendo ad animum suum: 'Vbi est modo fides tua? Vbi sunt uerba Christi quibus dicebat, "et si mortiferum quid biberint, non eis nocebit"?'

[32] In Winterbottom, *Three Lives*, Wulfstan's *uita* occupies 30 pages, Ælfric's 12. Wulfstan's cc. 38–40, 43–5 have no correlate in Ælfric.

Wulfstan, c. 19 (*cont.*)	Ælfric, c. 15 (*cont.*)
His et huiuscemodi uerbis accensa fides in eo omnem *letiferum haustum quem biberat extinxit*, furentisque ueneni dolore fugato *surrexit, abiens ad aulam hilari* uultu, nulla penitus signa palloris se intuentibus ostendens, nec quicquam *mali suo uenefico reddens* sed ei quod deliquit ignoscens. Sicque Dei uirtute dissipatum est malignum consilium clericorum, qui uidentes suam nichil praeualere nequitiam tandiu per diuersas gentis Anglorum prouincias huc illucque dispersi sunt quousque uitam finierunt.	His et huiuscemodi uerbis accensa fides in eo extinxit letiferum haustum quem bibebat, et maturius surrexit, abiens ad aulam satis hilaris, nil mali uenefico reddens suo.

There are two possible explanations of the close verbal relationship here: either Wulfstan was expanding Ælfric's text, or Ælfric was abbreviating Wulfstan. Consider the first possibility. Wulfstan takes Ælfric's chapter and (1) in order to tease out the implications of *dehinc denique* in Ælfric adds a *cum*-clause explaining that the events of the chapter happened when monks of all ages were flocking to the Old Minster, but otherwise takes care to preserve verbatim the wording of the sentence; (2) alters *prandebat* to *prandenti* then adds a parallel participial phrase (*omnemque* ... *exhibenti*); (3) keeps *illo extincto* but adds an explanation of what the clerics would do after Æthelwold's death (*seruos Dei* ... *congregati*) but again preserves the very wording of the sentence into which the words are interpolated; (4) expands the *ubi sunt* question in Ælfric by incorporating two *nonne*-questions, but takes care to preserve the very wording of Ælfric at the core of his sentence by slipping a few words in around each of Ælfric's words; (5) adds a sentence explaining what became of the poisoners after their plot had been frustrated. This process of expansion—all the while preserving the words and structure of Ælfric's sentence—must have been a pointlessly exacting exercise, and one might think that it would have been easier for a later amplifier of Ælfric's text simply to discard his precise wording and to start afresh. But this hypothetical process of expansion was even more complex. Recognizing that the poisoning story in Ælfric had an analogue in

Sulpicius Severus' *Vita S. Martini*, apparently unnoticed by Ælfric, Wulfstan will have had to weave the words from Sulpicius (*ueneni in se grassantis*, *omnis dolor fugatus est*, and so on) into the texture of Ælfric's prose, keeping all Ælfric's words but adapting those of Sulpicius to the Ælfrician grammatical context.[33] It must be admitted that this process of weaving verbal reminiscences into an already existing prose framework would have been taxing in the extreme. But if, on the other hand, Wulfstan's text is the earlier and Ælfric was the later abbreviator, all is simple. Ælfric need have done no more than draw a red pencil (so to speak) through the words in Wulfstan's text which he regarded as superfluous and then copy the remainder. He need hardly have altered a word.[34] And since this is the procedure followed by Ælfric in his other works of abbreviation, the most economical explanation is that Ælfric's *Vita S. Æthelwoldi* is an abbreviation of Wulfstan's *Vita S. Æthelwoldi*. Note, too, that this explanation squares exactly with the chronological evidence of Byrhtferth's *Vita S. Oswaldi* discussed above.[35]

Such a conclusion may seem obvious and inevitable; but the opposite view—that Wulfstan's *uita* is a later (hence post-1006) expansion of Ælfric—has had numerous supporters,[36] and it is worth while finally to consider the objections raised by these scholars to the priority of Wulfstan's text. The first, and most serious, objection, is that there is some information in Ælfric's text not found in Wulfstan[37] and therefore, so the argument goes, this information was omitted by Wulfstan while he was revising/expanding the text of Ælfric (there is, of course, a far larger amount

[33] See below, p. 35 n. 3.

[34] There are a few small changes of substance in this chapter which are characteristic of Ælfric's redaction: he added that Æthelwold drank *propter infirmitatem*; and he altered Wulfstan's *calix* to *anaphus*, 'cup' (a word commonly found in scholastic colloquies, and presumably therefore in colloquial use: it derives from a vernacular word; cf. OE *hnaepp*, 'bowl', and German *Napf*), possibly because he wished to remove the liturgical connotations of the word *calix* ('chalice'). The change of *ipsum* to *ipso* should probably be charged to the scribe of Ælfric's *uita*, since Ælfric would have known that the dative of *semet ipse* was *sibimet ipsi*, had he wished to make such a change; see below, p. 75 n. 8.

[35] The example given here (Wulfstan, c. 19 ~ Ælfric, c. 15) was chosen at random. Similar results can be obtained from the detailed analysis of any analogous chapters; cf. Winterbottom, 'Three lives of Saint Ethelwold', p. 193.

[36] There is a judicious assessment of the two positions by H. Gneuss, *Notes & Queries*, xx (1973), 479–80 (reviewing Winterbottom, *Three Lives*).

[37] Cf. the statement by William of Malmesbury, *Gesta pontificum*, ed. Hamilton, p. 406.

of information in Wulfstan which is omitted in Ælfric). Most of this information is relatively insignificant, and is of the sort which could be supplied almost unthinkingly by someone who had known Æthelwold while he was alive.[38] But one detail is perhaps more significant. In c. 33 Wulfstan tells the story of an Old Minster monk who stole something from the church and refused at first to confess this sin. Wulfstan does not name the monk, although he does give the name of another monk (Wulfgar) to whom the first monk related his story. Now Ælfric (c. 22) names the thieving monk as Eadwine.[39] But there may be good reason for Wulfstan's omission: namely that when he was writing *c.*996 Eadwine was still alive, and Wulfstan did not wish to cause a confrater any unnecessary embarrassment; but by the time Ælfric wrote his abbreviation a decade later, Eadwine had died, and there was no further need to conceal his name. Such a hypothesis cannot be proved, of course, but it suggests that there may be local and personal explanations for the fact that a piece of information omitted by Wulfstan was included by Ælfric. In any case this objection will not stand up to the weight of evidence in favour of the priority of Wulfstan's *uita*. A second objection pertains to the wording of Ælfric's preface, that he was writing *ne forte penitus propter inopiam scriptorum obliuioni tradantur*;[40] and these words, so it has been argued, are not the words of a later abbreviator, since the work being abbreviated would itself refute any suggestion of *inopia scriptorum*.[41] But the words are hardly to be taken literally, for they are a literary topos lifted verbatim from Priscian's prefatory letter to his *Institutiones grammaticae*: 'quippe in neglegentiam cadentibus studiis literarum propter inopiam scriptorum.'[42] These very words had already been used by an earlier Winchester writer, namely Lantfred, in the introductory *Epistola* to his *Translatio et miracula S. Swithuni*. They do not, therefore, imply that Ælfric thought he was the first writer to treat St Æthelwold's life:[43] he is merely making a conventional

[38] As, for example, the point mentioned above (n. 34) that Æthelwold always drank a little, after eating three or four morsels, *propter infirmitatem*.

[39] A detail first noted by Winterbottom, 'Three lives of Saint Ethelwold', p. 200 n. 14.

[40] Below, p. 71.

[41] So D. Whitelock, *EHD*, p. 903: 'he would not have written to the brothers of Winchester in the terms he does, if all that he had done was to abbreviate a work which they already possessed.'

[42] See above, p. lxxxvi n. 161; the borrowing from Priscian was first noted by Winterbottom, 'Three lives of Saint Ethelwold', p. 200 n. 17.

[43] Cf. the remark of Winterbottom (ibid., p. 194) that the phrase *ne tanti patris*

excuse for composing a Latin text. Finally, an objection pertaining to the vocabulary of Wulfstan's *uita*, namely that the word *canonicus* used by Wulfstan in c. 16 (but not by Ælfric, c. 12) was not used by any tenth-century Anglo-Latin authors, and hence that Wulfstan's *Vita S. Æthelwoldi* must be a post-Conquest fabrication and *ipso facto* posterior to Ælfric.[44] But this argument is false, for the word *canonicus* is several times used by Lantfred in his *Translatio et miracula S. Swithuni*, composed at Winchester *c.*975, and is also used by Wulfstan in his *Narratio metrica de S. Swithuno* composed there *c.*992 × 994.

None of the objections against the priority of Wulfstan's *Vita S. Æthelwoldi* will bear scrutiny, therefore; and the evidence to suggest that Ælfric's *Vita S. Æthelwoldi* is an abbreviation made *suo more* far outweighs them. Ælfric's *uita* can accordingly be accepted as a valuable witness to the state of Wulfstan's text within a decade of its completion. For this reason it is printed as Appendix A (below, pp. 70–80).

(d) *The sequence 'Dies sacra, dies illa'*

This sequence in honour of St Æthelwold is preserved in the two 'Winchester Tropers' (see above, pp. lxxxiii–lxxxiv), both of them written at the Old Minster: Oxford, Bodleian Library, Bodley 775 (Old Minster, s. xi^{med}) and Cambridge, Corpus Christi College 473 (also written at the Old Minster), where the sequence has been added in a hand of the later eleventh century.[45] The sequence had therefore been composed by the mid-eleventh century; in view of the manuscripts' origin, it was almost certainly composed at the Old Minster. The sequence alludes to a number of the miracles performed by Æthelwold during his lifetime, and these were evidently drawn from a *vita* of the saint. That the *vita* in question was Wulfstan's and not Ælfric's is clear from the allusion in stanza

memoria penitus obliuioni tradatur 'certainly *implies* the complete lack of previous documentation.'

[44] Robinson, *Times*, pp. 107–8. Robinson's other objections are equally groundless. For example, the point that word-play such as *Æthelwoldus*... *nomine*... *beniuolus* (c. 9) could not have been written by an Anglo-Saxon: on the contrary, such word-play is common in Anglo-Latin authors from Aldhelm, with his play on the name *Helmgils* as *casses* + *obses* (see M. Lapidge and M. Herren, *Aldhelm: The Prose Works* (Cambridge, 1979), p. 17), through Aediluulf, who rendered his own name in Latin as *clarus lupus* (*Æthelwulf De Abbatibus*, ed. A. Campbell (Oxford, 1967), p. 63, l. 796), to the 10th c.

[45] See above, pp. cxxviii–cxxx and n. 53.

10a to Æthelwold's breaking up of church-plate to feed the poor during the famine of 976:

> De famis angustia
> egenorum
> eripit milia.

This event is told by Wulfstan in c. 29, but is omitted altogether by Ælfric. The sequence establishes what could otherwise easily have been surmised, namely that there was a copy of Wulfstan's *Vita S. Æthelwoldi* at the Old Minster in the earlier eleventh century.

(a) *Goscelin of Saint-Bertin*

Goscelin of Saint-Bertin was a professional hagiographer who first came to England in the household of Bishop Hermann of Ramsbury, in 1058, or shortly thereafter; from then until his death at some unknown date in the very early twelfth century Goscelin was active writing saints' *uitae* on commission to various religious houses, in the first instance for Sherborne (the *Vita S. Wulfsini*, written *c.*1077 × 1079), then for Wilton, where Goscelin apparently acted as chaplain for the nuns (the *Vita S. Edithe*, *c.*1080), then for various East Anglian houses including Barking, and finally for St Augustine's, Canterbury, for which he composed a substantial corpus of historical and hagiographical writings.[46] His *uita* of St Wulfhild of Barking was written some time after 1086, probably at St Augustine's, Canterbury.[47] In this *Vita S. Wulfhilde* Goscelin has occasion to recount a miracle which occurred through Wulfhild's agency: once, when Æthelwold and his entourage visited Barking, drink was poured unceasingly and could not be exhausted.[48] The miracle is very similar to—and no doubt modelled on—a miracle told by Wulfstan in c. 12 of his *Vita S. Æthelwoldi*.[49] Hence Goscelin comments: 'talis etiam uirtus inexhausti poculi legitur affatim in uita eiusdem patris Adeluuoldi.'[50] From Goscelin's wording here

[46] See F. Barlow, *The Life of King Edward*, NMT (1962), pp. 91–111, and T. J. Hamilton, 'Goscelin of Canterbury: a critical study of his life, works and accomplishments' (Ph.D. thesis, Univ. of Virginia, 1973).

[47] M. Esposito, 'La vie de sainte Vulfhilde par Goscelin de Cantorbéry', *AB* xxxii (1913), 10–26.

[48] Ibid., p. 19.

[49] Note Esposito's comment: 'Cet incident n'est pas raconté dans les deux vies de S. Aethelwold par Aelfric et Wulfstan' (ibid., p. 19 n. 3). On the contrary it is found in both Wulfstan (c. 12) and Ælfric (c. 8).

[50] Ibid., p. 19.

it is not possible to determine whether he is referring to the text of Wulfstan or of Ælfric. Two points, however, are in favour of Wulfstan. First, Goscelin does not name the author of the *uita* in question (recall that Wulfstan's *uita* travelled anonymously in manuscript, whereas Ælfric's bears its author's name in its opening sentence). Secondly, whereas Wulfstan's *uita* enjoyed a very wide circulation, Ælfric's seems barely to have circulated at all (it survives in but one manuscript, and we have been unable to identify a single quotation from it in a later writer). On balance, therefore, it is more likely that Goscelin is referring to Wulfstan's *uita* than to Ælfric's. And this conclusion has the consequent implication that a copy of Wulfstan's *Vita S. Æthelwoldi* was available at Canterbury in the late eleventh century.

(f) *Orderic Vitalis*

Orderic Vitalis (1075–1142), best known as the author of the immense *Historia ecclesiastica*,[51] the bulk of which is concerned with events in England and Normandy in the period after the Norman Conquest, and with the history of the monastic foundation which housed him, namely Saint-Évroul in Normandy, was a scholar of wide-ranging interests and activities, as is clear not only from the range of sources quoted in the *Historia ecclesiastica*,[52] but also from manuscripts copied or annotated by Orderic himself. Orderic's handwriting was first identified by Léopold Delisle,[53] and is now known in more than a dozen manuscripts.[54] Among these manuscripts is Alençon, Bibl. mun. 14. The contents of this manuscript are miscellaneous and include various *uitae* of English saints (such as Alcuin's *Vita S. Willibrordi*), the anonymous Hiberno-Latin *Nauigatio S. Brendani*, various documents pertaining to Orderic's monastery of Saint-Évroul, and Amalarius, *De ecclesiasticis officiis*. Among the English saints' *uitae* near the beginning of the manuscript is a collection of Winchester materials on fos. 23–37 (see above, pp. xxiii–xxvii) including in particular liturgical and hagiographical texts pertaining to St Æthelwold. Among these texts is a copy of Wulfstan's *Vita S. Æthelwoldi* (fos. 23^{r}–34^{v}) in Orderic's

[51] Ed. M. Chibnall, *The Ecclesiastical History of Orderic Vitalis*, 6 vols., OMT (1968–80).

[52] Ibid. i. 48–77.

[53] L. Delisle, 'Notes sur les manuscrits autographes d'Orderic Vital', *Matériaux pour l'édition de Guillaume de Jumièges*, ed. J. Lair (Paris, 1910), with plates.

[54] There is a summary account in Chibnall, *The Ecclesiastical History of Orderic Vitalis*, i. 201–3.

own handwriting.[55] This copy is not an exact transcription of Wulfstan's work, but would be best described as a redaction of it: Orderic interfered with the text in various ways, revising sentences so as to remove ambiguity, replacing present participles by finite verbs, and so on. His most striking act of scribal interference is found in c. 40 of Wulfstan's text, where Orderic interpolated some seventy lines from Wulfstan's *Narratio metrica de S. Swithuno*. The evidence of Alençon 14, then, establishes that a copy of Wulfstan's *Vita S. Æthelwoldi* was available to Orderic at Saint-Évroul at some time early in the twelfth century. To judge from the liturgical materials relating to SS Æthelwold, Swithun, and Birinus which accompany it, the copy in question derived directly from the Old Minster, Winchester.

(g) *William of Malmesbury*

William of Malmesbury (d. *c.*1142) was a scholar of exceptionally wide learning, particularly in sources relevant to the Anglo-Saxon church.[56] It is not surprising that he should have been familiar with Wulfstan's *Vita S. Æthelwoldi*; indeed he is the earliest authority to refer to Wulfstan by name as the author of the *Vita S. Æthelwoldi*. Thus he states in his *Gesta regum*: 'huius [sc. Æthelwold's] uitam Wulstanus quidam, cantor Wintoniensis, discipulus eius scilicet et alumpnus, composuit stylo mediocri.'[57] William quoted from the work on several occasions. In the *Gesta pontificum*, for example, while discussing Bishop Ælfheah of Winchester, he quotes the lengthy passage from c. 8 concerning Ælfheah's prophecy during the ordination of Dunstan, Æthelwold, and Athelstan;[58] later in the same work he quotes the anecdote in c. 14 concerning the obedience demanded by Æthelwold of the monk Ælfstan at Abingdon.[59] In the *Vita S. Dunstani* William refers once again to Bishop Ælfheah's prophecy during the ordination,[60] and later in the same work paraphrases Wulfstan's description of Dunstan as an 'immovable column' (c. 14);[61] furthermore, he recounts Wulfstan's version of Dunstan's dream (c. 38) in which Dunstan saw a tree

[55] See below, pp. clxxx–clxxxi.
[56] See R. M. Thomson, *William of Malmesbury* (Woodbridge, 1987), esp. pp. 68–70.
[57] *Gesta regum*, ed. Stubbs, i. 166–7 (quoted above, p. xv).
[58] *Gesta pontificum*, ed. Hamilton, p. 165.
[59] Ibid., p. 181. [60] *Memorials*, pp. 261–2. [61] Ibid., p. 299.

covered in cowls.[62] The likelihood is that there was a manuscript of the *Vita S. Æthelwoldi* at Malmesbury in the early twelfth century (or was seen somewhere by William in his travels).

(h) *The* Libellus Æthelwoldi

The *Libellus Æthelwoldi* or 'Book of Æthelwold' is a Latin translation made by an anonymous monk at Ely during the episcopate of Hervey (1109–31) of a now lost treatise in Old English concerning the tenth-century endowment of Ely by Æthelwold. The *Libellus Æthelwoldi*[63] is preserved in two twelfth-century manuscripts and has been printed only once, by Thomas Gale in the late seventeenth century;[64] its content is moderately well known, however, from the fact that it was subsequently incorporated into the *Liber Eliensis*, a history of Ely compiled there during the years 1169 × 1174.[65] The prologue of the *Libellus Æthelwoldi* is concerned with Æthelwold himself, and for this purpose the author draws on the *prefatio* of Wulfstan's *Vita S. Æthelwoldi*, adding the advice that if anyone should wish to know more about Æthelwold, 'legat librum qui de ortu et de uita necnon de obitu eius contextus est.'[66] The *Libellus* also includes a paraphrase of c. 23 of Wulfstan's work (that concerned with the endowment of Ely).[67] The nature of the paraphrase in both cases makes it impossible to determine whether the manuscript used by the author of the *Libellus* was identical with any surviving manuscript, but it establishes at least that a copy of the work was available at Ely some time in the first half of the twelfth century.

(i) Chronicon monasterii de Abingdon

The *Chronicon monasterii de Abingdon* was compiled by an anonymous monk of Abingdon at some point during the decade 1154–64.[68] The work is essentially a cartulary, but the numerous charters

[62] Ibid., pp. 272–3.

[63] *BHL*, no. 2649.

[64] T. Gale, *Rerum Anglicarum Scriptorum Veterum II: Historiae Britannicae, Saxonicae, Anglo-Danicae Scriptores XV* (Oxford, 1691), pp. 463–88. A new edition, with translation and full commentary, by S. D. Keynes and A. Kennedy, is forthcoming in *Anglo-Saxon Ely: Records of Ely Abbey and its Benefactors in the Tenth and Eleventh Centuries* (Woodbridge); see also below, pp. 81–2.

[65] *BHL*, no. 2650; ed. Blake, *LE*. Appendix A (ibid., pp. 395–9) contains extracts from the *Libellus Æthelwoldi*. The poetic extracts are ptd. below, pp. 84–6 (Appendix B).

[66] *LE*, p. 395. Note that the wording here agrees with the colophon of MS. C (p. 68 n. *j*), which confirms our argument (p. clxxv) that C is from Ely.

[67] Ibid., pp. 396–7.

[68] *Chronicon Monasterii de Abingdon*, ed. J. Stevenson, 2 vols., RS (1858).

which it records are set in a narrative framework, much in the manner of other monastic histories which were compiled during the twelfth century.[69] In this case, the narrative stretches from Abingdon's foundation in the seventh century up to 1154. In order to eke out his narrative at points relating to the abbey's tenth-century endowment, the chronicler draws substantially on Wulfstan's *Vita S. Æthelwoldi*,[70] particularly on those chapters which discuss Æthelwold's abbacy at Abingdon, namely cc. 11 (quoted verbatim), 12 (paraphrased), 13 (quoted verbatim), and 14 (paraphrased). The extensive verbatim quotations of Wulfstan's text make it clear that the manuscript used by the Abingdon chronicler was not identical with any surviving manuscript; but at least there can be no doubt that a manuscript was available at Abingdon in the mid twelfth century.

(j) *The Abingdon Manuscript of the* Chronicon ex chronicis

Further evidence for the existence at Abingdon in the late twelfth century of a copy of Wulfstan's *Vita S. Æthelwoldi* is provided by a manuscript of the *Chronicon ex chronicis* which was copied there in the late twelfth century, now London, Lambeth Palace 42 (Abingdon, s. xii^{ex}).[71] The *Chronicon ex chronicis* was compiled at Worcester during the years 1124 × 1140 by the monk John.[72] It survives in a number of manuscripts,[73] including Lambeth Palace 42. What characterizes Lambeth Palace 42, however, is the fact that its scribe interpolated into the *Chronicon ex chronicis* a number of passages pertaining to tenth-century Abingdon, and these

[69] See A. Gransden, *Historical Writing in England c. 550—c. 1307* (London, 1974), pp. 269–95, esp. 273.

[70] The Abingdon version is listed as *BHL*, no. 1651. Gransden (ibid., p. 273) states categorically that the Abingdon chronicler used Ælfric rather than Wulfstan; but examination of the verbatim quotations from cc. 11 and 13 of Wulfstan's work will show that the statement is mistaken.

[71] M. R. James, *A Descriptive Catalogue of the Manuscripts in the Library of Lambeth Palace I* (Cambridge, 1930), pp. 58–60, and N. R. Ker, *Medieval Libraries of Great Britain* (2nd edn., London, 1964), p. 3.

[72] The text is ed. B. Thorpe, *Florentii Wigorniensis Monachi Chronicon ex chronicis*, 2 vols. (London, 1848–9); see also J. R. H. Weaver, *The Chronicle of John of Worcester, 1118–40* (Oxford, 1908), and Gransden, *Historical Writing*, pp. 143–8.

[73] M. Brett, 'John of Worcester and his contemporaries', *The Writing of History in the Middle Ages. Essays presented to Richard William Southern*, ed. R. H. C. Davis and J. M. Wallace-Hadrill (Oxford, 1981), pp. 101–26; see also the (unreliable) analysis by C. R. Hart, 'The early section of the *Worcester chronicle*', *Journal of Medieval History*, ix (1983), 251–315.

passages include a number of excerpts from Wulfstan's *Vita S. Æthelwoldi*, cc. 11, 12, 14, 18, and 21.[74] There is reason to think that the scribe of Lambeth Palace 42 drew on the same manuscript of Wulfstan's text as was used somewhat earlier by the author of the *Chronicon monasterii de Abingdon*.

(k) *The Peterborough Chronicle of Hugh Candidus*

Hugh Candidus was a monk at Peterborough in the late twelfth century.[75] The Chronicle[76] which has come down to us under his name resembles other twelfth-century monastic chronicles in that it attempts to trace the history of the monastery from its foundation up to the present day (in this case 1177) and in so doing draws on any documentary materials available, especially charters, in order to illustrate the growth of the endowment. At the appropriate point in his narrative Hugh mentions Æthelwold's endowment of Peterborough, and in order to set this endowment in proper historical perspective also mentions Æthelwold's refoundation and endowment of Ely, Thorney, Abingdon, and the New Minster, Winchester. Hugh's source for this material was Wulfstan's *Vita S. Æthelwoldi*, which at several points is quoted verbatim; as he explains, 'excerpsimus de huius sanctissimi antistitis . . . factis'. Those chapters of Wulfstan laid under contribution by Hugh include cc. 11, 13, 18, 20, 21, 22, 23, 25, and 27. It is possible to demonstrate that the manuscript used by Hugh is not identical with any surviving manuscript of the *Vita S. Æthelwoldi*, but at least we have sound evidence for the existence of a copy of Wulfstan's text at Peterborough in the late twelfth century. This much might perhaps have been surmised from evidence of a different sort. In a manuscript copied at Peterborough *c.*1100 and now preserved as Oxford, Bodleian Library, Bodley 163, there survives a booklist of the abbey's library, and this booklist includes the following item: 'Vita sancti Aðeluuodi.'[77] Without further specification it would not be possible to determine whether the *uita* in question was

[74] The Lambeth recension of the *Chronicon ex chronicis* (including the Abingdon interpolations) is ptd. H. Wharton, *Anglia Sacra*, 2 vols. (London, 1691), i. 164–6.

[75] Gransden, *Historical Writing*, p. 271.

[76] *The Chronicle of Hugh Candidus*, ed. W. T. Mellows (Oxford, 1949); there is a translation by C. and W. T. Mellows, *The Peterborough Chronicle of Hugh Candidus* (Peterborough, 1941).

[77] See M. Lapidge, 'Surviving booklists from Anglo-Saxon England', *Learning and Literature*, pp. 33–89, at 76–82.

Wulfstan's or Ælfric's. However, when John Leland visited Peterborough some four centuries later in the mid-1530s (? 1535) he made excerpts from a *Vita S. Æthelwoldi* which he found there, and this work was unquestionably Wulfstan's.[78] The evidence of Leland, combined with that of the booklist and of Hugh, suggests that a copy of Wulfstan's *Vita S. Æthelwoldi* was at Peterborough no later than *c.*1100, that it was used there shortly after 1177 by Hugh Candidus, and that it remained there until about 1535, when it was seen by Leland. Since the text used by Hugh Candidus cannot be identified with any surviving manuscript, we are obliged to assume that the Peterborough manuscript has been lost since Leland's day.

(l) *The Ely Breviary*

The Ely Breviary is found in Cambridge, University Library, Ii. 4. 20, written at Ely in the earlier thirteenth century.[79] It contains two sets of lections for feasts of St Æthelwold, and these have manifestly been compiled from Wulfstan's *Vita S. Æthelwoldi*. They are printed in full above (pp. cxxxi–cxxxiii). In view of the fact that one of the five surviving manuscripts of the *uita* may have an Ely provenance, namely, Cotton Caligula A. VIII (see below, pp. clxxi–clxxv), it would be useful to establish whether the lections in the Ely Breviary contained any readings peculiar to Caligula A. VIII. Unfortunately, however, most of the lections are drawn from the early chapters of Wulfstan's work whereas Caligula A. VIII is a mere fragment, containing only cc. 33 (part)–46. In any case the Ely Breviary confirms the earlier evidence of the *Libellus Æthelwoldi* that Wulfstan's *uita* was available at Ely.

(m) *John of Tynemouth*

The scholar and historian John of Tynemouth lived during the first half of the fourteenth century.[80] Little is known of his life, but it is clear that during the earlier part of his career he was vicar of the priory at Tynemouth, and that he was subsequently a monk of St. Albans. He travelled all over England in search of materials for

[78] J. Leland, *Collectanea*, ed. T. Hearne, 6 vols. (Oxford, 1715), i. 8–9 (excerpts from cc. 20–2).

[79] See above, p. cxxxi n. 54.

[80] The best account is still that of C. Horstman, *Nova Legenda Anglie*, 2 vols. (Oxford, 1901), i, pp. xxiii–liii.

his work on hagiography, and probably died of the plague in 1348 or 1349. He is best known for two massive scholarly enterprises: the *Historia Aurea*, a history of the world in twenty-three books, stretching from the Creation until the siege of Calais in 1347, and the *Sanctilogium Angliae, Walliae, Scotiae et Hiberniae*, a collection of 156 saints' *uitae*.

The *Historia Aurea* is preserved in three manuscripts,[81] but has never been printed, both because of its size and because much of it is derived from earlier sources, mainly (for the earlier parts) Higden's *Polychronicon*.[82] In book xxi, which covers the period 800–1060, John includes an account of King Edgar, Dunstan, and Æthelwold and the establishment of Benedictine monasticism throughout England. This account has several similarities to Wulfstan's *Vita S. Æthelwoldi*, particularly to cc. 16 and 18 of that work, but the debts are not extensive enough to permit certain conclusions.[83]

We are on firmer ground with respect to John's *Sanctilogium*. In this vast work John assembled *uitae* of whatever English, British, Scottish, and Irish saints he was able to discover during his lengthy searches for hagiographical manuscripts in English libraries. As John devised the work, the various *uitae* were arranged in the order of the liturgical year, and each *uita* was accompanied by antiphons and collects pertaining to each individual saint. There is only one surviving manuscript which preserves John's original arrangement (London, BL Cotton Tiberius E. 1), and this manuscript was badly damaged in the Cotton fire of 1731. However, an anonymous compiler rearranged all the *uitae* in alphabetical order (omitting the antiphons and collects),[84] and this alphabetical arrangement is preserved in three fifteenth-century manuscripts and was printed by Wynkyn de Worde in 1516.[85] Given the vast scale of the *Sanctilogium* it is not surprising that all the *uitae* which it contains should

[81] Cambridge, Corpus Christi College 5–6; London, Lambeth Palace, 10–12; and Oxford, Bodleian Library, Bodley 240. For convenience we have consulted CCCC 5–6.

[82] See V. H. Galbraith, 'The *Historia Aurea* of John, vicar of Tynemouth, and the sources of the St Albans chronicle (1327–77)', *Essays in History presented to R. L. Poole*, ed. H. W. C. Davis (Oxford, 1927), pp. 379–98; id., 'Extracts from the *Historia Aurea* and a French "Brut" (1317–47)', *EHR* xlii (1928), 203–17.

[83] Cambridge, Corpus Christi College 6, fos. 210^r–212^r (on King Edgar), esp. 210^v–211^r.

[84] P. J. Lucas, 'John Capgrave and the *Nova Legenda Anglie*: a survey', *The Library*, xxv (1970), 1–10.

[85] Rptd. Horstman, *Nova Legenda Anglie* (cited above, n. 80).

be more or less drastically abbreviated. The *Sanctilogium* includes a *uita* of St Æthelwold, and this *uita* is, as we should expect, an abbreviation of Wulfstan's *Vita S. Æthelwoldi*.[86]

(n) *John of Glastonbury*, Cronica

The *Cronica siue Antiquitates Glastoniensis Ecclesie* is a lengthy but derivative history of Glastonbury stretching from the time of its foundation until the mid-fourteenth century; it was compiled by one John, perhaps to be identified with John Seen, at Glastonbury shortly after 1342.[87] In cc. 65–8 of this work John has occasion to discuss Æthelwold and his programme of monastic renewal, and accordingly he quotes extensively from the following chapters of Wulfstan's *Vita S. Æthelwoldi*: cc. 7, 8, 9, 11, 14, 15, 18, 27, 38.[88] It is not possible to identify the manuscript used by John with any surviving manuscript of Wulfstan's work; but the evidence of the *Cronica* establishes the existence of a copy of that work at Glastonbury in the mid-fourteenth century; furthermore, the use made by John of Wulfstan's text suggests strongly that the entry 'Vita Sancti Adelwoldi' which occurs in a Glastonbury booklist of 1247 is also to be identified as Wulfstan.[89]

(o) *The Lansdowne Redaction*

At some point in the mid-fourteenth century, or slightly later, a compilation of English saints' *uitae* like that made by John of Tynemouth in his *Sanctilogium* was made at (or for) the nunnery of SS Mary and Ethelfleda at Romsey (Hants). The compilation survives in a single manuscript as London, BL Lansdowne 436; its medieval Romsey ownership is indicated by an ex-libris inscription on fo. 1^{v} and its contents have been carefully catalogued by the Bollandist Paul Grosjean.[90] The sources for the various saints' *uitae* in Lansdowne 436 are normally much abbreviated and are frequently recast. Among the contents of Lansdowne 436 is a *uita*

86 John's abbreviated *uita* of Æthelwold is listed as *BHL*, no. 2648, and ptd. Horstman, *Nova Legenda Anglie*, i. 432–8. The text in Tiberius E. 1 is accompanied by the collect ('Deus qui hodiernam diem') discussed above, pp. cxv–cxvi.

87 J. P. Carley, *The Chronicle of Glastonbury Abbey* (Woodbridge, 1985). On the authorship of the *Cronica*, see J. P. Carley, 'An identification of John of Glastonbury and a new dating of his chronicle', *Mediaeval Studies*, xl (1978), 478–83.

88 Carley, *The Chronicle*, pp. 122–8; cf. p. xlii.

89 T. W. Williams, *Somerset Medieval Libraries* (Bristol, 1897), p. 71.

90 P. Grosjean, 'Vita S. Roberti Novi Monasterii in Anglia abbatis', *AB* lvi (1938), 334–60, at pp. 335–9; see also Horstman, *Nova Legenda Anglie*, i, p. ix n. 2.

of Æthelwold (fos. 81r–85v), and the source of this *uita* was evidently Wulfstan's *Vita S. Æthelwoldi*. In compiling the *uita* of Æthelwold, the compiler sometimes recast chapters of Wulfstan's text, and on other occasions simply reproduced them verbatim. The structure of the Lansdowne *uita* is as follows: an introduction drawing material from cc. 1, 2, 6, 7, and 38 (Dunstan's vision of the tree covered with monastic cowls); then cc. 10–13; then a version of c. 14 including only the story of Ælfstan's obedience; then a version of c. 16; then cc. 17–19; then a brief interpolation on St Dunstan; then cc. 20–2; then an interpolation concerning the religious women at the Nunnaminster in the times of St Eadburh; and finally a summary version of cc. 23–8, 29–34, 37, and 40–1.[91]

(p) *The Breviary of Hyde Abbey*

The Hyde Breviary is preserved in two manuscripts from Hyde, both written *c.*1300 and both in the Bodleian Library, Oxford: Rawlinson, Liturg. e. 1* and Gough, Liturg. 8.[92] It includes two sets of lections for feasts of St Æthelwold (one for the deposition, one for the translation), both of which were drawn nearly verbatim from Wulfstan's *Vita S. Æthelwoldi* (see above, pp. cxxxiii–cxxxvi). Those for the deposition are concerned with Æthelwold's life, and are drawn from cc. 1, 6, 9, 10, 11, 14, 16, 25, 28, and 41; those for the translation are concerned with posthumous miracles and are drawn from cc. 42–3. The Hyde Breviary thus establishes what might have been surmised, namely that a copy of Wulfstan's *uita* was available at Hyde from *c.*1300 onwards, and no doubt earlier.

(q) *The* Liber monasterii de Hyda

The *Liber monasterii de Hyda* is a cartulary from Hyde Abbey, Winchester (formerly the New Minster), written probably in the first half of the fifteenth century.[93] As in the case of the twelfth-century monastic chronicles mentioned earlier, the various documentary materials in the *Liber de Hyda* are set in a narrative framework which was drawn from various historical and

[91] See below, p. clxxxi.

[92] *The Monastic Breviary of Hyde Abbey, Winchester*, ed. J. B. L. Tolhurst, 6 vols., HBS lxix–lxxi, lxxvi, lxxviii, lxxx (1932–42); see also above, p. cxxxiii.

[93] See G. R. C. Davis, *Medieval Cartularies of Great Britain: A Short Catalogue* (London, 1958), p. 121 (no. 1051); A. Gransden, *Historical Writing in England II: c. 1307 to the Early Sixteenth Century* (London, 1982), pp. 391–2. The text is ed. E. Edwards, *Liber Monasterii de Hyda*, RS (1866).

hagiographical sources. The work begins with a brief account of English history before King Alfred, then gives a full account of Alfred and the foundation of the New Minster. From that point events are treated in chronological order, arranged according to kings' reigns, as far as the reign of Cnut (the work ends incomplete at 1023). In his account of the reign of King Eadred the compiler treats Eadred's donation of the abbey of Abingdon to Æthelwold, and this account is drawn directly and verbatim from Wulfstan's *Vita S. Æthelwoldi*, cc. 10–12;[94] his subsequent discussion of the reign of King Edgar also includes a brief quotation from c. 17 of Wulfstan's work.[95] The manuscript used by the compiler cannot be identified among surviving manuscripts, but at least we have evidence that a copy of the *Vita S. Æthelwoldi*—perhaps that used earlier by the compiler of the lections in the Hyde Breviary—still existed at Hyde in the fifteenth century.

(r) *The 'South English Legendary'*

Another important witness to the circulation of Wulfstan's *Vita S. Æthelwoldi*, though not however to the Latin text *per se*, is the lengthy Middle English poem known as the 'South English Legendary'.[96] This poem enjoyed wide circulation in the later middle ages, and has been transmitted in a number of distinct recensions. One recension, known to editors as Z, includes a 'Life of Adelwolde' consisting of 110 lines of rhyming couplets.[97] The Z-recension probably originated at Worcester during the period *c.*1270 × *c.*1285;[98] it is preserved in a number of manuscripts (five of which include the 'Life of Adelwolde') but has never been printed integrally, with the result that the 'Life of Adelwolde' has not hitherto been printed; an edition is given below.[99] From this edition it may be seen that the 'Life of Adelwolde' was based on

[94] Edwards, *Liber Monasterii de Hyda*, pp. 151–2. The quotation from c. 10 is specified as such by the cartularist ('et ut habetur . . . decimo').

[95] Ibid., p. 180.

[96] See M. Görlach, *The Textual Tradition of the South English Legendary*, *Leeds Texts and Monographs*, vi (Leeds, 1974). There is an edition of one recension of the 'South English Legendary' by C. D'Evelyn and A. J. Mill, *The South English Legendary*, 3 vols., EETS, os ccxxxv–ccxxxvi, ccxliv (1956–9); but note that this recension does not include the 'Life of Adelwolde'.

[97] Listed in J. B. Severs and A. E. Hartung, *A Manual of the Writings in Middle English, 1050–1500*, 7 vols. (New Haven, Conn., 1967–86), no. 2837.

[98] Görlach, *The Textual Tradition*, pp. 32–8.

[99] See below, pp. 87–92 (Appendix C).

Wulfstan's *Vita S. Æthelwoldi*,[100] and hence that a copy of that work was available at Worcester in the late thirteenth century.[101]

From the various evidence listed above it will be clear that Wulfstan's *Vita S. Æthelwoldi* enjoyed a very wide circulation from the time of its composition until the fifteenth century, far wider in fact than one might have supposed from the relatively small number—five—of surviving manuscripts.[102] From later knowledge and use of the text we can infer that copies were available at the following centres: Ramsey (Byrhtferth); Cerne or Eynsham (Ælfric); the Old Minster, Winchester (the sequence 'Dies sacra, dies illa'); St Augustine's, Canterbury (Goscelin); Saint-Évroul in Normandy (Orderic Vitalis); Glastonbury (John of Glastonbury); Malmesbury (William); Abingdon (the *Chronicon monasterii de Abingdon*); Peterborough (Hugh Candidus); Ely (the *Libellus Æthelwoldi* and the Ely Breviary); St Albans (John of Tynemouth); Romsey (Lansdowne 436); Hyde Abbey, Winchester (the Hyde Breviary and the *Liber monasterii de Hyda*); and Worcester (the Z-recension of the 'South English Legendary'). It is perhaps worth noting that some of these houses were Winchester dependencies which had either been founded or refounded by Æthelwold himself—Hyde (formerly the New Minster), Abingdon, Ely, and Peterborough—and it is hardly surprising that copies of a *uita* in his honour should have been preserved at such places. But the distribution is by no means limited to such houses, and the evidence clearly suggests that Wulfstan's *Vita S. Æthelwoldi* was one of the most widely read of all pre-Conquest Anglo-Latin saints' *uitae*.

[100] As pointed out by Görlach, *The Textual Tradition*, p. 185.

[101] The 'Life of Adelwolde' was adapted by the compiler of the Chronicle ascribed to 'Robert of Gloucester': W. W. Wright, *The Metrical Chronicle of Robert of Gloucester*, RS (1887), ll. 5706–39.

[102] Another reference to a *Vita S. Æthelwoldi* deserves to be recorded, though its bearing on the reception of Wulfstan's text is unclear. In Thomas Walsingham's late 14th-c. continuation of the *Gesta Abbatum Monasterii Sancti Albani* (ed. H. T. Riley, 3 vols., RS (1867–9)), a *vita sancti Ethelwoldi* is quoted to the effect that a royal estate granted by King Offa had been called *Verolamium* up to the time of King Edgar (iii. 366: '. . . ut apparet per ea quae scribuntur in vita sancti Ethelwoldi, a tempore Regis Offae usque ad tempus Edgari Regis duravit nomen Verolamii civitatis'). But there is no mention of *Verolamium* in Wulfstan's *Vita S. Æthelwoldi*, and it is not clear what *uita* can be in question here.

VI. MANUSCRIPTS OF THE *VITA S. ÆTHELWOLDI*

Wulfstan's *Vita S. Æthelwoldi* is preserved in five manuscripts, none of which is earlier than the twelfth century.

A = London, BL Arundel 169, fos. 88ʳ–95ʳ. A manuscript of 103 folios in large quarto size (335 × 225 mm.), ruled and written in two columns, which may be dated on approximate palaeographical grounds to the first half of the twelfth century. The present manuscript is part of a once much larger passional or legendary (that is, a collection of saints' *uitae* arranged according to the dates of their liturgical feasts).[1] The feasts of the saints represented in Arundel 169 occur between 29 June (the *passiones* of Peter and Paul) and 2 August (the *passio* of Pope Stephen). Since these feasts occupy little more than a calendar month, it is apparent that the original passional must have been huge, consisting perhaps of some ten or more volumes. All of these except Arundel 169 have apparently been lost. Furthermore, there is good evidence that Arundel 169 was once much larger than it is at present. The principal scribe copied a list of contents on fo. 2ʳᵃ; subsequently the manuscript was foliated in black ink by a sixteenth-century antiquary, who then added his own folio-numbers against the original scribe's list of contents.[2] By comparing the antiquary's foliation with the modern pencilled foliation, and by comparing the present contents

[1] See G. Philippart, *Les Légendiers latins et autres manuscrits hagiographiques* (Turnhout, 1977), esp. pp. 37–44, and above, p. civ.

[2] The contents-list copied by the principal scribe is as follows (the antiquary's foliation is given in square brackets): 'Passio S. Petri apostoli [1]; Altercatio apostolorum [5]; Passio S. Marcelli [13]; Passio S. Pauli apostoli [9], Vita S. Marcialis episcopi et confessoris [15], Vita S. Theodbaldi confessoris [26], Vita S. Swithuni episcopi et confessoris [34], Passio SS. Processi et Martiniani [38], Vita S. Martini episcopi [39], Quedam gesta S. Gregorii episcopi [40], Passio S. Procobii [43], Passio S. Grilli episcopi [45], Passio .vii. fratrum [45], Passio SS. uirginum Rufine et Secunde [46], Translatio S. Benedicti abbatis [47], Vita S. Amalberge uirginis [53], Certamina S. Eugenii cum sociis suis [61], Translatio S. Swithuni episcopi [63], Passio S. Foce episcopi [70], Passio S. Margarete uirginis [73], Vita S. Praxedis uirginis [77], Passio S. Victoris martyris [77], Vita S. Wandregisili abbatis [78], Vita S. Marie Magdalene [86], Passio S. Apollinaris martyris [90], Passio S. Rufi martyris [no number given], Passio S. Cristine uirginis [94], Passio S. Iacobi apostoli [97], Passio S. Christofori martyris [99], Passio S. Cucufatis martyris [105], Passio SS. .vii. dormientium [107], Passio S. Pantaleonis martyris [111], Passio S. Felicis pape [114], Passio S. Germani episcopi [117], Passio SS. Machabeorum [127], Vita S. Athelwoldi episcopi [129], Passio S. Felicis martyris [136], Passio SS. Spei, Fidei et Caritatis [137], Passio S. Stephani pape [139], and Vita S. Alexi confessoris [142].'

with the original scribe's list of contents (and noting where a *uita* begins acephalous or ends incomplete) it is possible to determine the extent of the losses which have occurred in the manuscript since the sixteenth century. These include a quire of eight lost between fos. 25 and 26 (end of *Vita S. Marcialis*, beginning of *Vita S. Theobaldi*); a bifolium after fo. 36 (end of *Vita S. Goaris*, beginning of *Passio SS. Septem*); six leaves after fo. 79 (end of *Vita S. Marie Magdalene*, beginning of *Passio S. Cristine*); and three quires of eight after fo. 87 (end of *Passio S. Christophori*, beginning of *Passio SS. Machabeorum*).

The present contents of Arundel 169 are as follows:[3]

(date illegible)	*Passio S. Petri* (2^r–5^v)
(no date given)	*Altercatio SS. apostolorum Petri et Pauli cum Symone mago* (6^r–10^v)
(29 June)	*Passio S. Pauli apostoli* (10^v–14^r)
(29 June)	*Passio S. Marcelli* (14^r–15^v)
(30 June)	*Vita S. Marcialis* (15^v–25^v; ends incomplete)
	[quire of eight lost here]
	end of *Vita S. Theobaldi* (26^{r-v})
(no date given)[4]	*Vita S. Karilefi* (26^v–29^v)
(2 July)	*Vita S. Swithuni* (29^v–31^r)
(3 July)	*Passio SS. Processi et Martiniani* (31^r–32^r)
(4 July)	*Abbreuiatio de uita et uirtutibus S. Martini in translatione eius* (32^r–33^v)
(6 July)	*Pauca de uirtutibus beati Gregorii Neocesariensis episcopi* (33^v–34^r)
(6 July)	*Vita S. Goaris* (34^v–36^v; ends incomplete)
	[bifolium lost here]
	Passio SS. Septem (begins acephalous; ends 37^r)
(10 July)	*Passio Rufine et Secunde* (37^r–38^r)
(11 July)	*Translatio S. Benedicti* (38^r–43^r)
(10 July)	*Vita S. Amalberge* (43^r–51^r)

[3] The manuscript has never been catalogued; hence we give the detailed list of contents alongside the scribe's own list (above, n. 2). The collation is as follows (quire signatures are given in square brackets): i (fo. 1) + I^8 (fos. 2–9) [q. I]; II^8 (fos. 10–17) [q. II]; III^8 (fos. 18–25) [q. III]; IV^8 (fos. 26–33) [q. V]; V^8 (fos. 34–8; lacks 4, 5, 8 canc.); VI^8 (fos. 39–46) [q. VI]; VII^8 (fos. 47–54) [q. VII]; VIII^8 (fos. 55–62) [q. VII: *sic*]; IX^8 (fos. 63–79) [q. VIII; this is the last quire signature in the MS]; X^8 (fo. 71–8); XI^8 (fos. 79–80; lacks 2, 3, 4, 5, 6, 7); XII^8 (fos. 81–7); [three quires lost]; XIII^8 (fos. 88–95); XIV^8 (fos. 96–103).

[4] The date should be *kl. Iul.* (1 July).

(13 July)	*Certamina S. Eugenii Cartaginensis* (51^{r}–53^{r})
(15 July)	*Translatio S. Swithuni* (53^{r}–60^{v})
(14 July)	*Passio S. Foce* (60^{v}–63^{v})
(21 July)	*Passio S. Margarete* (63^{v}–67^{r})
(21 July)	*Vita S. Praxedis* (67^{r-v})
(21 July)	*Passio S. Victoris* (67^{v}–68^{v})
(22 July)	*Vita S. Wandregisili* (68^{v}–77^{r})
(22 July)	*Vita S. Marie Magdalene* (77^{r}–79^{v}; ends incomplete)
	[six leaves lost here]
	Passio S. Cristine (begins acephalous; 80^{r}–81^{v})
(25 July)	*Passio S. Iacobi* (81^{v}–82^{v})
(25 July)	*Passio S. Christophori* (82^{v}–87^{v}; ends incomplete)
	[twenty-four leaves, probably three quires of eight, lost here]
	Passio SS. Machabeorum (acephalous; ends 88^{r})
(no date given)[5]	*Vita S. Æthelwoldi* (88^{r}–95^{r})
(1 August)	*Passio S. Felicis* (95^{r}–96^{r})
(1 August)	*Passio SS. Spei, Fidei et Caritatis* (96^{r}–98^{v})
(2 August)	*Passio S. Stephani pape* (98^{v}–101^{v})
(17 July)	*Vita S. Alexi* (101^{v}–103^{v}; last half of column b is blank)

The departures from calendaric sequence, together with the disparities between the actual contents and the scribe's list of contents (which was evidently written *before* the manuscript which follows it), suggest that the scribe may have been compiling the passional as he went along; on this hypothesis he will have discovered a copy of the *Vita S. Alexi* only after he had passed the appropriate point in the calendaric sequence (that is, immediately after the *translatio* of St Swithun) where it should have been included. If the hypothesis is correct, it suggests that Arundel 169 was compiled and written at a centre with a substantial library, because the number of *uitae* in the original ten-or-so-volume work must have been exceptionally large.[6] The centre cannot yet be

[5] The date should be *kl. Aug.* (= 1 Aug.).

[6] Cf. the massive size of the passional in London, BL Cotton Nero E. 1, pts. 1–2 + Cambridge, Corpus Christi College 9 (see below, p. clxxv): which would nevertheless have been dwarfed by the original passional of which Arundel 169 is a remnant. Cf. also the fragmentary 13th-c. passional in BL Cotton Nero E. 1, pt. 2, fos. 189–222 (see below, p. clxxvi).

identified, but certain indications point tentatively to Winchester. It would appear that the core of the passional was a Frankish collection of saints' *uitae*; and to this core the *uitae* of two specifically Old Minster, Winchester, saints (Swithun and Æthelwold) were added. Furthermore, these are the only English saints represented in Arundel 169. On the other hand, the legendary is extant only for a part of the liturgical year (29 June–2 August), and there is no way of telling whether the *uitae* of other localizable English saints were included, although it is probably significant that certain English saints whose feast-days fell during July—such as Seaxburh (6 July), Hæddi (7 July), Grimbald (8 July), Mildrith (13 July), Kenelm (17 July), Eadburh (18 July), and Neot (31 July)—are not represented in Arundel 169. If this argument *ex silentio* is sound, then Arundel 169 is to be attributed to the Old Minster, Winchester.

C = London, BL Cotton Caligula A. VIII, fos. 125^r–128^v. A composite manuscript in small quarto size (225 × 165 mm.), whose contents and components require some detailed analysis, in default of an adequate catalogue description.[7] The construction of the manuscript is immensely complex, and it will be necessary to set out clearly the constituent parts of the present composite manuscript before proceeding to analyse that part of it which contains Wulfstan's *Vita S. Æthelwoldi*. As presently constituted, C consists of twelve parts, most of which (it would seem) were originally distinct, even though some may derive from the same scriptorium. The twelve parts may be listed as follows:

Four flyleaves, one removed to BL Royal 13. D. I*; the first now present is modern paper; the second two are parchment (i^2 [fos. 2–3]). There is a list of contents on fo. 3.

I. Fos. 4–27 (I^{10} [fos. 4–13]; II^4 [fos. 14–17]; III^{10} [fos. 18–27]). Contains a calendar recording the names of benefactors to the Premonstratensian house of Beauchief, Derbyshire, in various hands, with multifarious additions, s. xv. Sir Robert Cotton's ex-libris is on 4^r (it is not dated).

II. Fos. 28–58 (five quires: I^4 [fos. 28–31]; II^2 [fos. 32–3; both singletons]; III^8 [fos. 34–41]; IV^8 [fos. 42–9]; V^8 [fos. 50–8; fo. 54 is

[7] Dr David Dumville has generously placed at our disposal his collation of the manuscript, to which our own is entirely indebted; his full description will form part of his *Historia Brittonum 5: The 'Gildasian' Recension* (Woodbridge, forthcoming).

a paper slip inserted by Bale]). Contains an abbreviation of Part II of Symeon of Durham, *Historia regum*, the *Libellus de primo aduentu Saxonum*, a brief tract on the seven wonders of the world, and the 'Gildasian' recension of the *Historia Brittonum*.[8] Second half (probably last quarter) of the twelfth century. The origin is unknown, but on text-historical and art-historical grounds a northern origin seems probable. Sir Robert Cotton's ex libris (dated 1600) is on 28r.

III. Fos. 59–101 (five quires: i8 [fos. 59–66]; ii10 (fos. 67–76]; iii8 [fos. 77–84]; iv8 [fos. 85–92]; v8 [+ one after 8; fos. 93–101]); ruled for 33 lines per page. Contains Eadmer of Canterbury, *Vita S. Wilfridi*, a *Vita S. Werburgae*, and other miscellaneous hagiographical materials pertaining to Seaxburh and Eormenhild. Origin unknown; mid-twelfth-century date. The latter half of fo. 85v is erased, following the end of Eadmer's *Vita S. Wilfridi*, and fo. 86r 1–6 are painted out. The last half of fo. 101v is blank and the page shows signs of wear, suggesting that it may once have been the end of a book.

IV. Fos. 102–7 (two quires: i2 [fos. 102–3]; ii4 [fos. 104–7]). Brown ink but English script. Contains the *Miracula S. Wihtburgae*. The script of this part is far more compressed than that of the preceding part; by the same token, the parchment is prepared differently and ruled for a greater number of lines (40 as against 33). The latter half of fo. 107v is blank. Origin unknown; mid-twelfth-century date.

V. Fos. 108–20 (fos. 108–19 make a single quire of twelve [i12, + 1 after 12]; fo. 120 is apparently a singleton which has been erroneously attached to the following quire). Contains the *Vita S. Sexburgae*. Origin unknown; mid-twelfth-century date.

VI. Fos. 121–4 (i4 [fos. 121–4]; originally flyleaves?). Contains the anonymous *Vita S. Birini*.

VII. Fos. 125–8 (i4 [fos. 125–8]; originally flyleaves?). Contains a fragmentary text of Wulfstan's *Vita S. Æthelwoldi*. There is a stain on fo. 128v, for which there is no corresponding offset on fo. 129r, which suggests that fo. 128 may once have been the outer page of a separate book.

[8] For these contents, see H. S. Offler, *Medieval Historians of Durham* (Durham, 1958), p. 11, and C. W. Hollister, 'The Anglo-Norman civil war: 1101', *EHR* lxxxviii (1973), 315–33.

VIII. Fos. 129–52 (three quires; I^{8} [fos. 129–36]; II^{8} [fos. 137–44]; III^{8} [fos. 145–52]). Contains the *Vita SS. Benedicti et Scolasticae*; incomplete at end. Mid-twelfth-century date.

IX. Fos. 153–62 (one quire of ten); fo. 162^{r} (part) and 162^{v} blank. Contains the *Translatio S. Benedicti*. Mid-twelfth-century date.

X. Fos. 163–8 (one quire of six); fo. 168^{r} (part) and 168^{v} originally blank. Contains the *Vita S. Marie Magdalene*. Mid-twelfth-century date. On fo. 168^{v} appear the arms and ex libris of Robert Steward, prior of Ely, with the date 1531.

XI. Fos. 169–91 (three quires: I^{8} [fos. 169–76]; II^{10} [fos. 177–86]; and III^{4} [+ 1 after 4; fos. 187–91]. Contains the *Passio S. Katerine*. Mid-twelfth-century date.

XII. Fos. 192–209 (two quires: I^{16} [fos. 192–207] II^{2} [fos. 208–9]; two unnumbered flyleaves bound up with quire II, the first a blank parchment flyleaf, the second a modern paper one). Contains a Latin prose account of a vision of purgatory and hell seen by Edmund, a monk of Eynsham, in a script much later than the immediately preceding parts.[9] Origin unknown; fourteenth-century date.

It is not immediately clear how these twelve disparate parts are related, but some clue is provided by a note in a fifteenth-century hand entered on fo. 128^{v}, which, since it contains the key to understanding the construction of the present manuscript, needs to be quoted in full:

Liber ympnorum. Translacio sancti Benedicti et sancte Scolastice. Witburge Sexburge Magdalene Sancti Wilfridi Eboracensis. Sancte Werburge. Sancte Margarete. Katerine. Visio purgatorii monachi de Eyinersham.

In other words, there existed in the fifteenth century the following book:

1. Liber ympnorum: lost.
2. Translacio sancti Benedicti et sancte Scolastice: part VIII (fos. 129–52).

[9] See H. L. D. Ward, *Catalogue of Romances in the Department of Manuscripts in the British Museum*, 3 vols. (London, 1883–1910), ii. 503–4. The Latin text is a translation of a lost French poem, which in turn was a translation of a Latin account of the vision of a monk of Eynsham (AD 1196), on which see H. E. Salter, 'Vision of the monk of Eynsham', *The Cartulary of the Abbey of Eynsham*, 2 vols. (Oxford, 1907–8), ii. 257–371.

3. Witburge: part IV (fos. 102–7).
4. Sexburge: part V (fos. 108–20).
5. Magdalene: part X (fos. 163–8).
6. Sancti Wilfridi Eboracensis: part IIIa (fos. 59–85).
7. Sancte Werburge: part IIIb (fos. 85–101).
8. Sancte Margarete: lost.
9. Katerine: part XI (fos. 169–91).
10. Visio purgatorii monachi de Eyinersham: part XII (fos. 192–209).

The fifteenth-century book, that is to say, consisted of fos. 59–120 and 129–209 of the existing manuscript. The remainder of the present manuscript was presumably added to the fifteenth-century core when it came into the possession of Robert Cotton, who added to it the present parts I and II, both of which bear his ex-libris inscriptions. At the same time, some parts of the fifteenth-century book—nos. 1 and 8—were lost.

What then of the two parts (VI and VII) containing fragments of the *Vita S. Birini*[10] and Wulfstan's *Vita S. Æthelwoldi* respectively? Each of these two parts has a distinctly soiled appearance; part VII in particular is riddled with worm-holes. The most reasonable explanation of their appearance is that the two parts, each consisting of two bifolia, once served as flyleaves to the fifteenth-century book, with part VI as the rear flyleaves and part VII as the front.

The two bifolia which make up part VII were written by an English scribe probably *c.*1100; his script is characterized by the one-stroke suspension-marks, occasional tall-backed *a*s, horizontal serifs on minim strokes, wedge-shaped ascenders, and overall spindly appearance typical of English scribes of that period. The script of part VI (the *Vita S. Birini*) is of similar appearance and date, although it is not the production of the same scribe who wrote part VII. It is possible, but not provable, that parts VI and VII were once part of one manuscript which was broken up in the fifteenth century to provide flyleaves for the fifteenth-century book whose contents have been set out above.

It is not possible to localize part VII on the basis of its script. To judge from the contents of the fifteenth-century book, in particular

[10] *BHL*, no. 1361; a list of manuscripts of this work is given by T. D. Hardy, *Descriptive Catalogue of Materials Relating to the History of Great Britain and Ireland*, 3 vols. in 4 pts., RS (1862–71), i (1). 235–6 (no. 625).

the *uitae* of Ely saints such as Seaxburh, Werburh, Wihtburh, and Eormenhild, that book was an Ely book; and this supposition is confirmed by the ex libris of Robert Steward on fo. 168v. If the manuscript containing Wulfstan's *Vita S. Æthelwoldi* (and perhaps the *Vita S. Birini* as well) was broken up at Ely, then one might assume an Ely provenance for that manuscript as well. But that hypothesis could not be verified unless other parts of the same manuscript were to be identified (but cf. above, p. clix n. 66). In the present state of knowledge, the origin and provenance of Caligula A. VIII, part VII, must be left open.

G = Gotha, Forschungsbibliothek I. 81, fos. 94r–101r. A large collection of some sixty-four *uitae* of English and British saints. It consists of 230 folios in large quarto format (313 × 230 mm.), ruled in two columns. The manuscript was written at an unknown English centre in the second half of the fourteenth century (s. xiv²); its later provenance is also unknown. Its contents have been carefully catalogued by the Bollandist Paul Grosjean,[11] and there is no need to list them here. From Grosjean's description it is clear that the contents were arranged so as to form the sequence martyrs, then confessors, then holy women. Wulfstan's *Vita S. Æthelwoldi* is included among the *uitae* of confessors. The text in G is lacking Wulfstan's *praefatio* and begins directly with c. 1; G also lacks the rubrics to the individual chapters.

N = London, BL Cotton Nero E. I, pt. 2, fos. 209v–216v. The two volumes of Cotton Nero E. I, taken together with Cambridge, Corpus Christi College 9, constitute a massive two-volume passional or legendary of some 165 saints' *uitae* (now bound as three volumes) which, because these are the earliest manuscripts which preserve it, is known as the 'Cotton–Corpus legendary'.[12] This was originally compiled in Northern France during the second half of the ninth century; it was subsequently transmitted to England, where *inter alia* it was used by Ælfric in the late tenth century as the basis for his collection of 'Lives of Saints';[13] and in fact all five surviving manuscript copies of the 'Cotton–Corpus Legendary' are of English origin. The copy preserved in the Nero and Corpus manuscripts was written at Worcester in the third

[11] P. Grosjean, 'De codice hagiographico Gothano', *AB* lviii (1940), 90–103.

[12] See W. Levison, *MGH*, SS rer. Meroving. vii. 545–6, and above, p. civ n. 11.

[13] See above, p. civ n. 12.

quarter of the eleventh century.[14] Its original two-volume constitution was as follows:[15]

I. January to September (Nero E. i, pt. i, fos. 55–208; Nero E. i, pt. 2, fos. 1–155);
II. October to December (CCCC 9, pp. 61–458; Nero E. i, pt. 2, fos. 166–80).

However, once these two massive volumes were broken up, the resulting smaller volumes inevitably attracted accretions. Thus three Anglo-Latin saints' *uitae* were prefixed to Nero E. i, pt. i;[16] a liturgical calendar and four saints' *uitae* were prefixed to CCCC 9; and at some point in the mid twelfth century a substantial body of miscellaneous materials was added to the end of Nero E. i, pt. 2, following fo. 180.[17] Among these additional materials at the end of pt. 2 are: bounds to estates at Westbury, Withington, and elsewhere (fos. 181–4);[18] an originally separate and smaller manuscript containing a copy of the law of King Edgar in Old English (fos. 185–6); and a copy of the *Vita S. Bedae* (fos. 187–8). At the end of this miscellaneous collection of material has been added the remnant of what was once an entirely separate manucript, a Latin passional written in the first quarter of the thirteenth century: fos. 189–222. It is this entirely separate passional which contains the copy of Wulfstan's *Vita S. Æthelwoldi* on fos. 209^{v}–216^{v}. Because the manuscript context can often illuminate the transmission of the text itself, it is worth recording the contents of this now fragmentary passional:

Passio SS. Petri, Andreae, Pauli et Dionisii: 189^{r-v} [specified for the *idibus Mai* = 15 May]
Passio S. Peregrini: 189^{v}–190^{v}
Vita S. Framehildis: 190^{v}–192^{r}

14 Ker, *Catalogue*, p. 217 (no. 166); T. A. M. Bishop, *English Caroline Minuscule* (Oxford, 1971), p. 20 n. 1; and N. R. Ker, *English Manuscripts in the Century after the Norman Conquest* (Oxford, 1960), pp. 49, 53 and pl. 26.

15 See N. R. Ker, 'Membra disiecta, second series', *British Museum Quarterly*, xiv (1939–40), 82–3.

16 These are: Byrhtferth's *Vita S. Oswaldi* (fos. 1–23) and *Vita S. Ecgwini* (fos. 24–34), and Lantfred's *Translatio et miracula S. Swithuni* (fos. 35–52); the *uitae* are followed by the various epanaleptic hymns discussed above (p. xxviii). The passional itself begins with the list of contents on fo. 55^{r}.

17 See E. A. McIntyre, 'Early twelfth-century Worcester cathedral priory with special reference to the manuscripts copied there' (D.Phil. thesis, Oxford, 1978), pp. 29–51.

18 Listed S, p. 52.

Passio S. Torpetis: 192^{r}–194^{r}
Passio S. Dioscori: 194^{r}–195^{r}
Passio S. Potentiane: 195^{r-v} [specified for *.xiiii. kl. Iunii* = 19 May]
Eadmer's *Vita S. Dunstani*: 195^{v}–203^{v}
Passio S. Ædelberti: 203^{v}–204^{v}; ends incomplete [specified for *.xiii. kl. Iunii* = 20 May]
Vita S. Germani: 205^{r}–208^{v}; begins acephalous
Passio SS. Machabaeorum: 208^{v}–209^{v} [specified for *kl. Aug.* = 1 August]
Wulfstan's *Vita S. Æthelwoldi*: 209^{v}–216^{v}
Passio S. Felicis: 216^{v}–217^{v} [specified for *kl. Aug.* = 1 August]
Passio SS. Spei, Fidei et Caritatis: 217^{v}–219^{v} [specified for *kl. Aug.* = 1 August]
Passio S. Stephani: 220^{r}–222^{v} [specified for *.iiii. nonas Aug.* = 2 August]

The collation of this manuscript is as follows: I^{8} (fos. 189–96); II^{8} (fos. 197–204); III^{8} (fos. 205–12); and IV^{10} (fos. 213–22). It is clear that these folios constitute a small remnant of what was once a massive passional, perhaps one on the same scale as that preserved incomplete in Arundel 169. What remains of this Nero E. I passional consists of legends for part of May (15–20 May), and for the very end of July (the feast of St Germanus is on 31 July) and the first two days of August. A number of quires have evidently fallen out between our quires II and III (that is, between fos. 204 and 205). So little remains of this passional that it is not possible to form even a rough estimate of its original size; but like Arundel 169, it must have comprised some ten or twelve volumes.

As we have seen, the eleventh-century passional which constitutes the bulk of Nero E. I, pts. 1–2 + CCCC 9, was written at Worcester. It is possible, but not demonstrable, that the manuscript was still at Worcester when the various miscellaneous materials—including our fragmentary thirteenth-century passional—were added to the end of pt. 2; but in the present state of knowledge that can be no more than a conjecture. It is more prudent to consider the origin and provenance of the thirteenth-century passional as unknown.

T = London BL, Cotton Tiberius D. IV, pt. 2, fos. 121^{v}–130^{v}. A large collection of saints' *uitae*, arranged in no particular order, in large folio format (345 × 240 mm.; written space 305 × 190 mm.), ruled and written in two columns and now bound as two volumes. The *uitae* are not arranged according to the liturgical year. It is apparent that Tiberius D. IV is an English copy of a Frankish collection of saints' *uitae* (Frankish saints make up the majority of the contents: Remigius, Hilary, Vedastus, Amandus, Walaricus, Germanus of Paris, Germanus of Auxerre, Medardus, Martin, Richarius, Anianus, and so on). However, at the end of what is now pt. 2 of the manuscript were added four *uitae* of English saints: the anonymous *Vita S. Birini* (fos. 105ᵛ–110ᵛ), the anonymous *Vita* and *Miracula S. Swithuni* (fos. 111ʳ–121ᵛ), Wulfstan's *Vita S. Æthelwoldi* (fos. 121ᵛ–130ᵛ), and Osbern of Canterbury's *Vita S. Dunstani* (fos. 130ᵛ–153ʳ), a work composed *c.*1090. These English saints' *uitae* were followed by a copy of the *Miracula S. Laurentii* on fos. 153ʳ–157ʳ; fo. 157ᵛ, originally blank, was the end of the book. The manuscript is the work of a number of scribes. The script at the beginning of the manuscript is that characteristic of English scribes in the late eleventh century; it would seem, to judge from the appearance of scripts throughout the manuscript, that it was begun in the late eleventh century and continued perhaps into the early twelfth, when the *uitae* of the English saints were added. In any case a date of *c.*1100 (s. xi/xii) is appropriate for the book as a whole.

Three of the four English saints—Birinus, Swithun, and Æthelwold—were culted specifically at Winchester, and one may suspect that the manuscript was written there. This suspicion is confirmed by the fact that the manuscript has been bound up with nine leaves of another (originally distinct) manuscript containing a copy of Aediluulf's so-called *De abbatibus*,[19] together with some chronological materials from Jerome and Orosius; these nine leaves are now fos. 158–66 of vol. 2. The nine leaves have various Winchester connections. First, they were copied in the very early eleventh century by a scribe whose script closely resembles (and is perhaps identical with) that of Scribe I of CCCC 473 (the 'Winchester Troper' discussed above), who was active at the Old Minster *c.*1000.[20] Second, the original home of the nine leaves now attached to Tiberius D. IV was the manuscript known as the 'Winchester Bede', a copy of Bede's *Historia ecclesiastica* now

[19] See A. Campbell, *Æthelwulf: De Abbatibus* (Oxford, 1967), pp. ix–x.

[20] The identification was proposed by Holschneider, *Organa*, pp. 19–20; see also S. Potter, 'The Winchester Bede', *Wessex*, iii (2) (1935), 39.

Winchester, Cathedral Library, I.[21] The 'Winchester Bede' was certainly at Winchester in the fourteenth century, and was probably written there. It is not known when the nine leaves were detached from the 'Winchester Bede' and attached to Tiberius D. IV, but if the detachment took place at Winchester, it would imply a Winchester provenance for Tiberius D. IV; and this, taken in combination with the presence of the Winchester saints' *uitae* in the manuscript, would suggest that it originated at Winchester. But this suggestion falls short of absolute proof. In any event, it should be noted that Tiberius D. IV was very badly damaged during the Cottonian fire of 1731, and a good deal of the text of Wulfstan's *Vita S. Æthelwoldi* has been lost, particularly from the outer margins.

As we have seen, the number of surviving manuscripts of Wulfstan's *Vita S. Æthelwoldi* is surprisingly small, in view of the wide circulation which the work enjoyed from the time of its composition until the fifteenth century (see above, pp. cxliii–clxvii). Furthermore, none of the five surviving manuscripts can be assigned with confidence to a particular centre. Two of them (A and T) are perhaps from Winchester. Another (C) may perhaps have an Ely provenance, but nothing is known of its origin. Similarly, another (N) may perhaps have a Worcester provenance, but nothing is known of its origin. Nothing is known of the origin or provenance of the fifth (G). None of the five manuscripts is earlier than the twelfth century, and none preserves a highly accurate text. For this reason, it is essential to take into account other, later witnesses to the text, and to these we now turn.

VII. INDIRECT WITNESSES TO THE *VITA S. ÆTHELWOLDI*

We have seen that, although Wulfstan's *Vita S. Æthelwoldi* is preserved in relatively few manuscripts (five), there is abundant evidence that numerous later authors had access to copies of Wulfstan's text. Some of these later authors reproduced extensive portions of Wulfstan's text—albeit with individual and often idiosyncratic alterations—and they therefore may on occasion

[21] Ker, *Catalogue*, p. 465 (no. 396).

throw indirect light on the nature of Wulfstan's text. Five such indirect witnesses are in question.

Ælf = Ælfric's *Vita S. Æthelwoldi*[1] which we have seen to be a drastic abbreviation of Wulfstan's *uita* (above, pp. cxlvi–clv). Ælfric's work is preserved in a manuscript written *c.*1100 (Paris, BN lat. 5362, fos. 74^r–81^r) by a Norman scribe who manifestly misrepresented Ælfric's text in copying it,[2] to such a degree that at various points Ælfric's own wording is not recoverable. This, combined with the fact that Ælfric abbreviated Wulfstan's text so drastically, makes his testimony of doubtful value. Nevertheless there are several points, especially in c. 12, where Ælfric helps to illuminate the transmission of Wulfstan's text.

Ord = Orderic Vitalis' copy of Wulfstan's *Vita S. Æthelwoldi*, as preserved in Alençon, Bibl. mun. 14, fos. 28^r–34^v.[3] Although Orderic copied Wulfstan's text *in extenso*, his testimony is not always reliable. His script is meticulously neat and legible; as a scribe, however, he offends one's basic assumption about scribal fidelity in that he is prone to interfere with the text he is copying.[4] Thus he often reverses the order of two or more words. Sometimes he recasts a sentence to remove ambiguity: thus the implicit reference to Daniel in c. 5 is made explicit by Orderic.[5] Sometimes he revises a sentence so as to replace a present participle by a finite verb.[6] But his most striking act of scribal interference occurs in c. 40, where Wulfstan describes the dedication of the Old Minster on 20 October 980. Here Orderic interpolated some seventy lines from Wulfstan's *Narratio metrica de S. Swithuno*,[7] where Wulfstan

[1] Ptd. below, pp. 70–80 (Appendix A).

[2] See below, pp. 74–7 nn. 7–11.

[3] See above, pp. clvii–clviii. Orderic's redaction of the *Vita S. Æthelwoldi* was printed integrally by J. Mabillon, *Acta Sanctorum Ordinis S. Benedicti*, 9 vols. (Paris, 1668–1701), v. 606–24, and reprinted in *PL* cxxxvii. 81–104. See discussion of Ord by M. Winterbottom, 'Three lives of Saint Ethelwold', esp. pp. 195–9.

[4] Winterbottom, 'Three lives of Saint Ethelwold', pp. 195–6.

[5] For Wulfstan's *sicut ille refecit unum Dei hominem in lacu leonum, ita iste congruo tempore milia populorum pasceret*, Ord has substituted, *sicut ille refecit congruo tempore Danihelem prophetam in lacu leonum, sic iste milia populorum pasceret*.

[6] For example, in c. 20, he recasts Wulfstan's *ordinans illis abbatem discipulum suum Æthelgarum* as *Æthelgarum autem discipulum suum ordinauit illis abbatem*; in c. 24, Wulfstan's *rectorem illis et abbatem Godemannum proponens* is recast as *rectorem quoque illis et abbatem Godemannum preposuit*; in c. 29, Wulfstan's *protestans* is changed to *protestabatur*; and in c. 30, Wulfstan's *noctes insomnes . . . ducens* is changed to *noctes ducebat insomnes*. More changes of this sort could be cited.

[7] *Narratio*, Ep. spec. 45–114.

first describes Æthelwold's programme of reconstruction at the Old Minster, and then gives a detailed account of the dedication ceremony, including the names of those bishops who were present, information omitted from the prose *Vita S. Æthelwoldi*. Even here, however, Orderic was not content simply to copy the manuscript before him. To Wulfstan's metrical account of the nine bishops present at the dedication, and the three days' feasting which followed, Orderic added the following satiric couplet, no doubt of his own composition:

> Et tandem decimus Poca uenit episcopus illuc,
> nulla laboris agens, pocula multa bibens.

Satiric verse of this sort, which in its ingenious creation of the bibulous Bishop Poca looks forward to the poetry of the goliards, was practised on other occasions by Orderic, and may be seen as Orderic's personal contribution to Wulfstan's lively description of the ecclesiastical drinking-party. In spite of Orderic's alterations and interpolations, however, his copy of Wulfstan's *Vita S. Æthelwoldi* is valuable in providing a witness to a lost manuscript of earlier Winchester origin, and hence in throwing indirect light on the transmission of the text.

Ln = London, BL Lansdowne 436, fos. 81r–85v, a mid-fourteenth century collection of saints' *uitae* which belonged to the monastery of SS Mary and Ethelfleda at Romsey.[8] The scribe, who was probably the compiler of the collection, frequently took considerable liberties with the texts being copied, with the result that most of the texts in the collection are best to be described as redactions rather than copies of the *uitae* they represent. This is true of the text of Wulfstan's *Vita S. Æthelwoldi*. Of the forty-six chapters of the original, the Lansdowne redaction preserves faithful (frequently verbatim) copies of the following: 10, 11, 12, 13, 17, 18, 19, 20, 21, 29, 30, 31, 32, 33, 34, 37, 40, and 41; the remainder are handled with varying degrees of freedom and subjected to interpolations of various kinds.

Tyn = the *uita* of St Æthelwold included in John of Tynemouth's *Sanctilogium*.[9] John's *uita* is a drastic abbreviation of Wulfstan's text. The following chapters of Wulfstan are represented in some

[8] See above, pp. clxiv–clxv. [9] See above, pp. clxii–clxiv.

form (the *praefatio* is omitted): cc. 1–2, 5–7, 9, 11–12, 14–16, 18–20, 22–4, 27–30, 32–4, 36, 38–9, 41–3, and 45–6. Although John's abbreviation is drastic, and although he frequently alters Wulfstan's wording, the nature of the text he was redacting is visible at a number of important points, especially c. 12.

Hyd = the *Liber monasterii de Hyda*, a cartulary from Hyde Abbey, Winchester, probably written in the first half of the fifteenth century. As we have seen,[10] the cartularist included in his compilation a verbatim quotation of cc. 10–12 (as well as a brief excerpt from c. 17) of Wulfstan's text. The fact that the cartularist copied the passages verbatim makes him a useful witness, especially to the state of c. 12, which, as we shall see, was apparently revised by Wulfstan himself.

These five redactions each contribute in some way to our understanding of the transmission of Wulfstan's *Vita S. Æthelwoldi*. There are of course other later texts which preserve passages of Wulfstan's text, sometimes through verbatim quotation: the Chronicle of Abingdon, Hugh Candidus' Peterborough Chronicle, the *Cronica* of John of Glastonbury. The passages quoted in these works often enable us to determine that they derive from none of the surviving manuscripts; but beyond that, their evidence is of little value in determining the transmissional history of Wulfstan's text. We must therefore concentrate our attention on the five manuscript witnesses and the five indirect witnesses and attempt to determine how they are related to each other.

VIII. RELATIONSHIPS OF MANUSCRIPTS AND INDIRECT WITNESSES

It is worth stressing at the outset that there is no witness to Wulfstan's *Vita S. Æthelwoldi*, direct or indirect, earlier than the twelfth century; that is, that a century or more elapsed between the time Wulfstan wrote (and Ælfric abbreviated) and our earliest surviving manuscript. In these circumstances it is surprising that the transmitted text is as accurate as it appears to be.

All surviving manuscripts (and indirect witnesses, as far as can

[10] See above, pp. clxv–clxvi.

be determined) have some small amount of error in common which shows them to derive from a single archetype, conceivably Wulfstan's autograph. Thus in c. 14 all manuscripts (and Ælf and Ord), in describing Dunstan's tenure of the archiepiscopate, read *mansit in Cantia triginta et septem annis*. The number 37 is clearly an error for 27,[1] and it would appear that *triginta et septem* is an expansion of an original reading *.xxxvii.*, which in turn represents a copyist's error for the (correct) number *.xxvii.* Errors in the copying of Roman numerals are common in medieval manuscripts. It is of course possible that an error such as this is a simple *lapsus calami* by the author himself. Nevertheless, if there is one patent but detectable error in the text, more may be latent.

Let us begin by considering the evidence of the five manuscript witnesses. None of these manuscripts can have been copied from any other, for each omits words that the others preserve and makes errors that the others avoid. Thus, listing the witnesses in approximate chronological order:

T: c. 11, *om.* Frithegarus; c. 15, *om.* si; c. 19, *om.* qui . . . potest *after* potest; *om.* gentis; c. 24, *om.* precio *after* Giruiorum; c. 33, *om.* est *after* locutus; c. 34, *om.* una cum artificibus.

C: c. 33, *om.* deberet *and* nostram; c. 38, *om.* ad *after* regione; c. 41, *om.* mensis *and* psalmorum; c. 42, *om.* et dignissime.

A: c. 11, *om.* ei *after* placuitque; c. 28, *om.* uero *after* humilibus; c. 32, *om.* sibi *after* oleum, *om.* crismatis in uia iacentem; c. 38, *om.* haec *before* robusta; c. 39, *om.* quondam *after* presbiter; *om.* quatinus *after* colla subdere, *om.* patris *after* sancti.

N: c. 11, *om.* loci *after* praenotati, *om.* ut *after* contulit; c. 12, *om.* et *after* rex; c. 14, *om.* episcopi *after* Ælfeagi; c. 19, *om.* se *after* palloris; c. 29, *om.* et *after* saeculi; c. 39, *om.* et in *after* liberentur.

G: c. 11, *om.* est *after* ordinatus; c. 13, *om.* sanctae; c. 33, *om.* ante Deum.

Furthermore, common errors reveal a closer relationship between A and N,[2] and with these two manuscripts the Lansdowne recension (Ln) clearly belongs.[3] N and Ln stand especially close: both have the transpositions *eius frater* and *laudem Dei* in c. 10, and

[1] See below, p. 26 n. 1.

[2] Note also that in the manuscript passionals in which they are transmitted, they are preceded by the *Passio SS. Machabeorum* and followed by the *Passio S. Felicis*.

[3] Ln has errors peculiar to itself, which are probably due to the redactor: thus the reading in c. 19, *humilitatem* for *humanitatem* (cett.).

both omit *uero* after *reliquam* and before *praefati* in c. 11. Both N and Ln are linked with A through the following readings: c. 12 n. *f* (*letatus*), c. 18 n. *f* (*de*), c. 29 n. *a* (*pecunia*), and c. 41 n. *d* (*om.* uiri). The relationship between these three witnesses, two direct (AN), one indirect (Ln), suggests that they derive from one hyparchetype, which we shall call β; their relationships may be represented by a stemma (Fig. 1).

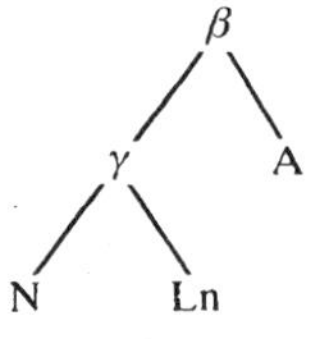

Fig. 1

In reconstructing the text, therefore, shared readings of β (that is, the agreement of AN(Ln)) are recorded, but their individual readings may be disregarded.[4]

Otherwise, the manuscripts are independent of each other: that is, we have to take account of four witnesses, T, C (where available), β, and G. But the picture presented by these four witnesses is further complicated by the evidence of Ælf, Ord, Tyn, and Hyd.

Various considerations prevent us from hypothesizing a simple unchangeable archetype directly reconstructible from these witnesses. First, both C and G, manuscripts otherwise unrelated, omit c. 40. Secondly, in c. 12, G joins Ælf, Ord, and Hyd in presenting the clause *clausis diligenter* (om. Ælf) *foribus ne quis fugiendo potationem regalis conuiuii deserere uideretur*; and all four (in slightly differing ways) present the reading *inebriatis suatim*,[5] which appears in Tβ (*def.* C) as *gaudentibus*. That is, Tβ alone show a toning-down of an originally over-sharp remark about the drinking habits of the Northumbrians. This is the only evidence that would support a stemma aligning G with Ælf, Ord, and Hyd against Tβ, and it is evidence too slim for so drastic a step. Taking it together

[4] Because A is a member of the sub-group of manuscripts including N and Ln, its individual readings are not recorded in the apparatus criticus (see below, p. clxxxvi); the same is true of N.

[5] Tyn here reads *inebriatis omnibus*.

with the behaviour of GC in c. 40, we should think rather in terms of changes in Wulfstan's autograph, as follows (see Fig. 2):

Stage 1: as seen in GC (and reflected in the indirect witnesses Ælf, Tyn, and Hyd), c. 12 had its sharp tone, but there was no c. 40.

Stage 2: deducible from Ord, in which c. 12 remained unchanged but c. 40 had been added.

Stage 3: seen in Tβ, where c. 12 had been toned down and c. 40 remained.

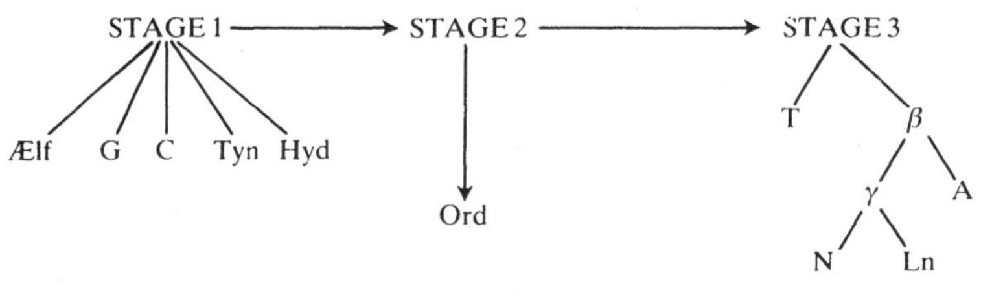

Fig. 2

The indirect witnesses thus help us to recover features of the transmissional history which are not fully evident in the five direct manuscript witnesses. On the other hand, because by their nature these indirect witnesses are redactions rather than copies of Wulfstan's text, their evidence at any point is not fully reliable. In reconstructing the text of Wulfstan's *Vita S. Æthelwoldi*, therefore, we have confined ourselves to the evidence of the direct witnesses TCβG.

IX. PREVIOUS EDITIONS OF WULFSTAN'S *VITA S. ÆTHELWOLDI*

Although Wulfstan's *Vita S. Æthelwoldi* has been printed on several occasions, the present edition is the first critical edition based on all manuscript witnesses.

The first edition was that of J. Mabillon, *Acta Sanctorum Ordinis S. Benedicti*, 9 vols. (Paris, 1668–1701), v. 606–24; 2nd edn. (Venice, 1733–40), v. 596–612. Mabillon's text was based solely on Alençon, Bibl. mun. 14 (= Ord); it is not, properly speaking, an edition of Wulfstan's text but of Orderic Vitalis' later redaction. Mabillon's text has been reprinted twice: by the Bollandists, *Acta Sanctorum*, Aug., i. 88–98; and in *PL* cxxxvii. 81–104.

More recently, an edition in the series of *Toronto Medieval Latin Texts* was prepared by M. Winterbottom: *Three Lives of English Saints* (Toronto, 1972), pp. 31–63. It is an editorial principle of texts in this series that they should be based on a single manuscript; Winterbottom's text is accordingly based principally on our T (BL Cotton Tiberius D. IV), with readings supplied from N (BL Cotton Nero E. I) where T is damaged or illegible.

Finally, there is a recent translation of Wulfstan's *uita*, based on Winterbottom's edition of 1972: D. Brearley and M. Goodfellow, 'Wulfstan's life of Saint Ethelwold: a translation with notes', *Revue de l'Université d'Ottawa*, lii (1982), 377–407.

X. EDITORIAL PROCEDURES IN THE PRESENT EDITION

Text and Apparatus Criticus

The text presented here is based on the five direct manuscript witnesses, but not on the various indirect witnesses (discussed above, pp. clxviii–clxxix). In the apparatus criticus we give:

1. a selection of variants from the late and corrupt G;
2. all variants of T where it is legible (where other variants are being recorded and T at such points is illegible, the fact is noted in the apparatus criticus; for a complete record of those places where T is damaged or illegible, see Winterbottom, *Three Lives*, pp. 31–63, where damage in T is signified by means of angle brackets; see also ibid., pp. 89–91);
3. all variants of β, that is, readings shared by NA; individual readings of N or A are usually ignored, except in some cases of personal names;
4. all variants of the fragmentary C.

Capitula

Only two manuscripts (C and T) include the capitula or chapter-headings found at the beginning of each chapter; in addition, T is preceded by a list of all forty-six capitula. We have not thought it necessary to print the list of these capitula from T *in extenso* (though readings from it are occasionally noted in the apparatus), but those prefacing each chapter in CT gave us pause, since there is some doubt that they were composed by Wulfstan. For example, in c. 40, there is a discrepancy between the chapter-heading (NOVEMBRIS, gen. sg.) and Wulfstan's text (*Nouembrium*, gen. pl.), a discrepancy which is odd if it was Wulfstan who composed the chapter-heading. However, it should be recalled that c. 40 was a later addition to the text made by Wulfstan, and the discrepancy may be the result of haste. Furthermore, we know that in his two longer poems—the *Breuiloquium de omnibus sanctis* and *Narratio metrica de S. Swithuno*—Wulfstan normally included prose capitula. On balance, therefore, it seems likely that the capitula in CT are by Wulfstan, and that the scribes of β and G omitted them independently. Accordingly, we have included the capitula in the present edition.

Orthography

As we have stressed, there is a century's lapse between the time Wulfstan completed his *Vita S. Æthelwoldi* (probably in 996 or shortly thereafter) and the date of the earliest manuscript witness (*c.*1100). That intervening century saw the Norman Conquest and its pervasive effect on English scriptorial practice. In matters of orthography, therefore, the surviving manuscripts of Wulfstan's *uita* reflect the practices of Norman scribes and twelfth-century (and later) English scriptoria more nearly than those of Wulfstan himself and of late tenth-century Winchester. If we wish to familiarize ourselves with the scriptorial practices (including such matters as orthography) of Wulfstan's Winchester, the safest guidance is given by manuscripts written at Winchester at that time. Several such manuscripts are in question, among them one which may have been partly written by Wulfstan himself (Cambridge, Corpus Christi College 473: see above, p. xxxvi). Most useful for our purposes, however, is London, BL Royal 15 C. VII (Old Minster, Winchester, s. x/xi), a manuscript containing Lantfred's *Translatio et miracula S. Swithuni* and Wulfstan's *Narratio metrica de S. Swithuno*. The text of the latter is so free from error and corruption that it may be thought to represent Wulfstan's autograph very closely, perhaps perfectly. If so, it can give us valuable guidance in the matter of Wulfstan's orthography.[1] Three aspects of this orthography require attention.

[1] See Holschneider, *Organa*, pls. xiv–xv.

1. *The use of* ae/ę. The scribe of Royal 15. C. VII consistently uses *ae* (never *æ*) in places where classical Latin practice requires it; he uses *ę* exceptionally rarely.[2] Accordingly, the prevalence of *ę* in the twelfth-century manuscripts of Wulfstan represents a later practice quite distinct from that of Wulfstan's own scriptorium. We have therefore normally written *ae* in place of manuscript *ę*, except in cases (such as *ęcclesia*) where the use of *ae* (hence *aecclesia*) would be philologically incorrect; here too the scribe of Royal 15. C. VII provides safe guidance.[3]

2. *English personal names*. The spelling of Anglo-Saxon names was a notorious source of difficulty for later (especially Norman) scribes. Fortunately, most of the names given in Wulfstan's *Vita S. Æthelwoldi* also occur either in Lantfred's *Translatio* or Wulfstan's *Narratio*, and we therefore have the guidance of the Royal scribe in these matters. Usually the spelling given by the late manuscripts can simply be normalized (for example, the use of *w*: this letter was introduced by Norman scribes in places where Anglo-Saxon scribes consistently wrote *uu*) by recourse to spellings in Royal 15. C. VII. Thus we write *Ætheluuold(us)*, not *Adelwold(us)* or *Ethelwoldus*; *Ælfeagus*, not *Elphegus*; *Æthelthryth(a)*, not *Edildrid(a)*; *Ealdulf*, not *Eldulf*; and so on.[4]

3. *The use of intrusive* p. In words such as *sollemnis*, *somnium*, *insomnis*, *damnatus*, etc., the practice of twelfth-century scribes was to insert *p*. The scribe of Royal 15. C. VII on the whole avoids the use of intrusive *p*, and we have accordingly normalized the spelling of our text by omitting it.

Punctuation

In accordance with OMT practice, the text has been punctuated on modern principles.

Biblical Quotations

Note that in the English translation of Wulfstan's text quotations from the Bible are taken from the Douai–Rheims version (1582–1609), as revised by Richard Challoner (1749–50).

[2] Holschneider, *Organa*, pls. xiv–xv: note that on pl. xiv occur the spellings *aliae* and *quae*; there is no example of a spelling with *ę*.

[3] Ibid., pl. xv (*ecclesiae*).

[4] Occasionally the spellings of names in the later manuscripts give rise to genuine critical variants; in such cases we have recorded the variants in the apparatus criticus.

WULFSTAN OF WINCHESTER

The Life of St Æthelwold

SIGLA OF MANUSCRIPTS CITED

A = London, BL Arundel 169, fos. 88^{r}–95^{r}
C = London, BL Cotton Caligula A. VIII, fos. 125^{r}–128^{v}
G = Gotha, Forschungsbibliothek I. 81, fos. 94^{r}–101^{r}
N = London, BL Cotton Nero E. I, pt. 2, fos. 209^{v}–216^{v}
T = London, BL Cotton Tiberius D. IV, pt. 2, fos. 121^{v}–130^{v}
β = readings shared by NA

[a]INCIPIT PRAEFATIO DE VITA GLORIOSI ET BEATI PATRIS ÆTHELWOLDI EPISCOPI, CVIVS SACRA MEMORIA CELEBRATVR IN KALENDIS AVGVSTI, QVA DIE FELICITER AD REGNA MIGRAVIT CAELESTIA.[b] Postquam mundi saluator Christus humano generi per aulam uirginalis uteri incarnatus apparuit, et, expleta suae pietatis ac nostrae salutis ineffabili dispensatione, ad paternae maiestatis sedem cum triumpho gloriae est regressus, multa per uniuersum orbem diffudit apostolicorum luminaria doctorum, qui euangelicae fidei inlustratione perfusi caecas ignorantiae tenebras ab humanis cordibus effugarent, et ut[c] credentium mentes igne superni amoris inflammarent, et, elongata diuturnae mendicitatis esurie, populorum turbas aeternae uitae epulis satiarent.[1] Ex quorum collegio beatus pater et electus Dei pontifex Ætheluuoldus, uelut lucifer inter astra coruscans, suis temporibus apparuit, multorumque coenobiorum fundator et ecclesiasticorum dogmatum institutor inter omnes Anglorum pontifices solus singulariter effulsit. De cuius ortu, gestis et obitu scire cupientibus aliqua narrare dignum duximus, et ne tanti patris memoria penitus obliuioni traderetur[d] ea quae praesentes ipsi uidimus et quae fideli seniorum relatione didicimus in his scedulis summatim perstrinximus,[2] illius sanctis confisi suffragiis hoc et nobis qui scripsimus et eis qui lecturi uel audituri sunt profuturum. EXPLICIT PRAEFATIO.

Incipit textus sequentis libelli de uita sancti Ætheluuoldi episcopi.[e]

1. DE ORTV ET TEMPORIBVS PARENTVM ILLIVS. Erant[f] igitur parentes sancti pontificis Ætheluuoldi ex ingenua Christianorum propagine oriundi, Wentanae ciuitatis urbani, temporibus senioris Eaduuardi[3] regis Anglorum florentes, in mandatis et

[a] *The Preface is omitted by G* [b] de uita . . . caelestia] uita sancti Athelwoldi *N;* in uita sancti Athelwoldi episcopi et confessoris *A* [c] *Apparently superfluous* [d] tradatur *T(?)* [e] *β gives the heading* Incipit uita sancti Athelwoldi episcopi et confessoris kalendas (kl *A)* Augusti; *there is no heading in G* [f] erat *G*

[1] The apostolic succession—from Christ to His apostles, then to martyrs and confessors—is a topos commonly found in prefaces of saints' *uitae*: see H. Hagendahl, 'Piscatorie et non Aristotelice', *Septentrionalia et Orientalia: Studia B. Karlgren dedicata* (Stockholm, 1959), pp. 184–93. Wulfstan will have known the topos from Sulpicius Severus, *Vita S. Martini*, c. 3, and Lantfred's preface to his *Translatio*.

[2] *Perstringo* is a word used elsewhere by Wulfstan in similar contexts; see *Narratio*, Ep. spec. 17, and below, c. 43; he may have been indebted for its use to Caelius Sedulius,

HERE BEGINS THE PREFACE TO THE LIFE OF THE GLORIOUS AND BLESSED FATHER, BISHOP ÆTHELWOLD, WHOSE SACRED MEMORY IS CELEBRATED ON THE FIRST OF AUGUST, THE DAY ON WHICH BEFELL HIS HAPPY DEPARTURE TO THE KINGDOM OF HEAVEN. After Christ, the Saviour of the world, had been incarnated by means of the temple of a virgin's womb and shown himself to the human race, he completed the ineffable stewardship that sprang from his affection for us and led to our salvation, before returning in glorious triumph to the seat of his father's majesty. Thereafter he spread throughout the world the light of many apostolic teachers; bathed in the brilliance of the faith proclaimed in the gospels, they were to banish the blind darkness of ignorance from men's hearts, set alight the minds of believers with the fire of heavenly love, and, driving away the hunger and poverty that had so long afflicted the mass of the peoples, fill them full with the banquet of eternal life.[1] Of the company of these teachers was the blessed father and elect of God, Bishop Æthelwold. He burst on his time brilliant as the morning star among the other stars; the founder of many monasteries and teacher of the Church's doctrines, he shone alone and unique among all the English bishops. For those who desire to hear of his birth, career, and death, I have thought it worth while to compose a narrative. Determined that the memory of so great a father should not be consigned to complete oblivion, I have in these pages touched[2] summarily on things that I saw with my own eyes or learned from older men whose account I could trust. My firm hope is that, thanks to Æthelwold's holy intercessory prayers, my book will be of use to its writer and to those who read it or hear it read. HERE ENDS THE PREFACE.

Here begins the text of the book that follows on the life of St Æthelwold the bishop.

1. OF THE ORIGIN AND TIMES OF HIS PARENTS. The holy bishop Æthelwold's parents were of noble Christian stock, dwelling at Winchester. They flourished in the time of Edward the Elder,[3] king of England, 'walking in the commandments and ordinances of

Carmen paschale i. 96 ('ex quibus audaci perstringere pauca relatu') or to Sulpicius Severus, *Dialogi* i. 9. 7 ('longum est, si omnia cupiam referre quae uidi: pauca perstringam').

[3] Edward the Elder was king 899–924. Wulfstan does not know the precise date of Æthelwold's birth; see above, p. xlii.

iustificationibus Domini sine querela fideliter incedentes.[1] Qui dum[a] cotidianis bonorum operum pollerent[b] incrementis, eximio Dei munere decorati sunt quo talem mererentur gignere sobolem, cuius eruditione et exemplis non solum populi praesentis aeui sed etiam futuri peruenirent ad noticiam ueri luminis, ut exuti caligine tenebrosi erroris gloria fruerentur aeternae claritatis.

2. DE VISIONE SOMNIORVM MATRIS EIVS. Itaque felix eius genitrix, cum eum in utero conceptum gereret, uidit huiuscemodi intempesta nocte somnium, quod erat certum futuri effectus praesagium. Visum namque sibi est se prae[c] foribus suae domus[d] sedere, et obtutibus suis adesse quoddam sublime uexillum, cuius summitas caelum tangere uidebatur: quod se inclinando honeste ad terram fimbriarum suarum uelamine circumdedit inpraegnatam, rursumque[e] procera altitudine erectum et inflexibili stabilitate robustum ipsum unde inclinabatur repetiit caelum. Expergefacta autem mulier rursus sopore deprimitur, et ecce repente uidit ex ore suo prosilire et auolare[f] quasi auream mirae magnitudinis aquilam, quae uolando cuncta Wentanae ciuitatis aedificia auratis pennarum remigiis[2] obumbrauit, et in alta caelorum se eleuando disparuit. Cumque mulier euigilans[g] secum miraretur attonita et somniorum uisionem[h] mente uolueret tacita nec per semet ipsam conicere posset eorum interpretationem, perrexit ad quandam Christi famulam, nomine Æthelthrytham,[3] moribus et aetate maturam, quae in praefata urbe nutrix erat Deo deuotarum uirginum, cui narrauit ex ordine quod sibi ostensum fuerat in nocturna uisione. At illa, sicut erat animo sagaci prudentissima, et interdum etiam futurorum Domino reuelante praescia, de nascituro infante multa praedixit, quae uera esse rerum exitus indicauit.[i]

[a] cum *G* [b] pollent *G* [c] pro *AG* [d] domus sue *G* [e] rursum *G* [f] euolare *G(?)* [g] uigilans *G* [h] somniorum uisionem] sompnionem *G* [i] comprobauit *G*

[1] Luke 1: 6 ('incedentes in omnibus mandatis et iustificationibus Domini sine querella').

[2] Cf. Vergil, *Aen.* i. 301, vi. 19.

[3] Wulfstan expresses himself rather vaguely on the subject of this Æthelthryth: does *nutrix Deo deuotarum uirginum* imply that she was abbess of the Nunnaminster, which was founded at approximately this time? Nothing is otherwise known of her. Wulfstan states

the Lord blameless'[1] and in all faith. Every day their strength in good works increased, and God marked them out with a particular gift: they were found worthy to produce a child of such character that, thanks to his learning and example, those who lived after him as well as his own contemporaries might come to knowledge of the true light, and, shedding the dark gloom of error, enjoy the glory of the brightness eternal.

2. ON WHAT HIS MOTHER SAW IN DREAMS. So his fortunate mother, while pregnant with him, saw at dead of night a dream that was an unerring indication of the future. She dreamed that she was sitting at the door of her house, and that she was presented with the sight of a banner on high. Its top seemed to touch heaven. It lowered itself with due honour to the ground, and veiled the pregnant woman in its fringes; then, straightening itself up to its former height and regaining its old strength and firmness, it returned to the sky from which it had come. The woman awoke, but, falling asleep again, she all at once saw what looked like an eagle of gold, leaping from her mouth and flying away. It was wonderfully large, and in its flight it shaded all the buildings in the city of Winchester with the gilded wings[2] that carried it along. It rose high in the air, and then disappeared. The woman woke up, thunderstruck with wonder, and pondered her dreams, without uttering a word. Then, because she could not imagine by herself what they might portend, she went along to a servant of Christ called Æthelthryth,[3] a woman ripe in years and experience, and the nurse of the virgins dedicated to God at Winchester. To her she told the full story of what had been shown her in her vision by night. Æthelthryth, being a sensible and sharp woman, and one to whom God at times revealed knowledge of the future, had many predictions to make of the child who was to be born; and the outcome showed their truth.

here that she was already ripe in years (*aetate matura*) during the reign of Edward the Elder (hence before 924: born *c.*900?); yet he later states (c. 22; below, p. 38 n. 1) that this same Æthelthryth was made abbess of the Nunnaminster at the time of its refoundation in *c.*964. She must have been rather elderly by then (over sixty?), and, if she was abbess in the early tenth century, one wonders what she had been doing in the years between then and the refoundation. She is not mentioned anywhere in *LVH*. Possibly Wulfstan has conflated two women of the same name.

3. DE INTERPRETATIONE SOMNIORVM EORVNDEM. Nos quoque eorundem somniorum coniectores esse possumus, in sublimi uexillo intelligentes sanctum uirum, qui tunc in utero portabatur, quandoque futurum militiae Dei signiferum, sicut et erat, quem multimoda reluctatione contra antiquum hostem pro defensione sanctae matris ecclesiae congredientem uidimus, ipsoque bellante, immo per ipsum Deo uincente, prauorum[a] machinamenta[1] ad nichilum redacta conspeximus. Et quia aquila ab acumine oculorum uocatur,[2] et testante sacro eloquio thesaurus desiderabilis[3] requiescit in ore sapientis, recte per auream aquilam, quae totam urbem alarum uelamento obumbrare uisa est, idem praeclarus uir totius sapientiae thesauro decoratus exprimitur. Qui perspicaci et inreuerberata[b] cordis acie diuina meditando, semper ad caelestia per contemplationem uolauit, et super ecclesiam, magni regis ciuitatem,[4] quam contrariae potestates inpugnare nitebantur, umbraculum paternae protectionis longe lateque expandit, et, consummato boni certaminis cursu, ad uisionem Dei in sanctorum comitatu peruenit: sicut in euangelio uoce dominica dicitur 'Vbicumque fuerit corpus, illuc congregabuntur aquilae',[5] quia ubi ipse redemptor noster est corpore, illuc procul dubio nunc colliguntur electorum animae, et in futurae resurrectionis gloria illuc quoque eorum colligentur et corpora. Haec de somniorum interpretatione breuiter diximus; nunc ad narrationis ordinem redeamus.[6]

4. QVOMODO MATER SENSIT VENISSE ANIMAM PVERI NASCITVRI. Quadam namque die cum mater eius stipata ciuibus staret in ecclesia, sacrae missae celebrationi interesse desiderans, sensit animam pueri quem gerebat in utero uenisse et in eum Dei nutu cuncta moderantis intrasse, sicut postea ipse sanctus qui nasciturus erat, iam episcopus, nobis gaudendo referebat.[7] Ex[c]

[a]]uorum *T*; prauarum *G* [b] inuerberata *β* [c] et *β*

---

[1] Cf. Prov. 6: 14 ('prauo corde machinatur malum').

[2] The etymology is from Isidore, *Etym.* xii. 7. 10: 'aquila ab acumine oculorum uocata.'

[3] Prov. 21: 20; cf. also 14: 33.

[4] The 'great city' here is the Church itself, symbolically Jerusalem; cf. Matt. 5: 35: '. . . per Hierosolymam, quia ciuitas est magni regis.' The *contrariae potestates* attacking the Church are presumably the secular clerics (below, cc. 16–20) who on one occasion attempted to poison Æthelwold.

[5] Matt. 24: 28; Luke 17: 37.

[6] Cf. Bede, *Historia abbatum*, c. 9: 'uerum his . . . breuiter praelibatis, redeamus ad

3. ON THE INTERPRETATION OF THESE DREAMS. We too may act as interpreters of these dreams. In the banner on high we can see that the holy man, then in his mother's womb, was one day to be standard-bearer in the army of God: as he indeed was, for we saw him putting up a versatile struggle in defence of Holy Mother Church against her ancient enemy, the devil; thanks to his warfare—or rather God's victory through him—we saw the machinations of the wicked[1] brought to nought. Then because the word *aquila* ('eagle') is derived from the sharpness (*acumen*) of an eagle's eyes,[2] and because, to cite Holy Writ, 'there is treasure to be desired'[3] resting in the mouth of the wise man, it is proper that a great man, marked out by the treasure of all wisdom, should be designated by the gold eagle whose overshadowing wings seemed to cover the whole city. For Æthelwold, who thought on divine things with a mind whose acute sight could not be averted, always flew in contemplation to the heavenly. He spread far and wide the shade of his fatherly protection over the church, the 'city of the great king',[4] which was under attack from hostile powers. And when he had completed the race of his good struggle, he came to the sight of God in the company of the saints; as the Lord says in the gospels: 'wheresoever the body is, thither will the eagles be gathered together,'[5] because where our Redeemer is in the body, there beyond question are now assembled the souls of the elect, and there too, at the glorious resurrection to come, their bodies will be assembled also. After these brief remarks on the interpretation of the dreams, let us now return to our narrative.[6]

4. HOW HIS MOTHER FELT THAT THE SOUL OF HER UNBORN SON HAD COME. Now one day his mother was standing in a crowd of people in church, wanting to take part in the celebration of holy mass, when she felt that the soul of the child whom she bore in her womb had come and entered him at the will of God who rules all. This is what I was told later by the very saint whose birth was then imminent, when he had become a bishop; and joyfully did he tell the tale.[7] It is clear from this that he was the 'elect of

ordinem narrandi' (Plummer, *VBOH* i. 373). Bede's phrase was recycled a number of times by Wulfstan's contemporary Byrhtferth: see M. Lapidge, 'Byrhtferth of Ramsey and the early sections of the *Historia regum* attributed to Symeon of Durham', *ASE* x (1981), 97–122, at pp. 106–7.

[7] On the possible circumstances in which Æthelwold recounted this miracle to Wulfstan, see above, pp. c–ci.

quo ostenditur eum Deo[a] electum[1] extitisse etiam antequam nasceretur, et animam procreati hominis non, ut quidam aestimant,[b] a patre uel a matre existendi initium sumere, sed, ut uere et absque omni dubietate creditur, a solo creatore uitalem spiritum uiuificari et singillatim unicuique dari.[2] Nascitur ergo futurus Dei pontifex, et fonte baptismatis in Christo renatus Æthelwuoldus a parentibus est appellatus, sanctique crismatis unctione confirmatus gratiae Dei in omnibus est commendatus.

5. QVOMODO PVER NATVS ⟨ET⟩[c] IN CHRISTO REGENERATVS QVADAM DIE SVBITO IN ECCLESIA CVM NVTRICE SVA INVENTVS EST. Accidit enim quadam sollemni die, cum more solito nutrix illius ad ecclesiam pergere[d] et orationi incumbere decreuisset, tam ualidam inundantis pluuiae tempestatem erumpere ut extra loci limen, ubi in gremio tenens eundem infantem sederat, pedem mouere non posset. Quae dum maerens amarissime fleret eo quod uotum piae intentionis soluere nequiret, caput humiliter omnipotentem Dominum rogatura[e] declinauit et confestim diuina miseratione consolari promeruit.[f] Nam nullam molestiam procellosae tempestatis sentiens subito inuenta est cum infantulo sedens in ecclesia quam adire disponebat, ubi sollemnia missarum presbiter celebrabat; et quod nulla ratione credere potuisset ut fieret, factum uehementer expauit, et omnes huius rei cognoscentes miraculum magnae admirationis stupor inuasit. Sicut enim propheta quondam ex Iudaea repente sublatus et in Chaldaea cum prandio est depositus,[3] sic beatus puer Æthelwuoldus sub momento cum nutrice in templo est praesentatus, ut sicut ille refecit unum Dei hominem in lacu leonum, ita[g] iste congruo tempore milia populorum pasceret in ecclesia sanctorum.

6. QVOD STVDIOSE ET DILIGENTER IN IPSA PVERITIA SACRIS LITTERARVM STVDIIS ANIMVM DEDERIT. Igitur cotidiano profectu creuit puer bonae indolis, et in ipsa mox pueritia sacris litterarum studiis

[a] Deo *om. G* [b] existimant *T* [c] *Supplied from Capitula* [d] pergeret *β* [e] omn. Dom. rog.] rogatura dominum *G* [f] meruit *G* [g] sic *G*

[1] The words *Deo electum* are a common biblical expression: Jer. 1: 5, Luke 23: 35, Col. 3: 12, and 1 Pet. 2: 4.

[2] Wulfstan here rejects the doctrine of traducianism, according to which the human soul was transmitted to the child by its parents; this doctrine was propounded by Tertullian (*De anima*, cc. 23–41) and Gregory of Nyssa, who are possibly the *quidam*

God'[1] even before his birth, and that the soul of a man, once begotten, does not, as some suppose, take its first rise from his father or mother; instead, as we believe in truth and without any doubt, the vital spirit is quickened by our Creator and none other, and is given individually to each man.[2] And so the future bishop of God was born; he was born again in Christ in the font of baptism, and named by his parents Æthelwold. Strengthened by the administration of the holy unction, he was commended to the grace of God in all things.

5. HOW THE BOY, BORN AND THEN REBORN IN CHRIST, WAS SUDDENLY FOUND ONE DAY WITH HIS NURSE IN CHURCH. One feast-day, when his nurse had, as was her custom, decided to go to church and pray, it chanced that so violent a downpour of rain broke forth that she could not set foot outside the door of the house where she sat with the baby in her lap. She was upset, and wept bitter tears because she could not fulfil the vow of her pious intent. She bowed her head in humble prayer to the Almighty Lord, and deservedly found speedy consolation from God's mercy. For, having felt no discomfort from the storm, she suddenly found herself with the baby, sitting in the church she had planned to visit, with the priest celebrating solemn mass. She was frightened out of her wits at an event so inexplicable, and all who learnt of the miracle were struck by wonder and astonishment. For just as once the prophet was suddenly taken up out of Judaea and set down with his dinner in Chaldaea,[3] so was the blessed child Æthelwold brought in a trice into the church with his nurse. Just as the prophet gave refreshment to a man of God in the lions' den, so Æthelwold was, when the time was ripe, to feed thousands of people in the church of the saints.

6. HOW EVEN AS A CHILD HE DEVOTED HIMSELF STUDIOUSLY AND INDUSTRIOUSLY TO STUDYING HOLY LITERATURE. And so every day this gifted child advanced. Soon, while still a boy, he was set to study religious literature; thus one who was destined to show others the

referred to by Wulfstan. By the late 10th c., however, traducianism had been a dead letter for centuries (it was condemned by Pope Anastasius II in 498), and the commonly held theological view was the creationism endorsed here by Wulfstan (see *DTC* xv. 1350–65). The same viewpoint is frequently endorsed by Ælfric; see below, p. 72 n. 2.

[3] The reference is to Habbakuk, who miraculously fed Daniel in the lions' den: Dan. 14: 32–8 (Bel & Dr. 33–8).

est traditus, ut qui aliis uiam salutis[1] erat[a] ostensurus ipse cum Maria secus pedes Domini humiliter sederet et uerbum ex ore illius salubriter audiret.[2] Erat enim agilis natura atque acutus ingenio, ita ut quicquid maiorum traditione[3] didicerat non segniter obliuioni traderet sed tenaci potius memoriae commendaret. Studebat etiam teneros pueritiae annos[4] morum honestate et uirtutum maturitate uincere, diuinis semper obsequiis omnia membra sua mancipare et ad Dei implendam uoluntatem totam mentis suae intentionem dirigere, sicque perceptis Christi muneribus recte uiuendo gratias exhibere ut ad maiora percipienda dignus mereretur existere.

7. QVOMODO ADOLESCENS ÆTHELSTANO REGI NOTVS EFFECTVS AD CLERICATVM ET SACERDOTIVM PERVENERIT. Cumque florentis adolescentiae contingeret aetatem,[5] praeconium sanctae[b] conuersationis eius Æthelstano regi,[6] filio praedicti regis Eaduuardi, fama uulgante nuntiatum est, iuuenemque[c] festinanter accersiri praecepit. Qui cum adductus staret in praesentia regis, inuenit gratiam in conspectu eius et in oculis optimatum eius, ibique indiuiduo comitatu multum temporis agens in palatio[7] plura a sapientibus[d][8] regis utilia ac proficua sibi didicit. Et demum, iubente rege, ab Ælfego Wintoniensi episcopo[9] secundum morem ecclesiasticum prius ad clericatus officium tonsoratus[10] ac deinde, paucis labentibus annorum curriculis,[11] in gradum sacerdotalem consecratus est.

[a] erat salutis *G* [b] sanctae *om. G* [c] is iuuenem *G* [d] a sapientibus] aspicientibus *T*

[1] Acts 16: 17.

[2] Luke 10: 39 ('et huic erat soror nomine Maria quae etiam sedens secus pedes Domini audiebat uerbum illius').

[3] Cf. Mark 7: 3 and 5 ('traditionem seniorum'); the phrase is ambivalent here, and could refer either to Æthelwold's elders or to the Church Fathers.

[4] On the chronology of Æthelwold's *pueritia*, which fell between the ages of 7 and 14 (Isidore, *Etym.* xi. 2. 3), see above, p. xlii.

[5] On the chronology of Æthelwold's *adolescentia*, which fell between the ages of 14 and 28 (Isidore, *Etym.* xi. 2. 3), see above, pp. xliii–xliv.

[6] Athelstan (924–39) was the first king of all England: see M. Wood, 'The making of King Æthelstan's empire: an English Charlemagne?', *Ideal and Reality in Frankish and Anglo-Saxon Society*, ed. P. Wormald *et al.* (Oxford, 1983), pp. 250–72, and D. N. Dumville, 'Æthelstan, first king of England', in his *Wessex and England from Alfred to Edgar* (Woodbridge, forthcoming). On the cultural achievements of the reign, to which the young Æthelwold was a witness, see M. Lapidge, 'Some Latin poems as evidence for the reign of Athelstan', *ASE* ix (1981), 61–98, and S. D. Keynes, 'King Athelstan's books' in *Learning and Literature*, pp. 143–201.

'way of salvation'[1] was himself with Mary able to sit humbly at the feet of the Lord, listening to the words of salvation from his lips.[2] He was naturally quick and sharp of mind, so that he did not lazily consign to oblivion what he learnt from the elders' teaching,[3] but rather stored it in a retentive memory. Further, he was keen to overcome his tender boyhood years[4] by good conduct and maturity in virtue; always to devote his whole body to the service of God, and give his mind undividedly to fulfilling the wishes of God; and by his correct life to show his gratitude for the gifts he had received from Christ, and to deserve to receive yet greater.

7. HOW AS A YOUTH HE BECAME KNOWN TO KING ATHELSTAN, AND ATTAINED THE STATION OF MINOR CLERIC AND PRIEST. When he reached the flower of youth,[5] rumour brought word of his holy life to King Athelstan,[6] son of King Edward, who had the young man sent for without delay. He was brought to the king; and standing in his presence he found favour in his sight and in the eyes of his thegns. He spent a long period there in the royal *burh* as the king's inseparable companion,[7] learning much from the king's *witan*[8] that was useful and profitable to him. In the end, at the king's command, he was first tonsured by Ælfheah, bishop of Winchester,[9] by the custom of the church, to clerical status,[10] then, after a few years had gone by, consecrated by him to the rank of priest.[11]

[7] For some possible documentary evidence of Æthelwold's presence at Athelstan's court in the early 930s, see above, p. xliii. The implication of Wulfstan's discussion is that Æthelwold pursued a secular career at court until he was ordained by Bishop Ælfheah. See also B. Yorke, 'Æthelwold and the politics of the tenth century', *Bishop Æthelwold*, pp. 65–88, at 71–4.

[8] The word *sapientibus* is a simple calque on the OE word *witan* (literally 'wise men').

[9] Ælfheah was bishop of Winchester 934–51; see M. A. O'Donovan, 'An interim revision of episcopal dates for the province of Canterbury 850–950, part II', *ASE* ii (1973), 91–113, at pp. 111–12.

[10] Wulfstan means that Æthelwold was tonsured into minor orders. On the tonsure of those in minor orders, see H. Leclercq, *DACL* xv. 2430–43, s.v. 'Tonsure'. It would be interesting to know why it was specifically at Athelstan's insistence (*iubente rege*) that Æthelwold took orders; it was also at the king's insistence (*praecipiente rege*) that he was obliged to remain with Bishop Ælfheah when his inclinations were to go to Glastonbury to become a monk.

[11] It is implied, if not stated, that Æthelwold became a priest during Athelstan's reign. Since the canonical age for the priesthood was 30, and since Athelstan died in 939, Æthelwold can have been born no later than 909 (see above, p. xlii). In any event, Æthelwold's consecration seems to have taken place between 934, the date of Ælfheah's accession to the bishopric of Winchester, and 939 (note also that he was not professed as monk until after he went to Glastonbury: below, c. 9).

8. DE PROPHETIA QVAM PRAEDIXIT SANCTVS ÆLFEAGVS EPISCOPVS DE TRIBVS SACERDOTIBVS. Ipse enim beatae recordationis pater Ælfeagus[1] inter cetera sibi conlata spiritalium[a] carismatum dona prophetiae spiritu pollebat;[2] et contigit eum ordinasse in ipso tempore[3] simul Dunstanum et Æthelwoldum et quendam, Æthelstanum[b] uocabulo, qui postmodum monachilem habitum deserens apostata fine tenus perdurauit. Completa autem missarum celebratione sanctus antistes Ælfeagus sibi adhaerentes ita alloquitur: 'hodie coram Deo tribus uiris manus imposui, eosque in sacerdotii ordinem consecraui: quorum duo ad episcopalem pertingent apicem, unus quidem primum in ciuitate Wigornensi, deinde in Cantia, quae est metropolis ecclesiae gentis Anglorum,[4] alter uero mihi quandoque successurus est in pontificii dignitatem, tercius autem per lubrica uoluptatum blandimenta miserabili fine tabescet.' Tunc Æthelstanus[c] interrogauit sanctum antistitem, propinquum suum, dicens: 'Num mihi continget esse unum ex duobus qui episcopali cathedra sublimandi sunt?' Cui respondit antistes: 'Non erit tibi pars neque sors in eo quem praefatus sum ordine, sed neque in ea sanctitate quam in humano conspectu uidebaris inchoasse permansurus es.' Cuius prophetiae uerba quam ueraciter essent prolata rei probauit euentus. Nam duo[d] (sicut dicit scriptura: 'Iustus iustificetur adhuc et sanctus sanctificetur adhuc')[5] ad pontificatus honorem peruenerunt, tercius uero, iuxta terribilem prioris sententiae cominationem quae dicit 'qui in sordibus est sordescat adhuc',[5] in fetore luxuriae uitam finiuit.

[a] spiritualium *NG* [b] Elstanum *T* [c] Elstanus *T* [d] duo *om. G*

[1] Bishop Ælfheah was culted to some modest extent at the Old Minster. The day of his deposition (12 Mar.) is recorded in two 11th-c. Winchester calendars (Cambridge, Trinity College R. 15. 32, and London, BL Cotton Vitellius E. XII: F. Wormald, *English Kalendars before* A.D. *1100*, HBS lxxii (1934), nos. 10 and 12 respectively) and his name is invoked among the confessors in one Winchester litany (see F. Wormald, 'The English saints in the litany in Arundel MS 60', *AB* lxiv (1946), 72–86, at p. 78, no. 93). Wulfstan elsewhere reports that his tomb was adjacent to the high altar of the Old Minster (*Narratio*, Ep. spec. 269); but since no masses or Offices in his name are found in surviving liturgical books, it is unlikely that his feast was fully commemorated.

[2] William of Malmesbury (*Gesta pontificum* ii. 75; ed. N. E. S. A. Hamilton, RS

8. ON THE PROPHECY GIVEN BY ST ÆLFHEAH THE BISHOP CONCERNING THREE PRIESTS. Now father Ælfheah himself, of blessed memory,[1] amongst the other spiritual gifts bestowed on him, was strong in the spirit of prophecy;[2] and it so happened that he ordained on one and the same day[3] Dunstan, Æthelwold, and one Athelstan, who afterwards deserted the monk's habit and remained a stubborn apostate to the end. After celebrating mass, the holy bishop Ælfheah said to those near him: 'Today, in the presence of God, I have laid hands on three men, consecrating them to the priesthood. Two will reach the peak as bishops, one of them first at Worcester, then in Canterbury, the metropolitan see of the English church,[4] while the second will one day be the successor to my own see. As for the third, he will waste away amid the treacherous blandishments of pleasure and come to a miserable end.' Then Athelstan had a question for the holy bishop, who was his kinsman: 'Shall I be one of the two to be raised to a bishop's throne?' The bishop replied: 'You will have no part or share in the career that I have mentioned; you will not even continue in the holy state which to men's eyes you seemed to have entered upon.' The outcome showed the truth of these prophetic words. For two (in the words of the scripture 'he that is righteous, let him be righteous still: and he that is holy, let him be holy still')[5] reached the honourable position of bishop; but the third fell under the dreadful threat of the sentence that precedes: 'he which is filthy, let him be filthy still,'[5] and ended his life amid the stink of luxury.

(1870), pp. 164–5) gives a second example of Ælfheah's prophetic powers, namely that on a certain Ash Wednesday Ælfheah decreed (as was his wont) fasting and abstinence from sexual intercourse. One of those present treated this decree as a joke, whereupon the bishop was heard to mutter, 'Contristas me, miser, nesciens quid uentura pariet dies.' The man was duly found dead in his room the following day, having been strangled.

[3] Wulfstan is vague as to when and where the ordinations took place: at the Old Minster, presumably? Does Wulfstan thereby imply that all three men were in minor orders among Ælfheah's cathedral clergy at Winchester? In any case the event took place before Dunstan became abbot of Glastonbury (see below, p. 14 n. 4).

[4] Dunstan was bishop of Worcester 957–9, then briefly bishop of London 959–60 (a detail omitted by Wulfstan), and finally archbishop of Canterbury 960–88. On his career, see Robinson, *Times*, pp. 81–103.

[5] Rev. 22: 11.

9. QVOMODO ÆTHELWOLDVS GLASTONIAM PERVENIT ET MONACHVS FACTVS QVALITER IBI DEO SERVIENS VIXERIT. Ætheluuoldus autem Christi famulus, nomine,[a] mente et opere beniuolus,[1] artam uiam quae ducit ad uitam[2] recto itinere gradiens, cotidiana Deo cooperante studuit melioratione succrescere, dans operam diligenter doctrinis et exemplis Ælfeagi susceptoris et ordinatoris sui. Aput quem praecipiente rege quo melius imbueretur aliquandiu commoratus est,[3] ac postmodum Glastoniam perueniens magnifici uiri Dunstani, abbatis eiusdem monasterii,[4] discipulatui se tradidit. Cuius magisterio multum proficiens, tandem monastici[b] ordinis habitum ab ipso suscepit,[5] humili deuotione eius[c] regimini deditus. Didicit namque inibi liberalem grammaticae artis peritiam[6] atque mellifluam metricae rationis dulcedinem,[d7] et more apis prudentissimae,[8] quae solet boni odoris arbores circumuolando requirere et iocundi saporis holeribus[e] incumbere, diuinorum carpebat flores uoluminum. Catholicos quoque et nominatos studiose legebat auctores, insuper uigiliis et orationibus perseueranter insistens, et abstinentia semet ipsum edomans, et[f] fratres ad ardua semper exhortans.[g] Qui cum pro merito

[a] et *ins.* G [b] monasticis G [c] eius *om.* G [d] dulcedine G
[e] oleri G [f] et *om.* G [g] exhortabatur G

---

[1] The onomastic play on Æthelwold's name: Wulfstan evidently took it as a compound of *æþel* ('noble') + *wolde* (pret. sg. of *willan*, 'to wish', 'to will'), hence 'nobly intentioned'; in fact the second theme is an orthographical variant of OE *weald* ('might', 'dominion').

[2] Matt. 7: 14.

[3] It is not clear why the king—still Athelstan, presumably—was commanding (*praecipiente*) Æthelwold to remain with Ælfheah. It was apparently only after Athelstan's death (27 Oct. 939) that Æthelwold was free to pursue his own inclination to become a monk, whereupon he went directly to Glastonbury to join his former colleague Dunstan (cf. above, p. 13 n. 3).

[4] The precise dates of Dunstan's abbacy are not known. The date *c.*940 is usually given for his election (see F. M. Stenton, *Anglo-Saxon England*, 3rd edn. (Oxford, 1971), p. 446, and *Heads*, p. 50), on the grounds that Dunstan's earliest biographer (.B.) states that it was early in the reign of King Edmund (939–46) that Dunstan was made abbot (*Vita S. Dunstani*, c. 14; *Memorials*, p. 25); but this biographer's chronology is frequently in error (he states, impossibly, that Dunstan was born during Athelstan's reign (c. 3; *Memorials*, p. 6), which would make him no more than 15 when he became abbot), and it is not clear that he is to be trusted on this point. The implication of Wulfstan's account is that Dunstan had preceded Æthelwold to Glastonbury while Athelstan was still alive, hence before 27 Oct. 939, and that Æthelwold later joined him as soon as he was free to do so. But the chronology (and indeed the identity) of Dunstan's immediate predecessors as abbots of Glastonbury is unclear (see J. A. Robinson, *Somerset Historical Essays* (London, 1921), p. 40), and it may be unwise to lay too much stress on Wulfstan's

9. HOW ÆTHELWOLD CAME TO GLASTONBURY, AND HOW HE LIVED THERE AS A MONK SERVING GOD. Æthelwold, servant of Christ, and 'well-intentioned' in name,[1] mind, and deed, proceeded straight along 'the narrow way which leadeth unto life'.[2] He was anxious, with God's help, to grow better with every day, and he studiously attended to the teaching and example of his patron and ordainer Ælfheah. With him he stayed for some time at the king's wish to improve his education.[3] Later he went to Glastonbury and became a disciple of the distinguished Dunstan, abbot of that monastery.[4] He profited greatly by Dunstan's teaching, and eventually received the habit of the monastic order from him, devoting himself humbly to his rule.[5] At Glastonbury he learned skill in the liberal art of grammar[6] and the honey-sweet system of metrics;[7] like a provident bee[8] that habitually flits around looking for scented trees and settling on greenery of pleasant taste, he laid toll on the flowers of religious books. He was eager to read the best-known Christian writers, and was in addition constant in vigils and prayer, taming himself by fasting and never ceasing to exhort his fellow monks to strive for the heights. Though he was

rather vaguely-worded narrative of the events. In any case, Dunstan presumably remained as abbot until he was exiled by King Eadwig in 956.

[5] Æthelwold 'eventually' was professed as monk: it would be interesting to know how long a novitiate is implied by the vague expression *tandem*.

[6] Something of Dunstan's interest in grammar may be deduced from the contents of his so-called 'class-book', now Oxford, Bodleian Library, Auct. F. 4. 32 (ed. in facsimile by R. W. Hunt, *Umbrae Codicum Occidentalium*, iv (Amsterdam, 1961)): the first part of that composite manuscript (fos. 1–18) contains a 9th-c. copy of Eutyches, *Ars de uerbo*. On Æthelwold's grammatical studies, see above, pp. lxxxvi–lxxxvii.

[7] Dunstan's proficiency in composing verse is witnessed by a small corpus of surviving Latin poetry: see M. Lapidge, 'The hermeneutic style in tenth-century Anglo-Latin literature', *ASE* iv (1975), 67–111, at pp. 95–7, 108–11, and 'St Dunstan's Latin poetry', *Anglia*, xcviii (1980), 101–6. On Æthelwold's studies in Latin metrics, see above, p. lxxxvii. Note that Wulfstan's wording here is clearly indebted to Aldhelm: see *Aldhelmi Opera*, ed. R. Ehwald, *MGH*, Auct. antiq., xv (Berlin, 1919), pp. 260 (*mellifluam dogmatum dulcedinem*), 500 (*artis grammaticae ratione*).

[8] The image of the clever bee gathering pollen like a scholar gathering knowledge is a common topos, and may have been known to Wulfstan from Aldhelm, prose *De uirginitate*, cc. 5–6, and 19 (*Aldhelmi Opera*, ed. Ehwald, pp. 233–4, 249), where the wording of the latter passage (*flores ex sacrorum uoluminum prato decerpens*) is close to Wulfstan's. Aldhelm does not, however, describe his bee as *prudentissima*, and Wulfstan may have drawn that term either from Cassian's description of the clever bee (*Institutiones* v. 4; ed. M. Petschenig, *CSEL* xvii (1888), p. 83) or from Asser, *De uita Ælfredi*, c. 76 (ed. W. H. Stevenson, *Asser's Life of King Alfred* (Oxford, 1904), p. 61). Æthelwold also used the image in the prohoemium to his *Regularis concordia*, c. 5, but the wording is not close to Wulfstan's.

sanctitatis ab omnibus amaretur et monasterii decanus[1] ab abbate suo constitueretur, nullum elationis incurrit periculum, sed tantae subiectis praebuit humilitatis exemplum ut cotidiano[a] manuum opere hortum excolendo laboraret et fratribus ad prandium poma ac diuersi generis legumina praepararet,[2] ut post spiritalem[b] animarum refectionem corporum quoque necessaria ministraret, prae oculis semper retinens illud dominicum: 'Quicumque uoluerit inter uos maior fieri sit uester minister, et qui uoluerit inter uos primus esse erit uester seruus,'[3] et illud: 'Quanto magnus es humilia te in omnibus et coram Deo inuenies gratiam.'[4] Haec et alia memoriae commendans scripturae testimonia per disciplinam subditos[5] et per humilitatem custodiebat[c] semet ipsum.

10. DE OBITV REGIS ÆTHELSTANI ET DE SVCCESSIONE FRATRVM EIVS IN REGNVM. Contigit interea uictoriosissimum regem Æthelstanum, quarto anno postquam[d] hostilem paganorum exercitum[6] maxima strage peremit,[7] obisse et fratrem eius Eadmundum pro eo regni gubernacula suscepisse. Cui post annos sex et dimidium crudeliter interempto[8] successit in regnum frater eius Eadredus,

[a] cotidianum *T* [b] spiritualem *NG* [c] custodiat *G* [d] plusquam *T*

---

[1] It is not clear whether, as *decanus*, Æthelwold was the senior monk next in authority to the abbot, or whether that authority would have been exercised by a *praepositus* ('prior'). Tenth-c. Anglo-Latin sources are ambivalent on this point. The *Regularis concordia* apparently envisages both officers within a monastic *familia*, with the *decanus* subordinate to the *praepositus* (see *Reg. conc.*, p. 39 and discussion by Symons, pp. xxx–xxxi). However, in .B.'s *Vita S. Dunstani*, c. 26, the important stations attained by Dunstan's pupils are given as 'praepositi uidelicet, decani, abbates, episcopi, etiam archiepiscopi' (*Memorials* p. 26), where from the reverse order it would appear that deans were regarded as senior to priors. In the *Consuetudines Floriacenses antiquiores*, cc. 4–6, it is the *decanus* who is second in command to the abbot, while the *praepositus* is of a lower station altogether (ed. Davril and Donnat, *CCM* vii (3). 11–13), and there is evidence for thinking that the stipulations of this customary were known to Æthelwold and his advisers (see above, p. lix). In any case Æthelwold did not let his high station go to his head and become like the type of haughty dean castigated by the *Regula S. Benedicti* as being *inflatus superbia*: 'quique decani, si ex eis aliqua forte quis inflatus superbia repertus fuerit reprehensibilis, correptus semel et iterum atque tertio si emendare noluerit, deiciatur . . .' (c. 21).

[2] The ideal of humility is explained in the *Regula S. Benedicti*, c. 7; the monastic fare prepared by Æthelwold is that specified by the *Regula*, c. 39 ('poma aut nascentia leguminum').

[3] Matt. 20: 26–7.

[4] Ecclus. 3: 20.

[5] The wording here, like much of this chapter, is indebted to the *Regula S. Benedicti*, cc. 34 ('districtiori disciplinae subdatur'), 60 ('disciplinae . . . subditum'), and 62 ('disciplinae subdendum').

universally loved for his holiness and was made dean[1] of the monastery by the abbot, he ran no risk of becoming proud; indeed he set those below him such a standard of humility that he performed manual labour every day, cultivating the garden and getting fruit and different kinds of vegetables ready for the monks' meal.[2] In this way he could follow up the spiritual refreshing of souls with ministry to the needs of bodies. For he always kept before his eyes the saying of our Lord: 'whosoever will be great among you, let him be your minister; and whosoever will be chief among you, let him be your servant,'[3] and also: 'The greater thou art, the more humble thyself, and thou shalt find favour before the Lord.'[4] Committing this text and others from the scriptures to his memory, he used discipline to guard those beneath him[5] and humility to guard himself.

10. ON THE DEATH OF KING ATHELSTAN AND THE SUCCESSION OF HIS BROTHERS TO THE KINGDOM. Meanwhile, it happened that the all-victorious King Athelstan died, in the fourth year after his destruction,[6] with great carnage,[7] of a hostile pagan army, and that his brother Edmund took over from him the reins of government. After six and a half years Edmund was cruelly murdered,[8] and his brother Eadred succeeded to the throne. Eadred was a particular

[6] Athelstan's great victory over an army of pagans, to which Wulfstan here refers, is clearly the Battle of *Brunanburh* (precise location not known), which is commemorated with a lengthy poem in the Anglo-Saxon Chronicle, s.a. 937 (also ed. A. Campbell, *The Battle of Brunanburh* (London, 1938)), and in which Athelstan and Edmund utterly routed a combined army of Scots, Welsh, and Norsemen (see A. P. Smyth, *Scandinavian York and Dublin*, 2 vols. (Dublin, 1975–9), ii. 62–88). In describing Athelstan as *uictoriosissimus* it is probable that Wulfstan had the concluding lines of the poem in mind (ll. 65–8). The implication is that Wulfstan had before him a manuscript of the Anglo-Saxon Chronicle; and this is confirmed by the chronology given in some manuscripts of that work, according to which *Brunanburh* was fought in 937 and Athelstan died in 940, which would account for Wulfstan's dating of his death to the *quarto anno* after the battle. There are grounds for thinking that MS A of the Chronicle—the so-called 'Parker Chronicle'—was at Winchester at this time: see Bately, *MS A*, pp. xiii–xiv. On Wulfstan's use of the Anglo-Saxon Chronicle, see above, p. cviii, and below, n. 8.

[7] The words *strage peremit* could form the cadence of a hexameter, and it is worth asking if Wulfstan was here also following a Latin poem on Athelstan's victory. No such poem survives; but in a Glastonbury booklist of 1247 there is an entry 'Bella Atheltani regis' (*Iohannis Glastoniensis Chronica*, ed. T. Hearne, 2 vols. (Oxford, 1726), ii. 438). Did Wulfstan have before him this lost Latin poem on Athelstan? Or is the hexameter cadence a case of stylistic embellishment by Wulfstan (cf. above, p. cxi)?

[8] Edmund reigned from Oct. 939 to 26 May 946. It is noteworthy that the Anglo-Saxon Chronicle also states, s.a. 946, that Edmund reigned six and a half years ('he hæfde rice seofoþe healf gear'): a further link between Wulfstan and the Chronicle.

qui erat Veteris Coenobii in Wintonia specialis amator atque defensor,[a][1] ut testantur ea quae ipso iubente fabricata sunt ornamenta, magna scilicet aurea crux,[2] altare aureum et cetera quae larga manu benignus illuc ad honorem beatorum apostolorum Petri et Pauli[3] direxit ibique aeternaliter ad Dei laudem et gloriam conseruari praecepit: qui etiam, si uita comes fieret, orientalem porticum eiusdem Wintoniensis ecclesiae deauratis imbricibus adornare disposuit.[4] Cuius regni tempore uir Domini Ætheluuoldus, adhuc cupiens ampliori scripturarum scientia doceri et monastica religione perfectius[b] informari, decreuit ultramarinas adire partes. Sed uenerabilis regina Eadgifu, mater regis memorati, praeuenit eius conamina,[5] dans consilium regi ne talem uirum sineret egredi de regno suo, insuper asserens tantam in eo fuisse[c] Dei sapientiam quae et sibi et aliis sufficere posset, quamuis ad alienae[d] patriae fines ob hanc causam minime tenderet.[e]

11. QVOMODO REGE EADREDO FAVENTE SANCTVS VIR ABBANDVNENSIS MONASTERII CVRAM SVSCEPERIT[f] EIVSQVE LOCI ABBAS ORDINATVS FVERIT. Quibus auditis delectatus rex magnam circa Dei famulum coepit habere dilectionem,[g] placuitque ei, suadente matre sua, dare sancto uiro quendam locum, uocabulo Abbandoniam, in quo modicum antiquitus habebatur monasteriolum,[h][6] sed erat tunc neglectum ac destitutum,[i] uilibus aedificiis consistens[7] et quadraginta

[a] defensor atque amator *G* [b] fectius *G* [c] esse *G* [d] alienos *T(?)* [e] tendisset *G* [f] susciperit *T* [g] delectationem *T* [h] haberetur monasterium *G* [i] atque destructum *G*

---

[1] Eadred reigned from May 946 to 23 Nov. 955. He was buried in the Old Minster (ASC s.a. 955 D). That he was a *specialis amator* is clear from the terms of his will (S 1515 = BCS 912): see F. E. Harmer, *Select English Historical Documents of the Ninth and Tenth Centuries* (Cambridge, 1914), pp. 34–5 (no. 21); the will is trans. *EHD*, pp. 554–6 (no. 107). Eadred left three Wiltshire estates (at Downton, Damarham, and Calne) to the Old Minster, as well as two golden crosses (see below, n. 2), two golden swords, and £400.

[2] The golden crucifix is now lost, but was presumably one of those bequeathed to the Old Minster by the terms of Eadred's will (see above, n. 1). On the munificence of Anglo-Saxon crucifixes, see C. R. Dodwell, *Anglo-Saxon Art: A New Perspective* (Manchester, 1982), pp. 210–13. It is also interesting to note that in a charter dated 949 (S 543 = BCS 879) King Eadred granted an estate on the Isle of Wight to his goldsmith Ælfsige for the service 'quam mihi auri argentique fabrica sollicite deseruit': possibly it was Ælfsige who made the golden crucifix in question.

[3] We know from Bede (*HE* iii. 7) that the Old Minster was dedicated to SS Peter and Paul, and Bede's information is confirmed by a number of early 8th-c. charters: S 254 = BCS 158, S 258 = BCS 179, S 284 = BCS 398, S 354 = BCS 565, S 444 = BCS 731, and others.

friend and champion of the Old Minster at Winchester,[1] as the ornaments manufactured at his orders bear witness: a great gold cross[2], a gold altar, and the other things that he graciously and generously sent there in honour of the blessed apostles Peter and Paul,[3] with instructions that they be preserved there in perpetuity to the praise and glory of God. He also planned, if he should live long enough, to decorate the eastern *porticus* of the same church at Winchester with gilded tiles.[4] During this reign, Æthelwold, the man of the Lord, in his continuing eagerness to know the scriptures more thoroughly and to receive a more perfect grounding in a monk's religious life, determined to go overseas. But the venerable queen Eadgifu, the king's mother, forestalled his plans,[5] advising the king not to allow such a man to leave his kingdom, and asserting moreover that he was so filled with the wisdom given by God that he had enough for others as well as for himself, even if he did not go to foreign parts for this purpose.

11. HOW WITH THE ENCOURAGEMENT OF KING EADRED THE HOLY MAN TOOK CHARGE OF THE MONASTERY OF ABINGDON AND WAS ORDAINED ABBOT OF THAT HOUSE. The king was pleased to hear this, and began to feel great affection for the servant of God. Swayed by his mother, he decided to give the holy man a place called Abingdon. Here there had of old been a small monastery,[6] but this had by now become neglected and forlorn. Its buildings were poor,[7] and its

[4] From the archaeological excavations carried out at Winchester in the 1960s it is known that, in the period before Æthelwold's massive rebuilding programme, the Old Minster was a simple double-cell structure, with an eastern chamber for the altar and the priest, and a chancel for the congregation (see M. Biddle, '*Felix Urbs Winthonia*: Winchester in the age of monastic reform', *Tenth-Century Studies*, pp. 123–40, at 136; and B. Cherry, 'Ecclesiastical Architecture', in *The Archaeology of Anglo-Saxon England*, ed. D. Wilson (London, 1976), pp. 151–200, at 160–4). It is not clear precisely how Eadred proposed to decorate the eastern *porticus* with golden tiles, or whether the reference is to a golden mosaic such as that found in the apse of the Carolingian church of Saint-Germigny-des-Prés; possibly the description is indebted to the gilded walls of Solomon's temple: 3 Kgs. (1 Kgs.) 6: 21–2 and 1 Chr. 29: 4 (*deaurandos parietes templi*).

[5] On Queen Eadgifu, see below, p. 21 n. 10. Yet again the Crown intervenes in Æthelwold's career: why?

[6] On the nature of the (7th-c.?) monastery built by Abbot Hean, there is the doubtful evidence of the 13th-c. treatise *De abbatibus Abbendoniae* (*Chron. Abingdon*, ii. 272–3); see F. M. Stenton, *The Early History of the Abbey of Abingdon* (Reading, 1913), pp. 2–3, 7; M. Biddle, H. T. Lambrick, and J. N. L. Myres, 'The early history of Abingdon, Berkshire, and its abbey', *Medieval Archaeology*, xii (1968), 26–69, at pp. 26–34; and A. Thacker, 'Æthelwold and Abingdon', *Bishop Æthelwold*, pp. 42–64, esp. 44–5.

[7] According to the (doubtful) evidence of the *De abbatibus Abbendoniae*, the monastery granted to Æthelwold consisted of twelve monks' dwellings and twelve chapels, all surviving from the time of Abbot Hean (*Chron. Abingdon*, ii. 277).

tantum mansas possidens; reliquam uero praefati loci terram, quae centum cassatorum lustris hinc inde gyratur, regali dominio[a] subiectam rex ipse possidebat.[1] Factumque est, consentiente Dunstano abbate, secundum regis uoluntatem, ut uir Dei Ætheluuoldus praenotati loci susciperet curam, quatinus in eo monachos ordinaret regulariter Deo seruientes. Venit ergo seruus Dei[b] ad locum sibi commissum: quem protinus secuti sunt quidam clerici de Glastonia, scilicet Osgarus,[2] Foldbirthus,[3] Frithegarus,[c4] et Ordbirthus de Wintonia,[5] et Eadricus de Lundonia,[6] eius discipulatui se subdentes. Congregauitque sibi in breui spacio gregem monachorum,[7] quibus ipse abbas, iubente rege, ordinatus est.[d8] Dedit etiam rex possessionem regalem quam in Abbandonia possederat,[9] hoc est centum cassatos, cum optimis aedificiis, abbati et fratribus ad augmentum cotidiani uictus, et de regio thesauro suo multum eos[e] in pecuniis iuuit; sed mater eius largius solatia munerum eis direxit.[10] Tantamque gratiam Dominus sibi

[a] domino *NG* [b] dei seruus *β* [c] Frithegarus *om. T* [d] est *om. G* [e] eis *G*

[1] The source for Wulfstan's statement that the original endowment consisted of forty hides is not known; on the hundred hides belonging to the royal fisc (which were subsequently donated to the abbey), see below, p. 21 n. 9.

[2] On Osgar, who later accompanied Æthelwold to Winchester (c. 17) and subsequently became abbot of Abingdon (c. 21), see below, p. 26 n. 3, 27 n. 4.

[3] The identity of Foldbriht is uncertain. He is not listed among the monks of Abingdon in *LVH* ('nomina fratrum Abbandunensis cenobii': pp. 59–61). The name is exceptionally rare, and it is possible, therefore, that this Foldbriht is identical with the Foldbriht who was abbot of Pershore *c.*970–88 (*Heads*, p. 58) and whose miraculous resuscitation at the hands of Bishop Oswald is recorded by Byrhtferth in the *Vita S. Oswaldi* iv. 8 (*HCY* i. 439). His obit is recorded in Oxford, Bodleian Library, Hatton 113 (a Worcester manuscript) against 22 Apr.; see Gerchow, *Gedenküberlieferung*, p. 339.

[4] Frithegar's identity is also problematical. He is listed in *LVH* among the 'nomina fratrum Abbandunensis cenobii' as being abbot (p. 60: 'Fryþegar abbas'), and his obit is recorded in Cambridge, Corpus Christi College 57 (Abingdon, s. x²): *obitus Freoþegari abbatis* (Gerchow, *Gedenküberlieferung*, p. 336); yet it is curious that later Abingdon sources know nothing of his abbacy there (see *Heads*, p. 23). An abbot Freoþegar—probably the same person—attests a charter of King Edgar dated 967 (S 749 = BCS 1283; *Burton*, no. 22). According to the so-called *Liber tertius* of the 'Evesham Chronicle', which was compiled in the early 13th c. by Thomas of Marlborough, one *Freodegarus monachus* was made abbot of Evesham by Ælfhere of Mercia at the time of the anti-monastic reaction in 976 (*Chronicon Abbatiae de Evesham*, ed. W. D. Macray, RS (1863), p. 79). Hart took this *Freodegarus* to be identical with the monk of Abingdon (*ECNENM*, pp. 335–6); but there are difficulties with the identification (on which see Sawyer, *Burton*, p. 36), and in any case it is perhaps unlikely that a follower of Æthelwold would have seemed to Ælfhere a suitable appointee to an abbacy. However, the excessive rarity of the name Frithegar (or Freothegar or Frithugar) lends some support to the identification.

[5] Ordbriht of Winchester subsequently had a very distinguished career, becoming abbot of Chertsey after Æthelwold's reformation of that house in 964 (see *Heads*, p. 38)

estate consisted of only forty hides of land. The remainder of the estate, which lies adjacent to it and consists of a further hundred hides, was the possession of the king and under his royal control.[1] At the king's wish, and with the consent of Dunstan, it came about that the man of God Æthelwold took charge of this place, with the aim of establishing monks there to serve God according to the rule. The servant of God accordingly came to the place he had been charged with. He was immediately followed by certain clerics in minor orders from Glastonbury, namely Osgar,[2] Foldbriht,[3] and Frithegar,[4] together with Ordbriht from Winchester,[5] and Eadric from London:[6] all submitting themselves to his teaching. Soon he had assembled a flock of monks,[7] and at the king's behest he was ordained their abbot.[8] The king also gave his royal estates in Abingdon,[9] the hundred hides, with excellent buildings, to the abbot and the monks to increase their everyday provisions, and he gave them much monetary help from his royal treasury; but his mother sent them presents on an even more lavish scale.[10] The

and subsequently bishop of Selsey (988 × 990–1007 × 1009); see Hart, *ECNENM*, pp. 350–1.

[6] Eadric is listed in *LVH* among the 'nomina fratrum Abbandunensis cenobii' in sixth place, as 'Eadric sacerdos' (*LVH*, p. 60; Gerchow, *Gedenküberlieferung*, p. 325), immediately after the abbots and hence in a position of some prestige. He does not seem to have obtained an abbacy, and nothing further is known of him.

[7] It would be interesting to know the size of Æthelwold's *grex monachorum*. According to the 13th-c. tract *De abbatibus Abbendoniae*, Æthelwold established fifty monks there (*Chron. Abingdon*, ii. 279: 'instituit et .l. monachos'), but this figure is almost certainly too high. Cf. the list of Abingdon monks in *LVH* under the heading 'nomina fratrum Abbandunensis cenobii', where forty-one names are given covering a period of five abbots from Osgar to Æthelwine, 964–1030 (*LVH*, pp. 59–61; Gerchow, *Gedenküberlieferung*, pp. 325–6).

[8] The precise date of Æthelwold's ordination as abbot is not known; a date of *c.*954 is usually given (*Heads*, p. 23) on the basis of John of Glastonbury's 14th-c. *Cronica* (see above, p. xliv).

[9] King Eadred's charter in favour of Abingdon, dated 955, is not preserved in its original form, but in a copy in the 12th-c. Abingdon Chronicle which may well have suffered interpolation (S 567 = BCS 906, *Chron. Abingdon*, i. 124–7; cf. Gelling, *ECTV*, no. 64, where it is described as a 'complete fabrication'). The grant included estates at Ginge, Goosey, Longworth, and Cumnor; but these amount in sum to only 80 hides.

[10] Queen Eadgifu (cf. above, c. 10) was the third wife of King Edward the Elder, whom she married in *c.*919, and the mother of Kings Edmund and Eadred (and hence the grandmother of Kings Eadwig and Edgar). Her munificence to Abingdon is mentioned in the Abingdon Chronicle (*Chron. Abingdon*, i. 130), but there is no surviving original charter in her name in favour of that house. She is known to have made donations to other ecclesiastical institutions (see S 1211–12). The latest charter in which she appears as witness is the 'New Minster Foundation Charter' (S 745 = BCS 1190; cf. above, pp. lxxxix–xc), dated 966; she presumably died shortly thereafter. For her career, see Hart, *ECNENM*, p. 315; A. Campbell, *Encomium Emmae Reginae*, Camden Third Series, lxxii (London, 1949), pp. 62–4; and M. A. Meyer, 'Women and the tenth-century English monastic reform', *RB* lxxxvii (1977), 34–61.

seruientibus contulit ut ad praefatum coenobium, quod antea rebus erat pauperrimum, omnes simul diuitiae putarentur adfluere,[1] et sic cuncta prosperis successibus occurrere ut palam sententia dominicae promissionis[a] impleri uideretur qua[b] dicitur: 'Primum quaerite regnum Dei et iustitiam eius, et[c] omnia adicientur uobis.'[2]

12. QVOD REX EADREDVS AD MONASTERIVM ⟨VENERIT⟩[d] ET HOSPITIBVS TOTA DIE BIBENTIBVS LIQVOR EXHAVRIRI NEQVIVERIT. Venit ergo rex quadam die ad monasterium, ut aedificiorum structuram per se ipsum ordinaret; mensusque est omnia fundamenta monasterii propria manu,[3] quemadmodum muros erigere decreuerat; rogauitque eum abbas in hospicio[4] cum suis prandere.[e] Annuit rex ilico; et contigit adesse sibi non paucos optimatum suorum uenientes ex gente Northanhimbrorum,[5] qui omnes cum rege adierunt conuiuium. Laetatusque[f] est rex, et iussit abunde propinare[g] hospitibus ydromellum,[6] clausis diligenter foribus ne quis fugiendo potationem regalis conuiuii deserere uideretur.[h] Quid multa? Hauserunt ministri liquorem tota die ad omnem sufficientiam conuiuantibus; sed nequiuit ipse liquor[i] exhauriri de uase, nisi ad

[a] passionis *G* [b] quia *G* [c] hec *ins.* *G* [d] *Supplied from Capitula* [e] prandere cum suis *G* [f] letatus *β* [g] propinari *G* [h] clausis . . . uideretur *G; om. Tβ* [i] liquor ipse *G*

[1] Some impression of the wealth of Abingdon at this time may be gleaned from the list of ecclesiastical furniture commissioned by Æthelwold and recorded in the Abingdon Chronicle: 'dedit [sc. Æthelwold] autem, ut ex antiquorum librorum accepimus attestatione, calicem unum aureum immensi ponderis . . . dedit etiam tres cruces admodum decoras ex argento et auro puro . . . ornauit etiam ecclesiam textis tam ex argento puro quam ex auro obrizo pariter et lapidibus pretiosissimis, thuribulis et phialis, peluibus fusilibus et candelabris ex argento ductilibus . . . tabulam fecit argenteam pretio adpretiatam trecentarum librarum, cuius materiam forma exsuperat artificialis . . . fecit etiam duas campanas propriis manibus . . . preterea fecit uir uenerabilis Athelwoldus quandam rotam tintinnabulis plenam quam "auream" nuncupant propter laminas ipsius deauratas' (*Chron. Abingdon*, i. 344–5). The tract *De abbatibus Abbendoniae* adds that the crosses were four feet high, that the *rota* or 'bell-wheel' was worth £40, and describes the *tabula* or 'altar-frontal' as follows: 'fecit et sanctus Athelwoldus tabulam supra altare, in qua erat sculpta et .xii. apostoli . . .' (*Chron. Abingdon*, ii. 278). Clearly Æthelwold's church at Abingdon was lavishly furnished, and it is a pity that all this furniture was broken up and confiscated by the Normans.

[2] Matt. 6: 33; Luke 12: 31.

[3] On kings and bishops and other dignitaries doing craft work *propria manu*, see Dodwell, *Anglo-Saxon Art*, pp. 49–50.

[4] In the *Regularis concordia* Æthelwold specifies that the abbot of a monastery is to be zealous in providing hospitality for guests in the monastery guesthouses: 'omnia igitur

Lord so bestowed his grace on his servants that men thought all the riches of the kingdom were flowing at once into a monastery that had formerly been poverty-stricken.[1] All seemed to be going so well that it looked as though what the Lord promised was being manifestly fulfilled: 'Seek ye first the kingdom of God, and his righteousness; and all things shall be added unto you.'[2]

12. THAT KING EADRED CAME TO THE MONASTERY, AND THOUGH THE GUESTS DRANK ALL DAY THE DRINK COULD NOT BE EXHAUSTED. One day the king visited the monastery to oversee the building works in person. With his own hand[3] he measured all the foundations of the monastery according to his plan for the erection of the walls. Then the abbot invited him to dine with his people in the hospice.[4] The king was quick to accept. Now it chanced that he had with him not a few of his Northumbrian thegns,[5] and they all accompanied him to the party. The king was delighted, and ordered the guests to be served with lavish draughts of mead.[6] The doors were carefully secured to make sure that no one should get out and be seen to be leaving the royal carousal. Well, the servants drew off drink all day to the hearts' content of the diners, but the level in the container could not be reduced below a palm's

humanitatis officia in hospitio pater ipse, si quomodo potuerit, uel fratrum quilibet deuotissime praebeat' (*Reg. conc.*, p. 62); cf. the 'New Minster Foundation Charter' (S 745 = BCS 1190), also probably drafted by Æthelwold: 'laicis in hospitio condecens exhibeatur humanitas.'

[5] Eadred's brief reign was marked by troubled dealings with the Viking kingdom of Northumbria and with its king Eric Bloodaxe. In 947 the *witan* of the Northumbrians pledged themselves to Eadred (ASC 947 D), but the following year they accepted Eric as king, whereupon Eadred invaded, ravaged, and subdued Northumbria, and forced the Northumbrian *witan* to come to his terms (ASC 948 D); Eric was finally expelled and murdered in 954 (ASC 954 D). The events described here by Wulfstan apparently took place in 954, and it is not surprising that the royal household should have included Northumbrian hostages as well as members of the Northumbrian *witan* which had pledged itself to Eadred; see also below, p. 24 n. 2.

[6] According to a 13th-c. interpolation in the Abingdon Chronicle, Æthelwold's abbacy at Abingdon was marked by the generous provision of food and drink—especially mead—for his monks. Æthelwold is said to have instituted a large measure of drink served in a flagon, which was taken twice daily, at lunch (*prandium*) and dinner (*cena*); the generous size of the flagon earned it the name *bolla Æthelwoldi* ('an Æthelwold beaker'). Moreover, on high-ranking feast-days, the monks were served mead: 'in festiuis etiam diebus constituit eis, siue in albis siue in cappis, hydromellum, uidelicet ad prandium inter sex fratres sextarium, et ad cenam inter .xii. fratres sextarium' (*Chron. Abingdon*, i. 346). See Knowles, *MO*, pp. 716–17, who doubts the general reliability of this report.

mensuram palmi,[1] inebriatis suatim[a] Northanimbris[2] et uesperi cum laetitia recedentibus.

13. QVOD REGNANTE EADGARO TEMPLVM PRAEDICTI COENOBII CONSTRVCTVM ET DEDICATVM FVERIT. Non tamen coepit[b] Ætheluuoldus abbas designatum sibi opus aedificare[c] in diebus Eadredi regis, quia celeriter ex hac uita migrauit die .VIIII. Kalendarum Decembris.[3] Sed regnante glorioso rege Eadgaro,[4] insigni et clementissimo, praepotente ac inuictissimo regis Eadmundi filio, honorabile templum in honore sanctae[d] Dei genitricis semperque uirginis Mariae in eodem construxit loco et consummauit, quod usque in hunc diem uisu melius quam sermone ostenditur.[5]

14. DE ORDINATIONE DVNSTANI ET QVOD ABBAS ÆTHELWOLDVS OSGARVM MONACHVM TRANS MARE DIREXERIT ET DE QVODAM FRATRE[e] ÆLFSTANO. Circa haec tempora eligitur abbas Dunstanus ad episcopatum Wigornensis ecclesiae,[6] iuxta prophetiam sancti Ælfeagi episcopi, sicut supra tetigimus.[f] Et post aliquot[g] annorum

[a] inebriatis suatim *G*; gaudentibus *Tβ* [b] coepit *om. G* [c] edificauit *G* [d] sanctae *om. G* [e] frater *T*; *corrected from Capitula* [f] tegimus *G* [g] aliqua *T (a deleted letter follows)*

[1] A similar miracle involving Æthelwold is recorded by Goscelin in his *Vita S. Wulfhildae*: on one occasion, when Æthelwold and his retinue visited Barking while Wulfhild was abbess there (dates unknown: *Heads*, p. 208), the drink was poured unceasingly and could not be exhausted (M. Esposito, 'La vie de sainte Vulfilde par Goscelin de Cantorbéry', *AB* xxxii (1913), 10–26, at p. 19). Goscelin attributed this event to Wulfhild's miraculous power, but he makes a cross-reference to Wulfstan's *Vita S. Æthelwoldi* at this point (see above, p. clvi), revealing that the present chapter was the source of Goscelin's story. Cf. also the story told in .B.'s *Vita S. Dunstani*, c. 10 (*Memorials*, p. 18), and Ovid, *Met.* viii. 679–80.

[2] The archaic adverb *suatim* ('in one's own fashion') is beloved of Anglo-Latin writers. It was used several times by Aldhelm in his prose *De uirginitate* (ed. Ehwald, pp. 246, 281, 318), and after him by pretentious authors such as Asser (*Asser's Life of King Alfred*, ed. Stevenson, pp. 46, 55, 93; see discussion at p. 278) and Byrhtferth. It also occurs in 10th-c. Anglo-Saxon glossaries (T. Wright, *Anglo-Saxon and Old English Vocabularies*, 2nd edn., rev. R. P. Wülcker, 2 vols. (London, 1884), i. 491, 514, where it is glossed *hiora ðeawe*). This is almost certainly the meaning which it has here in Wulfstan, although it is perhaps worth noting the existence of an adverb *suatim* meaning 'swinishly', which is, however, only attested once in all Latin, in the grammarian Nigidius Figulus, whose works did not survive the fall of Rome and were—it is quite safe to say—unknown to Wulfstan; Nonius Marcellus, who preserves the passage of Nigidius, *may* have been known in pre-Conquest England, but there is no sign of English transmission (L. D. Reynolds, 'Nonius Marcellus', *Texts and Transmission*, ed. id. (Oxford, 1983), pp. 248–52). It is interesting to ask why Wulfstan should have removed the remark about the Northumbrians' drinking habits from later drafts of his work (see above, p. clxxxiv): perhaps he felt it to be offensive, or else he wished to remove the unusual adverb *suatim*.

measure.[1] The Northumbrians became drunk, as they tend to,[2] and very cheerful they were when they left at evening.

13. THAT DURING THE REIGN OF EDGAR THE MINSTER CHURCH WAS BUILT AND DEDICATED. Abbot Æthelwold did not, however, start to build the structure the king had marked out for him in the days of Eadred, for the king died very soon afterwards, on 23 November.[3] But in the reign of glorious King Edgar,[4] the distinguished, merciful, powerful, and unconquerable son of Edmund, Æthelwold built and completed an impressive church in honour of the holy mother of God, ever-virgin Mary.[5] He used the same site, and his work is to this day better seen than described.

14. ON THE ORDINATION OF DUNSTAN, AND THAT ABBOT ÆTHELWOLD SENT THE MONK OSGAR OVERSEAS, AND ON A CERTAIN BROTHER ÆLFSTAN. About this time, Abbot Dunstan was chosen to be bishop of Worcester,[6] fulfilling the prediction of St Ælfheah the bishop which I mentioned earlier. After some years had gone by he

[3] Eadred died at Frome on 23 Nov. 955 and was buried in the Old Minster, Winchester (see above, p. 18 n. 1); he was succeeded by Eadwig (955–9). It is significant that Wulfstan omits any mention of Eadwig, who was not beloved of the monastic reformers *inter alia* for his exiling of Dunstan (.B., *Vita S. Dunstani*, cc. 22–4: *Memorials*, pp. 33–6).

[4] Edgar was king of all England from October 959 until his death on 8 July 975. Unlike Eadwig, Edgar was much beloved by Benedictine monks for his generosity towards their institution, and this is reflected in the string of superlatives used here by Wulfstan. Similar encomia are found in Lantfred, *Translatio*, c. 1, and Byrhtferth, *Vita S. Oswaldi* iii. 10 (*HCY* i. 425–6); see also that by Æthelwold himself in his OE treatise on 'King Edgar's Establishment of Monasteries' (*Councils & Synods*, i. 146–7).

[5] Wulfstan does not seem to know precisely when the church of St Mary at Abingdon was completed (he dates it vaguely to Edgar's reign: 959 × 975). Æthelwold supplies more precise information in his account of 'King Edgar's Establishment of Monasteries', where he states that Edgar commanded a glorious minster-church to be built at Abingdon within three years of his accession, hence by 962 (*Councils & Synods*, i. 148), but it is unlikely that the royal command was punctually obeyed (see below, p. 30 n. 1). There is no contemporary account of Æthelwold's church, but the 13th-c. tract *De abbatibus Abbendoniae* describes it as follows: 'tunc cepit sanctus Athelwoldus edificare ecclesiam hanc habentem formam: cancellus rotundus erat, ecclesia et rotunda, duplicem habens longitudinem quam cancellus; turris quoque rotunda erat' (*Chron. Abingdon*, ii. 277–8). The structure described here, of a tower-like rotunda with surrounding ambulatory and an eastern apsidal chancel, was clearly modelled on the chapel of Charlemagne's imperial palace at Aachen: see R. Gem, 'Towards an iconography of Anglo-Saxon architecture', *Journal of the Warburg and Courtauld Institutes*, xlvi (1983), 1–18, at pp. 8–9.

[6] Dunstan was elected bishop of Worcester probably in 957; although in 959 he was translated to London, he apparently held Worcester in plurality until 960. The vision of Bishop Ælfheah is described above, c. 8.

curricula factus archiepiscopus, mansit in Cantia triginta et septem annis[1] quasi columna inmobilis,[2] doctrina et actione praecipuus, angelico uultu decorus, elemosinis et prophetia praepollens: ad cuius tumbam caelestia saepe fieri miracula audiuimus. Ætheluuoldus autem misit Osgarum[3] monachum trans mare ad monasterium sancti patris Benedicti Floriacense,[4] ut regularis obseruantiae[a] mores illic disceret ac domi fratribus docendo ostenderet, quatinus ipse normam monasticae religionis secutus et una cum sibi subiectis deuia quaeque declinans gregem sibi commissum ad promissam caelestis regni perduceret patriam. In qua congregatione erat quidam frater Ælfstanus nomine, simplex et magnae oboedientiae uir, quem abbas iussit praeuidere cibaria artificum monasterii; cui seruitio ipse deuotissime se subdens coxit carnes cotidie et operariis sedulus ministrabat, focum accendens et aquam adportans et uasa denuo emundans, existimante[b] abbate illum hoc cum solatio et iuuamine alterius ministri peragere. Accidit namque quadam die, dum abbas more solito peragraret monasterium, ut aspiceret illum fratrem stantem iuxta feruens caldarium, in quo uictualia praeparabat artificibus, et intrans uidit omnia uasa mundissima ac pauimentum scopatum; dixitque ad eum hilari uultu: 'O mi frater Ælfstane, hanc oboedientiam mihi furatus es, quam me ignorante exerces. Sed si talis

[a] obseruacione *G* [b] estimante *G*

[1] Dunstan was elected archbishop of Canterbury in 960, and died on 19 May 988; he held the archbishopric for nearly twenty-eight years. Wulfstan's statement, that he stayed in Canterbury for 'thirty-seven years', is clearly an error; the reading *triginta et septem annis*—which is preserved in all manuscripts—should therefore correctly read *uiginti et septem*. It is not clear whether the error stems from Wulfstan himself, or entered the tradition at an early stage (see above, p. clxxxiii).

[2] On the image of the immovable pillar in 10th-c. English art and hagiography, see R. E. Deshman, 'The image of the living Ecclesia and the English monastic reform', *Sources of Anglo-Saxon Culture*, ed. P. E. Szarmach (Kalamazoo, Mich., 1986), pp. 261–82, at 275–7; Deshman points to occurrences of the image in Lantfred's *Translatio*, c. 3, Byrhtferth's *Vita S. Oswaldi* ii. 7 (*HCY* i. 416), and Adelard's *Vita S. Dunstani*, which describes Dunstan in terms similar to those used by Wulfstan: 'Hic Dunstanus iuxta interpretationem nominis sui, montanus utique lapis, ut mons immobilis, ut lapis angulari lapidi affixus, moueri non potuit' (*Memorials*, p. 67).

[3] Osgar was one of Æthelwold's principal disciples: he followed Æthelwold from Glastonbury to Abingdon (above, p. 20 and n. 2); he was with Æthelwold and the Abingdon monks at the beginning of Lent in 964 (c. 17); and he subsequently became abbot of Abingdon (c. 21; see below, p. 36 n. 4). The precise date of Osgar's sojourn at Fleury is unknown (it fell during the decade 954 × 964); he was presumably one of the monks of Fleury who advised Æthelwold in drawing up the *Regularis concordia* (see

became archbishop and stayed in Canterbury for thirty-seven years.[1] He was like a pillar that cannot be moved,[2] outstanding in learning and action, beautiful as an angel, strong in alms and prophecy. We have heard that God-sent miracles often occur at his tomb. Now Æthelwold sent the monk Osgar[3] overseas to the monastery of the holy father Benedict at Fleury,[4] to learn there the way of life according to the Rule and show it to his brothers when he taught them back at home. Thus Æthelwold could himself follow the regulations of monastic observance, and, avoiding together with those in his charge all byways, could bring the flock that had been entrusted to him to the promised homeland in the kingdom of heaven. Now in the fraternity was a monk called Ælfstan, a straightforward and highly obedient man whom the abbot had directed to oversee the food for the monastery craftsmen. He gave himself without stint to this job, cooking meat every day and serving it painstakingly to the workmen, lighting the fire, fetching water, and keeping the pans clean. The abbot thought he had the help of a second servant in these labours. One day the abbot was making his customary tour of the monastery. He happened to see this monk standing by a boiling cauldron in which he was preparing food for the craftsmen, and he went into the room. Finding all the pans sparkling and the floor swept, he said to him with a cheerful expression: 'O brother Ælfstan, you have stolen this service from me, in doing it without my knowing. But if

above, p. lix), and Lantfred, when he had returned to Fleury, addressed a letter to Winchester in which he specifically mentioned several of his books then in the possession of 'Abbot Osgar at Winchester' (*Memorials*, pp. 376–7; see above, p. xciv n. 192).

[4] On Fleury, see the valuable articles by H. Leclercq in *DACL* v. 1709–60, and J. Laporte in *DHGE* xvii. 441–76. On the relations between England and Fleury at this time, see L. Gougaud, 'Les relations de l'abbaye de Fleury-sur-Loire avec la Bretagne et les îles Britanniques (x[e] et xie siècles)', *Mémoires de la Société d'histoire et d'archéologie de Bretagne*, iv (1923), 4–30; D. Gremont and L. Donnat, 'Fleury, le Mont Saint-Michel et Angleterre à la fin du xe siècle', in *Millénaire monastique du Mont Saint-Michel*, ed. J. Laporte *et al.*, 4 vols. (Paris, 1966–7), i. 751–93, and L. Donnat, 'Recherches sur l'influence de Fleury au xe siècle', *Études ligériennes d'histoire et d'archéologie médiévales*, ed. R. Louis (Auxerre, 1975), pp. 165–74. Osgar will have been but one of several Englishmen at Fleury at this time: others included Oswald (later bishop of Worcester and York), Germanus (later abbot of Winchcombe), and the Leofnoth who appears as scribe in several Fleury manuscripts at this time: J. Vezin, 'Leofnoth: un scribe anglais à Saint-Benoît-sur-Loire', *Codices manuscripti*, iv (1977), 109–20. At a slightly later time an unidentified Englishman named Æthelgar was among the *familia* at Fleury: see A. Vidier, *L'Historiographie à Saint-Benoît-sur-Loire et les miracles de saint Benoît* (Paris, 1965), p. 190. There is good reason to think that Lantfred was a monk of Fleury (see above, p. xciv); one aspect of his influence at Winchester has been discussed recently by J. P. Carley, 'Two pre-Conquest manuscripts from Glastonbury abbey', *ASE* xvi (1987), 197–212, at pp. 204–10.

miles Christi es qualem te ostendis, mitte manum tuam in bullientem aquam et unum frustum de imis mihi impiger adtrahe.' Qui statim sine mora mittens manum suam ad imum[a] lebetis abstraxit frustum feruidum, non sentiens calorem feruentis aquae. Quo uiso abba[b] iussit deponi frustum, et nemini hoc indicare uiuenti. Illum uero fratrem postmodum abbatem uidimus ordinatum, qui etiam deinde pontificali honore sublimatus ecclesiae Wiltuniensi est praelatus et beato fine in Domino consummatus.[1]

15. QVOMODO HOSTIS ANTIQVVS SANCTVM VIRVM PER CASVM CVIVSDAM POSTIS EXTINGVERE CONATVS SIT. Erat namque sanctus Ætheluuoldus ecclesiarum ac diuersorum operum magnus aedificator,[2] et dum esset abbas et cum esset episcopus. Vnde tetendit ei communis aduersarius solitas suae malignitatis insidias ut eum si[c] ullo modo posset extingueret.[d] Nam quadam die, dum uir Dei in structura laboraret, ingens postis super eum cecidit et in quandam foueam deiecit confregitque paene omnes costas eius ex uno latere, ita ut nisi fouea illum susciperet[e] totus quassaretur.[f]

16. QVOD REX EADGARVS AD EPISCOPATVM WINTONENSIS ECCLESIAE SANCTVM VIRVM ELEGERIT. Conualuit tamen[g] uir sanctus de hac molestia, Dei omnipotentis adiuuante gratia, et elegit eum Eadgarus felicissimus Anglorum basileus[3] ad episcopatum Wintoniensis ecclesiae, antequam ecclesia praefati coenobii

[a] unum *G* [b] abbas *G (and A, perhaps after correction)* [c] si *om. T* [d] extinguere *T* [e] suscepisset *G* [f] quassatus fuisset *G* [g] autem *G*

[1] Wulfstan states that he saw Ælfstan ordained abbot, and that he subsequently became bishop of Ramsbury. Ælfstan was indeed bishop of Ramsbury from 970 until his death on 12 Feb. 981. An abbot Ælfstan occurs frequently as a witness to charters between 964 and 970 (see Hart, *ECNENM*, pp. 270–1). But the question is: where was Ælfstan abbot? A 12th-c. source, John ('Florence') of Worcester, states that he was abbot of Glastonbury, and this information is usually accepted (*Heads*, p. 50). The problem is that he is not mentioned in either of the two surviving lists of pre-Conquest Glastonbury abbots. A decisive solution to the problem is provided by Lantfred's *Translatio*. In c. 3 Lantfred describes the translation of St Swithun's remains (which took place on 15 July 971) and remarks that it was witnessed 'a domno presule Aðeluuoldo uenerabili atque abbatibus Ælfstano necne Æðelgaro precluibus et a fratribus Olimpicam in utroque coenobio ducentibus uitam.' The translation, that is to say, was a local Winchester affair, attended by the abbots and monks of the two Winchester monasteries (*utroque coenobio*). Æthelgar is well attested as abbot of the New

you are the soldier of Christ you look to be, put your hand in the boiling water and fetch me a bit of food from the bottom. Quick about it!' Ælfstan did not hesitate: he plunged his hand to the bottom of the pot and took out a hot morsel, without feeling the heat of the boiling water. Seeing what had happened, the abbot told him to put down the morsel and tell no living soul. Later I saw that monk ordained abbot; subsequently he was raised to the rank of bishop and put in charge of the see of Ramsbury, before completing a blessed life in the Lord.[1]

15. HOW THE ANCIENT ENEMY TRIED TO KILL THE HOLY MAN BY THE FALL OF A POST. St Æthelwold was a great builder of churches and other buildings,[2] both as abbot and bishop. It was from this direction that the enemy of us all laid a typically malign trap, hoping if at all possible to kill him. One day, when the man of God was toiling at building work, a huge post fell on him, knocking him into a pit. He broke almost all his ribs on one side, and would have been completely shattered but for the pit breaking his fall.

16. THAT KING EDGAR CHOSE THE HOLY MAN FOR THE BISHOPRIC OF WINCHESTER. However, the holy man recovered from this mishap, with the aid of the grace of Almighty God, and Edgar, most blessed monarch[3] of England, chose him for the bishopric of Winchester before the minster church at Abingdon was

Minster at this time (964–88: see *Heads*, p. 80); the obvious implication is that Ælfstan was abbot of the Old Minster. And this implication is confirmed by the list of Old Minster monks in *LVH* (p. 23; Gerchow, *Gedenküberlieferung*, p. 322), where Ælfstan's name is given in third place, immediately after Bishops Æthelwold and Ælfheah. Ælfstan's ordination as abbot, which was witnessed by Wulfstan, will have taken place in 964, soon after the expulsion of the secular clerics and the installation of Benedictine monks (below, c. 18).

[2] Æthelwold's building works at Abingdon are here described by Wulfstan; elsewhere (*Narratio*, Ep. spec. 35–60) Wulfstan describes Æthelwold's building-programme at the Old Minster, which included the provision of new walls, roofs, and a watercourse for the monks' dwellings, and, on the Old Minster itself, walls, roofs, and *porticus* ('side-chapels'). See *Winchester in the Early Middle Ages*, ed. M. Biddle, *WS* i. 306–8. Æthelwold also laid the foundations for an eastern *porticus*, but died before its completion.

[3] The word *basileus* (from Greek βασιλεύς) is frequently used of King Edgar in charters issued in his name: for example, S 682 = BCS 1058, S 683 = BCS 1054, S 689 = BCS 1080, S 691 = BCS 1079, S 695 = BCS 1076, S 699 = BCS 1068, S 739 = *Burton*, no. 21, S 745 = BCS 1190 (the 'New Minster Foundation Charter'), and others.

dedicaretur.[1] Et iubente rege consecrauit illum Dunstanus archiepiscopus Dorobernensis[a] ecclesiae, anno dominicae incarnationis nongentesimo sexagesimo tercio, sub die .III.[b] Kalendarum Decembrium, in uigilia sancti Andreae apostoli, quae tunc habebatur in dominica prima aduentus Domini et saluatoris nostri Iesu Christi.[2] Erant autem tunc in Veteri Monasterio, ubi cathedra pontificalis habetur, canonici[3] nefandis scelerum moribus implicati, elatione et insolentia atque luxuria praeuenti, adeo ut nonnulli illorum[c] dedignarentur missas suo ordine celebrare, repudiantes uxores quas inlicite duxerant et alias accipientes, gulae et ebrietati iugiter dediti. Quod minime ferens sanctus uir Ætheluuoldus, data licentia a rege Eadgaro,[4] expulit citissime detestandos blasphematores Dei de monasterio, et adducens monachos de Abbandonia locauit illic, quibus ipse abbas et episcopus extitit.[5]

17. DE COMMVNIONE QVAM CLERICI CANTAVERVNT QVANDO MONACHI DE ABBANDONIA VENIENTES AD INGRESSVM ECCLESIAE STETERVNT. Accidit autem sabbato in capite Quadragesimae,[6] dum monachi uenientes de Abbandonia starent ad ingressum ecclesiae, clericos missam finire, communionem canendo, 'Seruite Domino in timore,[7] et exultate ei cum tremore, apprehendite disciplinam,

[a] doruernensis *T* [b] tertia *βG* [c] eorum *AG*

[1] Æthelwold was consecrated bishop of Winchester on 29 November 963. According to notes made at Abingdon in the late twelfth century and added to the Abingdon copy of John of Worcester's *Chronicon ex chronicis*, now Lambeth Palace 42 (see above, p. clx), the church of St Mary at Abingdon was consecrated on 28 Dec., apparently in the same year: 'sed quia ecclesiam Abbendonensem ante susceptum episcopatum reliquerat [sc. Æthelwold], post sui consecrationem et ipsam una cum beato Dunstano et aliis nonnullis coepiscopis suis in honore Dei genitricis Mariae consecrauit .v. kal. Ian. [= 28 Dec.]' (H. Wharton, *Anglia Sacra*, 2 vols. (London, 1691), i. 166). The problem is that churches were normally dedicated on a Sunday, and 28 Dec. was not a Sunday in 963 (C. R. Cheney, *Handbook of Dates for Students of English History* (London, 1945), p. 141, table 29), nor was it in 964 and 965; the only two years in which 28 Dec. was a Sunday were 962 and 973. So the date of the consecration of the church cannot be determined on present evidence.

[2] It is true that in 963 the first Sunday of Advent fell on 29 Nov., the vigil of the feast of St Andrew (30 Nov.): see Cheney, *Handbook of Dates*, p. 141, table 29.

[3] The *canonici* here are cathedral canons, who, since they were not monks, are also referred to as secular clerics. As the life of a Benedictine monk was governed by the *Regula S. Benedicti*, so that of cathedral canons would properly be governed by the *Regula canonicorum* of Chrodegang of Metz (d. 766), a work which was translated into Old English under Æthelwold's supervision at Winchester (see above, p. xciv). However, the cathedral canons living at Winchester before 964 were clearly not following any such rule. Robinson (*Times*, pp. 170–1) argued that the word *canonicus* is not found in English

dedicated.[1] On the king's orders, he was consecrated by Dunstan, archbishop of Canterbury, in the year of the incarnation of our Lord 963, on 29 November, the vigil of the apostle St Andrew, held at that time on the first Sunday in the Advent of our Lord and Saviour Jesus Christ.[2] Now at that time there were in the Old Minster, where the bishop's throne is situated, cathedral canons[3] involved in wicked and scandalous behaviour, victims of pride, insolence, and riotous living to such a degree that some of them did not think fit to celebrate mass in due order. They married wives illicitly, divorced them, and took others; they were constantly given to gourmandizing and drunkenness. The holy man Æthelwold would not tolerate it. With permission from King Edgar,[4] he lost no time in expelling from the monastery such detestable blasphemers against God. He replaced them there with monks from Abingdon, to whom he was thus both abbot and bishop.[5]

17. ON THE MASS-CHANT WHICH THE SECULAR CLERICS SANG WHEN THE MONKS FROM ABINGDON WERE STANDING AT THE ENTRANCE TO THE CHURCH. Now it happened that on the Saturday at the start of Lent,[6] when the monks from Abingdon were standing at the entrance to the church, the clerics were finishing mass by chanting the *communio*, 'Serve ye the Lord with fear,[7] and rejoice unto him with trembling: embrace discipline, lest ye perish from the just

sources until after the 10th c., but it is used by Lantfred, *Translatio*, c. 1, and by Wulfstan here and in the *Narratio* i. 19.

[4] The support given by King Edgar to Æthelwold's monastic reform has been much discussed by historians: see especially E. John, *Orbis Britanniae, and Other Studies* (Leicester, 1966), esp. pp. 154–80.

[5] Æthelwold's appointment, as monk, to a bishopric, initiated a new and important phase in Anglo-Saxon ecclesiastical history. For a century, from 964 until the Norman Conquest, a substantial proportion of English bishops were also monks (see F. Barlow, *The English Church 1000–1066* (2nd edn., London, 1979), pp. 62–6), and the institution of the 'monk-bishop' or 'abbot-bishop' came to be regarded as characteristically English. Although since the beginnings of monasticism there were occasional monks who became bishops—St Cuthbert is an early English forerunner of Æthelwold in this respect—as an institution it was never as widespread in Europe as in late Anglo-Saxon England; see H. Frank, *Die Klosterbischöfe des Frankenreichs* (Münster, 1932).

[6] In 964 Easter Day fell on 3 Apr.; *sabbato in capite Quadragesimae* (= the first Saturday in Lent) was on 19 Feb. (Cheney, *Handbook of Dates*, p. 108).

[7] That the mass-chant for the *communio* of the mass on the first Saturday of Lent was *seruite Domino* in Æthelwold's day cannot be confirmed from contemporary service-books (there is no surviving pre-Conquest gradual or plenary missal from the Old Minster, and the so-called 'New Minster Missal', Le Havre 330, is defective for this part of the liturgical year). However, in the later Sarum Missal the chant *seruite Domino* is indeed proper for *Sabbato post cineres* (ed. J. W. Legg, *The Sarum Missal* (Oxford, 1916), p. 55), and the evidence of Wulfstan indicates that this same chant was proper in Æthelwold's day. The words of the chant derive from Ps. 2: 11–12.

ne pereatis de uia iusta', quasi dicerent:[a] 'Nos noluimus[b] Deo seruire nec disciplinam eius seruare; uos saltem facite, ne sicut nos pereatis de uia quae custodientibus iustitiam regna facit aperiri caelestia.' Quo audito fratres gauisi sunt, intelligentes a Domino suum iter esse prosperatum[c] et Dei nutu hunc psalmum propter illorum praesentiam fuisse decantatum. Moxque Dauiticum ad se traxerunt imperium, Osgaro exhortante eos atque dicente: 'Cur foris moramur? Faciamus sicut hortantur nos clerici, ingrediamur, et per uiam iustitiae gradientes Domino Deo nostro cum timore et exultatione famulemur, ut cum exarserit in breui ira eius[d] mereamur esse participes illorum de quibus subiungitur "beati omnes qui confidunt in eo."'[1]

18. DE EXPVLSIONE CLERICORVM DE VETERI MONASTERIO. Misit quoque[e] rex illuc cum episcopo quendam ministrorum suorum famosissimum, cui nomen erat Wulfstan æt[f] Delham,[2] qui regia auctoritate mandauit canonicis ut unum de duobus eligerent, aut sine mora dare locum monachis aut suscipere habitum monachici[g] ordinis.[h] At illi, nimio pauore conterriti et uitam execrantes monasticam, intrantibus monachis ilico exierunt. Sed tamen postmodum tres ex illis ad conuersionem uenerunt, scilicet Eadzinus,[3] Wulfsinus[4] et Wilstanus[5] presbiter: qui coenobium quod expulsi reliquerant humili corde repententes Christi iugo colla subdiderunt. Nam hactenus[i] ea tempestate non habebantur monachi in gente Anglorum nisi tantum qui in Glastonia morabantur et Abbandonia.

[a] diceret *N (and A before correction)* [b] nolimus *N*; nolumus *G (and A before correction)* [c] prosperatum suum iter esse *G* [d] eius *om. G* [e] itaque *G* [f] de *β*; e *G* [g] mona *(followed by a gap) A*; monachi *G* [h] habitus *G* [i] tenus *G*

[1] Ps. 2: 13.

[2] Wulfstan of Dalham (Suffolk) was one of the principal thegns of Edgar's reign, one who appears frequently as a witness to charters between 958 and 974. He was described as the *sequipedus* or 'close companion' of King Eadred (*LE* ii. 28, ed. Blake, p. 102); his importance is reflected in the fact that he was chosen by Edgar to expel the clerics from the Old Minster. He subsequently became the royal *discþegn* (S 768 = *Burton*, no. 23), and also performed the office of reeve or *praefectus* (S 796 = BCS 1301). He was steward of Queen Eadgifu's estates in East Anglia, which formed part of the endowment of Ely (see below, c. 23). He is described in the following complimentary terms in the *Libellus Æthelwoldi*, c. 2: 'unus qui regi erat a secretis, nomine Wlstanus de Dalham, uir prudens, consilio pollens, celitus inspiratus'. On his career, see Blake, *LE*, p. xiii; Hart, *ECNENM*, p. 379; and Keynes and Kennedy, *Anglo-Saxon Ely* (forthcoming).

way', as if to say: '*We* have not wished to serve God or keep his discipline: but *you* must do so, lest like us you perish from the way which opens the kingdom of heaven to those who preserve justice.' Hearing this, the brethren were glad, for they perceived that their journey had been speeded by the Lord and that it was God's will that this psalm had been sung, because they were there. They straightway applied to themselves the order given by David, for Osgar exhorted them thus: 'Why are we wasting time outside? Let us do as the clerics encourage us. Let us go in, follow the way of justice, and serve the Lord our God with trembling and joy, so that "when his wrath is kindled in a short time" we may deserve to share with those of whom the psalm goes on to say: "Blessed are all they that put their trust in him."'[1]

18. ON THE EXPULSION OF THE SECULAR CLERICS FROM THE OLD MINSTER. The king also sent there with the bishop one of his agents, the well-known Wulfstan of Dalham,[2] who used the royal authority to order the canons to choose one of two courses: either to give place to the monks without delay or to take the habit of the monastic order. Stricken with terror, and detesting the monastic life, they left as soon as the monks entered. Still, three of them were converted later, Eadsige,[3] Wulfsige,[4] and Wilstan[5] the priest. They humbly made their way back to the monastery they had left on their expulsion, and bowed their necks to Christ's yoke. Up to then there had been no monks in England at that time, except those dwelling at Glastonbury and Abingdon.

[3] The return of Eadsige to become a monk at the Old Minster under Æthelwold's discipline was seen by contemporaries as an event of great importance. We know from Ælfric that Eadsige was a kinsman of Æthelwold ('Life of Swithun', c. 5: 'þeah þe se sanct wære gesib him for worulde'). After the expulsion from the Old Minster in 964, Eadsige went to live in the vicinity of Winchcombe. In 969 St Swithun appeared in a dream to a certain smith, who was instructed to report the revelation to Eadsige; for his part, Eadsige was to report it to Æthelwold (Lantfred, *Translatio*, c. 1). Eadsige apparently did so, and the translation of St Swithun's remains in 971 served as the pretext for a reconciliation between Æthelwold and his kinsman. Eadsige subsequently was appointed sacrist of Swithun's shrine (Lantfred, *Translatio*, c. 20). He is listed simply as 'Eadsige monachus' in the list of Old Minster monks in *LVH* (p. 25, no. lvii; Gerchow, *Gedenküberlieferung*, p. 323). The day of his death is known (27 July: *LVH*, p. 271; Gerchow, op. cit., p. 333), but not the year. He had apparently died by 996, for Wulfstan includes a lengthy eulogy on him in the *Narratio* ii. 131–50.

[4] Wulfsige is listed as 'Wulfsige monachus' in *LVH* (p. 25, no. liv; Gerchow, *Gedenküberlieferung*, p. 323); nothing further is known of him.

[5] Wilstan is listed as 'Wilstan sacerdos' in *LVH* (p. 25, no. liii; Gerchow, *Gedenküberlieferung*, p. 323); nothing further is known of him.

19. QVOMODO VIR SANCTVS VENENVM BIBERIT ET CALORE FIDEI SVCCENSVS POTVM MORTIS EXTINXERIT. Deinde cum praedicti fratres in Veteri Coenobio regularis uitae normam seruare coepissent et multi illuc ad Dei famulatum senes conuersi, iuuenes adducti et paruuli oblati confluerent,[1] ex inuidia clericorum datum est episcopo uenenum bibere in aula sua[2] cum hospitibus prandenti omnemque eis humanitatem exhibenti, quatinus illo extincto seruos Dei expellerent, rursumque in unum congregati libere pristinis frui potuissent[a] flagitiis. Erat namque ei[b] moris statim post tres aut quattuor offulas modicum quid bibere; bibitque[c] nesciens adportatum sibi uenenum totum quod erat in calice, et statim in pallorem facies eius inmutata est et uiscera illius nimium ui grassantis ueneni cruciabantur. Surrexit autem uix a mensa exiens[d] ad lectulum, serpsitque uenenum per omnia membra eius,[e] iam instantem minitans sibi mortem.[3] At ille tandem recogitans coepit exprobrare semet ipsum, dixitque ad animum suum: 'Vbi est modo fides tua? Vbi sunt cogitationes sensus tui? Nonne uerba Christi uera sunt et fidelia, quibus in euangelio pollicetur dicens: "Et si mortiferum quid biberint credentes, non eis nocebit"?[4] Nonne ipse qui haec loquitur praesens est diuinitate, licet absens sit corpore?[5] Ipse procul dubio, ipse hoc ueneni[f] uirus in te euacuare potest qui semper omnia potest.'[g] His et huiuscemodi uerbis accensa fides in eo omnem letiferum haustum quem biberat extinxit, furentisque ueneni dolore fugato surrexit, abiens ad[h] aulam hilari uultu, nulla penitus signa palloris se intuentibus ostendens, nec quicquam mali suo uenefico reddens sed ei quod deliquit ignoscens. Sicque Dei uirtute dissipatum est malignum consilium[i] clericorum, qui uidentes suam nichil praeualere nequitiam tandiu per diuersas gentis[j] Anglorum prouincias huc illucque dispersi sunt quousque uitam finierunt.

[a] possent *G* [b] namque eis *N*; ei namque *T* [c] bibit ergo *G* [d] exiliens *G* [e] eius *om. G* [f] ueneni *om. G* [g] qui . . . potest *om. T* [h] in *G* [i] concilium *(sic)* malignum *G* [j] gentis *om. T*

---

[1] On the three classes of monks, see Knowles, *MO*, pp. 417–23. The meaning of *senes conuersi* here is not entirely clear; elsewhere *conuersi* refers to lay brethren who were admitted to the monastery too late to qualify for orders; but Wulfstan may be thinking of secular canons who—like those mentioned in the previous chapter—were 'converted' to Benedictine monasticism in their maturity (c. 18: *ad conuersionem uenerunt*).

[2] The precise location of the bishop's palace is unknown, and this is the earliest reference to it in Winchester sources (see Biddle, *Winchester in the Early Middle Ages*, p. 323). The later bishop's palace was at Wolvesey in the south-east corner of the walled

19. HOW THE HOLY MAN DRANK POISON AND, SET ALIGHT BY THE HEAT OF HIS FAITH, OVERCAME THE LETHAL DRAUGHT. Later, after the brethren had begun to observe the rule of regular life in the Old Minster, and many flocked there to serve God, old men who had been professed, novices, and child oblates,[1] the envy of the clerics caused the bishop to be given poison to drink when he was dining with guests in his own hall[2] and showing them every kindness. The clerics intended, upon his death, to drive away the servants of God and regroup to form a new assembly, free to indulge their former shameful practices. It was Æthelwold's custom, after eating three or four morsels, at once to drink a little. On this occasion he drank, quite unawares, all the poison brought to him in a goblet. His face instantly grew pale, and his innards underwent terrible torture as the poison took its toll. However, he mananged with an effort to rise from the table and make his way to his bed. The poison crept through all his limbs, threatening immediate death.[3] But he eventually took thought and began to reproach himself, saying to his heart: '*Now* where is your faith? Where are the thoughts of your understanding? Is not Christ's promise in the gospel true and trustworthy: "And if believers drink any deadly thing, it shall not hurt them"?[4] He who spoke these words is surely here in his godhead, even if he is absent in the body.[5] He without a doubt, he can rid you of this virulent poison, for he can always do all.' The faith kindled by these and similar words overcame all the deadly draught he had taken. The pain caused by the raging of the poison was banished, and he got up, departing to the hall with a cheerful face and showing absolutely no sign of pallor to those who looked at him. He did not in return do any harm to his poisoner, but forgave him his sin. So, by God's miraculous power, the evil plan of the clerics was brought to nought; they saw their wickedness had no effect, and they were scattered through the different provinces of England till the end of their lives.

burh; excavations conducted from 1963 to 1971 revealed 'that the twelfth-century structures were preceded by an earlier complex beginning in the later tenth century' (ibid.). A full account of Wolvesey is forthcoming in *WS* vi; note that Æthelwold's palace had adjacent sleeping-quarters.

[3] The description of the poisoning of Æthelwold is modelled on Sulpicius Severus, *Vita S. Martini*, c. 6: 'sed cum *uim* ueneni in se *grassantis* uicina iam morte sensisset, *imminens* periculum oratione repulit statimque omnis *dolor fugatus* est.'

[4] Mark 16: 18.

[5] Cf. 1 Cor. 5: 3 ('ego quidem absens corpore, praesens autem spiritu') and Col. 2: 5 ('etsi corpore absens sum, sed spiritu uobiscum sum').

20. DE EXPVLSIONE CANONICORVM DE NOVO MONASTERIO. Exinde Christi aquila[1] antistes Ætheluuoldus expandit aureas alas suas,[a] et, annuente rege Eadgaro, canonicos de Nouo expulit Monasterio,[2] illucque monachos introduxit regulariter conuersantes, ordinans illis abbatem discipulum suum Æthelgarum,[3] qui postmodum prouinciae Australium Saxonum episcopus ac deinde, sancto Dunstano ad caelestia regna translato, Cantuariorum archipraesul effectus est.

21. QVOD IN ABBANDONIA OSGARVM CONSTITVERIT ABBATEM. In Abbandonia uero Osgarum pro se constituit abbatem,[4] ditatusque est locus ille sexcentis et eo amplius cassatis,[5] insuper et aeternae libertatis suffultus priuilegiis, diuina simul et regia auctoritate conscriptis, quae laminis aureis sigillata inibi usque hodie conseruantur.[6]

22. QVOD IN COENOBIO NONNARVM SANCTIMONIALES ORDINAVERIT. In tercio quoque Wintoniensi coenobio, quod Anglice Nunnamenster appellatur, in honore semper uirginis Mariae Deo consecratum, mandras[b] sanctimonialium[7] ordinauit, quibus

[a] alas suas aureas *G* [b] monasterium *G*

---

[1] Cf. above, c. 2.

[2] This expulsion also took place in 964: see ASC 964 A. The event was duly solemnized by the 'New Minster Foundation Charter' (S 745 = BCS 1190) issued two years later in 966. This charter is lavishly written in gold lettering and is prefaced by an illumination of King Edgar: see above, pp. xlvii–xlviii, as well as Temple, *AS Manuscripts*, no. 16, and Wormald, in *Collected Writings I*, ed. J. J. G. Alexander, T. J. Brown, and J. Gibbs (London, 1982), pp. 105–10, who concludes that the charter was 'a creation of Ethelwold, made after the event, a solemn commemoration to be preserved on the altar as a memorial'.

[3] Æthelgar was abbot of the New Minster from 964 (*Heads*, pp. 80–1); he was elevated to the see of Selsey and consecrated on 2 May 980 (though he apparently held the abbacy in plurality until 988). On the death of Dunstan on 19 May 988, Æthelgar became archbishop of Canterbury, the first of Æthelwold's pupils to achieve such high station. He died on 13 Feb. 990, a fact surprisingly omitted by Wulfstan. According to *LVH* he was an outstanding patron of the New Minster (p. 31: 'egregius et insignis ipsius monasterii fautor et instructor'; Gerchow, *Gedenküberlieferung*, p. 324); the same source reports (*LVH*, pp. 8–10) that he built a magnificent tower at the New Minster which was the embodiment of meaningful numerical symbolism. On the probable structure of this tower, see R. N. Quirk, 'Winchester New Minster and its tenth-century tower', *Journal of the British Archaeological Association*, xxiv (1961), 23–35, and R. Gem, 'Towards an iconography', pp. 15–18. On Æthelgar's career in general, see Hart, *ECNENM*, pp. 283–4.

[4] Æthelwold was consecrated bishop of Winchester on Sunday 29 Nov. 963, and most sources assume that Osgar was appointed abbot immediately thereafter (see

20. ON THE EXPULSION OF THE CANONS FROM THE NEW MINSTER. Thereupon Bishop Æthelwold, the eagle[1] of Christ, spread his golden wings, and with the permission of King Edgar drove the canons from the New Minster,[2] introducing there monks living according to the Rule and ordaining as their abbot his pupil Æthelgar,[3] who later became bishop of the province of the South Saxons and then, after Dunstan's translation to the kingdom of heaven, archbishop of Canterbury.

21. THAT HE MADE OSGAR ABBOT AT ABINGDON. As to Abingdon, he made Osgar abbot there in his stead.[4] The place was enriched by the gift of six hundred and more hides,[5] and it was further underpinned by the granting of privileges of perpetual liberty, written on God's and the king's authority. They are kept there to this day, sealed with gold leaves.[6]

22. THAT HE ESTABLISHED NUNS IN THE NUNNAMINSTER. He had plans too for the third monastery at Winchester, known in English as the Nunnaminster and dedicated to God in honour of ever-virgin Mary. Here he established flocks of nuns,[7] placing over

Heads, p. 23; but note that the date given for Osgar's consecration—28 Dec. (963)—derives from a misreading of a passage in the Abingdon copy (Lambeth Palace 42) of John ('Florence') of Worcester, where the date properly refers to the consecration of the church of St Mary, not Osgar's ordination). The position of c. 21 in Wulfstan's narrative rather implies that he did not become abbot until some time later in 964. He first witnesses charters as abbot in 964 (S 725 = BCS 1143; S 731 = BCS 1135), and then continuously until 979 (a list is given in Hart, *ECNENM*, pp. 355–6). John records his death in 985 (his successor Eadwine was ordained in 985: ASC 985 C), and his obit is given as 24 May in the calendar in Cotton Titus D. xxvii (*LVH*, p. 271; Gerchow, *Gedenküberlieferung*, p. 333). In combination these facts suggest that during the last five years of his life Osgar was too ill to participate in the king's council; see also above, pp. 20 n. 2, 26 n. 3.

[5] The precise size of the Abingdon endowment at this time is unknown, and it is not clear whence Wulfstan derived his figure of 600 hides. There is an authentic charter of 993 in King Æthelred's name (S 876 = *Chron. Abingdon*, i. 358–66) confirming the privileges and estates granted to Abingdon by earlier monarchs, but these do not total anything near 600 hides.

[6] Unfortunately this charter has not been preserved. To judge from the surviving 'New Minster Foundation Charter', the Abingdon charter will have been lavishly illuminated and written in gold lettering (this is presumably what is meant by *laminis aureis sigillata*).

[7] The phrase *mandras sanctimonialium* is taken from Æthelwold's *Regularis concordia*, c. 3: 'coniugique suae Ælfthrithae sanctimonialium mandras ut impauidi more custodis defenderet cautissime praecepit' (ed. Symons, p. 2).

matrem de qua superius paululum[a] tetigimus Æthelthrytham[1] praefecit,[b] ubi regularis uitae norma hactenus obseruatur.[c]

23. QVOMODO IN PROVINCIA ORIENTALIVM ANGLORVM ELIGENSE COENOBIVM REGVLARITER INSTITVERIT. Nec solum in finibus Occidentalium Saxonum uerum etiam in remotis Britanniae partibus sanctus antistes Æthelauoldus ad Dei omnipotentis seruitium monachos adgregare curauit. Est enim quaedam regio famosa in prouincia Orientalium Anglorum sita, paludibus et aquis in modum insulae circumdata, unde et a copia anguillarum quae in eisdem paludibus capiuntur Ælig nomen accepit.[2] In qua regione locus omni ueneratione dignus habetur, magnificatus nimium reliquiis et miraculis sanctae Æthelthrythae reginae et perpetuae uirginis ac sororum eius;[3] sed in ipso tempore erat destitutus et regali fisco deditus.[4] Hunc ergo locum famulus Christi pro dilectione tantarum uirginum magnopere uenerari coepit, datoque precio non modicae pecuniae emit eum a rege Eadgaro, constituens in eo monachorum gregem non minimum.[5] Quibus ordinauit abbatem Byrhtnodum praepositum suum,[6] et eiusdem loci situm monasterialibus aedificiis decentissime renouauit,[7] eumque terrarum possessionibus affluentissime locupletatum[d] et

[a] superius paululum] paululum superius *N*; superius *A* [b] perfecit *T* [c] prefuit *T* [d] locupletauit *G*

[1] The identity of this woman is unknown, as are the dates at which she was abbess (see *Heads*, p. 223). Rather surprisingly, she is not mentioned among the 'nomina feminarum illustrium' in *LVH* (pp. 57–9; Gerchow, *Gedenküberlieferung*, p. 325). Wulfstan took her to be identical with the *nutrix* who attended Æthelwold's early years (above, c. 2 and n. 3); if so, she will have been elderly (over 60) at the time the Nunnaminster was refounded in 964.

[2] The information about the site of Ely, as well as the (still accepted) etymology, is drawn from Bede, *HE* iv. 19 (17): 'in similitudinem insulae uel paludibus, ut diximus, circumdata uel aquis, unde et a copia anguillarum, quae in eisdem paludibus capiuntur, nomen accepit.'

[3] On St Æthelthryth (St Audrey) and her sisters, especially Seaxburh, see Bede, *HE* iv. 19 (17), whence Wulfstan derives his information. Æthelthryth was a daughter of King Anna of the East Angles who in 660 married King Ecgfrith of Northumbria on the condition that she remain celibate. When the king wished to revoke this agreement in 672, Æthelthryth—supported by Bishop Wilfrid—first entered the double house at Coldingham and then founded Ely in 673; she died in 679. Because of the close links between Winchester and Ely, she was fully commemorated in the liturgy of Winchester (see above, p. lxxxii, for pontifical blessings in the 'Benedictional of St Æthelwold'). Ælfric composed an English 'Life of St Æthelthryth' based on the chapter in Bede (see above, p. cxlix).

[4] It has recently been argued that during the Viking period when English

them Æthelthryth,[1] whom I briefly mentioned above. Here the procedures of life according to the Rule are followed to this day.

23. HOW HE ESTABLISHED THE MONASTERY OF ELY IN EAST ANGLIA ACCORDING TO THE RULE. The holy bishop Æthelwold was concerned to bring monks together in the service of Almighty God not only within Wessex but also in remote parts of Britain. There is a well-known spot in East Anglia, surrounded like an island by swamps and water. From the quantity of eels taken in these marshes it has been given the name Ely.[2] Here there is a place held to deserve all reverence, for it is made glorious by the relics and miracles of St Æthelthryth, queen and perpetual virgin, and her sisters.[3] But at this time it was abandoned and pertained to the royal fisc.[4] The servant of Christ began to reverence this place greatly, out of his love for the distinguished virgins, and he paid a large sum of money to buy it from King Edgar.[5] In it he established a large group of monks, ordaining his prior Byrhtnoth as abbot.[6] He renovated the place as it deserved, giving it monastery buildings,[7] and enriched it lavishly with possessions

monasteries such as Ely (which lay within the Danelaw) ceased to function, the monastic estates were absorbed, by default or exchange, into the royal fisc, and, subsequently, during the monastic reform, the estates were granted back to the monasteries by the king: R. Fleming, 'Monastic lands and England's defence in the Viking Age', *EHR* c (1985), 247–65.

[5] The endowment of Ely by King Edgar and Æthelwold is the subject of the 12th-c. Latin text called the *Libellus Æthelwoldi* (see above, p. xlviii), which was produced at Ely between 1109 and 1131 from a now lost late 10th-c. account of the endowment in Old English. The *Libellus Æthelwoldi* has not been printed integrally since 1691; a new edition by S. D. Keynes and A. Kennedy is forthcoming as *Anglo-Saxon Ely* (see below, p. 81). It is a very extensive text which was largely incorporated into the *Liber Eliensis* (*LE* ii. 4–49), and it reveals more clearly than any other text the immense amount of energy and the large number of financial transactions which went into Ely's endowment, and which are perhaps belied by Wulfstan's bland, one-sentence account of the process. There are also four surviving royal charters, all dated 970, in favour of Ely: S 776 = BCS 1265, S 779 = BCS 1267, S 780 = BCS 1268 and S 781 = BCS 1269. The refoundation probably took place in 970 (see *LE*, p. 74 n. 3).

[6] Byrhtnoth was abbot of Ely from the time of its refoundation, probably in 970, until his death on 5 May 996 × 999 (see *Heads*, p. 44). He witnesses a number of charters between 970 and 996 (list in Hart, *ECNENM*, pp. 306–7), and was involved in the business of increasing the Ely endowment, as is seen from the number of times he is mentioned in the *Libellus Æthelwoldi*. He may have been prior at the Old Minster from 964 until his elevation to Ely in 970.

[7] See T. D. Atkinson, *An Architectural History of the Benedictine Monastery of St Etheldreda at Ely* (London, 1933), pp. 1–6, at 2: 'It was refounded by Ethelwold . . . We have no descriptions of the buildings nor has a single fragment survived.'

aeternae libertatis priuilegio confirmatum omnipotenti Domino commendauit.[1]

24. QVOD IN PROVINCIA QVOQVE GIRVIORUM DVO MONACHORVM COENOBIA CONSTRVXIT, QVORVM VNVM BVRH, ALTERVM VERO THORNIG APPELLATVR. Alterum quoque locum in regione Giruiorum[2] precio[a] optinuit a rege et nobilibus terrae, positum in ripa fluminis Nen, cui lingua Anglorum quondam Medeshamstede nomen imposuit, nunc autem consuete Burh appellatur.[3] Cuius loci basilicam congruis domorum structuris ornatam[4] et terris adiacentibus copiose ditatam[5] in honore beati Petri principis apostolorum consecrauit,[6] ibique simili modo cateruam monachorum coadunauit, Ealdulfum[7] eis praeficiens abbatem monachum suum, qui post excessum domini Osuualdi pontificis ecclesiae Eboracensis archiepiscopatum suscepit. Tercium nichilominus adquisiuit precio locum iuxta crepidinem praedicti fluminis situm, qui propter spineta circumquaque succrescentia Thornig solito nuncupatur Anglice uocabulo, quem pari conditione monachis aptissimum delegauit,[8] rectorem illis et abbatem Godemannum[9]

[a] precio *om. T*

---

[1] Æthelwold's charter to Ely granting perpetual immunity has not survived; presumably it was like those issued to the New Minster (above, p. 36 n. 2) and to Abingdon (above, p. 37 n. 6).

[2] The Gyrwe (Latin *Gyruii*) were the East Anglian people who inhabited the fens around Ely and Peterborough, as we learn from the *Liber Eliensis* (ed. Blake, p. 3): 'Giruii sunt omnes Australes Angli in magna palude habitantes, in qua est insula de Ely.' They are mentioned several times by Bede (*HE* iii. 20; iv. 6, 19) as the people living in the vicinity of Peterborough, and it is likely that Wulfstan took the name from Bede. On the meaning of the name, see E. Ekwall, 'OE "Gyrwe"', *Beiblatt zur Anglia*, 1922, 116–18.

[3] On the early history of Medehamstede, see F. M. Stenton, *Preparatory to Anglo-Saxon England*, ed. D. M. Stenton (Oxford, 1970), pp. 179–92.

[4] Although excavations carried out at Peterborough in the 1880s recovered something of the Saxon church, it has unfortunately not been possible to identify any remains from the period of Æthelwold's refoundation: see J. T. Irvine, 'Account of the pre-Norman remains discovered at Peterborough Cathedral in 1884', *Associated Architectural Societies Reports*, xvii (1883–4), 277–83, and Taylor and Taylor, *AS Architecture*, ii. 491–4.

[5] For Æthelwold's endowment of Peterborough, see Hart, *ECEE*, pp. 110–13, 243–7, and E. King, *Peterborough Abbey, 1086–1310: A Study in the Land Market* (Cambridge, 1973), pp. 6–12. One substantial record of Æthelwold's endowment of Peterborough survives as S 1448 = BCS 1128; this undated grant (datable only to Æthelwold's bishopric) includes, in addition to a number of estates, a large amount of ecclesiastical furniture (including silver crucifixes, candelabra, bells, etc.), and twenty-one books. For another example of Æthelwold's generosity to Peterborough, see below, p. 42 n. 2.

[6] It is not known precisely when Peterborough was refounded. The sequence of chapters in Wulfstan would suggest 964 × 971, and the earliest datable charter pertain-

in land. He confirmed this grant with a privilege conferring perpetual liberty;[1] and dedicated it to the Almighty Lord.

24. THAT IN THE PROVINCE OF THE GYRWE TOO HE BUILT TWO MONASTERIES, CALLED *BURH* (PETERBOROUGH) AND THORNEY. He purchased another place too from the king and noblemen of the land. It was in the district of the Gyrwe[2] on the banks of the River Nene, once called in English *Medeshamstede* but now ordinarily known as *Burh* (Peterborough).[3] He extended the church here by constructing appropriate residential buildings,[4] enriched it lavishly with estates nearby,[5] and consecrated it in honour of the blessed Peter, chief of the apostles.[6] Here, as at Ely, he brought together a troop of monks, appointing as their abbot his monk Ealdwulf,[7] who took over the archbishopric of York after the death of the Lord Bishop Oswald. He purchased yet a third place on the banks of the same river, normally called Thorney in English from the thorn-bushes growing freely all round it, and made it entirely suitable for the monks to whom he handed it on the same terms.[8] He placed over it as ruler and abbot Godemann,[9]

ing to the refoundation is dated 971 (S 782 = BCS 1270). For that reason *c*.970 (Hart, *ECNENM*, p. 326) seems slightly more satisfactory than *c*.966 (*Heads*, p. 59).

[7] Ealdwulf was apparently abbot from the time of the refoundation—whenever that was—until his elevation to the bishopric of Worcester in 992. In spite of this long abbacy he witnesses only three charters as abbot: S 840 = KCD 633 (dated 982), S 942 = KCD 712, and S 944 = KCD 713, both dated 990 × 992. His background is unknown, but Hugh Candidus reports the interesting story that while still a layman, Ealdwulf had unintentionally killed his only son by falling drunkenly asleep on top of him; as penance, Æthelwold imposed on him the financial burden of restoring the monastic buildings at Peterborough (*Chronicle*, ed. Mellows, pp. 29–31). On the death of Bishop Oswald on 28 Feb. 992, Ealdwulf became bishop of Worcester; he subsequently was consecrated as archbishop of York on 12 Apr. 995 (Worcester and York were customarily held in plurality). See Hart, *ECNENM*, pp. 325–8, and *Heads*, p. 59.

[8] The precise date of the foundation of Thorney is not known. The date 973 is given in the *Liber uitae* of Thorney (London, BL Add. 40000, fo. 11^r: see *Heads*, p. 73). A document purporting to be the foundation charter of Thorney (S 792 = BCS 1297) is also dated 973, but this is not authentic in the form in which it has been preserved. On the other hand Wulfstan places the foundation of Thorney before the translation of St Swithun (c. 26), which took place on 15 July 971, so a date of *c*.970 seems preferable to 973.

[9] Godemann was a pupil of Æthelwold who is best known as the scribe of the 'Benedictional of St Æthelwold' and the author of the thirty-eight Latin hexameters which serve as its preface (see above, p. xcv). It is not known when he was appointed abbot of Thorney. He does not witness charters as abbot until after 990, and it has been suspected (on the basis of a note in the unprinted 14th-c. Thorney annals preserved in Cambridge, UL Add. 3020: *Heads*, p. 74) that Æthelwold retained the abbacy until his death in 984. Wulfstan's statement refutes that suspicion, but we are still in ignorance of the precise date of his appointment. In any event, he witnesses charters sporadically until 1013, and apparently died then or soon after; see Hart, *ECNENM*, p. 338.

praeponens, constructumque monasterium[1] in honore Dei genitricis et uirginis Mariae dedicauit et bonorum omnium possessione gratulanter ditauit.[2]

25. DE FAMILIARITATE EIVS CVM REGE. Erat autem uir Dei Ætheluuoldus a secretis Eadgari incliti regis,[3] sermone et opere magnifice pollens, in plerisque locis ecclesias dedicans et ubique euangelium Christi praedicans, iuxta ammonitionem Ysaiae prophetae dicentis: 'Clama, ne cesses, quasi tuba exalta uocem tuam, et adnuntia populo meo scelera eorum, et domui Iacob peccata eorum.'[4]

26. DE REVELATIONE SANCTI ANTISTITIS SWITHVNI, QVEM SANCTVS ÆTHELWOLDVS IN ECCLESIAM TRANSTVLIT ⟨SVB DIE⟩[a] IDVS IVLII. Cuius[b] praedicationem maxime iuuit sanctus antistes[c] Suuithunus eodem tempore caelestibus signis declaratus et infra templi regiam gloriosissime translatus ac decentissime[d] collocatus.[5] Ideoque gemina simul in domo Dei fulsere luminaria, candelabris aureis superposita: quia quod Ætheluuoldus salubri uerborum exhortatione praedicauit, hoc Suuithunus miraculorum exhibitione mirifice decorauit.

27. QVOD ET ALIA MVLTA PER DVNSTANVM ET ÆTHELWOLDVM CONSTRVCTA SINT COENOBIA. Sicque factum est, consentiente rege, ut partim Dunstani consilio[e] et actione, partim[f] Ætheluuoldi sedula cooperatione, monasteria ubique in gente Anglorum,[g] quaedam monachis, quaedam sanctimonialibus, constituerentur sub abbatibus et abbatissis regulariter uiuentibus.[6] Circumiuitque famulus

[a] *Supplied from Capitula* [b] huius *TA* [c] antistes sanctus *G* [d] decenter *T* [e] concilio *G* [f] partem *G* [g] in gente Anglorum] ubique *G*

---

[1] Nothing of Æthelwold's monastery remains visible, and Thorney has not yet been properly excavated.

[2] For Æthelwold's endowment of Thorney, see Hart, *ECEE*, pp. 146–209, and S. Raban, *The Estates of Thorney and Crowland: A Study in Medieval Monastic Land Tenure* (Cambridge, 1977), pp. 6–20. One authentic document in Æthelwold's name and in favour of Thorney survives as S 1377 = BCS 1131 (roughly dated 963 × 975), an Old English deed of exchange by which Æthelwold consigned to Peterborough and Thorney estates forfeited by a woman accused of practising witchcraft; it is translated in *EHD*, pp. 562–3 (no. 112).

[3] Byrhtferth, *Vita S. Oswaldi* iii. 11 (*HCY* i. 426–7) reports that 'instructus ⟨namque erat⟩ idem rex ad cognitionem ueri regis ab Æþeluuoldo sanctissimo episcopo Wintoniensis ciuitatis', which seems to imply that Æthelwold was some sort of tutor to Edgar, and Æthelwold himself says as much in the *prohemium* to the *Regularis concordia*: 'abbate quodam [sc. Æthelwold] assiduo monente et regiam catholicae fidei uiam

dedicated the completed monastery[1] to the virgin Mary, mother of God, and was glad to make it rich in all sorts of property.[2]

25. ON HIS FRIENDSHIP WITH THE KING. The man of God Æthelwold was an intimate of the distinguished king Edgar.[3] He was splendidly strong in word and deed, dedicating churches in many places and everywhere preaching the gospel of Christ in accordance with the instruction of the prophet Isaiah: 'Cry aloud, spare not, lift up thy voice like a trumpet, and shew my people their transgression, and the house of Jacob their sins.'[4]

26. ON THE REVELATION OF THE HOLY BISHOP SWITHUN, WHOM THE HOLY ÆTHELWOLD TRANSLATED INTO THE CHURCH ON 15 JULY. His preaching was greatly aided by the holy bishop Swithun's being at this time marked out by signs from heaven and gloriously translated to receive proper burial within the church.[5] So it was that at one and the same time two lamps blazed in the house of God, placed on golden candlesticks; for what Æthelwold preached by the saving encouragement of his words, Swithun wonderfully ornamented by display of miracles.

27. THAT MANY OTHER MONASTERIES TOO WERE BUILT BY DUNSTAN AND ÆTHELWOLD. And so it came about, with the king's agreement, that thanks both to Dunstan's counsel and activity and to Æthelwold's unremitting aid, monasteries were established everywhere in England, some for monks, some for nuns, governed by abbots and abbesses who lived according to the Rule.[6] The

demonstrante' (*Reg. conc.*, p. 1). These statements need not imply formal tuition, but make it clear that Æthelwold was Edgar's adviser in spiritual matters.

4 Isa. 58: 1.

5 Æthelwold's translation of St Swithun's remains is the subject of Lantfred's *Translatio*, esp. cc. 1–3; it will be discussed fully in Lapidge, *The Cult of St Swithun*. Wulfstan was thoroughly familiar with Lantfred's work—he rendered it into hexameters as his own *Narratio*—and is frequently indebted to it for turns of phrase. Here the phrase *infra templi regiam* is taken from the *Translatio*, c. 2.

6 In addition to the monasteries then founded or refounded which Wulfstan names, the Anglo-Saxon Chronicle specifically mentions Chertsey and Milton Abbas (ASC 964 A) as foundations of King Edgar. To the initiative of Dunstan may be due the south-western foundations of Cerne, Tavistock, and Cranborne, but the evidence for these is uneven. To the initiative of Æthelwold one may also attribute the founding of St Neots (see above, p. l n. 46). Wulfstan does not mention in this connection the activities of Bishop Oswald, whose foundations included Westbury-on-Trym, Pershore, and Ramsey; he also refounded Winchcombe. Evesham, too, was probably refounded at this time, as were various women's houses such as Romsey. See, in general, Knowles, *MO*, pp. 48–52.

Christi Ætheluuoldus singula monasteria, mores instituens, oboedientes ut in bono proficerent uerbis ammonendo et stultos ut a malo discederent uerberibus corrigendo.

28. QVOD SANCTVS ÆTHELWOLDUS LENITATIS BLANDIMENTO SEVERITATEM DISCIPLINAE TEMPERAVERIT. Erat namque terribilis ut leo discolis[1] et peruersis, humilibus uero et oboedientibus se quasi agnum mitissimum exhibebat, ita serpentinae prudentiae temperans seueritatem ut columbinae simplicitatis non amitteret lenitatem.[2] Quem si quando zelus rectitudinis cogeret ut iura disciplinae subiectis imponeret, furor ipse non de crudelitate sed de amore processit, et intus paterna pietate dilexit quos foris quasi insequens castigauit. Pater erat et pastor monachorum, peruigil sanctimonialium protector et uirginum, uiduarum consolator, peregrinorum susceptor, ecclesiarum defensor, errantium corrector, pauperum recreator, pupillorum et orphanorum adiutor: quod plus impleuit opere quam nostra paruitas sermone possit euoluere.

29. QVOMODO FAMIS TEMPORE MVLTITVDINEM PAVPERVM AB IPSIS FAVCIBVS MORTIS ERIPVERIT. Accidit enim quodam tempore ut acerba fames uniuersam Britanniae regionem uehementer premeret et inopiae magnitudo plerosque dira clade extingueret.[3] Vir autem Domini misertus super turbam fame ualida pereuntium omnem pecuniae portionem quam habebat in usus pauperum expendit. Cumque pecunia deficeret, tolli iussit ornamenta quaeque et argentea uasa perplurima de thesauris ecclesiae, praecepitque ea minutatim confringi et in pecunias[a] redigi,[4] intimo cordis suspirio protestans se aequanimiter ferre non posse muta metalla integra perdurare, hominem uero ad imaginem Dei creatum et[b] precioso Christi sanguine[c] redemptum mendicitate et inedia perire.[5] Emptis ergo cibis sustentauit innumerabilem multitudinem egenorum,

[a] pec(c)unia *β* [b] et *om. G* [c] sanguine Christi *G*

[1] The rare word *discolus* is a Graecism originally from δύσκολος ('intractable', 'perverse'), but latinized in the Vulgate at 1 Pet. 2: 18.

[2] Cf. Matt. 10: 16 ('estote ergo prudentes sicut serpentes et simplices sicut columbae').

[3] This is probably the great famine of 976: see ASC 976 C.

[4] It is clear from the archaeological record that, in Æthelwold's day, precious-metal objects were often hacked up into pieces of definite weight and used as the equivalent of

servant of Christ Æthelwold toured the individual houses, laying down standards of conduct; the obedient he encouraged by words to advance in good, the foolish he corrected with lashes to make them depart from evil.

28. THAT ST ÆTHELWOLD TEMPERED THE SEVERITY OF HIS DISCIPLINE WITH COAXING GENTLENESS. Indeed he was terrible as a lion to malefactors[1] and the wayward; but to the humble and obedient he showed himself the meekest of lambs, tempering the severity of a serpent's cunning in such a way as to preserve the gentleness of an innocent dove.[2] If ever zeal for the right compelled him to impose the discipline of the law on his subjects, his very rage proceeded from love, not from cruelty, and inwardly he loved with a father's tenderness those whom he seemed on the surface to be correcting and harrying. He was a father and shepherd to his monks, an unsleeping champion of nuns and virgins, consoler of widows, receiver of pilgrims, defender of churches. He set right those who had gone astray, refreshed the poor, helped wards and orphans. And all this he carried out in deeds more fully than I could hope to unfold in my poor words.

29. HOW DURING A FAMINE HE SNATCHED A HOST OF POOR PEOPLE FROM THE VERY JAWS OF DEATH. Once it happened that a bitter famine afflicted the whole of Britain,[3] and there was a dreadful toll of men dying from lack of food. The man of God took pity on the throng of those perishing in the harsh famine, and he spent all the money he had on the needs of the poor. When the money ran out, he ordered the collection of all ornaments and many silver vessels to be brought from the church treasuries, and had them broken in pieces and turned into money,[4] protesting with deep and heartfelt sighs that he could not tolerate dumb metal being preserved untouched while man, created in the image of God and redeemed by the precious blood of Christ, perished of poverty and lack of sustenance.[5] He bought up food and supported a countless host of the

coinage; such metal, known as 'hacksilver', is frequently found in Viking Age hoards. See, *inter alia*, M. Stenberger, *Kulturhistorisk leksikon for nordisk middelalder*, vi. 37–9 and P. H. Sawyer, *The Age of the Vikings*, 2nd edn. (London, 1971), pp. 92, 192–3.

[5] Bede tells a similar story of King Oswald breaking up a silver dish in order to feed the poor (*HE* iii. 6). There are clear verbal parallels between Wulfstan's account and Bede's; Bede writes of the silver dish: '. . . sed et discum *confringi* atque eisdem *minutatim* diuidi *praecepit*.'

qui periculum famis euadere cupientes ad eum undique confugerant, et eos qui semineces in plateis et compitis omni solatio destituti iacebant refocilando subleuauit,[a] ab ipsis faucibus mortis eripiens miseros, praebens quoque cibaria cotidiana[b] singulis, donec misericordia Dei de caelo in terram prospiceret et humano generi solita pietate subueniens malum inopiae temperaret. In cuius pietatis opere sectatus[c] est imitabile exemplum beati Laurentii leuitae et martyris,[1] qui, instante persecutionis tempore, thesauros et facultates ecclesiae dispersit deditque pauperibus, ut iustitia eius maneret in saeculum saeculi et 'cornu eius exaltaretur in gloria'.[2]

30. QVOD INTER HAEC VIR SANCTVS INFIRMITATES SAEPE IN VISCERIBVS ET IN CRVRIBVS SVSTINVERIT.[d] Verum quia Dominus, sicut dicit scriptura, quem diligit corripit et omnem filium quem recipit flagellat,[3] uir Dei infirmabatur frequenter in uisceribus, morbumque tumoris[e] sustinebat in cruribus,[4] noctes plerumque insomnes prae dolore ducens, et in die, licet pallidus, tamen quasi sanus et nil molestiae sentiret ambulans, memor apostolicae consolationis qua dicitur 'quia uirtus in infirmitate perficitur';[5] et rursum 'quando enim infirmor, tunc fortior sum et potens',[6] et iterum 'libenter gloriabor in infirmitatibus meis, ut inhabitet in me uirtus Christi'.[5] Et quamuis acri pulsaretur molestia, minime tamen esu carnium quadrupedum aut auium usus est,[7] nisi semel, cogente maxima infirmitate, per tres menses, quod et fecit iussu Dunstani archiepiscopi,[f] et iterum in infirmitate qua obiit.

31. QVOD IVVENES DOCERE SEMPER DVLCE HABVERIT. Dulce namque erat ei adolescentes et iuuenes semper docere, et Latinos

[a] et *ins.* *β* [b] cotidiana cibaria *β* [c] imitatus *G* [d] sustin[*T* (perpessus fuerit *Capitula*) [e] morborumque tumores *G* [f] archiepiscopi *om.* *G*

[1] The story of St Laurence bequeathing his wealth to the poor was well known in Anglo-Saxon England from its occurrence in a *passio* (*BHL*, no. 4753) incorporated in the 'Cotton-Corpus Legendary', a 9th-c. Frankish compilation which was used by Ælfric for his 'Lives of Saints' (see above, p. cv) and was therefore probably known to Wulfstan. The *passio* is ptd. H. Delehaye, 'Recherches sur le légendier romain', *AB* li (1933), 34–98; for the story of Laurence distributing his wealth, see p. 83: 'beatus Laurentius coepit per regiones curiose quaerere, ubicunque sancti clerici uel pauperes essent absconsi; et portans thesauros, prout cuique opus erat, ministrabat.'

[2] Ps. 111 (112): 9.

[3] Heb. 12: 6 ('quem enim diligit Dominus castigat; flagellat autem omnem filium quem recipit'); cf. Prov. 3: 12.

needy, who had fled to him from every quarter in their longing to escape the danger of starvation. Those who lay about half-dead and quite untended in the streets and at the crossroads he brought back to life and consoled, snatching the wretches from the very jaws of death, and giving each his daily bread until such time as God should mercifully look out from heaven upon earth, relieve the sufferings of mankind with his customary pity, and ease the dearth. In this work of love Æthelwold followed the splendid example of St Laurence,[1] deacon and martyr, who, in a crisis during the persecution, dispersed the treasures and riches of the church and gave to the poor, so that his righteousness might endure for ever and 'his horn be exalted with honour.'[2]

30. THAT AMIDST THIS THE HOLY MAN HAD OFTEN TO PUT UP WITH ILLNESS IN HIS INNARDS AND LEGS. But as the scripture says: 'Whom the Lord loveth he chasteneth, and scourgeth every son whom he receiveth.'[3] And the man of God was frequently ill internally, and he suffered a malign swelling in his legs.[4] The nights he often spent without sleep because of the pain, but by day, though he looked pale, he moved about as though he were fit and felt no discomfort. For he remembered the apostle's consolation: 'For my strength is made perfect in weakness,'[5] and again: 'For when I am weak, then am I more strong and powerful,'[6] and again: 'Gladly therefore will I glory in my infirmities, that the power of Christ may rest upon me.'[5] And though he was grievously discomfited, he would not eat any flesh or fowl,[7] except once for a period of three months, forced to it by a grave illness and on the instructions, too, of Archbishop Dunstan, and again during the illness of which he died.

31. THAT HE ALWAYS FOUND IT PLEASANT TO TEACH YOUNG MEN. It was always agreeable to him to teach young men and the more mature students, translating Latin texts into English for them,

[4] Elsewhere Wulfstan (*Narratio* i. 859–61) gives a compassionate picture of Æthelwold on the occasion of the translation of St Swithun, attending the ceremony propped up by two attendants (presumably because of the pain in his legs):

> Et dictis iam finis erat, geminisque ministris
> aetatem propter nimiam hinc inde leuatus
> surgit . . .

[5] 2 Cor. 12: 9. [6] Ibid. 12: 10 ('cum enim infirmor, tunc potens sum').

[7] Cf. the stipulation in the *Regula S. Benedicti*, c. 36: 'sed et carnium esus infirmis omnino debilibus pro reparatione concedatur.'

libros Anglice eis soluere, et regulas grammaticae artis ac[a] metricae rationis tradere, et iocundis alloquiis ad meliora hortari.[1] Vnde factum est ut perplures ex discipulis eius fierent sacerdotes atque abbates et honorabiles episcopi, quidam etiam archiepiscopi, in gente Anglorum.[2]

32. DE AMPVLLA PAENE VACVA QVAE IN ITINERE OLEO PLENA INVENTA EST. Placuit inter haec omnipotenti Deo ut caelesti etiam monstraretur indicio quod ei beneplacitum esset habitare in sancto suo.[3] Nam cum iter quoddam sacer[b] antistes ageret ut in agro Dominico semen uerbi Dei spargeret, contigit clericum eius, cui sanctum crisma fuerat designatum, minus olei quam necessitas poscebat accepisse, et hoc parum quod acceperat in ipso itinere perdidisse. Cumque Christi famulus ad destinatum peruenisset locum, post missae[c] celebrationem postque dulcia sanctae praedicationis alloquia,[4] iussit ex more ad confirmandos pueros oleum sibi exhibere.[d] Sed clericus qui ampullam se secum[e] ferre aestimabat repente quod eam perdidisset agnouit. Turbatus[f] ergo celerrime repetiit iter unde[g] uenerat, et diligenter huc illucque circumspiciens inuenit ampullam crismatis in uia iacentem oleo plenam, cuius nec medietas quidem paulo ante quicquam liquoris habuerat. Qua assumpta 'cum timore et gaudio magno'[5] reuersus est,[h] sancto antistiti satisfaciens et caelestis stillicidii miraculum ueraci relatione pandens. Quod Dei nutu gestum esse probatur, ut qui spiritus sancti gratia perfundebatur, eiusque unctione corda et facies multorum exhilarabat, ipse non solum interius sed etiam exterius oleo supernae laeticiae[i] remuneraretur.

33. DE MONACHO QVI FVRTVM COMMISIT ET SOLO SERMONE VIRI DEI LIGATVS ET ABSOLVTVS EST. Quidam monachus[6] sub eius magisterio degebat qui daemoniaco[j] instinctu furti reatum perpetrauit. Vnde et omnem congregationem magnae tristiciae dolor inuasit,

[a] et *T* [b] sanctus *β* [c] missarum *T* [d] exhiberi *G* [e] secum ampullam se *G* [f] turbatur *T* [g] quo *G* [h] reuersus est magno *G* [i] leticie superne *G* [j] demonico *G*

[1] On Æthelwold's teaching and students, see above, pp. xcii–xcix.

[2] The archbishops included Æthelgar, archbishop of Canterbury 988–90 (above, p. 36 n. 3), and Ealdwulf, archbishop of York, 995–1002 (above, p. 41 n. 7). The bishops and abbots in question are too numerous to list conveniently here.

[3] Ps. 67 (68): 17 ('in quo beneplacitum est Deo habitare in eo').

passing on the rules of grammar and metric, and encouraging them to do better by cheerful words.[1] Many of his pupils accordingly became priests, abbots, and notable bishops, some even archbishops, in England.[2]

32. ON THE ALMOST EMPTY FLASK WHICH WAS FOUND ON THE ROAD FULL OF OIL. Meanwhile, it pleased Almighty God to have it shown by a sign from heaven too that it was pleasing to him to dwell in his holy man.[3] When the sacred bishop was going on a journey to scatter the seed of God's word in the Lord's field, it happened that the cleric in minor orders whom he had entrusted with the holy ointment took less oil than was needed and lost even this on the way. When the servant of Christ had come to his destination, he celebrated mass, spoke the sweet words of his holy sermon,[4] and then, as usual, ordered the oil for confirming the boys to be given him. But the cleric who imagined that he was carrying the flask suddenly realized he had lost it. In his dismay he hurriedly retraced his steps, and after a careful search in various places found the flask of oil lying in the road full of oil, though shortly before it had not even been half full of liquid. The cleric retrieved the flask and returned 'in fear and great joy',[5] excusing himself to the holy bishop and telling him the true story of the miraculous supply of oil from heaven. It is certain that this took place at the will of God, so that one who was flooded with the grace of the Holy Ghost and brought happiness to the hearts and faces of many by its unction should himself be rewarded both within and without by the oil of joy from above.

33. ON A MONK WHO STOLE AND WAS BOUND AND THEN RELEASED BY THE MERE WORD OF THE MAN OF GOD. There was a monk[6] living under his rule who was inspired by the devil to commit a theft. The whole fraternity was saddened and grieved at this; everyone was

[4] Perhaps a reminiscence of a hexameter here, perhaps Venantius Fortunatus, *App.* x. 1 (*dulcibus alloquiis*).

[5] Matt. 28: 8.

[6] The monk is not named by Wulfstan; Ælfric, however, supplies his name as Eadwine (c. 22; below, p. 77). For a possible reason why the name was omitted by Wulfstan, see above, p. cliv. No monk named Eadwine is given among the Old Minster monks in *LVH* (pp. 22–9; Gerchow, *Gedenküberlieferung*, pp. 322–4); however, an *Edwine* is included among the New Minster monks in the same source (p. 32; Gerchow, op. cit., p. 324).

dum quisque[a] suspectus ab altero fratre geri putaret quod se nequaquam fecisse procul dubio sciuit. Pro qua re sanctus antistes in conuentu fratrum modesta correptione[b] mandauit ut, si quis furti illius[c] sibi conscius esset, rem quam abstulerat quantotius cum Dei benedictione[d] redderet, aut in loco tali eam proiceret ubi inueniri potuisset. Ille uero frater obstinato corde se ipsum indurauit, et mandatum uiri Dei seruare neglexit. Transactis itaque tribus diebus et tribus noctibus, cum res furata minime[e] esset inuenta, locutus est[f] uir sanctus[g] in capitulo coram omni multitudine fratrum, terribili indignatione et comminatione inquiens: 'Noluit sacrilegus ille pecuniam quam furatus est[h] reddere cum benedictione sicut iussimus; reddat eam modo cum Dei omnipotentis[i] maledictione, et sit ipse ligatus, non solum in anima sed etiam in corpore, nostra auctoritate.' Quid multa? Dixerunt fratres 'amen', et ecce monachus ille sedens inuisibiliter ligabatur, brachiis sibi inuicem adhaerentibus sub cuculla sua, mansitque stupidus, cogitans quid agere deberet.[j] Omnia tamen reliqua membra sua[k] mobilia et ad usum apta habebat, exceptis brachiis, quae uir sanctus auctoritate sibi a Deo collata ligauit et inutilia reddidit. Tandem finito capitulo surrexit miser ille sic ligatus, et exiens post sanctum episcopum confessus est ei secreto se fuisse reum, seque latrocinii perpetrasse reatum, nichil tamen ei de ligatione qua tenebatur adstrictus indicans. Episcopus autem uidens eum nimio terrore correptum, sicut ei moris erat paenitentibus et flentibus clementer ignoscere et misericordiae uisceribus[1] condolere, blando sermone respondit: 'Modo saltem bene fecisti, licet sero, confitendo peccatum tuum; habeto nunc nostram[l] benedictionem.' Et statim soluta sunt brachia illius, episcopo nesciente. At ille exiens inde uehementer gauisus est, narrauitque per ordinem de sua ligatione et solutione cuidam fratri, uocabulo Wulfgaro,[2] qui ammonuit hoc magis silentio esse celandum et congruo postmodum[m] tempore detegendum. Qua ex re datur intelligi cuius meriti ante Deum[n] uir iste fuerit, qui solo sermone tantam uirtutem, licet nesciens, ostendit. Nam quia pastoralem sancti regiminis curam fide et moribus digne custodiuit, profecto beati

[a] quisquis *G* [b] correctione *β* [c] *C begins with this word, although the first recto is not always easy to read* [d] benedictione dei *C* [e] res furata minime] furto ablata non *G* [f] est *om. T* [g] dei *β* [h] es *C* [i] omnipotentis dei *G* [j] agere deberet] ageret *C* [k] membra sua reliqua *β (with* reliqua *above the line) G, perhaps rightly* [l] nostram *om. C* [m] postmodum congruo *β* [n] ante Deum *om. G.*

under suspicion, and thought that another brother must have done what he knew for certain he had not done himself. The holy bishop therefore issued a restrained reprimand to the assembled brothers, ordering that if anyone knew himself guilty of the theft he should with God's blessing give back what he had stolen with all speed, or drop it where it could be found. But the brother was obstinate, hardened his heart, and would not obey the man of God's order. Three days and nights went by without the stolen object being found. The holy man addressed all the fraternity in the chapter-house, fearsomely angry and full of menace: 'Despite my order, this sacrilegious thief has refused to restore with my blessing the money he took. Now let him return it with the curse of Almighty God upon him, and be bound in body as well as soul by my authority.' Well, the brethren said 'amen', and behold, the monk was invisibly tied up in his seat, his hands attached to each other beneath his cowl. He sat there in a daze wondering what to do. All the rest of his limbs he could move and use, but his hands the holy man had bound and rendered useless by the authority conferred on him by God. In the end, chapter over, the wretch got up, tied up as he was, and going out after the holy bishop confessed to him in secret that he was the guilty one and had committed the theft, though he did not tell him anything of the bonds that held him fast. The bishop saw his extreme terror. It was his practice to be merciful to those who wept and showed penitence, and to feel sympathy for them 'through bowels of mercy'.[1] So he replied kindly: 'It is late in the day, but now at least you have acted wisely in confessing your sin. Now have our blessing.' Immediately his hands were freed, though the bishop was unaware of it. The monk went away delighted, and told another monk the whole story of his binding and loosing. This other monk, who was called Wulfgar,[2] advised him to keep it quiet and only reveal it later at an appropriate moment. The incident lets us perceive the merit in God's eyes of a man who by a mere word and without being aware of it could perform such a miracle. He brought the proper faith and conduct to the shepherd's care of his holy rule, and surely for that

[1] Luke 1: 78 ('per uiscera misericordiae').

[2] Two oblates, each called 'Wulfgar puer' are listed among the monks of the Old Minster (*LVH*, p. 28, nos. xxxvi, xliii; Gerchow, *Gedenküberlieferung*, p. 323); the same list includes one 'Wulfgar agnus' (ibid., no. xxxviii). Any of these may have been the monk in question here. Furthermore, there was a monk named Wulfgar among the New Minster community at this time (*LVH*, p. 32, no. xlvii; Gerchow, op. cit., p. 324).

Petri principis apostolorum uicem ligando atque soluendo optinuit.[1]

34. DE MONACHO QVI DE SVMMO TEMPLI CVLMINE CECIDIT ET NIL MALI PASSVS INCOLVMIS SVRREXIT. Igitur cum uir Dei magno conamine Veterem renouare decreuisset Ecclesiam, iussit fratres frequenter laboribus una cum artificibus[a] et operariis insistere, quibus certatim laborantibus opus aedificii paulatim in sublime excreuit, plurimis hinc inde suffultum oratoriis, in quibus sanctorum uenerantur suffragia cunctis fideliter accedentibus profutura. Contigit autem quadam die, dum fratres starent ad summum culmen templi cum caementariis, ut unus illorum, Godus[2] nomine, caderet a summis[b] usque ad terram. Qui mox ut terram attigit, incolumis surgens stetit, nil mali passus de tanta ruina, seque crucis signaculo benedixit, admirans quid illic ageret uel qualiter illuc uenisset.[c] Et cunctis qui aderant uidentibus ascendit ad locum ubi antea steterat, et accipiens trullam operi quod inchoauerat diligentius insistebat. Cui ergo hoc miraculum adscribendum est nisi illi cuius iussu ad opus oboedientiae exiuit? Qui idcirco laedi non potuit quia hunc in casu suo uiri Dei meritum portauit et a periculo ruinae incolumem protexit.

35. DE MONACHO QVI SE VIRO DEI IN LEGENDO ASSIMILARE PRAESVMPSIT. Tempore quodam hiemali, cum fratres secundum regulae edictum temperius ad uigilias surgerent[3] et nocturno interuallo psalmodiae et lectioni inseruirent, quidam monachus, nomine Theodricus,[4] ad Dei hominem perrexit, uolens indiciis de quadam necessitate ei indicare, eumque luminis candelabrum manu tenentem repperit et legentem et sedula agilitate palpebrarum seniles obtutus acuentem: ibique diutius stetit, adtendens quam studiose oculos paginae infigeret. Surrexit tandem uir sanctus a lectione,[d] et ille frater residens accepit candelam coepitque legere, probans utrum et ipse posset oculos suos sanos ad legendum tam diligenter acuere sicut episcopum suos caligantes

[a] una cum artificibus *om. T* *(perhaps a variant in the original)* [b] a summis] assummis *T* [c] ueniret *βCG* [d] a lectione uir sanctus *β*

[1] Cf. Matt. 16: 19.

[2] Godus is listed among the monks of the Old Minster as a deacon (*LVH*, p. 26, no. xcii; Gerchow, *Gedenküberlieferung*, p. 323); nothing further is known of him.

[3] Wulfstan is here quoting the *Regularis concordia*, c. 29: 'Secundum uero regulae edictum *temperius ad Vigiliam surgatur*' (*Reg. conc.*, p. 26); the reference is to the *Regula S. Benedicti*, c. 11.

reason was the successor of the blessed Peter, chief of the apostles, in binding and loosing.[1]

34. ON THE MONK WHO FELL FROM THE TOP OF THE CHURCH ROOF AND GOT UP UNHARMED, HAVING SUFFERED NO INJURY. When the man of God had decided to go to great lengths to renovate the Old Minster, he ordered the brethren to take a frequent part in the work together with the craftsmen and labourers. All vied to work on the building, and gradually it grew very high. It was supported on either side by several oratories, where men beg for the help of saints, which is forthcoming to all who approach them with faith. However one day, when the brethren were standing with the masons on the topmost roof of the church, one of them, who was called Godus,[2] had the ill luck to fall right to the ground. When he reached it he at once got up uninjured and stood there, having suffered no harm from such a fall; he blessed himself with the sign of the cross, wondering what he was doing there and how he had got there. Everyone present watched as he climbed to the point where he had previously stood, took a trowel, and set himself with even more energy to the work he had begun. To whom should we ascribe this miracle if not to the man who had commanded him to go out to do this work of obedience? The monk could not sustain harm, because the deserts of the man of God bore him up in his fall and kept him uninjured from so dangerous a drop.

35. ON THE MONK WHO PRESUMED TO VIE WITH THE MAN OF GOD IN READING. One winter's day, when the monks, as the Rule lays down, 'rose earlier for Vigils'[3] and gave themselves over to singing psalms and reading in the night interval, a monk named Theodric[4] came to the man of God wanting to tell him by signs about some important matter. He found him with a candlestick in his hand, reading, and sharpening his aged sight by keeping his eyelids hard at work. There he stood for some while, watching how closely Æthelwold fixed his eyes on the page. At length the holy man rose from his reading, and the monk sat down, took the candle and started to read, testing whether he could make his healthy eyes as sharp at reading as he had seen the bishop do his dim ones. But

[4] Theodric is not listed among the earliest group of Old Minster monks in *LVH* (pp. 22–9; Gerchow, *Gedenküberlieferung*, pp. 322–4); a *Theodric* occurs among the late additions to the list of New Minster monks (p. 52), but he is unlikely to be the monk in question here. It is not a common English name at this time.

fecisse uiderat. Sed illa temeritas non inpune euenit illi. Nam sequenti nocte, cum membra sopori dedisset, apparuit ei quidam uultu incognitus, terribili comminatione dicens ad eum:[a] 'Qua temeritate praesumpsisti exprobrare[b] episcopum[c] praeterita nocte in legendo?' Cumque tremefactus se hoc fecisse negaret, ille toruis intuens in eum luminibus[d] 'Non potes' inquit 'me fallendo ludere,[e] sicut aestimas; sed hoc signum tuae praesumptionis habeas': et haec dicens incussit uiolenter ictum oculis eius digito suo, statimque dolor oculorum ualidus secutus est, qui eum multis diebus uehementer affligebat, donec satisfactione culpam deleret quam incaute in sanctum uirum commisit.

36. DE CANDELA QVAE EPISCOPO OBDORMIENTE SVPER FOLIVM LIBRI ARDENS IACVIT ET TAMEN PAGINAM MINIME LAESIT. Item accidit, cum famulus Christi nocturno tempore lectioni operam daret, eum ob nimiam uigilantiam[f] obdormisse, et candelam ardentem de candelabro super librum in quo legerat cecidisse. Quae tandiu ardens super folium iacebat donec unus frater, nomine Leofredus,[1] adueniret. Qui festinus accepit candelam adhuc flammantem de libro, et intuitus aspexit fauillas ipsius candelae per multas lineas iacentes, et exsufflans eas inuenit paginam inlaesam. Qua in re meritum sancti uiri patuit, quia ardentem candelam flamma consumpsit et tamen uim uirtutis suae ne paginam laederet amisit.

37. QVOD NON OMNIA VIRTVTVM EIVS OPERA VALEANT EXPLICARI. Haec Christo largiente breuiter retulimus ut et praesentes et futuros quosque[g] fideles ad amorem et reuerentiam tanti patris humili deuotione incitaremus. Ceterum non facile nobis occurrit explicare quanta uel qualia sanctus Ætheluuoldus[h] sustinuerit[i] pro monachorum defensione pericula, aut quam benigno diligebat affectu studiosos[j] et oboedientes fratres, aut quantum in structura monasterii elaboraret, ecclesiam reparando aliasque domos aedificando, aut quam peruigil erat in orationibus, et quam deuote hortabatur fratres ad confessionis remedium, aut quam multa milia

[a] ad eum] ei *G* [b] exprobare *NCG* [c] episcopo *TG* [d] ait *ins. T* [e] illudere *C corr.*, *G* [f] uigiliam *G* [g] quousque *G* [h] Ath. sanctus *G* [i] sustinuit *β* [j] studiose *G (omitting* et*)*

[1] Leofred is not listed among the Old Minster monks in *LVH*. However, a *Leofred leuita* is found among the New Minster monks (*LVH*, p. 31, no. xix; Gerchow, *Gedenk-*

such presumption did not go unpunished. The following night, when he had given his body up to sleep, there appeared to him someone whose face he did not recognize, who asked with fearful menace: 'With what temerity did you dare to reproach the bishop last night in reading?' The monk trembled and said he had not done this. But the other glared at him and said: 'You cannot play with me or deceive me, as you imagine: take that as the mark of your presumption.' With these words he jabbed his finger sharply into Theodric's eyes. Severe eye pains followed at once, and troubled him badly for many days, till his penance removed the guilt which he had unwittingly incurred towards the holy man.

36. ON THE CANDLE THAT LAY BURNING ON THE PAGE OF A BOOK WHEN THE BISHOP WAS ASLEEP AND YET DID IT NO HARM AT ALL. It also happened that, when the servant of Christ was devoting himself to reading at night, he fell asleep because he had stayed awake too long, and that a burning candle fell from the candlestick on the book in which he had been reading. It lay alight on the page until a brother, whose name was Leofred,[1] came along. He quickly removed the candle, still alight, from the book. On examination he saw hot ash from the candle lying across many lines of the writing. Blowing them away he found the page undamaged. Here the merit of the holy father was made obvious: the flame wore away the candle as it burned, but it lost its force and could not harm the page.

37. THAT NOT ALL HIS VIRTUOUS WORKS CAN BE RELATED. Christ has made it possible for me to give a brief account of these facts; I hope in my humble piety to encourage all believers, now and in the future, to love and reverence the great father. But I do not find it easy to relate all the extraordinary dangers St Æthelwold underwent in defence of his monks; with what kindness he loved diligent and obedient brethren; how hard he laboured at the monastery buildings, repairing the church and building other structures; how he stayed awake to pray; how devotedly he encouraged the brethren to find aid in confession; or how many thousands of souls

überlieferung, p. 324); it is probably this same Leofred whose obit is recorded in the calendar in Cotton Titus D. XXVII (*LVH*, p. 271). This miracle involving Leofred has a close parallel in Odilo of Cluny's exactly contemporary *Vita S. Maioli* (*PL* cxlii. 955), but it is not possible to ascertain that there was any contact between the two authors.

animarum diabolo subtraxerit easque Deo redditas caelo intulerit. Sed ex his paucis plura cognosci possunt quae a nobis enarrari nequeunt.

38. DE ARBORE QVADAM MAGNA CVCVLLIS INNVMERIS ONVSTA ET DE EIVS INTERPRETATIONE QVAE IN SOMNIS SANCTO DVNSTANO OLIM FVERAT OSTENSA. Oportebat namque impleri somnium quod Dunstanus ille gloriosus et angelicus Anglorum gentis archiepiscopus olim de eo se uidisse perhibebat. Nam cum[a] esset abbas monasterii Glastoniensis[b] et sub eius regimine militaret omnipotentis Dei famulus Ætheluuoldus, sicut supra narrauimus, uidit in somnis, extra dormitorium positus, quasi quandam mirae celsitudinis arborem, quae ramos suos expandere uisa est ad orientem et occidentem, septentrionem et meridiem, super uniuersam Britanniae regionem uasta[c] longitudine et latitudine extensam. Cuius arboris rami innumeris erant maioribus atque minoribus cucullis onusti, ipsa uero arbor in summo cacumine gestabat unam pergrandem[d] cucullam, quae manicarum uelamento supereminens protegebat ceteras et ingenti proceritate supergrediens uniuersas ipsum contingebat caelum. Vir autem Domini[e] Dunstanus, super tali uisione uehementer attonitus, interrogabat haec sibi demonstrantem canis angelicis decoratum presbiterum, dicens: 'Quaeso, uenerande senior, quae est haec robusta et sublimis arbor cuius rami longe lateque expansi tam innumerabiles cucullas sustinere cernuntur?' Cui ille respondit: 'Arbor haec quam uides, abba Dunstane, situm designat huius insulae: magna autem cuculla, quae in[f] huius arboris summitate erigitur, ipsa est monachi tui Ætheluuoldi, qui in hoc monasterio deuote Christo famulatur; reliquae uero cucullae, quibus hi rami uidentur onusti, multitudinem designant monachorum qui eius eruditione sunt instruendi et undique in hac regione ad[g] omnipotentis[h] Dei seruitium congregandi, eiusque ducatu peruenturi sunt ad gloriam regni caelorum et ad societatem cum Christo regnantium spirituum beatorum.' Quo accepto responso uir sanctus euigilat, uisionem tacitus secum considerans, eamque postmodum fideli relatione fidelibus indicans. Quae succedente tempore fama uulgante multis[i] innotuit et tandem ad nostrae quoque paruitatis noticiam peruenit.[1]

[a] adhuc *ins.* *T* [b] glaestiniensis *C*; Glestoniensis *G* [c] mra *(sic)* *T*
[d] pregrandem *T* [e] Domini *om.* *G* [f] in *om.* *G* [g] ad *om.* *C*
[h] omnipotentum *G* [i] multis *om.* *G*

he won from the devil, restoring them to God and bringing them to heaven. But from the little that I have related it is possible to infer more that I cannot narrate.

38. ON A GREAT TREE LOADED WITH COUNTLESS COWLS, AND THE INTERPRETATION OF IT, ONCE SHOWN IN A DREAM TO ST DUNSTAN. In fact there had to be fulfilled a dream which the glorious and angelic archbishop of England, Dunstan, recounted that he had once had concerning Æthelwold. When Dunstan was abbot of Glastonbury and the servant of Almighty God Æthelwold was, as I related above, a soldier under his command, Dunstan saw, while asleep outside the dormitory, what looked like a tree of wonderful height, which appeared to stretch its branches to east, west, north, and south, extending far and wide over all Britain. The branches of the tree were loaded with countless cowls, some bigger, some smaller. But the tree itself carried on its topmost point one very large cowl, which protected the others with the covering of its jutting sleeves, and was so much higher than the rest that it reached heaven itself. The man of God Dunstan, thunderstruck at a sight like this, asked a priest with white hair like an angel's who was showing him the spectacle: 'Tell me, venerable old man, what is this strong and tall tree whose branches spread so far and wide and can be seen to support so countless a number of cowls?' He replied: 'The tree you see, abbot Dunstan, denotes this island. The big cowl standing at the top of this tree is that of your monk Æthelwold, who is Christ's devoted servant in this monastery. The other cowls that seem to burden these branches denote the many monks who are to be instructed by his scholarship and assembled from all quarters for the service of Almighty God in this district. Eventually they will come, with him as their leader, to the glories of the kingdom of heaven and the society of the blessed spirits who rule with Christ.' After hearing this reply, the holy man woke up, pondering silently on the vision and later giving a faithful account of it to the faithful. As time went on, rumour spread it, and it became known to many; and in the end it came to the knowledge of my insignificant self as well.[1]

[1] This same vision of Dunstan is later recounted by William of Malmesbury in his *Vita S. Dunstani*, c. 17 (*Memorials*, pp. 272–3). The dream is ultimately inspired by that of Nebuchadnezzar in Dan. 4.

39. DE VISIONE VIRI DEI IN QVA APPARVIT EI[a] NAVIS QVAEDAM MAXIMA PISCIBVS ET ANGVILLIS PLENA. Nec minus et aliud oportebat impleri somnium, quod ipse uir Dei sanctus Ætheluuoldus de se nobis quadam uice referebat, inquiens: 'Putabam me stare iuxta litus maris, ubi mihi uidebatur adesse quaedam maxima nauis, in qua multitudo copiosa piscium, et maxime anguillarum, conclusa tenebatur ab imo usque ad summum. Cumque mecum tacitus cogitarem quid sibi uellet hoc somnium quod uidebam, repente audiui uocem meo nomine me uocantem mihique dicentem: "Ætheluuolde, Ætheluuolde, hoc tibi mandatum caelitus a Deo missum est: 'Excita hos pisces, quibus haec nauis quam cernis impleta est, et orationibus tuis effice ut sint homines, sicut antea fuerunt.'" Cuius iussioni mox ego obtemperans steti pro eis ad orationem, et lacrimarum imbre perfusus ingemiscens dixi: "Domine Iesu,[b] cui nichil est inpossibile, respice propitius ad animas diabolica fraude deceptas, quae a sensu humanae rationis alienatae sunt et more bestiali in lubrico huius saeculi caeno miserabiliter inuoluuntur. Ne, quaeso, bone Iesu, permittas ut de eis triumphans glorietur humani generis inimicus, sed per tui[c] nominis omnipotentiam resuscitentur ad uitam, ut somnum aeternae mortis euadentes te uerum et unicum mundi saluatorem cognoscant, et deinceps semper ad tranquillum salutis tuae portum confugientes ab omnibus mundi perturbationibus immunes existant[d] et sub tua gubernatione securae[e] permaneant. Tuum est enim, Christe, mortuos uiuificare, et imaginem tuam quam creasti in decorem suum pristinum reformare, qui uenisti in hunc mundum peccatores saluos facere, et dira mortis supplicia passus in cruce[f] fundere dignatus es sanguinem tuum preciosum pro salute omnium nostrum." Cum haec et his similia orationis uerba conpuncto corde et spiritu humilitatis effunderem, ecce quos antea pisces in luto faecis et in lacu miseriae uideram inuolutos,[1] subito homines effectos et a morte resuscitatos uideo,[g] surrexitque de naui et perrexit festinanter ad terram copiosa hominum multitudo, quorum multos specialiter agnoueram:[h] inter quos unus retrorsum[i] cadens iterum in anguillam uersus est, ille uidelicet Æthelstanus,[2] qui mecum presbiter quondam fuerat ordinatus, quem deinceps nullo modo excitare nec ut homo fieret

[a] et *T* [b] Iesu *om. N;* Christe *ins. A* [c] sancti *ins. NCG* [d] perturbationibus immunes existant] periculis eruantur *T* [e] securi *CG* [f] crucem *N (and A before correction);* cr[*T* [g] uidero *G* [h] noueram *G* [i] retrorsus *G*

39. ON THE VISION OF THE MAN OF GOD IN WHICH THERE APPEARED TO HIM A VERY LARGE SHIP FULL OF FISH AND EELS. Another dream too had to find fulfilment, which the man of God, St Æthelwold, himself told us once of himself: 'I thought that I was standing by the seashore, and that near me was a very large ship, in which from top to bottom was trapped a vast host of fish, particularly eels. I was silently wondering what this dream could mean, when suddenly I heard a voice calling me by name and saying: "Æthelwold, Æthelwold, God sends you this command from heaven: 'Rouse these fish which fill the ship you see, and cause them by your prayers to be men as they were before.'" I obeyed this command at once, and stood before them to pray. Bathed in tears and groaning I said: "Lord Jesus, for whom nothing is impossible, look favourably on souls practised upon by the devil's deceit, which have been estranged from the understanding of human reason, and like beasts are pitifully plunged in the slippery mire of this world. Do not, good Jesus, I pray you, allow the enemy of the human race to gloat in triumph over them, but may they through the almighty power of your name be brought back to life. May they leave the sleep of eternal death and recognize you as the true and sole Saviour of the world; may they always thereafter find refuge in the quiet harbour of your salvation, and, untouched by all the troubles of the world, remain for ever free of care under your guidance. You have the power, Christ, to give life to the dead, and to bring back your image, which you created, to its former beauty: you who came into this world to save sinners and who after suffering the terrible penalty of death on the cross deigned to shed your precious blood for the salvation of us all." I poured out these and similar words of prayer from a conscience-stricken heart and in a spirit of humility. And behold the fishes I had seen plunged in "the miry clay" and "an horrible pit",[1] I now saw suddenly made men and revived from death. There arose from the ship and came swiftly to land a great host of men, many of whom I recognized personally. One fell backwards and was turned into an eel again: it was the Athelstan who had once been ordained priest along with me.[2] I could not thereafter rouse him at all, or make him become

[1] Ps. 39 (40): 3 ('et eduxit me de lacu miseriae et de luto fecis').
[2] Cf. above, c. 8.

poteram efficere. Reliqui uero omnes unanimiter leuauerunt uocem in caelum, manibus plaudentes et gratias omnipotenti Deo referentes quia per eius ineffabilem clementiam et per meae paruitatis aduentum meruerunt a morte ad uitam reuocari et humanae rationi quam amiserant restaurari. Ego autem gaudens in Domino et congratulans illis euigilo; hancque uisionem uobis, O filioli mei, idcirco refero ut et uos cum bonorum operum cultu perseueretis in sancto proposito, quo per gratiam Dei possitis in eorum numero computari qui mihi licet indigno commissi sunt, ut de saeculi huius caenolenta uoragine liberentur et in aeterna beatitudine sine fine saluentur.' Haec quae notauimus somnia[a] tunc quidem uisa sunt: sed ex eo tempore usque hodie impleri non cessant, dum quique diuino[b] feruentes amore festinant mundum relinquere et coenobialem uitam ducere et dum populares quique satagunt a malo declinare et bonum facere et humiliter regi regum, Christo, colla subdere, quatinus et monachi simul et laici sequentes sancti patris Ætheluuoldi uestigia caelestis regni sempiterna mereantur adipisci gaudia.

40.[c] DE VETERIS ECCLESIAE NOVA DEDICATIONE QVAE FACTA EST DIE .XIII. KALENDARVM NOVEMBRIS. Anno dominicae incarnationis nongentesimo octogesimo renouata et constructa est ecclesia Veteris Coenobii, nouem pontificibus eam sollemniter et cum magna gloria dedicantibus: quorum primi et praecipui arcem tenebant Dunstanus archiepiscopus et ipse sanctus[d] Ætheluuoldus episcopus, sub die .XIII. Kalendarum Nouembrium, in praesentia regis Æthelredi et in conuentu omnium paene ducum, abbatum, comitum primorumque optimatum uniuersae gentis Anglorum, qui eandem biduo cum omni gaudio celebrauerunt dedicationem.[1] Exinde superna pietas sancto pontifici tantam contulit gratiam ut sublimes illi saecularium potestatum principes, duces, tyranni atque iudices et omnes qui ei hactenus contrarii et in uia Dei resistere uidebantur subito uelut oues ex lupis efficerentur et eum

[a] omnia *T(?)* [b] diuino *om. G* [c] *The chapter is omitted by CG* [d] sanctus *om. N*, ipse sanctus *om. A*

[1] The dedication of the rebuilt Old Minster, on 20 Oct. 980, is described in full by Wulfstan, *Narratio*, Ep. spec. 61–114. Wulfstan there lists the nine bishops who were present. These included Dunstan, Æthelwold, and a further seven: two bishops named Ælfstan (any two of Ælfstan of London (959 × 964–996), of Rochester (955 × 964–995), and of Ramsbury (970–81, on whom see above, p. 28 n. 1)); Æthelgar of Selsey (see above,

a man. However, all the others raised their voices to heaven with one accord, clapping their hands and thanking Almighty God because, through his ineffable clemency and the arrival of my insignificant self, they had merited recall from death to life and restoration to the human reason they had lost. I rejoiced in the Lord and wished them joy: then I awoke. I tell you this vision, my dear sons, so that you too may cultivate good works and continue in your holy purpose. Thus by the grace of God you may come to be counted in the number of those who have been entrusted to my unworthy self to be freed from the filthy gulf of this world and find salvation without end in eternal blessedness.' What I have noted down seemed then to be mere dreams. But from that time till today they have never ceased to be fulfilled: everyone ablaze with the love of God is hurrying to leave the world and lead a monastic life, and the common people are anxious one and all to depart from evil, do good and bow their necks in humility to Christ, king of kings, so that both monks and laity together, following the footsteps of the holy father Æthelwold, may deserve to attain the lasting joys of the heavenly kingdom.

40. ON THE NEW DEDICATION OF THE OLD MINSTER THAT TOOK PLACE ON 20 OCTOBER. In the year of the Lord's incarnation 980 the church of the Old Minster was renewed and rebuilt. It received a solemn and splendid dedication from nine bishops, of whom the first and highest dignitaries were Archbishop Dunstan and the holy bishop Æthelwold in person. The date was 20 October, and there were present King Æthelred and virtually all the ealdormen, abbots, thegns and leading noblemen of the whole race of the English.[1] For two days they celebrated the dedication in all joy. Furthermore, God in his love gave such grace to the holy bishop that those high lay dignitaries, ealdormen, potentates, and judges, and all who had previously seemed his enemies, standing in God's path, were suddenly made, as it were, sheep instead of wolves: they

p. 36 n. 3); Æscwig of Dorchester-on-Thames (975 × 979–1002); Ælfheah of Lichfield (975–1002 × 1004); Æthelsige of Sherborne (978–991 × 993); and Athulf of Hereford (d. 1013 × 1016). On the ceremony itself, see D. J. Sheerin, 'The dedication of the Old Minster, Winchester, in 980', *RB* lxxxviii (1978), 261–73. In his *Narratio* Wulfstan concludes the description of the feasting which took place (this modelled on Vergil, *Aen.* i) with the opinion that such a dedication-ceremony had never before taken place in England ('numquam tanta fuit talisque dicatio templi / in tota Anglorum gente patrata reor').

miro affectu uenerarentur, eiusque genibus colla summittentes ac dexteram illius humiliter exosculantes orationibus se uiri Dei in omnibus commendarent.

41. DE OBITV SANCTI PATRIS IN KALENDIS AVGVSTI ET DE SEPVLTVRA EIVS IN DIE .III. NONARVM MENSIS[a] EIVSDEM. Eodem uero tempore quo sanctus antistes Ætheluuoldus de hac mortali uita erat exiturus et laborum suorum praemia a Deo percepturus, uenit ad uillam quae consueto nomine Beaddingtun[1] appellatur, sexaginta milibus ab urbe Wintonia distans. Ibi ergo cum aliquandiu moraretur, acri coepit infirmitate grauari, et sacrati olei liquore perunctus dominici corporis et sanguinis perceptione exitum suum muniuit. Sicque ualefaciens et dans pacem filiis suis inter uerba orationis spiritum caelo reddidit in Kalendis Augusti, anno[b] dominicae incarnationis nongentesimo octogesimo quarto, episcopatus autem sui uicesimo secundo, regni moderamina gubernante Æthelredo rege Anglorum. Testati uero nobis sunt[c] qui ibi praesentes aderant exanime corpus sancti uiri[d] subita inmutatione fuisse renouatum, lacteo candore perfusum[e] roseoque rubore uenustum, ita ut quodam modo septennis pueri uultum[f] praetendere uideretur, in quo iam quaedam resurrectionis gloria per ostensionem mutatae carnis apparuit. Iam uero dici non potest quanta ad exequias eius hominum multitudo conuenerit. Vndique certatim ex uicinis oppidis et castellis simul in unum diuites et pauperes, ultimum uale pastori suo dicturi, confluxerant. Omnes cum dolore et amaro animo sequebantur feretrum incomparabili thesauro preciosum, sacrosanctis euangeliis et crucibus armatum, palliorum uelamentis ornatum, accensis luminaribus et hymnis caelestibus atque psalmorum[g] concentibus hinc inde uallatum. Quibus sequenti die Wintoniam ingredientibus, obuiam corpori tota simul ciuitas unanimiter occurrit. Hinc eiulantes[h] turbas conspiceres monachorum, inde pallida agmina uirginum; hinc audires in excelso uoces psallentium clericorum, inde gemitum flentium pauperum et ululatum uociferantium egenorum, qui, pastoris sui praesentia se priuari non sustinentes, dabant infinitos lacrimarum clamores ad caelum. Perductus est ergo uir Dei cum caelestibus exequiis in ecclesiam beatorum apostolorum Petri et Pauli ad

[a] mensis *om.* *C* [b] scilicet *ins.* *T* [c] sunt nobis *G* [d] uiri *om.* *β* [e] prefusum *T* [f] multum *G* [g] psalmorum *om.* *C* [h] querulentas *T*; euigilantes *A before correction*

revered him with extraordinary affection, and, lowering their necks to his knee and humbly kissing his hand, commended themselves in all things to the prayers of the man of God.

41. CONCERNING THE DEATH OF THE HOLY FATHER ON 1 AUGUST AND HIS BURIAL ON 3 AUGUST. Now at the time when the holy bishop Æthelwold was destined to leave this mortal life and receive from God the rewards for his labours, he came to a town commonly known as Beddington,[1] sixty miles from Winchester. Staying there for a while, he fell seriously ill; he was anointed with the holy oil, and fortified his departure from this life by receiving the Lord's body and blood. And so, bidding farewell to his sons and granting them his peace, he gave up his spirit to heaven while still praying. It was 1 August, in the year of our Lord's incarnation 984, the twenty-second of his bishopric, and Æthelred, king of the English, was on the throne. Those who were present have witnessed to us that the holy man's corpse was suddenly changed and renewed: it was suffused with a whiteness as of milk, and became lovely with a rosy redness, so that his face looked in a way like that of a seven-year-old boy; in this observed change of the flesh appeared even on earth some hint of the glory of the resurrection. It is not possible to say what a countless multitude flocked to his funeral. From every direction had assembled rich and poor alike from neighbouring towns and boroughs vying to say their last farewell to their shepherd. It was with grief and bitterness at heart that they all followed behind the bier, precious with its incomparable treasure, armed with the holy gospels and crosses, decked with veiling cloths, protected on each side by lit candles, hymns to God and chanted psalms. When the procession came next day into Winchester, the whole city with one accord met the body. Here you might have seen wailing troops of monks, there pale-faced companies of virgins; here you might have heard the voices of the clergy singing on high, there the groans of the weeping poor and the wailing of the shrieking needy, who could not bear to lose their shepherd's presence, and poured endless tears and cries to heaven. So the man of God was led in heavenly funeral to the church of the blessed apostles Peter and Paul, and to his bishop's seat. The

[1] Beddington lies 2 miles west of Croydon in Surrey; it was an estate granted by King Edgar to Æthelwold and the Old Minster (S 815 = BCS 1155).

sedem suam[a] episcopalem, et expletis uigiliarum missarumque sollemniis sepultus est in cripta ad australem plagam sancti altaris, ubi eum requiescere debere, sicut ipse nobis retulit, olim sibi caelitus ostensum est.

42. QVOMODO SANCTVS VIR ANTEQVAM LEVARETVR E TVMVLO MANIFESTAVIT SE VRBANO CVIDAM ÆLFHELMO PLVRIMA CAECITATE MVLTATO. Anno duodecimo post obitum gloriosi pontificis Æthel-uuoldi placuit supernae dispensationi illum per caelestia signa reuelari eiusque ossa de sepulchri munimine leuari, ut lucerna quae ad tempus sub modio latebat[1] super candelabrum poneretur quatinus luceret omnibus qui in domo Dei[b] sunt. Est enim ciuitas quaedam modica, commerciis abunde referta, quae solito Walinga-ford[c] appellatur, in qua uir strenuus quidam morabatur, cui nomen erat Ælfhelmus,[2] qui casu lumen amittens oculorum caecitatem multis perpessus est annis. Huic in somnis tempore gallicinii sanctus Ætheluuoldus antistes adstitit eumque ut maturius Wintoniam[d] pergeret et ad eius tumbam gratia recipiendi uisus accederet ammonuit, dicens: 'Idcirco te in stratu tuo recubantem[e] uisito et quae tibi uentura sunt praenuntio ut per tuae salutis signum manifestetur quia me oportet leuari[f] de tumulo in quo[g] iaceo.' Qui haec audiens et uocem secum loquentis agnoscens[h] sancto patri gratias egit quod[i] eum uisitare dignaretur; et quia ubi sepultus esset penitus ignorauit, qualiter sepulchrum eius scire et adire potuisset diligenter inquisiuit: cui[j] protinus uir Dei nomen alumni et monachi sui innotuit, cuius hactenus homo ille nescius extitit, eique dixit: 'Cum festinus Wintoniam perueneris et Veteris Coenobii ecclesiam intraueris, accersiri fac ad te monachum quendam Wulfstanum, cognomento Cantorem. Hic cum ex ore tuo uerba meae legationis audierit, te mox indubitanter ad meum perducet tumulum, ibique recipies lumen oculorum tuorum.' Quid multa? Credulus uir ille uerbis et promissionibus sacri pontificis Wintoniam citius adiit, ecclesiam intrauit, fratrem praedictum accersiuit, accersitumque postulauit ut missatica beati patris impleret, narrans ei et cunctis adstantibus ordinem uisionis.[k] Erat enim uespera in qua natiuitas sacratissimae Dei genitricis et

[a] suam sedem *G* [b] Dei *om. G (and C before correction)* [c] Uuealinga ford *C*; Walingeford *G A before correction)* [d] Wintoniam maturius *G* [e] recumbantem *N (and* [f] leuare *G* [g] nunc *ins. β* [h] agnoscentis *G* [i] quo *G* [j] cuius *G* [k] ordine uisionem *G*

solemnities of vigils and masses complete, he was buried in the crypt to the south of the holy altar, where, as he told me himself, a sign from heaven had long ago shown that he should rest.

42. HOW BEFORE THE HOLY MAN WAS RAISED FROM HIS TOMB HE SHOWED HIMSELF TO A CITIZEN CALLED ÆLFHELM WHO WAS AFFLICTED WITH SEVERE BLINDNESS. In the twelfth year after the death of the glorious bishop Æthelwold, it pleased God in his high counsels that he should be marked out by signs from heaven, and that his bones should be raised from the enclosure of the tomb; thus the candle that for the time lay hidden under a bushel[1] would be put on a candlestick, that it might give light unto all that are in the house of God. For in a small but busy market town commonly known as Wallingford there dwelt an industrious man called Ælfhelm,[2] who had chanced to lose the sight of his eyes and had endured blindness for many a year. To this man the holy Æthelwold appeared in his sleep at cock-crow; he told him to hurry to Winchester and go to his tomb to receive back his sight. 'I visit you,' he said, 'as you lie in your bed and tell you of your future in order that by the sign of your recovery it may be made clear that I must be raised from the tomb in which I lie.' Ælfhelm, hearing this and recognizing the voice of the speaker, thanked the holy father for deigning to visit him. He was quite ignorant of the position of the grave, and made careful inquiry as to how he could recognize and visit it. Straightway the man of God told him the name of a pupil and monk of his, previously unknown to Ælfhelm, saying: 'When you have made all haste to Winchester and entered the church of the Old Minster, get them to fetch you a monk called Wulfstan *Cantor*. When he hears from you the details of my message, he will take you at once and without question to my tomb. There you will get back the sight of your eyes.' Need I say more? Ælfhelm believed the words and promises of the holy bishop, and hurried to Winchester. He went into the church, summoned Wulfstan, and on his appearance asked him to act on the blessed father's message; and he told him and all the bystanders the whole story of the vision. It was the evening on which the entire world

[1] Cf. Matt. 5: 15.
[2] This Ælfhelm is otherwise unknown.

perpetuae uirginis Mariae per totum mundum sollemniter et dignissime[a] celebratur. Ille uero frater admirans inter spem et timorem[1] se medium posuit, et uicino oboedientiae pede iussis sancti pontificis humiliter obtemperans ad antrum sarcofagi perduxit caecum, qui pernox ibidem in oratione permansit, et mane facto iam amplius ductore non indigens ad propria cum gaudio reuersus est uidens, corde et animo Dominum benedicens.

43. DE SANCTI PRAESVLIS TRANSLATIONE QVAE FACTA EST SVB DIE .IIII. IDVVM SEPTEMBRIVM ET DE MIRACVLIS AD EIVS SEPVLCHRVM PATRATIS.[b] Haec reuelatio longe lateque diuulgata est, quae tam euidenti miraculo fuerat comprobata. Exinde famulus Christi praedicto fratri Wulfstano et plerisque aliis per nocturnam uisionem manifestus apparuit, illisque per haec et haec indicia aperuit[c] quia supernae complaceret uoluntati eum de tumulo transferri et digne in ecclesia collocari. Venerandus ergo[d] pontifex Ælfeagus,[2] successor eius, animo sagaci talia secum pertractans, humillimas alacri corde Christo omnipotenti gratias reddidit eo quod suo tempore dignaretur caelestibus signis sanctum suum mirificare. Nec mora, fratrum cleri plebisque multitudine congregata, reliquias sancti praesulis Æthelwuoldi sub die .IIII. Iduum Septembrium honorifice transtulit easque in choro ecclesiae collocauit, ubi in magna ueneratione habentur usque in praesentem diem, ubi etiam nobis intuentibus caelestia sunt perpetrata miracula, e quibus duo breuiter ad firmitatis indicium perstrinximus.

44. DE INFIRMA PVELLA QVAE IBI SANITATEM RECEPIT. Erat eo tempore in Wentana ciuitate puella quaedam paruula, cuiusdam Æthelwueardi[e][3] domestici[f] filia, quae nimis infirmabatur et usque ad mortem paene torquebatur. Haec a matre deducta ad uiri Dei tumulum obdormiuit paululum.[4] Protinus euigilans sana surrexit et gaudens cum genitrice domum rediit.

[a] et dignissime *om. C* [b] *C gives the heading* quod non omnia uirtutum eius opera ualeant explicari *(see ch. 37)* [c] apparuit *G* [d] autem *G* [e] Aðeluerði *T*; Æthelwueardi *C*; Etheluerti *G*; Athelstani *N(A)* [f] uiri *ins. T*

[1] Cf. Vergil, *Aen.* i. 218 ('spemque metumque inter dubii').

[2] Ælfheah was Æthelwold's successor as bishop of Winchester (984–1005); he was elevated to the archbishopric of Canterbury in 1005 and brutally murdered by the Danes at Greenwich on 19 Apr. 1012. He is principally known from notices in the Anglo-Saxon

celebrates with all due solemnity the birthday of the most holy mother of God, ever-virgin Mary (8 Sept.). The monk was amazed, and torn between hope and fear.[1] With obedient foot he humbly obeyed the holy bishop's commands, and took the blind man to the burial chamber. There Ælfhelm stayed all night praying. In the morning he no longer needed a guide, and returned homewards, his sight restored, rejoicing and blessing the Lord in heart and mind.

43. ON THE TRANSLATION OF THE HOLY BISHOP WHICH TOOK PLACE ON 10 SEPTEMBER, AND ON THE MIRACLES PERFORMED AT HIS TOMB. This revelation, which had been confirmed by so plain a miracle, was noised abroad far and wide. Then the servant of Christ appeared in a clear vision by night to Brother Wulfstan and many others, making it known to them by various signs that it pleased the heavenly will that he should be moved from his grave and given proper burial in the church. The venerable bishop Ælfheah,[2] his successor, therefore put his sage mind to the consideration of the matter, and cheerfully gave the most humble thanks to Almighty Christ because it was in his time that he thought fit to exalt his saint with signs from heaven. There was no delay. At a great gathering of monks and minor clergy Ælfheah, with due honour, translated the remains of the holy bishop Æthelwold on 10 September, and laid them to rest in the choir of the church. There they are held in great awe to the present day. In my own sight heavenly miracles have been performed there, two of which I have briefly touched upon to add weight to my assertion.

44. CONCERNING A SICK GIRL WHO WAS CURED THERE. There was at that time in the city of Winchester a small girl, daughter of a house-servant called Æthelweard.[3] She was very ill, and suffered agonies that brought her close to dying. Her mother took her to the tomb of the man of God, and she slept there awhile.[4] The moment she awoke, she stood up cured, and joyfully went home with her mother.

Chronicle (s.a. 984, 994, 1006, 1011, 1012, 1023) and from Osbern's *Vita S. Elphegi* (ed. H. Wharton, *Anglia Sacra*, 2 vols. (London, 1691), ii. 122–47); see also N. Brooks, *The Early History of the Church of Canterbury* (Leicester, 1984), pp. 278–81, 283–5.

[3] This Æthelweard is otherwise unknown.

[4] The phrase *obdormiuit paululum* is lifted from Lantfred, *Translatio*, c. 2.

45. DE QVODAM CAECO PVERVLO QVI ET IPSE IBIDEM ILLVMINATVS EST. Puer etiam quidam paruulus, Ælfsini[1] cuiusdam mansueti et modesti uiri filius, in ipsa infantia lumine est priuatus, et maternis ulnis ad uenerandi patris Ætheluuoldi sepulchrum perductus. Mirum dictu, mox caligo caecitatis abscessit, et oculos pueri ueniens splendor lucis aperuit, omni populo congaudente et tota deuotione Christo gratias agente.

46. DE LIGATO QVODAM FVRE QVI SOLO SERMONE VIRI DEI ABSOLVTVS EST. Nec silentio praetereundum est quod praedictus sancti uiri successor,[a] Ælfeagus antistes, quendam furem pro multiplici reatu flagellis caesum mitti iussit[b] in cippum acrioribus suppliciis cruciandum. Cumque diu sic in poenis iacuisset damnatus, quadam nocte uenit ad eum in uisione sanctus Dei pontifex Ætheluuoldus et ait illi: 'Miser, cur tanto tempore sic in trunco iaces extensus?'[c] At ille recognoscens sanctum uirum, quem saepe uiderat in uita mortali, respondit: 'Dignas, domine mi, sustineo poenas, et iusto iudicio episcopi sic torqueor, quia frequenter[d] in furtis deprehensus sum et ab eis non cessaui, sed mala quae feci iterum atque iterum repetiui.' Tum sanctus 'Cessa' inquit 'uel modo,[e] miser, a furtis, cessa, et sis solutus a nexu compedis huius.' Surrexit ilico miser ille absolutus, et exiens inde uenit et procidit ante pedes[f] Ælfeagi episcopi, narrauitque ei rem gestam circa se per ordinem, et ille pro honore tanti patris siuit[g] eum abire indemnem. Constat ergo sanctum hunc, aeternae uitae coniunctum, uirtute meritorum suorum posse nos a peccatorum nostrorum uinculis soluere et ad caelestia regna perducere, cui adhuc in carne degenti caelitus est concessa potestas ligandi atque soluendi, praestante Domino nostro[h] Iesu Christo, qui cum Deo coaeterno patre et spiritu sancto uiuit et regnat Deus, per infinita saecula saeculorum.[i] Amen.[j]

[a] sanctus *ins.* *G* [b] iussisset *T* [c] iaces sic in trunco extentus *G* [d] sepe *T* [e] uel modo] amodo *β* [f] sancti *ins.* *G* [g] sinit *C* [h] nostro *om.* *G* [i] seculorum secula *G* [j] Explicit uita sancti Athelwoldi episcopi *N*; *no colophon in T*; Finit libellus de ortu uita et obitu et de translatione gloriosi et beati patris nostri Atheluuoldi episcopi per omnia mente et opere beniuoli *C*; Explicit uita sancti Ethelwoldi episcopi et confessoris *A*; Explicit uita beati patris Aethelwoldi Wintoniensis episcopi qui ibidem iacet *G*

45. CONCERNING A LITTLE BLIND BOY WHO IN THE SAME PLACE HAD HIS SIGHT RESTORED. Also a little boy, son of a gentle and modest man called Ælfsige,[1] had lost his sight as a baby. He was taken in his mother's arms to the tomb of the venerable father Æthelwold. Wonderful to relate, the fog of blindness at once departed, and brilliant light came to open the boy's eyes, to the joy of the whole people, who with complete devotion paid thanks to Christ.

46. CONCERNING A BOUND THIEF WHO WAS FREED BY A MERE WORD FROM THE MAN OF GOD. Nor must I pass over in silence how Bishop Ælfheah, who was, as I have said, Æthelwold's successor, had a thief, who was guilty on many counts, whipped and sent to the stocks for sterner tortures. When he had long lain thus undergoing his punishment, there came to him one night in a vision Æthelwold, holy bishop of God, who said to him: 'Wretch, why do you lie so long stretched out in the stocks?' The man had often seen him in his mortal life, and he recognised him. 'My lord,' he replied, 'I am suffering as I deserve. I am being tortured like this on the just judgement of the bishop, because I was often caught stealing, and did not cease from it, but repeated my crime over and over again.' Then the saint said: 'Cease even now, wretched man, from your thefts, cease and be freed from the bonds of these shackles.' The poor man at once got up, freed. He went from there and fell before the feet of Bishop Ælfheah, and told him what had happened to him, in due order. Ælfheah, out of respect for the great father, let him go free. It is clear then that this saint, while enjoying his eternal life, is able by the virtue of his merits to release us from the chains of our sins and take us to the heavenly kingdom: the same who while still dwelling in the flesh had granted him by heaven the power of binding and loosing, through the gift of our Lord Jesus Christ, who lives and reigns with God, coeternal Father, and the Holy Spirit, God for ever and ever, Amen.

[1] This Ælfsige is otherwise unknown.

APPENDIX A

ÆLFRIC'S *VITA S. ÆTHELWOLDI*

ÆLFRIC'S *Vita S. Æthelwoldi* (*BHL*, no. 2646) is an abbreviation of Wulfstan's earlier *uita* of Æthelwold. It is dedicated to Cenwulf, who was bishop of Winchester for a brief period during the year 1006, and was therefore compiled some time between 1004 (Ælfric states in his *Prologus* that twenty years have elapsed since Æthelwold's death in 984: *transactis uidelicet uiginti annis post eius migrationem*) and 1006. The principal characteristic of Ælfric's work is that it drastically abbreviates Wulfstan's *uita* and, above all, eliminates what Ælfric conceived as Wulfstan's unnecessary verbosity. Because Ælfric's *uita* throws important light on the transmission of Wulfstan's *Vita S. Æthelwoldi*, we offer here a new text.

Ælfric's *Vita S. Æthelwoldi* is preserved uniquely in Paris, BN lat. 5362, fos. 74^{r}–81^{r}, a manuscript written *c.*1100 by a Norman scribe, either in England or possibly in Normandy (the later provenance of the manuscript is Fécamp). It contains texts of a number of Latin hagiographical writings that were used in one way or another by Ælfric in his own hagiography (see above, pp. cxlviii–cxlix), and may be regarded therefore as a later copy of a lost hagiographical commonplace-book compiled by Ælfric for his own use. In most respects the text of the *Vita S. Æthelwoldi* is an accurate one, but in its orthography it represents the scriptorial practices of Norman scribes, particularly as regards the spelling of Old English names and the use of the letters *k* and *w*. We have normalized the spelling in accordance with the editorial principle stated above (pp. clxxxvii–clxxxviii), namely that from manuscripts written at Winchester *c.*1000 and from other writings of Ælfric it is possible to achieve a more accurate sense of Ælfric's own orthography than that purveyed by the Norman scribe of BN lat. 5362. In particular, we reproduce MS *e* as *ae*, except where it is philologically incorrect (e.g. in the first syllable of *ecclesia*: see above, p. clxxxviii); we also print *sublimis* for MS *sullimis*, *namque* for *nanque*, *tandem* for *tamdem*, *membra* for *menbra*, and *monachus* for *monacus*, since the preferred spelling in each case is attested in others of Ælfric's writings, particularly his pedagogic works (the *Grammar*, *Glossary*, and *Colloquy*). In the case of Old English names, we have printed the normalized form and recorded the manuscript reading in the apparatus, except in the case of *Atheluuold*(*us*), which we print consistently as *Æthelwuold*(*us*), without comment (cf. above, p. clxxviii). The chapter-division is that of previous editors; note that, at the end of each chapter, we give in square brackets the number(s) of the corresponding chapter(s) in Wulfstan's *Vita S. Æthelwoldi* from which it is drawn.

Ælfric's *Vita S. Æthelwoldi* has been printed on three previous occasions: in *Chron. Abingdon*, ii. 255–66; in the Bollandists' *Catalogus codicum hagiographicorum latinorum ... qui asseruantur in Bibliotheca Nationali Parisiensi*, 4 vols. (Brussels, 1889–93), ii. 356–63; and in Winterbottom, *Three Lives*, pp. 17–29. It has been translated by Whitelock, *EHD*, pp. 903–11.

1. INCIPIT PROLOGVS IN VITA SANCTI ÆTHELWOLDI. Ælfricus[a] abbas, Wintoniensis alumnus, honorabili episcopo Cenulfo[b] et fratribus Wintoniensibus salutem in Christo.[1] fo. 74r

Dignum ducens denique aliqua de gestis patris nostri et magnifici doctoris Æthelwuoldi memoriae modo commendare, transactis uidelicet uiginti annis post eius migrationem, breui quidem narratione meatim sed et rustica, quae apud uos uel alias a fidelibus didici huic stilo ingero, ne forte penitus propter inopiam scriptorum obliuioni tradantur.[c] Valete. EXPLICIT PROLOGVS, INCIPIT VITA.

2. Erant autem parentes sancti Æthelwuoldi habitatores ciuitatis Wentae, tempore | Eaduuerdi regis Anglorum florentes, eximio Dei dono fo. 74v decorati quo talem meruissent prolem generare, cuius documentis non solum praesentis aeui populi sed etiam futuri caligine caruissent erroris. Ergo felix eius genitrix, dum in utero eum haberet, huiuscemodi somnium, praesagium futuri effectus, uidit. Visum namque sibi est se sedere prae foribus domus suae, et adesse obtutibus eius quoddam sublime uexillum, cuius summitas caelum tangere uideretur, quod inclinando se honorifice circumdedit fimbriis propriis inpregnatam. Rursus itaque mulier oppressa somno eadem nocte uidit quasi auream aquilam de ore ipsius exire et auolare, tam ingentem ut uideretur tota ciuitas eius auratis pennis obumbrari. Horum autem somniorum, sicut rei probauit euentus, coniectores facile esse possumus, in sublimi uexillo intelligentes filium eius quem gestabat in utero signiferum fore militiae Dei, sicut et erat, et in aquila aurea praeclarum uirum, sicut Dominus in euangelio ait, 'ubicumque fuerit corpus, illuc congregabuntur et aquilae.' [cc. 1–3.]

3. Iterum ipsa mater quadam die stans in ecclesia stipata ciuibus, causa sanctam missam audiendi, sensit uenisse animam pueri, quem gestabat in

[a] Alfricus *MS* [b] Kenulfo *MS* [c] tradentur *MS*

[1] Cenwulf, sometime abbot of Peterborough, was bishop of Winchester for part of a year in 1006; at that time Ælfric was presumably abbot of Eynsham (*Heads*, p. 48). He similarly describes himself as a student of Æthelwold in the preface to his *Grammar*: 'sicut didicimus in scola Aðelwoldi, uenerabilis praesulis, qui multos ad bonum imbuit' (ed. Zupitza, p. 1).

utero, et intrasse in eum, sicut postea ipse sanctus, qui nasciturus erat, iam episcopus, gaudendo nobis narrauit. Ex quo ostenditur eum electum Deo extitisse etiam antequam nasceretur, et animam hominis non a patre
fo. 75ʳ uel a matre uenire sed a solo creatore | unicuique dari.[2] [c. 4.]

4. Nato uero infante uocauerunt eum parentes eius Ætheluuoldum, cum sacrosancto baptismate ablueretur. Accidit namque quadam solenni die, sedenti matre[3] domi et in gremio infantem tenente, tempestuosam auram adsurgere, in tantum ut ipsa, sicuti decreuit, adire ecclesiam nequiret; sed cum gemebunda orationi se dedisset, subito inuenta est in ecclesia sedens cum infantulo ubi missam presbiter celebrabat. [cc. 4–5.]

5. Creuit autem puer, et in ipsa pueritia sacris litterarum studiis traditus est. Qui adolescens factus Æthelstano[d] regi, filio Eaduuerdi, fama uulgante notus factus est; et eius comitatui diu adhaerens, cum esset acer ingenio, plura a sapientibus regis utilia sibi didicit; et demum, iubente rege, ab Ælfego Wintoniensi episcopo tonsoratus et in gradum sacerdotalem consecratus est. Ipse uero Ælfegus prophetiae spiritu pollebat; et contigit eum ordinasse simul Dunstanum et Ætheluuoldum et quendam, Æthelstanum[e] uocabulo, qui postmodum monachilem habitum deserens apostata fine tenus perdurauit. Post missam autem dixit episcopus Ælfegus sibi adhaerentibus: 'Hodie consecraui tres sacerdotes, quorum duo ad episcopalem apicem pertingent, alter in mea sede, alter alia diocesi.' Tunc Æthelstanus, 'sum ego', inquit, 'ex illis duobus qui ad episcopalem dignitatem peruenturi sunt?' 'Non', dixit Ælfegus, 'nec in sanctitate quam inchoabas permansurus es': sicut nec fecit. [cc. 6–8.]

6. Ætheluuoldus uero, multum melioratus doctrinis et exemplis
fo. 75ᵛ Ælfegi, ordinatoris sui, cui iu|bente rege studiose ad tempus adhaesit, postmodum Glæstoniam perueniens magnifici uiri Dunstani, abbatis eiusdem monasterii, discipulatui se tradidit. Cuius magisterio multum proficiens, tandem monastici ordinis habitum ab ipso suscepit, humili deuotione eius regimini deditus. Didicit namque inibi grammaticam artem et metricam et libros diuinos seu auctores, nimium insuper uigiliis et orationibus insistens, et abstinentia semet ipsum edomans, et fratres semper ad ardua exortans. [c. 9.]

[d] Aetelstano *MS* [e] Aetelstanum *MS*

[2] The doctrine that the soul came from God, not from the father or mother, is one which interested Ælfric; cf. *Homilies of Ælfric: A Supplementary Collection*, ed. J. C. Pope, 2 vols., EETS, os cclix–cclx (1967–8), i. 240 (ll. 227–34): 'Nu ge magon tocnawan þæt ure sawla ne cumað of fæder ne of meder, ac se heofonlica Fæder gescipð þone lichaman and hine geliffæst mid sawle.' See also M. R. Godden, 'Anglo-Saxons on the mind', *Learning and Literature*, pp. 271–98, at 284–5. The fact that the same statement is found in Wulfstan (see above, p. 8 n. 2) may well suggest that Ælfric and Wulfstan derived the doctrine from Æthelwold, their teacher.

[3] Ælfric (by inadvertence?) has altered Wulfstan's *nutrix* here to *mater*.

7. Elapso denique multo tempore postquam monachilem susceperat gradum, disposuit ultramarinas partes adire, causa imbuendi se[f] sacris libris seu monasticis disciplinis perfectius; sed praeuenit uenerabilis regina Eadgiuu, mater regis Eadredi, eius conamina, dans consilium regi ne talem uirum sineret egredi de regno suo. Placuit tunc regi Eadredo, suadente matre sua, dare uenerabili Ætheluuoldo quendam locum, uocabulo Abbandun, in quo monasteriolum habebatur antiquitus, sed erat tunc destitutum ac neglectum, uilibus aedificiis consistens et quadraginta tantum mansas possidens; reliquam uero terram eiusdem loci (hoc est centum cassatos) praefatus rex iure regali possidebat. Factumque est, permittente Dunstano, secundum regis uoluntatem, ut Ætheluuoldus praefati loci susciperet curam, ut in eo scilicet monachos ordinaret regulariter Deo seruientes. Venit ergo praedictus seruus Dei ad locum sibi commissum: quem statim secuti sunt quidam clerici de Glastonia, hoc est Osgarus, Foldbirchtus, Frithegarus, et Ordbirchtus de Wintonia et Eadricus de Lundonia, eius | discipulatui se subdentes. Congregauitque fo. 76r
sibi in breui spatio gregem monachorum, quibus ipse abbas, iubente rege, ordinatus est. [cc. 10–11.]

8. Dedit etiam rex possessionem regalem quam in Abundonia possederat, hoc est centum cassatos, cum optimis aedificiis, abbati et fratribus ad augmentum cotidiani uictus, et in pecuniis multum eos iuuit; sed mater eius largius. Venit ergo rex quadam die ad monasterium, ut aedificiorum structuram per se ipsum ordinaret; mensusque est omnia fundamenta monasterii propria manu, quemadmodum muros erigere decreuerat; rogauitque eum abbas in hospitio cum suis prandere. Annuit rex ilico; et contigit adesse sibi non paucos uenientes ex gente Northanhymbrorum, qui omnes cum rege adierunt conuiuium. Laetatusque est rex, et iussit abunde propinare hospitibus medonem,[4] clausis foribus, ne quis fugiendo potationem regalis conuiuii deserere uideretur. Quid multa? Hauserunt ministri liquorem tota die ad omnem sufficientiam conuiuantibus; sed nequiuit ille liquor exhauriri de uase, nisi ad mensuram palmi, inebriatis Northanhymbris suatim ac uesperi recedentibus.[5] [cc. 11–12.]

9. Non coepit tamen abbas designatum sibi opus aedificare in diebus Eadredi regis, quia cito obiit, sed regnante Eadgaro honorabile templum in honore sanctae Mariae genitricis Dei semperque uirginis construxit loco et consummauit, quod uisu melius quam sermone ostenditur. Circa

[f] seu *MS*

[4] Note that Ælfric replaced Wulfstan's word *ydromellum* with the less ostentatious *medonem*.

[5] Ælfric was clearly following Wulfstan's original version of this passage, before the unflattering reference to the Northumbrians' drinking habits had been suppressed (see above, p. clxxxiv).

haec tempora eligitur Dunstanus ad episcopatum Wigornensis ecclesiae; et post annorum curricula factus archiepiscopus mansit in Cantia triginta fo. 76v et septem annis, | quasi columna immobilis, doctrina, elemosinis, prophetia praepollens: ad cuius tumbam etiam frequenter fieri miracula audiuimus. [cc. 13–14.]

10. Ætheluuoldus autem misit Osgarum monachum trans mare ad monasterium sancti Benedicti Floriacense, ut mores regulares illic disceret ac domi fratribus docendo ostenderet, quatinus ipse regularem normam secutus, una cum sibi subiectis, deuia quaeque declinans, gregem sibi commissum ad patriam perduceret promissam. In qua congregatione erat quidam frater, Ælfstanus nomine, simplex et magnae oboedientiae uir, quem abbas iussit praeuidere cibaria artificum monasterii; cui seruitio ipse deuotissime se subdens coxit carnes cotidie et operariis ministrabat, focum accendens et aquam adportans et uasa denuo emundans, existimante abbate illum hoc iuuamine ministri peragere. Accidit namque quadam die, dum abbas more solito peragraret monasterium, ut aspiceret illum fratrem stantem iuxta caldarium feruens, praeparantem uictualia artificibus, et intrans uidit omnia uasa mundissima ac solum scopatum. Dixit ei hilari uultu: 'O mi frater, hanc oboedientiam mihi furatus es, quam me ignorante exerces. Sed si es talis miles Christi qualem te ostendis, mitte manum in bullientem aquam et unum frustum de imis mihi adtrahe.' Qui statim sine mora mittens manum ad imum lebetis abstraxit frustum feruidum, nil sentiens calorem feruentis aquae. Quo uiso abbas iussit deponi frustum, et nemini hoc indicare uiuenti. Illum uero fratrem postmodum abbatem audiuimus[6]
fo. 77r factum, et deinde | episcopum Wiltoniensis[g][7] ecclesiae ueraciter uidimus. [c. 14.]

11. Erat namque Ætheluuoldus magnus aedificator, et dum esset abbas et cum esset episcopus; unde tetendit ei communis aduersarius insidias, ita ut quadam die, dum in structura laboraret, ingens postis super eum caderet et in quandam foueam deiecit confregitque paene omnes costas eius ex uno latere; et nisi fouea eum susciperet totus quassaretur. Conualuit tamen de hac molestia Deo auxiliante, et elegit eum

[g] Wintoniensis *MS*

---

[6] Ælfric changes Wulfstan's *uidimus* to *audiuimus*. The precise date when Ælfstan was consecrated abbot of the Old Minster is unknown, but must have fallen between 964 and 971 (see above, p. 28 n. 1). Wulfstan, who would then have been an oblate at the Old Minster, would have witnessed the consecration; but Ælfric, who was evidently younger than Wulfstan, only heard of it. Nevertheless, Ælfric proudly adds that he saw (*ueraciter uidimus*) Ælfstan consecrated bishop of Ramsbury, an event which took place in 970.

[7] The MS reading here, *Wintoniensis*, is an error for *Wiltoniensis* (Ramsbury), almost certainly through scribal inadvertence; it is inconceivable that Ælfric could have made an error such as this, unless by a slip of the pen.

Eadgarus felicissimus rex Anglorum ad episcopatum Wintoniensis ecclesiae, antequam ecclesia praefata dedicaretur, et eo iubente ordinauit illum Dunstanus, archiepiscopus Dorouernensis ecclesiae. [cc. 15–16.]

12. Erant autem tunc in Veteri Monasterio, ubi cathedra episcopalis habetur, male morigerati[h] clerici, elatione et insolentia ac luxuria praeuenti, adeo ut nonnulli eorum[i] dedignarentur missas suo ordine celebrare, repudiantes uxores quas inlicite duxerant et alias accipientes, gulae et ebrietati iugiter dediti. Quod minime ferens uir sanctus Ætheluuoldus, data licentia a rege Eadgaro, expulit citissime nefandos blasphematores Dei de monasterio, et adducens monachos de Abundonia[j] locauit illic, quibus ipse abbas et episcopus extitit. [c. 16.]

13. Accidit autem, dum monachi uenientes de Abundonia starent ad ingressum ecclesiae, clericos intus finire missam, communionem canendo, 'Seruite Domino in timore, et exultate ei cum tremore, adprehendite disciplinam, ne pereatis de uia iusta,' quasi dicerent: 'nos noluimus Deo | seruire nec disciplinam eius tenere; uos saltem facite, ne fo. 77v
sicut nos pereatis.' Monachi uero audientes cantum illorum dixerunt mutuo: 'Cur moramur foris? Ecce ortamur ingredi.' [c. 17.]

14. Misit quoque rex quendam ministrorum suorum famosissimum, Wulfstanum uocabulo, cum episcopo, qui regia auctoritate mandauit clericis ocissime dare locum monachis aut monachicum suscipere habitum. At illi execrantes monachicam uitam ilico exierunt de ecclesia; sed tamen postmodum tres ex illis conuersi sunt ad regularem conuersationem, scilicet Eadsinus, Wulfsinus, Wilstanus. Nam hactenus in gente Anglorum ea tempestate non habebantur monachi nisi in Glastonia et Abundonia. [c. 18.]

15. Dehinc denique, ex inuidia clericorum, datum est episcopo uenenum bibere in sua aula, in qua cum hospitibus prandebat, ut illo extincto libere pristinis quiuissent frui flagitiis. Erat namque ei moris mox post tres aut quattuor offulas propter infirmitatem quid modicum bibere; bibitque nesciens adportatum sibi uenenum omne quod anaphus habebat, et statim in pallorem facies eius immutata est et uiscera eius[k] nimium ui ueneni cruciabantur. Surrexit tunc uix a mensa exiens ad lectulum, serpsitque uenenum per omnia membra eius, mortem minitans sibi. At ille tandem coepit exprobrare semet ipso,[8] dicendo ad animum suum: 'Vbi est modo fides tua? Vbi sunt uerba Christi quibus dicebat, "et si mortiferum quid biberint, non eis nocebit"?' His et huiuscemodi uerbis

[h] morierati *MS* [i] uel illorum *added above in main hand MS* [j] habundonia *MS* [k] uel illius *added above in main hand MS*

[8] Wulfstan here has *semet ipsum*, acc. (after *exprobrare*); the change to *ipso* may simply be due to scribal inadvertence. If the dative after *exprobrare* was intended, one would expect *sibimet ipsi*.

fo. 78r accensa fides in eo extinxit letiferum haustum[9] | quem[l] bibebat, et maturius surrexit, abiens ad aulam satis hilaris, nil mali uenefico reddens suo. [c. 19.]

16. Exinde expandit Ætheluuoldus alas suas, et, annuente rege Eadgaro, expulit[m][10] clericos de Nouo Monasterio, ordinans ibi Æthelgarum discipulum suum abbatem, et sub eo monachos regulariter conuersantes, qui postmodum archiepiscopus in Cantia effectus est. [c. 20.]

17. In Abundonia uero Osgarum abbatem fecit, ditatusque est locus ille sexcentis et eo amplius cassatis. In Monasterio namque Nonnarum ordinauit sanctimoniales, quibus matrem praefecit Ætheldritham. Est igitur locus in regione quae uocatur Elig, nobilitatus nimium reliquiis et miraculis sanctae Ætheldrithae[n] uirginis ac sororum eius; sed erat tunc destitutus et regali fisco deditus. Quem emebat Ætheluuoldus a rege, constituens in eo monachos perplures, quibus praefecit patrem, Brithnothum[o] nomine, discipulum suum; locumque affluentissime ditauit aedificiis ac terris. Alterum uero locum adquisiuit a rege et a nobilibus terrae, situm in ripa fluminis Nen, qui lingua Anglorum antiquitus Medehamstede,[p] modo consuete Burh nominatur, quo simili modo monachos congregauit, Ealdulfum[q] eis abbatem praeficiens, qui postmodum archiepiscopatum Eboracae ciuitatis obtinuit. Tertium quoque locum pretio adquisiuit iuxta praedictum flumen, Thorniae Anglice nuncupatum, quem eadem conditione monachis delegauit; constructoque
fo. 78v monasterio abbatem eisdem, Godemannum[r] uocabulo, | constituit, ac possessionibus habundanter ditauit. [cc. 21–4.]

18. Erat autem Ætheluuoldus a secretis regis Eadgari, magnifice pollens sermone et opere, ubique praedicans euangelium Christi iuxta ammonitionem Isaiae prophetae dicentis, 'Clama, ne cesses, quasi tuba exalta uocem tuam, et adnuntia populo meo scelera eorum, et domui Iacob peccata eorum.' Cuius praedicationem maxime iuuit sanctus Suuithunus eodem tempore reuelatus; quia quod Ætheluuoldus uerbis edocuit, hoc Suuithunus miraculis mirifice decorauit. Sicque factum est, consentiente rege, ut partim Dunstani consilio et actione, partim Ætheluuoldi, monasteria ubique in gente Anglorum, quaedam monachis,

[l] quod *MS* [m] expulsit *MS* [n] Aeldrite *MS* [o] Brinthothum *MS* [p] Medelhamstede *MS* [q] Aldulfum *MS* [r] Godomannum *MS*

[9] Wulfstan rightly takes *haustus* as masculine. It is not clear why it should be construed as neuter (note MS *quod*) by Ælfric, and the change is presumably due to the scribe. We have accordingly emended the transmitted *quod* to *quem*. Ælfric also presumably wrote *biberat* with Wulfstan.

[10] The transmitted form *expulsit* is an error for *expulit* (the reading found in Wulfstan's text). That the error is scribal, and not due to Ælfric, is clear from his discussion of *expello* in his *Grammar* (ed. Zupitza, p. 180; cf. p. 110); and cf. above, c. 12.

quaedam monialibus, constituerentur sub abbatibus et abbatissis regulariter uiuentibus. [cc. 25–7.]

19. Circuiuitque Æthelwuoldus singula monasteria, mores instituens, oboedientes ammonendo et stultos uerberibus corrigendo; eratque terribilis ut leo inoboedientibus seu discolis, mitibus uero et humilibus mitior columba. Pater erat monachorum ac monialium, uiduarum consolator et pauperum recreator, ecclesiarum defensor, errantium corrector: quod plus opere impleuit quam nos possimus sermone enarrare. [cc. 27–8.]

20. Infirmabatur saepe in uisceribus et cruribus, insomnes noctes ex dolore ducens, et in die, licet pallidus, tamen quasi sanus ambulans. Minime tamen esu carnium quadrupedum aut auium usus est, nisi semel, cogente maxima infirmitate, per tres menses, quod et fecit iussu Dunstani | archiepiscopi, et iterum in infirmitate qua obiit. Dulce namque fo. 79r erat ei adolescentes et iuuenes semper docere, et libros Anglice eis soluere, et iocundis alloquiis ad meliora hortari; unde factum est ut perplures ex eius discipulis fierent abbates et episcopi in gente Anglorum. [cc. 30–1.]

21. Contigit aliquando clericum eius, cui designatum erat ampullam eius ferre, minus olei accipere quam necessitas poscebat,[s][11] et hoc ipsum in itinere perdidisse. Veniens autem episcopus ad locum destinatum, cum uellet habere crisma, non habuit. Turbatus tunc clericus repedauit iter quo uenerat, et inuenit ampollam plenam olei iacentem, quae nec medietatem antea habuerat. [c. 32.]

22. Quidam monachus sub eo degens, Eaduuinus uocamine,[12] marsupium cuiusdam hospitis instinctu daemonico furatus est; de quo episcopus in capitulo omni congregationi dixit, ut si quis illud raperet cum sua benedictione iterum redderet, aut in talem locum proiceret ut inueniretur. Iterum transactis tribus diebus, non inuenta pecunia, locutus est episcopus omnibus fratribus dicens: 'Noluit noster fur cum benedictione rem furatam reddere sicut iussimus; reddat modo cum maledictione, et sit ille ligatus,

[s] poposcebat *MS*

[11] The transmitted form *poposcebat* is a solecism, created from *poscebat* and *poposcerat*. Again, it is difficult to think that the error is Ælfric's; cf. his *Grammar*, ed. Zupitza, p. 181. We have accordingly emended to *poscebat*, the reading in Wulfstan.

[12] The name of the monk—*Eaduuinus uocamine*—is not found in Wulfstan. Two explanations are possible: either the words were found in the copy of Wulfstan used by Ælfric, but had fallen out of the 12th-c. manuscripts on which our text of Wulfstan is constructed; or else Ælfric supplied the detail from his own personal knowledge of the event. In favour of the latter explanation is the fact that Ælfric also tells us that the object of the theft was a guest's purse, a detail not found in Wulfstan. In any event, the only Eadwine listed among the Old Minster monks in the *Liber uitae* of Hyde is found fairly high up in the list—higher even than Wulfstan, Lantfred, and Ælfric—as no. xxiii (*LVH*, p. 25; Gerchow, *Gedenküberlieferung*, p. 323), and it is perhaps unlikely that he is the Eadwine in question.

non solum in anima sed etiam in corpore, nostra auctoritate.' Quid fo. 79ᵛ multa? | Dixerunt fratres 'Amen', et ecce fur ille sedens inuisibilit.. ligabatur, brachiis sibi adhaerentibus sub cappa sua, mansitque sic stupidus usque horam tertiam,[13] cogitans quid agere deberet. Omnia tamen membra mobilia, exceptis brachiis, habebat, quae auctoritate episcopus sibi a Deo collata inutilia reddidit. Surrexit tamen miser ille sic ligatus, et exiens post episcopum coactus confessus est ei secreto se rem illam habere, nichil dicens de eius ligatione. Tunc dixit ei episcopus blande, sicut ei moris erat: 'Bene fecisti saltem modo, licet sero, confitendo reatum tuum; habeto nunc nostram benedictionem.' Et statim soluta sunt brachia eius, episcopo nesciente. At ille exiens inde laetus effectus narrauit per ordinem de eius ligatione et solutione cuidam fratri, Wulfgarus uocabulo, qui ammonuit hoc silentio magis tegendum. [c. 33.]

23. Igitur cum episcopus magno conamine uellet Veterem renouare Ecclesiam et iussisset[t] fratres frequenter laboribus una cum artificibus insistere, contigit quadam die, dum monachi starent ad summum tectum templi cum cymentariis, ut caderet unus monachus, Godus uocabulo, a summis usque deorsum. Qui statim cum terram attigisset, surrexit, nil | fo. 80ʳ mali passus de tanta ruina, ascenditque ad opus ubi antea steterat, et accipiens trullam fecit quod incoauerat. Cui ergo hoc miraculum adscribendum est nisi illi cuius iussu ad opus exiuit? [c. 34.]

24. Quidam etiam monachus, nomine Teodricus, iuit ad episcopum nocturno interuallo, uolens indiciis de quadam necessitate ei indicare, et repperit eum legentem cum candela et sedula agilitate palpebrarum seniles acies acuentem; stetitque diu ammirans quam studiose oculos paginae infigeret. Surrexit tunc episcopus a lectione, et ille frater accepit candelam coepitque legere, probans si potuisset suos sanos oculos tam diligenter acuere ad lectionem sicut episcopus fecit suos caligantes. Sed illa temeritas non impune illi euenit. Nam sequenti nocte, cum se sopori dedisset, apparuit ei quidam uultu incognitus, terribili comminatione dicens ei: 'Quomodo ausus fuisti exprobrare episcopum praeterita nocte in legendo?', et haec dicens incussit ictum oculis eius digito, et continuo dolor oculorum ualidus secutus est, qui eum multis diebus nimis affligebat, usque quo satisfactione culpam deleret quam incaute in sancto uiro commisit. [c. 35.]

25. Item accidit, cum episcopus legeret noctu, eum ob nimiam uigilantiam obdormisse, et candelam ardentem super paginam cecidisse; | fo. 80ᵛ arsitque super folium usque quo unus frater adueniens accepit candelam

[t] iusset *MS*

---

[13] That the thief remained paralysed until Tierce (*usque horam tertiam*) is another detail not found in Wulfstan, and presumably supplied by Ælfric from his knowledge of the event.

flammantem de libro, et intuitus aspexit fauillas candelae iacentes per multas lineas, et eas exsufflans inuenit paginam inlaesam. [c. 36.]

26. En fateor plane quod non facile mihi occurrit scribere quanta uel qualia sanctus Ætheluuoldus perpessus sit pro monachis et cum monachis, et quam benignus extitit erga studiosos et oboedientes, aut quanta in structura monasterii elaboraret, reparando ecclesiam aliasque domos aedificando, aut quam peruigil erat in orationibus, et quam benigne ortabatur fratres ad confessionem. Sed ex his paucis possunt plura cognosci quae a nobis narrari nequeunt.[14]

Obiit autem uicesimo secundo anno sui episcopatus, in kalendas Augusti, regnante Æthelredo[u] rege Anglorum, sepultusque est in ecclesia beatorum Petri et Pauli ad sedem eius episcopalem. Ad cuius mausoleum miracula fieri audiuimus, et antequam ossa eius eleuarentur de tumulo sed et postea, ex quibus duo tantum huic breuitati insero. [cc. 37, 41.]

27. Erat quidam ciuis Oxnofornensis,[15] Ælfhelmus[v] uocamine, caecitate plurimis annis multatus, qui ammonitus in somnis ad sancti Ætheluuoldi mausoleum ire, dicebaturque ei nomen monachi Wintoniensis, cuius inscius hactenus extitit, qui eum ducere deberet ad sancti praesulis tumbam. | Quid plura? Iuit ipse Wintoniam, et aduocato fo. 81r
monacho ex nomine, sicut in somnis didicerat, uidelicet Wulfstanum, cognomento Cantor,[16] rogans sibi ductor fieri ad sarcophagum sancti, enarrauitque ei ordinem uisionis. Perduxit tunc monachus ad tumulum sancti caecum, sed non indigens ductore reuersus est uidens. [c. 42.]

28. Narrauit quoque nobis[17] Ælfegus episcopus, successor sancti Ætheluuoldi, quod ipse quendam furem flagellatum misisset in neruum, et cum diu sic in poenis iacuisset, uenit ad eum in uisione sanctus Ætheluuoldus, dicens ei: 'Cur, miser, sic in trunco iaces tam diu extensus?' At ille recognoscens sanctum, quem saepe uiderat in uita mortali, respondit: 'Dignas, domine mi, luo poenas, et iusto iudicio episcopi sic torqueor, quia non cessaui a furtis.' Tum sanctus, 'Cessa uel modo', inquit, 'miser, cessa, et sis solutus a nodis nerui huius.' Surrexit

[u] Aelhelredo *MS* [v] Aelfelmus *MS*

---

[14] Ælfric omits the two lengthy visions described by Wulfstan in cc. 38–9. Also, significantly, he omits c. 40 (concerning the dedication of the Old Minster) which, as we have seen (above, p. clxxxv), was added later by Wulfstan, and was not in the redaction of the text used by Ælfric.

[15] In Wulfstan, Ælfhelm is said to be a citizen of Wallingford, not of Oxford; there is no obvious reason for the change.

[16] The grammatical concordance in this sentence is astray: note *monacho* (abl.), *Wulfstanum* (acc.), and *Cantor* and *ductor* (nom.); cf. also c. 22 (*cuidam fratri Wulfgarus uocabulo*). It is not clear whether the fault is Ælfric's or the scribe's; but note that the sentence-structure is also faulty (no main verb for *aduocato* and *rogans* to modify).

[17] Ælfric adds a personal detail (*narrauit nobis*) not found in Wulfstan, though in other respects their accounts of this miracle are identical.

ilico fur ille absolutus, et uenit ad episcopum Ælfegum, narrauitque ei rem gestam circa se per ordinem, et ille indemnem dimisit eum abire. [c. 46.]

29. Claret ergo fides sanctae trinitatis et uere unitatis tam miris signis meritis sanctorum suorum, cui est honor et imperium per aeterna saecula. Amen.

APPENDIX B

POEMS ON ST ÆTHELWOLD FROM THE *LIBELLVS ÆTHELWOLDI*

THE *Libellus Æthelwoldi* (properly the *Libellus quorundam insignium operum beati Æthelwoldi*) was compiled anonymously at Ely in the earlier twelfth century at the instigation of Hervey, bishop of Ely (1108–31). It is an account of Æthelwold's refoundation and endowment of Ely. The bulk of the work is taken up with a record of the estates granted to and belonging to Ely, and this part of it is evidently based on a (now lost) account in Old English dating from the late tenth century. For his account of the refoundation itself, the author draws (as we have seen: above, p. clix) on Wulfstan's *Vita S. Æthelwoldi*. At certain points in the work, the author has inserted seven poems in praise of Æthelwold, and since these poems are an unambiguous witness to the veneration in which Æthelwold was held in twelfth-century Ely, we have thought it worth while to reproduce them here.

The *Libellus Æthelwoldi* survives in two manuscripts, both of twelfth-century date: Cambridge, Trinity College O. 2. 41 (Ely, 1139–40), pp. 1–64 (= C), and London, BL Cotton Vespasian A. XIX (Ely, s. xii^{med}), fos. 2^{r}–27^{v} (= L); the two were probably both copied independently from the original. The text itself has been printed integrally only once, by Thomas Gale in his *Rerum Anglicarum Scriptorum Veterum II: Historiae Britannicae, Saxonicae, Anglo-Danicae Scriptores XV* (Oxford, 1691), pp. 463–88, from the Trinity College manuscript (which Gale himself owned). The *Libellus Æthelwoldi* was subsequently incorporated into the late twelfth-century *Liber Eliensis*, an extensive history of Ely, its saints and its endowments, in the manner of the monastic chronicles which were being compiled elsewhere in England in the twelfth century. The *Liber Eliensis* is available in a good modern edition (ed. E. O. Blake (London, 1962)); but since the compiler of the *Liber Eliensis* omitted substantial parts of the *Libellus Æthelwoldi*, including the seven poems on St Æthelwold, it is of little use for our purposes. A new edition of the *Libellus Æthelwoldi* is a great desideratum, therefore, and it is welcome news that such an edition is in preparation: S. D. Keynes and A. Kennedy, *Anglo-Saxon Ely: Records of Ely Abbey and its Benefactors in the Tenth and Eleventh Centuries* (Woodbridge, forthcoming).

In the mean time, it may be useful to record some observations concerning the authorship of the Æthelwold poems in the *Libellus*, for they may have implications for the authorship of the work as a whole. These observations are prompted by the recent publication of a metrical *uita* of St Æthelthryth, Ely's patron saint. The poem is preserved uniquely in Cambridge, Corpus Christi College 393, a manuscript which was written at Ely between 1116 and 1131; that is, precisely at the time when the *Libellus Æthelwoldi* was being compiled. All the contents of the manuscript are concerned with Ely and its saints; of relevance to us is the poem on St Æthelthryth on fos. 35^{r}–56^{r}. The poem is preceded by a rubric (on fo. 34^{v}) explaining that the author of the poem was one Gregory ([*libellus*] ... *quem uersifice composuit Gregorius Eliensis monachus*), about whom nothing is known but the name and what can be gleaned from the poem. Gregory's poem on St Æthelthryth consists of nearly 1,000 hexameters and is divided into three books, the first treating the life and times of the seventh-century foundress, the second concerned generally with the late Anglo-Saxon period and with Æthelwold's endowment of Ely, and the third with miracles which occurred in Gregory's own day. The poem has been edited by P. A. Thompson and E. Stevens, 'Gregory of Ely's verse life and miracles of St Æthelthryth', *AB* cvi (1988), 333–90. Gregory and the poet of the Æthelwold verses in the *Libellus Æthelwoldi* were, therefore, exact contemporaries at Ely. Their verse is stylistically very similar and in the same form, leonine hexameters with bisyllabic rhyme, which was then fashionable. Moreover, the two share so many similarities of theme and phrasing that the suspicion must arise that Gregory was the author of the Æthelwold verses. For example, in Book II Gregory describes the happy times when monasticism flourished in England in bygone days; the point is made by two hexameters beginning with the word *tunc*:

Tunc opulenta bonis fuit Anglia religionis;
Tunc habuit ciues celestes Anglia diues. (ii. 33–4.)

So too in the first of the Æthelwold poems printed below, the 'golden age of Æthelwold' is emphasized by a series of hexameters beginning *Tunc*. Gregory subsequently describes how the devil destroyed the peace of holy men by sending the Viking hordes:

Sed studiis istis inuidit perfidus hostis,
Ecclesiae celebrem studuit turbare quietem.
Dum pacem turbat, sanctorum frangere temptat
Propositum ... (ii. 35–8.)

Compare the third of the Æthelwold poems, where it is the *inimicus* who destroys the 'peace of the saints':

Pacem sanctorum sic rumpere sepe uirorum,
Sic solet antiquus turbare bonos inimicus.

Note how both poems use the same phrase, *turbare* (*pacem*). In Gregory's poem the peace at Ely is restored by Æthelwold himself:

Sed factis celebris Ædgari tempore regis,
Presul Æðelwoldus, nulli pietate secundus,
Presul Wintonie, digno sublimat honore
Restauratque locum, nouat agminibus monachorum. (ii. 95–8.)

These sentiments are precisely those of the Æthelwold poems, especially nos. i, ii, iv, and vi. But the similarities go beyond mere sentiments. The Æthelwold poet, in order to explain the golden age of the church in Æthelwold's time, says, curiously, that 'at that time both Martha and Mary shone in the church' (i. 9). This unusual expression (based of course on Luke 10: 38–42) is also used by Gregory in his description of St Æthelthryth:

Martha prius uita fuit, inde fit ipsa Maria;
Est bona pars Marthe, pars optima dicta Marie. (i. 125–6.)

Similarly, the Æthelwold poet's description of the beauties of the site of Downham, an estate granted to Ely by Æthelwold (vi), is closely matched by Gregory's description of the beauties of Ely (i. 283–369). Both places are said to abound in wild animals which provide prey for hunters: compare Gregory's wording—'Deuia siluarum *uenatibus apta ferarum*' (i. 313)—with that of the Æthelwold poet ('. . . crebris *uenatibus aptas* . . . claudit genus omne *ferarum*'). Both places abound in bird life, and both poets give a list of birds in question; both lists include the nightingale, turtle-dove, and magpie (*pica*). In this passage Gregory begins one of his hexameters (i. 353) with the words *Instar habet*, a phrase which recurs in the Æthelwold poet's description of the bird-song at Downham (*Instar habet* cythare'). Another feature which links the poets is their interest in Greek mythology: compare the Æthelwold poet's reference to the Atlantides and the garden of the Hesperides (vi. 18–20) with Gregory's catalogue of Greek myths at the beginning of his poem (i. 1–10), for example. The poems are also linked by features of metrical technique, such as the use of pentasyllabic words to fill the last two feet of the hexameter. It is possible that a thorough study of the metrical technique of the two works would provide decisive evidence on the question of authorship, but this is not the place to undertake such study. For us it is enough to note the similarities between Gregory's verse and that of the Æthelwold poems printed here, and to raise the possibility that it was indeed Gregory who composed them.

The seven poems are edited here from both manuscripts. After each poem we give in square brackets the chapter-number from which it is taken in the forthcoming edition of the *Libellus Æthelwoldi* in Keynes and Kennedy, *Anglo-Saxon Ely*.

i. *On England in the Golden Age of St Æthelwold*

In mundo uere tunc aurea secla fuere:
Tunc uer eternum decus enituitque supernum;
Tunc et spinetum fuerat ceu suaue rosetum;
Lactea currebant tunc flumina, mella fluebant;[1]
Tunc et sponte dabat tellus quod quisque rogabat;
Pura fides, pax, uerus amor tunc emicuere;
Fraus, tumor et liuor, periuria tunc latuere;
Tunc et libertas sedes habuit sibi certas;
Tunc et in ecclesia fulserunt Martha, Maria;[2]
Tunc erat ordo bonus, cum floruit iste patronus.
[c. 3.]

ii. *Brief Prayer addressed to St Æthelwold*

Institor o diues, felix per secula uiues!
Celica sumpsisti, dum tu terrena dedisti.
Ecce tenes celum, quo nostrum dirige uelum,
Conciues tecum quo conregnemus in euum. [c. 4.]

iii. *On the Devil's Snares*

Pacem sanctorum sic rumpere sepe uirorum,
Sic solet antiquus turbare bonos inimicus,
Sic armat mundum contra sanctos furibundum,
Vt[a] pars iustorum succumbat mole malorum,
Ni Domini pietas dignetur ponere metas,
Ne, dum temptentur,[b] nimium temptando grauentur. [c. 5.]

iv. *On St Æthelwold*

O quantus uir erat, quem gratia tanta replerat,
Esset ut in mundo uiuens Christo sine mundo!
Felix ille pater, quem nescit spiritus ater,[3]
Pectore sub cuius mundi uis nil habet huius.
O decus ecclesie, uas nobile philosophie,
Cuius ad exemplum Christi fies homo templum!
Vir pie, sancte, bone pater, Ædeluuolde,[c] patrone,
Inter opes secli sitiebas gaudia celi.[4]

[a] V- *omitted by rubricator of C* [b] *read* temptantur [c] Aðeluuode *L*

[1] The land of 'milk and honey': Exod. 3: 8–17. [2] Luke 10: 38–42.
[3] The cadence *spiritus ater*: Juvencus, *Euang.* ii. 45; Caelius Sedulius, *Carm. pasch.* iv. 160. [4] The cadence *gaudia celi*: Paulinus of Nola, *Carm.* xxi. 839.

Mundus uilescit, tibi dum dos celica crescit,
Qua[c] nos dotari felix dignare precari. [c. 7.]

v. *On the Moral Excellence of St Æthelwold*

Omine felici condignum censeo dici,
Qui seruit Christo, mundo dum uiuit in isto,
Sicut Ædeluuoldus fecit presul uenerandus.
Ex utero matris se moribus exuit atris,
Proposito saluo, dum matris uixit ab aluo.
Instituit uitam diuina lege peritam.
Composuit mores, essent totidem quasi flores.
Excoctus digne, dum purificatur in igne,
Purior extractus, resplenduit illius actus,
Dumque suum cursum direxit ad ethera sursum,
Per uite portus eternos uenit ad ortus. [c. 9.]

vi. *On Æthelwold's Donation to Ely of an Estate at Downham*

Esse locum memorant quem mella liquentia rorant:
Dunham dixerunt, qui nomen ei posuerunt.
Deliciis plenus, locus uber, letus, amenus,
Vber ager gratis sat confert fertilitatis.
Piscosi fluuii iuxta noscuntur haberi.
Stat uiridis lucus, crebris uenatibus aptus;[5]
Floribus est pictus, congesto cespite cinctus;
Aggere terrarum claudit genus omne ferarum.[6]
Hic canit omnis auis, dum uentilat aura[7] suauis:
Pica loquax, murule,[d] turdi, turtur, philomele,
Instar habent cythare,[e] dum certant garrulitate!
Regia splendescit, qua silua decora patescit,
In cuius claustris loca perflat uentus ab austris,
Copia qua residet, felix opulentia ridet.
Hic loca formosa, uiridaria sunt speciosa:
Hiisque locis nempe uilescunt Tessala Tempe.[8]
Ortus ibi crescit, qui fructus quosque capescit.[f]
Ortus Athlantiadum[g] describitur aureus esse
Et satis Hesperidum reor aurea poma fuisse:
Aurea poma quidem nasci dicuntur ibidem.
Aut est translatus huc qui fuit aureus ortus
Aut ita res agitur, quod hic illius instar habetur! [c. 11.]

[c] Q- *omitted by rubricator of C* [d] *read* merule [e] cithare *L* [f] *read* capessit [g] Athalantiadum *C*

[5] The phrase *uenatibus aptus*: cf. Ovid, *Ars amat.* i. 253, *Her.* v. 17.

[6] The cadence *genus omne ferarum* is very frequent in classical Latin verse: Vergil, *Georg.* iv. 224; Ovid, *Met.* x. 705 and *Her.* x. 1; Statius, *Theb.*. v. 391; etc.

[7] The phrase *uentilat aura*: cf. Ovid, *Amores* i. 7. 54.

[8] The cadence *Tessala Tempe*: Statius, *Achill.* i. 237 (cf. Horace, *Carm.* i. 7. 4).

vii. *Prayer to St Æthelwold*

Qui dispensator, qui fidus erat[h] operator,
Qui cultor Christi, pater Ædeluuolde, fuisti,
Non decus argenti, speciem non excolis auri,
Non fodis in terris, sed nosti condere celis
Diuitias et opes, ubi nil temptant male fures,
Quo regnas tutus, thesauros ipse secutus,
Quos premittebas, quos tam bene distribuebas.
Interes eternis opibus gazisque supernis,
Pace fruens Christi, quem prudens excoluisti:
Quo nobis certus patronus adesto misertus! [c. 34.]

[h] *read* eras

APPENDIX C

THE MIDDLE ENGLISH 'LIFE OF ADELWOLDE'

THE lengthy Middle English poem known as the 'South English Legendary', a massive collection of some ninety saints' lives in rhyming verse, was probably composed somewhere in the West Midlands in the second half of the thirteenth century. It enjoyed enormously wide circulation, and is extant in a number of distinct recensions. One of these recensions, known to editors as Z, probably originated at Worcester during the period *c.*1270 × *c.*1285 (see M. Görlach, *The Textual Tradition of the South English Legendary* (Leeds, 1974), pp. 32–8). The Z recension, which alone contains the 'Life of Adelwolde', has never been printed integrally. The result is that the 'Life of Adelwolde' is also unprinted. An edition was recently produced by A. Butterfield ('The Middle English Lives of Saint Aethelwold', MA Diss., U. of Bristol, 1983), but this has not been published; we are grateful to Dr Butterfield for making a typescript of her edition available to us. Because the 'Life of Adelwolde' sheds some light on the later transmission of Wulfstan's *Vita S. Æthelwoldi* and because it is chronologically one of the last witnesses to the medieval veneration of St Æthelwold, we have thought it useful to include a text here as part of our saint's dossier.

The poem survives in five manuscripts (see Görlach, op. cit., pp. 185–6): Aberystwyth, National Library of Wales, 5043 (fragment, *c.*1400), fo. 3^{r-v}; Cambridge, Trinity College, R. 3. 25 (605) (*c.*1400), fos. 136^{v}–137^{v}, 235^{r}–236^{r} (another copy); London, BL Add. 10626 (*c.*1400), fos. 5^{v}–7^{r}; London, Lambeth Palace Library, 233 (*c.*1400), fo. 153^{v}; and Oxford, Bodleian Library, 'Vernon' manuscript (SC 3938–42) (*c.*1390), fos. 38^{v}–39^{r}. Of these, that which preserves the most complete and accurate text is London, BL Add. 10626. In its present state Add. 10626 is now a mere fragment of eleven leaves from a once much larger manuscript; it contains the Middle English lives of Oswald, Æthelwold, Ecgwine, and Eustace.

Our edition is based on the copy in Add. 10626, though at a few places we have corrected its readings by reference to the other manuscripts. Because the scribes of Middle English verse took liberties in copying a text (liberties which would be unthinkable, say, in the transmission of a Latin poem), by giving words in a dialectal form familiar to them, by altering the order of words, sometimes by recasting entire lines, every individual manuscript version of a Middle English poem is in effect a scribal recension. For this reason, in giving the (lightly emended) text of Add. 10626, we have not attempted to provide an apparatus of variants from the other four manuscripts. We reproduce the virgules from Add. 10626, since they give a clear notion of how at least one medieval reader of the poem phrased the lines.

fo. 5v Seint Adelwolde þe bischepe / in Englond was ybore.
In chylhade wel ȝong he gan / to forsake synne and hore;
þo he was suþþe of more age / by leve nolde he nouht
þat he nolde monke be / for þeron was al his þouht.
To þe hous he wente of Glastyngbury / þat bote newe þo nas;
Seint Donston he fonde abbot þere / þe ferst abbot þat þer was.
Of hym he toke þe abyte / and monke þer bycom;
Swyþe wel his ordere he hulde / and gode ȝeme þerto nom.
Bytwene Seint Donston and hym grete love / þer wex ynow,
For to clennesse and holy lyf / or eyþer oþer drow.
Gretelyche bytwene hem þey speke / ȝy oure Lorde hem ȝeve þe grace
Anoþer abbey sumware to rere / ȝif þey hadde a place.
fo. 6r þe kyng Adelred þat was þo / on a day þer forþe com,
And þis holy man Seint Adelwold / from Glastyngbury þe wey to hym nom,
And prayde hym of a place in Barkschyre / þat muche his now in mone,
Vyve myle bysyde Oxinforde / þat me clepeþ Abyndone,
þe kyng hym granted anon. / Seint Adelwold gan bylde faste
And lette þere bygynne a feyre abbey / þat hyderto doþe laste.
Verst abbot he was þere hymsylf / and monkes to hym nom.
In þis maner Abyndone / ferst to abbey com.
A day as þis holy man / aboute þe werke stode
Forto arere þis gode abbey / þat so noble his and gode,
þe devel, þat haþe to eche godnesse / strong envye and onde,
To desturbly þis holy werke / in eche maner he gan fonde.
As þis gode man þeraboute stode / he sewede hym faste
And a post þrewe adoun on hym / and sone to grounde him caste.
Ac by a lytel he stode / as oure Lorde hym ȝaf þe grace,
He hadde be elles flesch and bon / al tobrused in þe place.
Ac wit þe dunt of þe post / he vel doun in þe put,
And þe post lay hym above / and hym byneþe ydut.
Ac ȝut as þe post hym smote / he ne myhte ascape so
þat he ne brake almest alle his rybbes / in his o syde atwo.
þe folke come to hym sone / and of þe put hym nom,
And he of all his brusynge / hole man sone bycom.
Welle þat þe schrew haþe grete wraþe / and onde also
And fondeþ desturbly alle men / þat godenesse wolde do.
þis gode man rered up þis abbey / and abbot was þer longe
And gode men þat wolde monkes be / he gan hem feyre avonge.
Seint Donston þat abbot was / of þe hous of Glastyngbury
Erchebischepe was ymade / suþþe at Canterbury.

þorw þe kyng of Englond / Edgar þat was þo;
Suche holy men as he was / þe kyng wilnede after mo.
So hit byfel þat þe bischepe of Wynchestre was ded,
þe kyng Edgar and Seint Donston / þerof nome or red,
And þis holy man Seint Adelwold / bischepe þey made þere
To warde þat bischeperiche / þe folke to wisse and lere.
His bischeperiche he wuste wel / and fondede fer and ner
Fram synne to wyte his bischeperiche / and dude al his power.
At þe heye chirche of Wynchestre / þere his see was ydo fo. 6v
þat me clepede þe churchedras / as me doþ ȝut also.
Canons þere were seculers / þo[a] he þyder ferst com:
Ferce men and proude ynow / þat muche were in hordom.
Seint Adelwolde bygan anon / to sette aȝen hem faste
And out of þe hous and of or rentus / eche after oþer caste,
And monkes vette at Abyndone / holy men and bolde
And made þere a priorie / here order for to holde.
Of Seint Swythyn þe hous was / as hit his ȝut also,
So þat monkes of Abyndon / þerinne were ferst ydo;
þe priorie of Seint Swythyn / þat so riche and gode his
Of þe hous of Abyndon / in þis maner come ywis.
And Seint Adelwolde ferst abbot was / of þat housus boþe two,
Of Wynchester and of Abyndone; / and bischepe he was also.
Seint Oswald was þat tyme / bischepe of Wircestre,
Seint Donston of Canterbury, / Seint Adelwolde of Winchestre.
Luþer persons he founde fele / as me may ȝut ynowe,
þat her chirchis spendeþ in foly / and to synne drowe.
Wit þe kyng þey nome hor rede, / þat eche person scholde chese
To wite hym chast fram lecherie / or his chirche lese.
þis þre bischepus wende aboute / in Englond wel faste
And luþer persons al to grounde / out of here chirches caste.
Here chirches and or oþer gode / wel clene þey hem bynome,
And bysette hit in oþer gode men / þorw þe pope of Rome.
.viii. and .xl. abbeys of monkes / and of nonne
In Englonde þey rered wit tresoure / þat of persons was ywonne.
In þe toun of Wynchestre / Seint Adelwold rered also
Anoþer hous of blake monkes / þat ȝut stondeþ boþe two;
þe þridde hous he rered also / þere of Seint Marie,
Of wemmen in relygioun, / and made a nonnerie.
Suþþe of Edgar þe gode kyng / þorw oure Lordes grace
In þe Ile of Hely he boute / a feyre place,
And bygan þere a noble hous / of monkes, þat ȝut his,
And þerto a bischeperiche / to þe priorie ywis.
Of þe kyng Edgar suþþe also / anoþer place he boute,
A feyre abbey þere he bygan / and monkes þerinne broute,
þat me clepeþ þe abbey Borw, / and grete hous witalle his; fo. 7r
þe chirche he bygan of Seint Peter / þat also his ȝut ywis.

[a] þe *MS*

Ȝut he boute an oþer stede / of þe kyng Edgar also,
And þe abbey of þorney / and monkes gan þere do;
Of oure Lady þe chirche his / as he hit bygan þo.
þese abbeys Seint Adelwolde / bygan, and wel mo,
þe tresoure þeron he bysette / þat he of persons nom:
Wel bet was hit þeron bysette / þan on here horedom!
Seint Swythyn þe holy man / þat longe was byfore
Bischepe ybe of Wynchestre, / or Seint Adelwolde were ybore,
At his chirche fel aday / of hym miracle ynow
þerfore fram eche syde / þe folke þyderward drow;
For miracle of Seint Swythin / þat þey herde on eche syde
þe prechyng of Seint Adelwolde / me leved þe bet wel[b] wyde.
þis holy man Seint Adelwolde / began to be feble and olde,
And he hadde ny to and twenty ȝer / his bischeperiche holde;
He wex syke as oure Lorde wolde / and deyde at te ende,
And to þe joye of hevene sone / his soule gan wende.
He deyde on Lammasse day / þan his / his day ywis,
Ac for þe feste of Seint Petre / þe Lasse of hym ys.
Nyne hundred ȝer and fourscore[c] / and .iiii. ȝer byfore
Hit was[d] þat oure Lorde Crist / of his moder was ybore,
By þe kyngus day Adeldred / Seint Adelwolde[e]
Out of þis lyve wende her / as þe boke us haþe ytolde.
Now oure Lorde Iesu Crist, / kyng of alle þynge,
For love of Seint Adelwolde / to þe joye of hevene us brynge.

[b] wy *MS* [c] fourtene *MS* [d] *after* was *MS adds* after [e] Adelwode *MS*

Notes. In the following notes, our principal concern has been to determine the relationship of the Middle English poem to Wulfstan's *Vita S. Æthelwoldi*, rather than to treat the poem as an object of interest in its own right. In general it follows the outline of Wulfstan's *uita* fairly closely, but the poet at many places qualified a statement in Wulfstan by reference to the state of the church in his own day, and this led him frequently to introduce anachronisms. We have not attempted to comment in detail on the language of Add. 10626; but note that the scribe uses various characteristic spellings: *wit* ('with'), *or* (for *hor*, 'their'), *his* ('is'), and *ȝy* ('if').

1–4. Wulfstan, c. 6.

5–10. Wulfstan, c. 9; but Wulfstan makes no mention of the *grete love* which grew up between Dunstan and Æthelwold, nor that they incited each other to holiness.

11–17. Wulfstan, c. 11. The name of King Eadred is wrongly given as *Adelred* (13), though the error is probably the poet's, since it is found in all five manuscripts. The statement that Abingdon is located in Berkshire, 5 miles from Oxford, is the ME poet's addition.

17–20. Wulfstan, c. 13. The statement that the abbey church begun by Æthelwold was still extant in the late 13th c. (18: *þat hyderto doþe laste*) seems to be confirmed by the 13th-c. tract *De abbatibus Abbendoniae* (*Chron. Abingdon*, ii. 277–8); but it is equally possible that the ME poet was simply recasting Wulfstan's wording ('quod usque in hunc diem uisu melius quam sermone ostenditur').

21–36. Wulfstan, c. 15.

39–46. The election of Æthelwold is in Wulfstan, c. 16; the emphasis on Dunstan is paralleled elsewhere in the 'South English Legendary', namely in the 'Life of Dunstan', ll. 133–5 (*The South English Legendary*, ed. C. D'Evelyn and A. J. Mill, 3 vols., EETS, OS ccxxxv–ccxxxvi, ccxliv (1956–9), i. 208):

> Hit bivel þat þe erchbissop of Kanterburi was ded
> þe pope and þe king Edgar þerof nome hore red
> And made þe gode sein Donston erchbissop þere . . .

50. The compound *churchedras* does not seem to occur elsewhere in Middle English, and was possibly coined by the poet.

51–62. Wulfstan, c. 15. The ME poet introduces several anachronisms of word and thought: that the livings of the cathedral canons were referred to as 'rents'; that the Old Minster was a 'priory'; and that it was referred to as St Swithun's priory. The word *rente* is a ME loanword from OFr *rente*, and is not attested earlier than the 12th c.; the 'rents' due to the church of Winchester and its officers are first recorded in the Winchester Survey of 1148 (*WS* i. 69–141; cf. p. 8). The ME poet is also mistaken in stating that Æthelwold was 'first abbot' (61) of Winchester as well as of Abingdon (a statement which has no basis in Wulfstan); in fact the abbot of the Old Minster during Æthelwold's episcopacy was the Ælfstan who later became bishop of Ramsbury (see above, p. 28 n. 1).

63–74. The passage on the three great monastic reformers has no correlate in Wulfstan; but passages with nearly identical wording are found elsewhere in the 'South English Legendary': in the 'Life of Oswold', ll. 123–30 (ed. D'Evelyn and Mills, i. 75) and in the 'Life of Dunstan', ll. 139–50 (ibid. i. 209). The emphasis on Oswald, who is not mentioned by Wulfstan, is understandable in a work composed at Worcester. The source of the statement that these three men established forty-eight monasteries—which is repeated in all three lives in the 'South English Legendary'—is unknown. The number is surprisingly high. Byrhtferth in his *Vita S. Oswaldi* (III. 11; *HCY* i. 426) refers to 'more than forty' monasteries, but it is difficult to determine which these might have been. An attempt is made by Knowles, *MO*, p. 52.

75–6. The New Minster; Wulfstan, c. 20.

77–8. The Nunnaminster; Wulfstan, c. 22.

79–82. Ely; Wulfstan, c. 23. That Æthelwold established a bishopric at Ely attached to the priory, is an anachronism; the first bishop of Ely, Hervey, was elected in 1108.

83–6. Peterborough; Wulfstan, c. 24. That anything of Æthelwold's monastery was visible there in the late 13th c. seems very doubtful; see above, p. 40 n. 4.

87–9. Thorney; Wulfstan, c. 24.

90–2. Wulfstan, c. 27.

93–8. Wulfstan, c. 26. The ME poet has here closely reproduced Wulfstan's balance between the preaching of Æthelwold on one side and the miracles of St Swithun on the other. The corresponding passage in Ælfric (c. 18) is less close here, which confirms that it was Wulfstan, not Ælfric, that the ME poet was following.

103-4. Lammas Day is 1 Aug. *Lammas*, from OE *hlafmæsse* ('loaf-mass'), was a harvest-festival at which loaves made from newly-ripened corn were consecrated; the day was also the feast of St Peter in Chains (*ad uincula*), referred to here as 'St Peter the Less', presumably to distinguish it from St Peter *in cathedra* on 22 Feb.

108. The 'boke' in question is evidently Wulfstan's *Vita S. Æthelwoldi*.

INDEX OF MANUSCRIPTS

INDEX OF QUOTATIONS AND ALLUSIONS

A. BIBLICAL ALLUSIONS

B. CITATIONS FROM CLASSICAL, PATRISTIC AND MEDIEVAL SOURCES

GENERAL INDEX

Printed in the USA/Agawam, MA
August 13, 2019

709268.008